PLACING LATIN AMERICA

Contemporary Themes in Geography

THIRD EDITION

Edited by
Edward L. Jackiewicz
and
Fernando J. Bosco

ROWMAN & LITTLEFIELD
Lanham • Boulder • New York • London

Published by Rowman & Littlefield
A wholly owned subsidiary of The Rowman & Littlefield Publishing Group, Inc.
4501 Forbes Boulevard, Suite 200, Lanham, Maryland 20706
www.rowman.com

Unit A, Whitacre Mews, 26-34 Stannary Street, London SE11 4AB, United Kingdom

British Library Cataloguing in Publication Information Available

Library of Congress Cataloging-in-Publication Data

Names: Jackiewicz, Ed, editor. | Bosco, Fernando J., 1971– editor.
Title: Placing Latin America : contemporary themes in geography / edited by
   Edward L. Jackiewicz and Fernando J. Bosco.
Description: Third edition. | Lanham : Rowman & Littlefield, [2016] |
   Includes bibliographical references and index. | Description based on
   print version record and CIP data provided by publisher; resource not
   viewed.
Identifiers: LCCN 2015049136 (print) | LCCN 2015043658 (ebook) | ISBN
   9781442246836 (electronic) | ISBN 9781442246812 (cloth : alk. paper) |
   ISBN 9781442246829 (pbk. : alk. paper)
Subjects: LCSH: Human geography—Latin America. | Globalization—Economic
   aspects—Latin America. | Latin America—Economic conditions.
Classification: LCC GF514 (print) | LCC GF514 .P53 2016 (ebook) | DDC
   304.2098—dc23
LC record available at http://lccn.loc.gov/2015049136

Printed in the United States of America

Contents

List of Figures, Tables, and Textboxes   vii

Introduction   1
Fernando J. Bosco and Edward L. Jackiewicz

Chapter 1: Physical Geography: Contemporary Human-Environment Relationships
in Latin America and the Caribbean   9
Benjamin F. Timms and James J. Hayes

Chapter 2: The Making of a Region: Five Hundred Years of Change from Within
and Without   25
Edward L. Jackiewicz and Fernando J. Bosco

Chapter 3: Cycles of Economic Change: Political Economy from Neocolonialism
to the Bolivarian Revolution   39
Edward L. Jackiewicz and Linda Quiquivix

Chapter 4: Urban Latin America: Evolving Forms and Functions   53
Zia Salim and Fernando J. Bosco

Chapter 5: Economic and Geopolitical Vulnerabilities and Opportunities   77
Thomas Klak

Chapter 6: Mass and Alternative Tourisms in Latin America and the Caribbean   95
Edward L. Jackiewicz and Thomas Klak

Chapter 7: Natural Resources   113
Christian Brannstrom

Chapter 8: Drug Geographies: A Cultural Historical Profile   133
Kent Mathewson

Chapter 9: Nongovernmental Organizations: Scale, Society, and Environment   147
J. Christopher Brown

Chapter 10: Latin American Social Movements: Places, Scales, and Networks of Action   159
Fernando J. Bosco

Chapter 11: Urban Environmental Politics: Flows, Responsibility, and Citizenship   175
Sarah A. Moore

Chapter 12: Children and Young People: Inequality, Rights, and Empowerment   189
Kate Swanson

Chapter 13: US-Mexico Borderlands   205
Altha J. Cravey

Chapter 14: Transnational Latin America: Movements, Places, and Displacements   219
Araceli Masterson-Algar

Chapter 15: Remapping Latin America: US Latino Immigration and Immigration
Enforcement on Localized Scales   233
Joseph Wiltberger

Index   251

About the Contributors   257

Figures, Tables, and Textboxes

Figures

1.1. Geomorphic regions of Mexico. 12

1.2. Tectonic features of the Central American and Caribbean regions. Plate boundaries illustrate approximate locations of major faults and subduction zones. Black triangles indicate subduction zones, arrows indicate relative direction of plate movement. 13

1.3. Geomorphic regions of South America. 14

1.4. Major biomes and climate types of South America. Shaded areas represent generalized biomes. Each biome is related to at least one major climate type (see text for descriptions). The map illustrates the broad relationship between biomes and climate, not precise spatial boundaries. For detailed maps of biomes and climate, specific texts on physical geography, climate, and biogeography are recommended. 16

1.5. Boundaries of the Cockpit Country Forest Reserve in the karst landscapes of western Jamaica. 20

2.1. Audiencias and their date of origin. 29

2.2. Viceroyalties of Spanish America. 30

4.1. Major cities of Middle America and the Caribbean. 55

4.2. Major cities of South America. 56

4.3. Machu Picchu, iconic and relatively intact, spectacularly showcases pre-Columbian architecture and craftsmanship. 57

4.4. Spanish ports and convoy routes in the Colonial Era. 58

4.5. The *Plaza de Armas* in Cuzco, Perú (top half of picture) shows colonial influences in what used to be an Inca capital, while more eclectic modern symbols and architecture occupy and surround the *Plaza de Mayo* in Buenos Aires, Argentina (bottom half of picture). 59

4.6. New condominium and office towers surround the old docks in Puerto Madero, Buenos Aires. 60

4.7. Two architectural imports in Mexico City: The Torre *Latinoamericana* and the *Palacio de Bellas Artes*. 61

4.8. An improved model of Latin American city structure. 66

4.9. Stark contrasts in São Paulo: the boundary between the *Paco dos Reis* gated development and the *Paraisopolis* favela marks a pronounced difference in urban landscapes and lifestyles. 69

4.10. Curitiba's innovative Bus Rapid Transit system features dedicated bus lanes, high capacity bi-articulated buses, and elevated "tube" stops designed to speed passenger boarding by providing pre-boarding fare payment and same-level boarding through multiple doors. At peak times, some buses run as frequently as every 90 seconds. 72

5.1. A 2014 Summit of Latin American and Caribbean leaders with China's President Xi Jinping (front, fourth from left). 79

5.2. When KFC, followed by Subway and Pizza Hut, arrived in Dominica in 2006, it illustrated the reach of fast food chains to what are otherwise very peripheral locales. Both old and young, tourists and locals are drawn to fast food's seductive combination of salt, sugar, and fat, just as in the United States (Pollan 2006). According to Dominica's national epidemiologist, citizens are now suffering from diseases long associated with poor diets in the United States, such as diabetes, hypertension, coronary heart disease, stroke, high cholesterol, and colorectal cancer (Ricketts 2011). Further, whereas money spent on international fast food largely goes abroad, money spent at the fresh fruit and vegetable market at right supports local farmers and vendors. 81

5.3. Peasants who clear Guatemala's Petén rainforest have difficulty making a living off the land, so they sell their cleared land to ranchers. Massive inequalities and inadequate state support for sustainable agriculture results in environmental destruction and land use inefficiencies. Guatemala has vast natural resources but also massive problems of hunger. 88

6.1. Quintana Roo and the Yucatán Peninsula. 99

6.2. A cruise ship docks for the day at the port of St. John's, the capital of Antigua and Barbuda. 103

6.3. Map of cruise ship routes through the Caribbean, west vs. east routes and ports of call. 106

6.4. Author with his two "bodyguards" entering the Rocinha favela, Rio de Janeiro. 108

7.1. Tying up bell peppers destined for US markets in a greenhouse in the Bajío. 116

7.2. Bananas in Sixaola, Costa Rica, being readied for export. Note the calipers for measuring bananas to export criteria. 117

7.3. Irrigated grape plantation in Petrolina, Brazil. 118

7.4. John Deere tractor dealership in Luis Eduardo Magalhães, Bahia state, a booming region in Brazil's northeast soy belt.   119

7.5. Fibria barge filled with eucalyptus leaving plantation area.   120

7.6. Emblem on uniforms of the forest guards of the Lower Lempa in El Salvador, sponsored by a non-governmental organization specializing in mangrove protection, shows the symbolic importance of mangroves to local residents.   121

7.7. Oil production in Venezuela, Mexico, and Brazil (2000–2013, thousand barrels per day).   122

7.8. Anti-fracking grafitto on a park bench along Avenida Argentina in Neuquén, Argentina.   123

7.9. Soy production in South America, 1975–2013 (hectares).   125

8.1. Hierarchy of psychoactive substances in Latin America.   135

8.2. Drugs and the triangular trade system.   140

8.3. Mexican drug cartel territories.   143

9.1. Rondonia and Matto Grosso, Brazil.   153

10.1. Silhouettes of the "disappeared" are painted on the ground in the Plaza de Mayo in downtown Buenos Aires.   164

10.2. The Madres de Plaza de Mayo in the city of La Plata during one of their weekly marches.   166

10.3. The international reach of the Madres de Plaza de Mayo: volunteer support groups are spread out across Argentina, North America, Europe, and Australia.   168

10.4. Hijos goes global: countries in Latin America and Europe where groups of sons and daughters of disappeared people have organized.   170

11.1. Market area during a garbage crisis in Oaxaca.   176

11.2. City of Oaxaca and surrounding municipalities.   179

11.3. Oaxaca's dump.   180

12.1. Young children collecting plants and bringing animals to pasture in Andean Ecuador.   194

12.2. Street working children in Quito, Ecuador.   197

13.1. The US-Mexico border region.   206

13.2. Checkpoint at *El Tortugo*, thirty miles south of the borderline at Sasabe, Sonora.   214

14.1. Performance of the group from Guanajuato 'Los Tiempos Pasados' on September 15, 2007, at the Moline Public Library.   226

14.2. Visit of the Mexican Consulate to Casa Guanajuato on August 2, 2007.   226

14.3. Casa Guanajuato leading the Migrant March in May 2006.   227

15.1. "Latino/a-America," by Pedro Lasch.   235

15.2. Percent change in Hispanic or Latino population by county in the contiguous United States: 2000–2010.   237

Tables

3.1.   Latin America's Leading Exports, 1913 and 2005   41

4.1.   National Rate of Urbanization and Population in Selected Main
        Metropolitan Areas (Both as a Percentage of Total Population)   63

4.2.   Megaslums in Latin America and the Caribbean   71

6.1.   International Tourist Arrivals (000's)   100

6.2.   International Tourism Receipts and Population   101

6.3.   Modifiers Used to Describe Alternative Tourisms   103

10.1.   Some Latin American Social Movements and Their Organizations   160

13.1.   Comparison of the Old and New Factory Regimes   210

Textboxes

1.1.   Gold Mining in the Peruvian Amazon   15

1.2.   Geohazards and Vulnerability in Central America   18

1.3.   Caribbean Reforestation   19

1.4.   Coffee and Water Resources in Colombia   22

2.1.   The Panama Canal as an Example of US Domination   35

3.1.   Brazil's Bolsa Família   47

4.1.   Caribbean Cities   62

4.2.   Planning for Urban Sustainability   72

10.1.   The Madres de Plaza de Mayo in Argentina   165

12.1.   Work and Play   193

12.2.   Street Working Children   198

12.3.   Street Children and Public Space   198

15.1.   The Impact of the 287(g) Program in North Carolina   243

Introduction

Fernando J. Bosco and Edward L. Jackiewicz

ALMOST TWO DECADES INTO the twenty-first century, Latin America finds itself deeply integrated in economic, social, political, and cultural networks that transcend regional and national boundaries and span the world. Transnational networks of migrants link villages in Central and South America with cities all across North America, international tourism links the local economies of places throughout the region to the consumption patterns and needs of visitors from places in the "global North," and the transnational strategies of firms and corporations reach more places in the region than ever before. Such increased global interconnections of places and people take place while Latin American countries continue to experience profound changes in their political, economic, and social organization. Some countries are challenging the basic tenets of globalization, while others are embracing them more directly. Grassroots social and political movements are active participants in promoting political and social change from the ground up in the region, strengthening civil society and continuing with processes of democratization. Add to this the ebb and flow of relations of Latin American countries with the United States and other global powers such as China. On the one hand, the push for greater economic integration and free trade continues to increase. On the other hand, persistent attempts to tighten security along the US border to control immigration from the region work against notions of hemispheric integration. These are some of the contemporary themes that provide the driving force for this third edition of *Placing Latin America*, a collection of essays written from an explicit geographic perspective in an effort to summarize and contextualize the global and local dimensions of economic, political, cultural, and social change in the region.

The geographic perspective that informs this volume pays close attention to the richness and diversity of places in Latin America, from cities to border regions to nations. *Placing Latin America* examines the nexus of economy, politics, society, and culture and documents how these interactions manifest themselves geographically in different places and environments in the region. The approach of *Placing Latin America* is geographic and thematic, but it is not regional in the traditional sense. Much has changed in the discipline of geography in the past decades, and geographers writing about Latin America have been thinking geographically about a host of new issues, from environmental politics to Latin American enclaves in the United States, from tourism to the illicit drug trade, from children and young people's livelihoods to new transnational cultural practices. These issues have joined more common research topics that have been central to geographers working on Latin America for quite some time, such as natural resources and economic development, migration, and urbanization, to name a few. But given the dynamic character of the region, even writing about development and urbanization in Latin America today involves revisiting some conventional ideas and reexamining them in light of changing local, regional, and global conditions. Thus, the contributors to this volume were asked to think about Latin America's most pressing and interesting issues and themes and to write about them in summary chapters that are rich in detail, that are conceptually current, and that provide room for further thought, reading, and exploration.

This third edition of *Placing Latin America* has been thoroughly updated to provide an account of the diverse geographies of the region. Two new chapters (on natural resources and on Latinos and Latin Americans in the United States) join the other revised and updated thirteen chapters, reflecting the rapid changes that the region has experienced in the past five years. In this volume, we speak of geograph*ies* (in the plural form) because of the way in which we document the juxtapositions of environments, landscapes, and social relations that are characteristic of the region today. For example, some chapters in the book explain the struggles of indigenous people, peasants, and other marginalized rural and urban populations as they compete for resources (e.g., access to land, availability of water) with more powerful social actors. Other chapters document the ways in which neoliberalism and global economic restructuring have resulted in changes to urban form and urban governance in cities across the region, providing new opportunities for some residents but also excluding many others, such as poor urban dwellers, from access to key amenities. We have asked authors of this volume to make these tensions, between the larger forces and effects of globalization and the inspiring and creative ways in which different people respond to such challenges, explicit in their contributions.

Two important themes of this volume are issues of continuity and change in Latin America. The contributors to this volume were asked to highlight the changing and dynamic geographies of Latin America and at the same time to recognize the historical legacy and the continuity of many place-based phenomena across the region. Despite the changes and challenges confronting Latin America, some things have remained constant over the years, some would say to a fault. A few decades ago, scholars writing on the development trajectories of Latin America drew heavily from theories of economic dependency that emphasized that most of the region was mostly an exporter of primary products under the watchful eye of the United States, mired in extreme poverty and inequality, and a source of cheap labor for transnational corporations. Many such conditions still remain, but there have also been alternative accounts of the trajectories of economic and social development in the region that have attempted to explain the myriad ways in which national and local governments, NGOs (nongovernmental organizations), and people in the region have been working to change long-standing structural inequalities, rethinking strategies for social change, and imagining alternative futures.

The diversity of experiences of continuity and change in Latin America's economic development mirrors the structure and ideas that inspire many of the chapters in this volume. As geographers, we are keenly aware of, and most interested in, the way all of these issues of continuity and change play out on the landscapes of the region. The contributors to *Placing Latin America* recognize that studying the past can help shed light on contemporary conditions. They also recognize that change is possible, and that human agency can go a long way in affecting and modifying deep-seated structural conditions. Thus, many of the chapters in this volume are about conversations between the past and the present, and about changes in the present that challenge the problems of "historical persistence" (Adelman 1999) that so many scholars have described as characterizing Latin America.

As geographers or scholars who follow a geographic perspective, the contributors to this volume also explain situations of continuity and change in Latin America by paying close attention to the relations between people and place and society and space. For example, it is difficult to understand environmental politics and the mobilization of social movements in contemporary Latin America without recognizing people's claims to land and territory, or in other words, the need for people to have their own spaces for (re)production and representation. Overall, we are interested in how people experience globalization in place, and we are also particularly interested in how people attempt to change their conditions and create new geographies. We are also interested in understanding and positioning issues of continuity and change across geographic scales, from the global and hemispheric to the regional and the local.

Latin America: Bounded Region or Open Place?

A volume on the dynamic human geographies of Latin America begs the question of where Latin America begins and ends. What exactly is the extent of Latin America? There are some common (but also contested) answers to this question. Many geographic textbooks on Latin America define the region as a coherent unit that extends from the southernmost tips of Argentina and Chile in Tierra del Fuego to Mexico in the north, thus including both South America and Middle (or Central) America. This definition emphasizes the shared experience of Iberian colonialism (Spain and Portugal) and its legacy in the region as a unifying force that holds the region together despite the different trajectories that countries have followed since independence.

While some scholars include the Caribbean as part of Latin America, many others treat it as a distinct region. The argument is that the economic and cultural histories of the lands of the Caribbean are fundamentally different from those of mainland Latin America. Many point to the larger African legacy and the impact of other European colonial powers in the Caribbean landscape as two fundamental variables that render the Caribbean a separate geographic realm, distinct from the rest of Latin America. Yet, it could be easily argued that emphasizing the African heritage in the Caribbean as a differentiating factor is misleading because this position fails to recognize the many ways in which Africans and African customs and traditions have played a significant role in shaping the character of places in Latin America, from Brazil to the Pacific coast of Colombia to the Atlantic region of Costa Rica, to name just a few. There are many other places where there might be no visible traces of an African past because of the brutality of slavery and independence and "frontier" wars, yet an African influence is undeniably a part of many unique Latin American cultural traits. This can be observed in food and musical traditions all the way to the Southern Cone; even Argentine tangos and milongas owe much of their style to African rhythms.

It is not the intention of this volume to enter into an in-depth debate about the boundaries of the region, but it should be noted that the idea of Latin America that inspires this collection is one of an expanded region. We are not really interested in delineating boundaries; rather we are more interested in the flows and connections between places that are made by shared social, cultural, economic, political, and environmental dimensions and that create Latin American spaces in Middle and South America, in the Caribbean, and even beyond. As geographers, we are inspired by ideas of place as open and porous and notions of place as an expression of the global in the local. Latin America seems to us a perfect example of a porous region that is difficult to pin down in terms of tangible boundaries, in particular in the context of contemporary globalization. For example, this volume includes discussion of the Caribbean in the context of Latin America and with respect to natural resources, tourism, and economic development; the trends the authors recognize in the Caribbean (in terms of tourist flows, economic strategies for development, and so on) are shared also by other places in continental Latin America.

This volume also goes beyond the imagined but also very real line that separates Latin America from lands farther north: the boundary between Mexico and the United States of America. On the one hand, this border is tangible, material. One can visit the border region from either side—though it is far easier to cross the border coming from the United States than the other way around. In this sense, the border acts as the real boundary between Latin America and North America. On the other hand, the border also is an artificial line, the product of the territorial geopolitics of modern nation-states. The border also is a porous contour that over the years has allowed those Latin Americans who have crossed it to begin creating Latin American spaces in North America (those places that in the United States we recognize as "Latino" and "Hispanic"). This is why in this volume we do not talk about a border, but rather about a border region that extends along the official boundary between the United States and Mexico. That transnational border region is also a part of different Latin American human geographies. Latin American cultural critic Nestor Garcia Canclini describes Latin American cultures as "hybrid cultures" (1990), an intertwining of premodernity, modernity, and postmodernity; of races and ethnicities; of religions; of symbolisms; of colonial pasts and postcolonial presents. Following Garcia Canclini, we see the border region from a geographic perspective and as a hybrid place that also encapsulates such intricate mixtures. But then again, because we recognize the openness of place in the context of globalization, the border region between the United States and Mexico is no more of a hybrid place than São Paulo in Brazil or Puerto Vallarta in Mexico. Thus, we see all of Latin America as a hybrid and open region, constantly changing and being transformed in the context of globalization and extending beyond traditional boundaries to reach new places through the growing transnational experiences and lives of people.

Placing Latin America: Overview of Chapters

We have organized this third edition of *Placing Latin America* so that the first four chapters provide a general overview of the physical and human geographies of the region, from key dimensions of the natural environment to historical foundations of politics, economies, and cities. Subsequent chapters engage in more detail and depth with themes that are mentioned in the first four chapters and develop new ones.

In chapter 1, James Hayes and Benjamin Timms offer insight into the opportunities and challenges created by the physical environment of the region, highlighting the climatic and landscape diversity that characterize Latin America. The authors emphasize human environment relations, focusing on struggles and conflicts that range from the local to the regional level, as exemplified by their case studies of socioeconomic and environmental vulnerability in Central America and of reforestation in the Caribbean.

In chapter 2, the editors provide a broad historical overview of a series of events that have been crucial in shaping the region. Jackiewicz and Bosco pay particular attention to geopolitical issues such as the territorial evolution of Latin America from colonial times to the present. The chapter explains that colonialism had lasting effects on Latin America, influencing everything from the demarcation of political boundaries to political, economic, and social systems. The chapter also highlights Latin America's transition, over time, from a place contested by different colonial powers to a region of independent nation-states that at specific times and places experiences situations resembling different forms of neocolonialism. Rather than attempting to provide a detailed historical account, the chapter offers a simpler narrative of key foundational events and moments in the historical geographies of the region to help the reader approach many of the following chapters dealing with contemporary issues in more detail.

Chapter 3, by Ed Jackiewicz and Linda Quiquivix, provides an overview of the economic changes that occurred during the twentieth century and the pattern of development trajectories followed by different countries in the region. The authors present a typology of developmental trajectories for the region and suggest that Latin America today may be witnessing the transition to a new, uncertain phase of political and economic development characterized by a "turn to the left" and an antiglobalization stand. But, as the authors are also quick to point out, the presence of foreign capital and sentiments against it are nothing new in Latin America; the current neoliberal transformation and challenges to it are only the latest chapters in the saga of continuity and change in the region.

In chapter 4, Zia Salim and Fernando J. Bosco provide an account of the diversity of urban experiences in Latin America, from both historical and contemporary perspectives. The authors explain that Latin America is one of the most highly urbanized regions in the world and that Latin American cities are dynamic and exciting places that are becoming increasingly more global, in particular as economic development and tourism grow in the region. But high rates of urbanization also put enormous pressure on the social, economic, and environmental conditions of cities, and the capacities of city governments to respond to such challenges are sometimes limited. As a result, many Latin American cities experience increasing social inequalities and social polarization as well as challenging urban environments, a theme that is developed again later in chapter 11. Overall, Salim and Bosco remind us that the past, present, and future of Latin American cities cannot be separated from the larger economic and political contexts of the countries in the region.

In chapter 5, Thomas Klak further develops the theme of continuity and change in Latin America through an analysis of the risks and vulnerabilities of trade dependency as well as of new opportunities for economic development, in particular in the context of the region's embrace of neoliberalism as a developmental strategy. Klak takes on some of the themes of geopolitics and economic development discussed in chapters 2 and 3 and focuses specifically on Central America and the Caribbean. He points out that over the last two decades three factors have reshaped the region's vulnerabilities and opportunities: a decline of US engagement with the region, the influences of a new hemispheric bloc championed by Venezuela, and the rise of Chinese influence. He illustrates the fragility of economic development strategies in the region with examples from agricultural production (such as banana plantations), labor-intensive but low-value-added assembly manufacturing (such as maquiladoras), and even advanced consumer services (such as online gambling and tourism). Klak argues that despite the apparent diversity of economic activity in the region, there is still a marked lack of sustained social and economic development. Much like the authors in chapter 3, Klak remains suspicious of neoliberalism as capable of producing sustained development for everyone because of the model's connections with powerful economic interests both locally and abroad. Klak, however, considers ecotourism as a possible sustainable development strategy for countries of Central America and the Caribbean.

In chapter 6, Ed Jackiewicz and Thomas Klak collaborate to explore the range of tourist experiences that have become integral to Latin America economic and cultural development. The tourism industry is examined from both the macro level (by conceptualizing tourism as an export industry) and micro level (the relations between tourists and locals). The authors present case studies ranging from mass tourism in Cancún to retirement tourism in Belize to urban tourism in Old San Juan and the *favelas* of Rio de Janeiro. The themes in this chapter build on discussions of sustainable development from chapter 5, where tourism is seen as a catalyst for positive change if it connects with a range of local productive activities such as small-scale agriculture, fishing, or forestry.

Chapter 7, by Christian Brannstrom, deals with a key topic in geographic discussions of Latin America: the existence, use, exploitation, and conservation of natural resources. As the author's conversation about natural resources transverses the region, one theme—conflict—remains constant. Brannstrom filters the abundant natural resources found throughout through the lens of political economy at geographic scales ranging from the global to the local. Whether it be oil from Mexico, soybeans from Brazil, or one of the many other crops that Latin America provides the global marketplace, conflict is apparent but not without some civil unrest. Brannstrom uses several examples to illustrate how workers have responded to the extraction of resources and exploitation of resources that aggravate the "open veins" of the region.

In chapter 8, Kent Mathewson analyzes how psychoactive drugs have been and continue to be both a force and a factor in the production of Latin America's economic, political, and cultural conditions. Mathewson's goal is to show what a comprehensive geography of drug making, taking, and trading for Latin America might entail. His comprehensive analysis is unique in its historical and geographic approach and shows how entire Latin American landscapes and livelihoods have been made and remade in relation to the cultivation of drugs and how local, regional, and national economies have been affected by the imperative of drug commerce. Mathewson's chapter demonstrates one particular way in which the relations between society, culture, and economy are an active part of the construction of unique human geographies in the region.

The remaining chapters in this volume examine the interactions between people, place, and politics in Latin America, with an eye toward developing a geographic perspective on contemporary Latin American civil society. In chapter 9, J. Christopher Brown examines the growing role that NGOs play in Latin American civil society. He ties what he calls an ongoing "associational revolution" in the region to the development of the "politics of scale." Brown documents the efforts of NGOs to effect change in people's livelihoods in the region, and he explains how these often formal modern institutions that have roots in pre-Columbian civilizations operate at local, national, and global levels. He argues that NGOs respond to the challenges presented by the actions of the state and capitalism and that their actions reveal much about how ordinary citizens confront globalization.

Whereas Brown's focus is on formal organizations, in chapter 10 Fernando J. Bosco focuses exclusively on informal ones, specifically on social movements, which are the responses of civil society to perceived injustices. Like Brown, Bosco takes an explicitly geographic perspective to describe those acts of resistance that take place outside the sphere of formal institutions. He focuses on the ways in which Latin American social movements can be understood in relation to the symbolic places they create and that help sustain them and in connection to the spatial strategies that they enact in order to change society. Bosco provides several examples, from indigenous movements in Guatemala, Ecuador, and Bolivia to human rights movements in Argentina, Chile, and El Salvador. He finds a common thread in the explanation of their mobilization through an analysis of the social movements' strategies in places such as plazas and historic sites and of their networking with other actors of civil society across scales.

Adding to the analysis of the dynamism of civil society in the region, Sarah Moore provides a narrative regarding urban environmental politics in Latin America in chapter 11, continuing with the discussion of urban environmental issues that was introduced in chapter 4. Moore ties the ecological and environmental changes that are occurring in urban areas of Latin America in the context of neoliberal adjustment and restructuring to the environmental activities of residents and citizens of the region's urban areas. Focusing on conflicts over the management of trash in Oaxaca, Mexico; access to water in Bolivia; and successful environmental management in Curitiba, Brazil, she illustrates the complexity of the relationship between urban ecologies and urban politics and, again, reaffirms how geography is woven into the mobilization of civil society.

In chapter 12, Kate Swanson offers us a critical perspective on Latin America through an examination of the daily lives of children and young people. Swanson draws from the growing literature on children's geographies and offers vivid examples from the experiences of children and young people in Bolivia, Ecuador, and Mexico, to name few. The case studies in her chapter make explicit connections to many of the themes explored throughout this volume, from the impacts of neoliberalism and economic restructuring on families and children to the importance of NGOs and their efforts to improve the lives of the many disadvantaged children throughout the region. All together, the chapters in this third section of the volume focus on the struggles of people to shape their own geographies. They provide clear examples of the dynamism of contemporary Latin American civil society and explain how, in order to improve livelihoods, Latin Americans are resisting some of the detrimental dimensions of global capitalism and neoliberalism and attempting to find alternatives believed to be more just and equitable.

The final three chapters of this volume continue emphasizing people, place, and politics but specifically highlight transnational dimensions of the lives of Latin Americans and of the Latin American experience. In chapter 13, Altha Cravey provides an in-depth account of the US-Mexico borderlands region, a region that in recent years has become more treacherous as migration to the north increases and the tangible effects of neoliberalism are intensified with the industrialization of the border. Adding to the discussion of assembly manufacturing already introduced in chapter 5, Cravey provides a detailed and socially oriented account of the maquiladoras that have settled in the border region in the context of the North American Free Trade Agreement (NAFTA). She is particularly interested in explaining how globalization affects daily life for people in the border region, and she focuses explicitly on issues of gender, class, and household dynamics. Cravey is also interested in the informal economy of the region, and her accounts of drug and people smuggling further illustrate the discussion of the effects of neoliberalism and economic reform that other authors tackle in this collection. Cravey successfully shows how the border region is a place that operates at multiple scales simultaneously: it is place that penetrates deep into ordinary spaces of both the United States and Mexico, but it is also a place to live, where many people work and raise families.

This theme continues into chapter 14, where Araceli Masterson-Algar explores the concept of transnationalism from both theoretical and empirical perspectives, illustrating the cultural and economic significance of this concept. She draws on case studies of Mexicans in the United States and Ecuadorians in Spain to show how their transnational lives have economic, political, and cultural impacts in both their places of origins and their new destinations. Finally, in chapter 15, Joseph Wiltberger continues the discussion of transnationalism with a chapter that describes how the growing presence and influence of Latinos in the United States challenges us to reconceptualize the space, place, and borders of Latin America. Wiltberger's focus is also on emerging trends involving local-level officials in federal immigration enforcement efforts in the United States. As he explains, these efforts have emerged in response to social and economic concerns surrounding unauthorized immigration, and they are having a significant impact on the lives of Latino immigrants and the Latino population in the United States as a whole. At the end of the chapter, Wiltberger explains the different ways in which Latino immigrant advocates are working for changes that will hopefully lead to recognizing and valuing the contribution of immigrants who have cultural ties to Latin America. Together, the last three chapters of the volume speak to the idea of an "expanded" Latin America, focusing on the way in which Latin American spaces are fluid, crossing artificial and imagined boundaries as Latin American people carry their traditions with them to different places, whether in the US-Mexico border region, in the streets of a Latino neighborhood in the southern United States, or in cities in Europe such as Madrid.

Note to the Reader

The chapters in this third edition of *Placing Latin America* describe the continuity and change of a variety of geographic patterns in the region, the conditions that give rise to such patterns, and the actions of people (in the region and abroad) that either challenge or reaffirm such patterns. While this introduction makes explicit some of the many points of connection among all the chapters, the book can be read in different ways. Readers are encouraged to approach this collection either by reading it in its entirety and in the order presented or by choosing chapters according to a thematic preference. We have asked each of the contributors to write chapters that would be satisfying to the reader if read individually and that also would make independent contributions to our knowledge of the diverse geographies of the region. The contributors have different writing styles, but all the chapters are clear and approachable and follow a similar structure. Each chapter contains a list of key terms and concepts that the authors consider essential in their discussion. All chapters also ground the key terms and ideas discussed through clear examples and case studies. Finally, at the end of each chapter, the authors provide a list of suggested readings, films, websites, or other resources that are meant to lead the reader to further engage with the topics discussed. We hope such references become additional resources that, together with the chapters in this collection, will lead readers to their own conclusions regarding how to *place* the geographies of Latin America.

References

Adelman, J. (Ed.) *Colonial Legacies: The Problem of Persistence in Latin American History.* New York: Routledge, 1999.

García Canclini, Nestor. *Culturas híbridas.* Mexico City: Editorial Grijalbo, 1990.

Chapter 1

Physical Geography

Contemporary Human-Environment Relationships in Latin America and the Caribbean

Benjamin F. Timms and James J. Hayes

LATIN AMERICA AND the Caribbean have an amazing diversity of landforms, climates, and biomes that stretch from the driest desert on earth, the Atacama in Chile, to the world's largest watershed with the greatest annual discharge of fresh water, the Amazon basin. One can travel from tropical rain forest–clad coastlines to snow-capped peaks reaching over 20,000 feet in a single day! In this chapter, we explain the geographical factors responsible for such diversity, setting the stage for the following chapters' coverage of contemporary human-geography topics that are related to the physical geography of this vast and mesmerizing region. In the process, we include case studies of contemporary human-environment relationships that exhibit our negative impacts on the natural environment, but also highlight promising avenues to mitigate such impacts.

Human-Environment Interaction

The physical environment has tremendous influence on human livelihoods. Some geographers in the nineteenth and early twentieth centuries promoted the concept of environmental determinism, whereby the physical environment determined how human societies formed. According to this largely discredited theory, people living in the Amazon basin developed low-density hunter-gatherer societies because of the preponderance of diseases in tropical wet climates and relatively poor soils (due to nutrient leaching by high rainfall and nutrient uptake by vegetation). However, recent research has challenged this claim through archaeological evidence of advanced pre-Colombian urban civilizations that modified the environment to support much larger numbers of inhabitants than previously understood. These advanced societies were devastated by introduced Old World diseases, which greatly reduced their populations and ability to govern (Mann 2008). This exhibits modern geography's focus on the physical environment as less deterministic and more a source of possibilities that cultural groups utilize in developing different cultural landscapes, a concept referred to as "environmental possibilism."

These debates fall under one of the main concepts in geography: human-environment relationships. This is a phrase that attempts to capture the relationship between humans and the environment without the traditional separation of "humans" from "nature" as disparate topics. We see examples of human-environment interactions in cultural landscapes throughout Latin

America—ways of life that would not exist without the particular physical geography with which they evolved and the particular cultural strategies for making a living there. Prior to European contact, the Aztec in Mexico developed floating gardens called *chinampas*, expanding its civilization and population in wetland areas; the Taino people of the Caribbean developed *conucos*, agricultural techniques particularly suited to the topography and soils of both karst and volcanic tropical island landscapes; the Inca of the Andes developed sophisticated technology and techniques for developing domesticated potatoes and other wild crops as well as collecting and distributing water in the high, arid environment. Each of these cultures had a long history prior to contact with Europeans, but the arrival of the Europeans marked the beginning of a drastic upheaval in this history, altering ecosystems and influencing cultural changes that resulted in new human-environment relationships and hybrid cultural landscapes.

The idea of humans being part of (rather than in control of) an environmental system has gained increasing importance as we recognize the impact of overexploitation of environmental goods and the problems associated with the distribution of those goods to a growing world population. Sustainability is the catchword today (see chapters 5 and 6), not just for environmental activists but also for businesses and governments that are recognizing the potential for exhausting or overusing the environmental systems that currently, but may not always, sustain them. Of course sustainability is only important if one is concerned about the quality of life on earth in the future, and individuals, corporations, and governments may ignore potential future problems of resource availability while focusing on short-term goals and economic growth.

In spite of our growing awareness of our interconnections and dependence on the environment, human institutions exist that create incentives for unsustainable behavior. This raises questions beyond those applying more directly to the physical environment—questions of socioeconomic equity and fairness. As much as our chapter is about the physical geography of Latin America and the Caribbean, it is also about the interaction between humans and the environment, which our case studies exhibit as a multifaceted relationship.

Tectonics, Landforms, and the Creation of Mineral Wealth

The landforms and geology of Latin America range from the highest mountain peaks in the Western Hemisphere to broad lowland basins, from ancient weathered plateaus to geologically recent coastal alluvial plains. This diversity of features has been created over billions of years through the forces of plate tectonics that shaped the geography of what has become Latin America. In this section, we will discuss these processes and the resultant landforms for each region—Mexico, Central America, the Caribbean Islands, and South America.

The theory of plate tectonics is based on a puzzle of continental and oceanic tectonic plates being driven in different directions by convection cells in the underlying molten mantle. The major tectonic plates for Latin America include the continental plates of North America, South America, and the Caribbean and the oceanic Pacific, Cocos, and Nazca plates. As the divergent plate boundary of the Mid-Atlantic Ridge pushes the North American and South American plates westward, they form a convergent plate boundary as they run into and are subducted beneath the Caribbean plate, resulting in the volcanic islands of the Lesser Antilles. The northern boundary between the Caribbean and North American plates forms a transform plate boundary, which is partly responsible for the mountainous terrain of the Greater Antilles islands of Jamaica, Hispaniola, and Puerto Rico. It is also responsible for an active earthquake zone that most recently resulted in the disastrous Haitian earthquake in 2010, which killed up to two hundred thousand people. Further west on the Pacific coast, the South American plate and the Caribbean plate converge on the Nazca and Cocos oceanic plates, where the latter two are subducted under the South American and Caribbean plates, respectively, resulting in the rugged mountains of the Central American Volcanic Axis and the ever-rising Andes mountain range along the western edge of South America. Further north, the North American plate boundary with the Pacific plate creates the transform and divergent boundaries responsible for the Gulf of California and the Baja Peninsula in northwest Mexico.

It is at these plate boundaries that we find active landform creation with fertile volcanic soils at the subduction zones, where population densities have always been high due to the increased agricultural productivity of these fertile soils. In addition, exceptional deposits of mineral wealth were created as a result of tectonic and volcanic activity as the Andes were formed. Famous examples include the copper and tin in Andean countries, most notably in Chile's Chuquicamata copper mine, and the famous, but exhausted, deposits of silver at Potosí in Bolivia. However, these boundaries also result in the geohazards of volcanic activity and earthquakes, such as the previously mentioned Haitian earthquake and the massive 8.8 magnitude Chilean earthquake, which also occurred in 2010.

Inland from these tectonic plate boundaries we find older landforms. In Mexico, located on the North American tectonic plate, the northern part of the country is dominated by the Western Sierra Madre and Eastern Sierra Madre, with the Mexican Plateau lying between them. These mountains are historically noted for the silver wealth, and the Mexican Plateau ends in the south with the Neovolcanic range, with active volcanoes reaching over 18,000 feet in elevation within sight of Mexico City. East of here lies the wide Gulf Coastal Plain and Yucatan Peninsula, a flat region of limestone origin that formed under the sea and was uplifted above the surface. Unequal chemical weathering of the limestone base results in karst landscapes with sinkholes and underground river systems. These karst landscapes re-merge in the Caribbean in Cuba and the Bahamas.

Away from the tectonic plate boundaries in South America lie the oldest portions of the Latin American landmass—the Precambrian cratons—which form the ancient core onto which the rest of the South American continent has been accreted over its long geologic history. These ancient cratons, or continental shields, have been subjected to unimaginable forces of heat and pressure since the time of their formation. For billions of years, tectonic processes have acted upon them in creating, destroying, and re-creating continents in new arrangements on the earth. Approximately three billion years old, the cratons form the Guyana and Brazilian Highlands and the Patagonia region at the southern end of South America. The Guyana and Brazilian Highlands are separated by the Amazon basin, and Patagonia is separated from the Brazilian Highlands in the south by the Paraña-Plata river system basin (see figure 1.3). It is this geologic activity that has formed additional mineral wealth in South America, including diamonds and gold found in the Guyana and Brazilian Highlands, the iron ore mined in the Carajás region of the Brazilian Highlands, and the bauxite deposits in Guyana, Suriname, and Venezuela, which is exported for use in making aluminum.

Between the young Andes Mountains and ancient cratons of the Guyana and Brazilian Highlands lies an extensive lowland, including the Amazon basin, which has filled in with sediment deposited by erosion from the rocks where they were formed in the Andes and continental shields. This includes alluvial diamond and gold deposits found in the Amazon basin, which has brought economic rewards but has also resulted in environmental degradation. Finally, we must mention the rich petroleum and natural gas deposits found in the Amazon basin. Although these fossil fuels were formed by very different processes, the geologic and biogeographic history of South America contributed to the conditions for the deposition, sedimentation, and compression of organic remains to form these carbon-rich fuels.

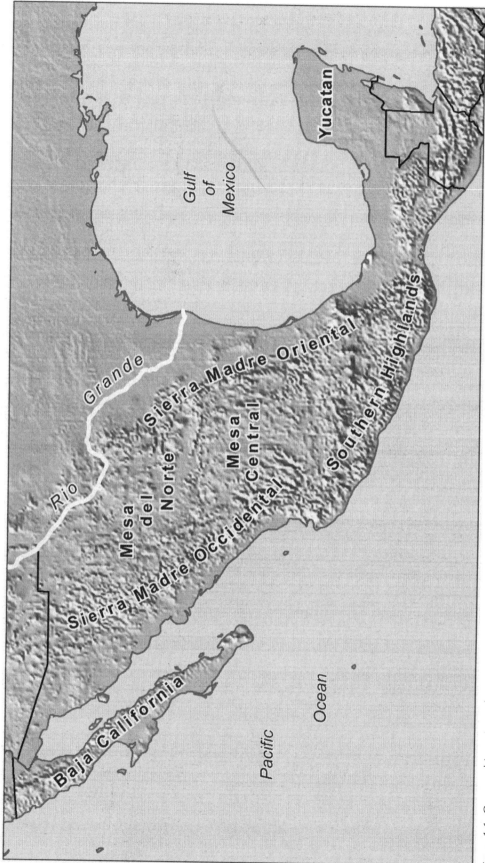

Figure 1.1. Geomorphic regions of Mexico. Map made with Natural Earth; free vector and raster map data at www.naturalearthdata.com/.

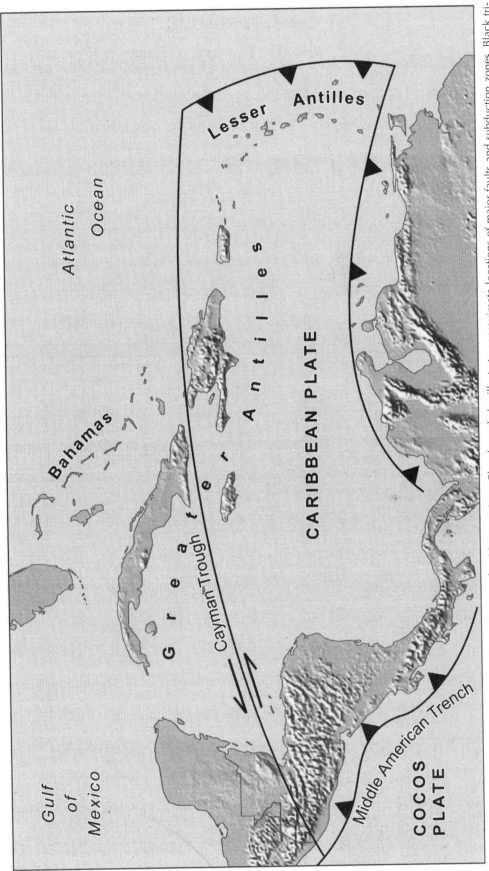

Figure 1.2. Tectonic features of the Central American and Caribbean regions. Plate boundaries illustrate approximate locations of major faults and subduction zones. Black triangles indicate subduction zones, arrows indicate relative direction of plate movement. Shaded relief map data made with Natural Earth.

Figure 1.3. Geomorphic regions of South America. Made with Natural Earth.

Textbox 1.1. Gold Mining in the Peruvian Amazon

Deforestation in the Amazon basin has long been a topic of intense interest, particularly since the early 1970s, when researchers such as the anthropogeographer Emilio Moran began studying the impacts of the Brazilian government's settlement schemes (Moran 1981). Under these programs, the government laid out road networks throughout the Amazon with planned settlements and land allocations to poor farmers and large cattle ranchers. The result of increased access led to environmental degradation based on human settlement patterns.

Recently, a new route of access to the Amazonian rainforest has been constructed. The Interoceanic Highway connects the Atlantic ports of Brazil with the Pacific ports of Perú. While concerns about the replication of settler frontiers as seen in the Brazilian Amazon are well founded, of recent interest is the access this new highway will grant for global commodity markets such as gold, oil and natural gas, beef, and soybeans. Prices for each of these commodities have risen dramatically over the past decade, resulting in increased production. The expansion of these industries in the Amazon basin threatens not only the tropical rainforest but soils, water, air, and landforms as well.

A prime example is gold mining in the Peruvian Amazon. Fueled by the recent global recession, gold prices have skyrocketed 360 percent over the past decade, and Perú has increased its gold mining production in concert, making Perú one of the top five gold-producing countries in the world. In a recent study applying remote sensing techniques to measure land-cover change, deforestation from artisanal mining (small-scale, informal operations) outpaced deforestation from settler expansion between 2003 and 2009 (Swenson et al. 2011). The pattern of deforestation created by artisanal gold mining is very different from that created by agricultural settlers as it is located primarily along waterways where alluvial gold is located. To extract this gold from the surrounding sediment, the amalgamation process requires the use of mercury. The result has been "deforestation, acid mine drainage, and air and water pollution from arsenic, cyanide, and mercury contamination" (Swenson et al. 2011, 1).

Hence, while the Interoceanic Highway has provided access to global commodity markets, the pattern of environmental damage from artisanal gold mining is focused along rivers and water sources. Not only does this affect the natural environment, it is detrimental to human health (Diringer et al. 2015). Of course, global commodity prices are cyclical and changes in the global economy could lead to lower gold prices, lessening the incentive to expand production. But gold is not the only commodity in the Peruvian Amazon; it has vast reserves of oil and natural gas, much of which have already been leased to foreign corporations. The increased access to the Amazon basin that the Interoceanic Highway has granted Perú does not bode well for sustainable management of this region's environmental resources.

Climate, Biomes, Human Modification, and Vulnerability

Climate (the long-term patterns of temperature and precipitation) and biomes (the dominant forms of natural vegetation and wildlife) are intricately related, along with the soils and topography resulting from the previously discussed geologic processes (see figure 1.4). Here climate and biomes are discussed alongside each other. Interspersed are further case studies exhibiting human modifications to biomes, both in their negative aspects and possibilities for future positive responses, and human vulnerability to climatic events.

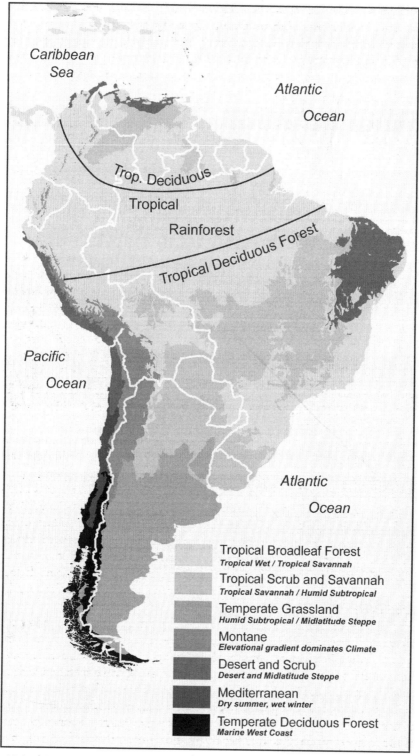

Figure 1.4. Major biomes and climate types of South America. Shaded areas represent generalized biomes. Each biome is related to at least one major climate type (see text for descriptions). The map illustrates the broad relationship between biomes and climate, not precise spatial boundaries. For detailed maps of biomes and climate, specific texts on physical geography, climate, and biogeography are recommended. Created with World Wildlife Fund Ecoregions of the World spatial data (Olson et al. 2004).

Climates vary with distance from the equator, north and south, in an approximately symmetrical pattern. Tropical wet climates with consistently rainy conditions and stable warm temperatures dominate within 10 degrees north and south of the equator due to the high prevalence of incoming solar radiation at the equator and the convergence of the northeast trade winds in the Northern Hemisphere and the southeast trade winds in the Southern Hemisphere. These moist, warm winds are so named as they helped sailing vessels transverse the Atlantic Ocean from Europe to the Caribbean during the colonial era (at least for the northeast trade winds). As they approach the equator from the northeast and southeast, respectively, they converge and create the Intertropical Convergence Zone (ITCZ). Here, along with high surface temperatures, a low-pressure zone of ascending air is formed, leading to adiabatic cooling and condensation that results in the some of the highest precipitation amounts on earth. Interestingly, since the air at the equator is ascending to higher altitudes, surface wind speeds decline to the point that the region was called the Doldrums, with no prevailing winds, and sailing vessels often sat in place for long periods of time until they drifted out of the region into areas with more prevailing winds to power them.

The natural biome associated with the tropical wet climates is the tropical rain forest, also referred to as the *selva*. Here, a high diversity of species forms a complex structure including a large number of tree species that forms the canopy—a dense layer of intermixed tree crowns, which shades the forest floor below—and giant tree species, known as "emergents," that extend above the canopy to reach sunlight. Below the canopy is an understory of shade-tolerant trees that can thrive in low-light, high-humidity conditions. While tropical rain forests, particularly in the Amazon basin, contain possibly 50 percent of the world's biodiversity, the ground-level vegetation in the rain forest is relatively sparse (due to the low-light conditions), and the soil has low fertility, primarily due to rapid uptake of nutrients by the many plants, fungi, and invertebrates as well as leaching from heavy rainfall. Hence, most of the biodiverse flora and fauna exists within the canopies.

Just north and south of the tropical wet climates are the tropical savannah climates, which still have high temperatures and precipitation due to their location within the tropics, but are defined by their pronounced dry seasons and lower overall precipitation amounts. In the Northern Hemisphere, this dry season occurs roughly during the months of November through May, and in the Southern Hemisphere the opposite is true from June through October. Tropical savannah woodlands predominate here, with a higher proportion of trees closer to the equator and gradually transitioning to more grasslands as one moves further north or south. Trees tend to drop their leaves and become dormant as a strategy to cope with the dry seasons. This leaf drop allows sunlight to penetrate the tree canopy to the forest floor, allowing green plants to flourish near ground level and resulting in a more dense understory than found in the tropical rain forest.

While this climate and biome pattern is relatively symmetrical east of the Andes in South America, there are exceptions due to the unique landforms and prevailing winds in this region. For example, the Caribbean islands experience orographic processes that create a windward and leeward pattern of precipitation. The warm and moist northeast trade winds are forced to rise over the mountainous interiors of the Greater Antilles and high volcanic islands of the Lesser Antilles, resulting in heavy precipitation on the northeast windward side of these islands and coincident tropical rainforest biomes. The southwestern coasts, in contrast, lie in the rain shadow of the interior mountains and, hence, are much drier and transition into a tropical savannah woodland biome. Similar orographic processes can also be seen in Central America, in the Guianas of northern South America, and along the coastline of Brazil near Rio de Janeiro

Textbox 1.2. Geohazards and Vulnerability in Central America

The physical geography of Central America has rendered it susceptible to extreme natural phenomena such as earthquakes, volcanic eruptions, landslides, and tropical storms, particularly in the Caribbean and Central America where hurricanes are a prominent threat from June through November. As natural events, they are considered disturbances and part of the natural order; however, they become natural *disasters* when human populations are impacted. Of course, human activity also affects the intensity of natural disasters through settlement patterns, land-use and land-cover change, alterations to the hydrologic system, and anthropogenic contributions to global climate change, all of which can detrimentally affect natural systems. There is a growing acceptance that while the proximate cause of these disasters is the actual natural event, there are socioeconomic processes that increase vulnerability for affected populations and, simultaneously, natural systems (Klein 2007).

A poignant case was Hurricane Mitch, which struck Central America in October of 1998. Central America a has long history of socioeconomic inequality, particularly in access to land, where the past century has witnessed export-oriented agricultural industries appropriating most of the flat and fertile lands in the region, forcing impoverished rural populations onto steep slopes in the interior mountains that are vulnerable to landslides and flooding (Stonich 2008). With the vast majority of the rural population eking out a farming existence on these marginal hillside locations, this geographic settlement pattern led to widespread deforestation that degraded natural biomes, disrupted the hydrological cycles, and further exacerbated the vulnerability of these communities to flooding and landslides.

While these socioeconomic factors would aggravate the effects of any severe weather event, the potential for global climate change to increase human vulnerability to natural hazards may have been revealed as a result of Hurricane Mitch and an unusually strong El Niño Southern Oscillation (ENSO) event in 1998. ENSO events occur when warmer ocean waters in the Pacific migrate to the coast of South America, changing global precipitation patterns. Global climate change, particularly global warming, is increasing the frequency and intensity of these ENSO events, which result in drought for Central America during the early growing season in the spring and summer, but also increase the potential for powerful storm activity such as hurricanes in the autumn and winter.

In the spring and summer of 1998, a drought attributable to ENSO led to fires that ravaged Central America, further degrading hillside vegetation. Then, in October of 1998, Hurricane Mitch arrived and stalled over the region. Fed by warm moist air associated with ENSO, it unleashed torrents of rain, causing massive flooding and landslides that killed an estimated eleven thousand people and left up to a million people homeless. Afterward, the focus of disaster recovery on the tourism industry in Honduras ignored the underlying socioeconomic processes that had created vulnerability for the impoverished and heavily impacted populace, leaving them less resilient to withstanding future natural disasters (Stonich 2008). In another case, the devastation was used as an opportunity to relocate indigenous Lenca residents from within Celaque National Park in Honduras, resulting in impoverishment and increased vulnerability as well (Timms 2011). While, in this case, we discussed hurricanes, these same socioeconomic factors also apply to the study of volcanic eruptions and earthquakes throughout Latin America and the Caribbean, such as comparisons of the 2010 destructive earthquakes in impoverished Haiti (with widespread destruction and suffering) and relatively wealthy Chile (where the impacts were much less severe).

Textbox 1.3. Caribbean Reforestation

The natural biomes of the Caribbean islands have been heavily modified by humans over the past five hundred years, primarily due to plantation agriculture and small hillside agriculture that have left virtually no old-growth forest remaining. However, recent changes in the global political economy have rendered the agricultural sector in the Caribbean uncompetitive with industrialized agriculture in other world regions. When combined with societal advancement through demographic and migration transitions that have resulted in slower population growth, aging farmers, and increased migration to urban areas by younger generations, farm abandonment has become a noted reality. The question then becomes, will the islands of the Caribbean progress through a forest transition with reforestation occurring in these emptying rural areas?

Recent research suggests that this may indeed be the case. In the Cockpit region of central Jamaica, our research found a net decrease in forest of 1 percent between 1987 and 1998. We attribute this net deforestation to the expansion of small fields for growing yams for export. However, from 1998 to 2011 the trend reversed, with a reforestation rate of 2 percent (Timms et al. 2013). While these net changes appear minimal, they do indicate a changing of trends indicative of a forest transition. The average age of farmers in the region has risen, and these farmers are less inclined to undertake the difficult work of hiking to fields within the reserve. Additionally, interviews with farmers during fieldwork in Jamaica showed that young people are less inclined to enter into farming and are instead migrating to urban areas, coastal tourism destinations, and abroad to engage in alternative forms of employment.

While demographic trends such as a decreasing natural increase rate and emigration play an important part in this pattern, it is also influenced by changes in the global political economy. Neoliberal restructuring and trade liberalization from the 1990s through the present decimated the agricultural sector in Jamaica as small farmers found themselves unable to compete with the influx of cheap agricultural imports (Timms 2009). Further, yam production decreased substantially over the last decade. Hence, younger populations are disregarding farming as a suitable career option, which is motivating them to seek employment elsewhere (see chapters 3 and 5) as the older farmers retire or scale back production, allowing forest to regrow on their abandoned plots.

What this suggests is the possibility of a forest transition occurring in Jamaica, and similar processes are at work throughout the region. Several recent studies have uncovered drastic declines in land under cultivation and substantial increases in forest cover throughout the Caribbean (Helmer et al. 2008). In the Lesser Antilles, the loss of a guaranteed banana market in Europe due to the rulings of the World Trade Organization (see chapter 5) has led to a crash in banana exports and corresponding decline in banana farmers from thirty-five thousand in 1992 to less than four thousand in 2008 (Klak et al. 2011). Much of these abandoned banana lands are reverting to forest as many of these ex–banana farmers are now migrating abroad for work to support families back home with remittances, creating "phantom landscapes" (see chapter 5).

More research is needed in multiple locales to determine if reforestation will be sustained, particularly since changes in the global political economy, such as the rise in world food prices making agriculture more lucrative (Timms 2009), may reverse these gains in forest cover. Further, it is difficult to reconcile the impoverishment of rural populations, which drives the forest transition in the Caribbean, with the positives of increased forest cover. But from an environmental perspective, it may signal a "conservation by abandonment" trend.

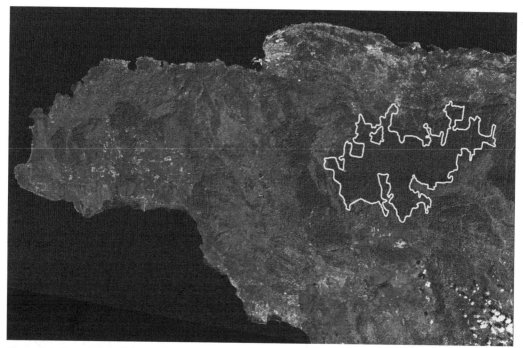

Figure 1.5. Boundaries of the Cockpit Country Forest Reserve in the karst landscapes of western Jamaica.

where the coastline has a tropical wet climate while the interior regions exhibit a tropical savannah climate. The natural biomes of these areas should correspond to their climatic matches, but human modifications have altered these natural biomes.

Around 30 degrees north and south of the equator, the dominant air pressure pattern changes from the ascending low pressure storms of the ITCZ, and corresponding high rainfall, to descending high pressure dry conditions. In turn, climates transition to steppe and eventually desert climates at these latitudes. Corresponding biomes also transition from shrub and sparse grasslands in the steppes with ten to eighteen inches of rainfall a year to more extreme xerophytic plants, which are more efficient at preserving water, in the deserts with less than ten inches of annual rainfall. Following this symmetrical pattern of climates and biomes, we find steppe climates in the Mexican Plateau and Gran Choco of central South America and deserts further north in the borderlands between the Mexico and the United States.

In addition, we also find desert climates both on the west coast of Mexico (on the Baja Peninsula) and in the Atacama Desert in South America that stretches from southern Ecuador to northern Chile. Both of these are related to their locations relative to the previously mentioned 30 degree latitudinal location and the presence of cold ocean currents. On the Baja Peninsula, the cold California Current denies the landmass relatively moist air, resulting in dry conditions. On the other side of the equator, the cold Perú Current off the coast of South America achieves the same affect. Adding in the rain shadow effect of the Andes, which blocks moisture from the Tropical Atlantic Ocean, the Atacama Desert is considered the driest desert in the world with some areas having never experiencing recorded rainfall.

While most of Latin America and the Caribbean lie within the tropics, there are regions that extend beyond them, including the northern steppe and desert regions of the Mexican Plateau and the Patagonian region of southern South America. In the latter we also find mid-latitude temperate climates. In the far southern reaches of Paraguay and Brazil, and including all of Uruguay and Argentina south through the Pampas region, we find a humid subtropical climate similar to what one can find in the southeast of the United States and much of eastern China. This climate is influenced by warm Atlantic Ocean currents and is characterized by warm wet summers and mild winters. In conjunction with the South American lowlands of the Paraña-Plata watershed, this climate and biome region is renowned for its excellent soils, vast grasslands, and the human activities of grain farming and livestock ranching.

On the west coast, the Atacama Desert transitions southward into the mild midlatitude Mediterranean climate of central Chile, which is characterized by wet winters and mild dry summers. The corresponding Mediterranean biome will be more diverse than deserts, including some trees and more shrubs and grasses, but these will also have some traits similar to desert plants like the ability to access and store water and minimize its loss. The Central Valley of Chile is noted for its production of Mediterranean crops such as grapes and irrigated fruits and vegetables, similar to what one finds in the Central Valley of California. Further south, the climate transitions into a marine west coast climate with predominantly cool, humid conditions. The vegetation also transitions into temperate rain forest, which mirrors the climate and vegetation patterns of the Pacific Northwest of the United States and Canada.

Of final note are the highland climates of the north-south trending Andes and the mountains of the Central American Volcanic Axis. The elevation gradients imposed by these mountains result in rapidly changing temperatures, precipitation, and vegetation forms as elevation increases, which is referred to as *altitudinal zonation*. Noting that the following elevation ranges are general and vary with latitude, at the lowest levels below 3,000 feet in elevation lies the *tierra caliente* (hot lands), which typically have tropical wet or tropical savannah climates, with their associated vegetation characteristics. Above this zone up to around 8,000 feet in elevation is the *tierra templada* (temperate lands), which are cooler and have quite pleasant climates with deciduous and, at higher elevations, coniferous forests. It is in this zone that many of the cities of Central America and South America are located, and it is also known for coffee production. Further up in elevation, to perhaps 12,000 feet, lies the *tierra fria* (cold lands) with decreasing trees and increasing amounts of grasses and shrubs. At this point, cooler weather crops such as wheat and potatoes are cultivated. Finally, the highest altitudinal zone is the *tierra helada* (frozen lands), primarily in the Andes, which is above the tree line and where one finds small indigenous communities growing such crops as quinoa and grazing livestock such as llamas, alpaca, and sheep. At the highest elevations one finds tundra vegetation and eventually barren rock and glaciers.

Conclusion

The physical geography of Latin America and the systems it forms with human culture are diverse and complex. The tectonic history and geology of Latin America have produced a wealth of natural mineral resources. Initially these resources were utilized by indigenous populations, later extracted by Europeans during the colonial era, and today increasingly exploited by Latin American states and foreign corporations as they ride the boom of the recent spike in commodity prices. Of increasing concern is potential conflict over resource exploitation among foreign interests, state governments, and individual citizens themselves. And what about the environmental costs? Similarly, natural biomes such as tropical rain forests have also suffered from long-term human modifications driven by both global commodity needs such as lumber, gold, iron ore, soybeans, and petroleum and domestic needs of arable land for farmers and the

Textbox 1.4. Coffee and Water Resources in Colombia

The mountains of Colombia's coffee-growing region are covered with green vegetation, often shrouded by clouds and fog, receive consistent rainfall, and have humid conditions all year, yet water conservation is a growing concern here. Colombia has been experiencing a severe drought and many communities have little or no clean water. Drought is partly a natural phenomenon—unusually low rainfall—and partly human—exacerbated by unsustainable management choices. Ranching, farming, urban, and industrial water use can all affect water sustainability. While the connection between water and coffee may seem obvious—you need water to make a cup of coffee—it takes an impressive amount to make one cup. It takes about 140 liters (37 gallons) of water to produce one cup (125 ml/4.2 oz.) of brewed coffee, and most of that is used before it leaves the farm (Chapagain et al. 2007).

Most of the 140 liters of water that goes into our cup of coffee comes in the form of rainfall on coffee fields and although this may seem "free," it has a price. This rainfall has economic value in the commodity crop it helps produce, but consumers do not pay for this water—local people and the environment pay. Rainfall that goes into coffee growing is exported to other countries where coffee is roasted and consumed. In this way, rainfall is diverted from local watersheds and ecosystems and from supporting human health, biodiversity, and environmental services. Because most coffee is grown in monoculture plantations where native forest has been removed, rainfall that would have been retained in the soil, in local food products, rivers and lakes, and in the forest canopy, is "lost" to higher rates of evapotranspiration and economic exportation. Runoff from coffee plantations can also carry high amounts of agricultural chemicals that pollute rivers and lakes.

In Colombia, and other humid countries, water is used to remove the pulp of the coffee "cherry" from the "bean" that becomes your roasted coffee. In less-humid locations coffee cherries are dried whole and the dried pulp is removed by machines, but in humid regions, the higher moisture and rain prevent drying and ruin the harvested coffee. A typical operation using "wet-method" processing will use 40 liters of water to process 1 kilogram of coffee cherries. While this wet process uses relatively little water compared to the total 140 liters required for our cup (most of it goes into growing the plant that the cherries came from), it is an intensive and wasteful process, directly impacting water quality and availability for human use and for native plants and animals.

Wet-method water use is a small fraction of the total water used; however, it has a large environmental impact because it is taken directly from surface water sources, further reducing availability for humans, and it creates high amounts of water pollution when it is released back into rivers and streams. Wet-method water output contains high concentrations of organic pollutants, and can have high acidity, both of which upset local ecosystems and cause problems for human water management.

Awareness of the water intensity of coffee production is growing, but much still needs to be done to keep local water local, maintain functioning ecosystems, and make fair pricing include the environmental costs of lost water and water pollution. Work by Cenicafé (The National Coffee Research Center in Colombia) has led to techniques to reduce water consumption and pollution throughout the production process, and groups such as Rainforest Alliance and UTZ are emphasizing integrated sustainable agriculture to reduce waste and pollution. Every bean purchased from sources that use and promote sustainable practices makes a difference in coffee's impact on people and the environment.

damming of rivers for hydroelectric energy. But in light of these concerns, there are rays of hope. Brazil has cut its deforestation rate in half over the past decade by enforcing conservation laws and monitoring forest change through utilizing geospatial technologies such as remote sensing (Hansen et al. 2013).

On a slightly different note, global climate change presents considerable challenges to the people and biomes of the region. Vulnerability to climatic variability and extremes is something that cultures in Latin America have adapted to in the past, yet increasing population density, changing patterns of land use, global market forces, and climate change are all making populations more vulnerable to climatic variability. Rising sea levels threaten Caribbean beach tourism, increasing variability in precipitation stresses small farmers without access to irrigation, and more powerful and frequent tropical storms are a constant concern for people made vulnerable by socioeconomic and ecological marginality.

Our discussion of human-environment interaction in Latin America has had to be limited, though there is much more to explore and even the few topics raised here provide fertile ground for more detailed investigation. Not only must we understand the myriad of negative impacts we have on the natural environment—be it deforestation, land degradation, water quality and quantity, or global climate change—we must also seek out ways to mitigate these negative repercussions of human activity and restore these natural systems. In this chapter, we not only provided a broad background on the physical geography of this region but highlighted case studies of contemporary human-environment relationships—some of which are alarming, such as gold mining in the Amazon and geohazards in Central America, and some of which give rise to hope, in the case of Caribbean reforestation and efforts to reduce water use and pollution in coffee production.

Key Terms

altitudinal zonation: The change in climates and biomes with increased elevation in mountain regions.

biome: A large terrestrial ecosystem characterized by specific plant communities and formations; usually named after the predominant vegetation in the region.

environmental determinism: The belief that human activities are governed by the environment rather than social conditions.

environmental possibilism: Belief that the environment sets limitations, but humans have the capacity to choose between a range of possible responses to physical conditions.

Suggested Readings

Hecht, S. and A. Cockburn. *The Fate of the Forest: Developers, Destroyers, and Defenders of the Amazon.* Updated edition. Chicago: University of Chicago Press, 2011.

Miller, S. W. *An Environmental History of Latin America.* New York: Cambridge University Press, 2007.

Roberts, J. T. and N. D. Thanos. *Trouble in Paradise: Globalization and Environmental Crises in Latin America.* New York: Routledge, 2003.

References

Chapagain, A. K. and A. Y. Hoekstra. "The Water Footprint of Coffee and Tea Consumption in the Netherlands." *Ecological Economics* 64 (2007): 109–18.

Diringer, S. E., B. J. Feingold, E. J. Ortiz, J. A. Gallis, J. M. Araújo-Flores, A. Berky, W. K. Y. Pan, and H. Hsu-Kim. "River Transport of Mercury from Artisanal and Small-Scale Gold Mining and Risks for Dietary Mercury Exposure in Madre de Dios, Peru." *Environmental Science: Processes & Impacts* (2015) DOI: 10.1039/C4EM00567H.

Hansen, M. C., P. V. Potapov, R. Moore, M. Hancher, S. A. Turubanova, A. Tyukavina, D. Thau, S. V. Stehman, S. J. Goetz, T. R. Loveland, A. Kommareddy, A. Egorov, L. Chini, C. O. Justice, J. R. G. Townshend. "High-Resolution Global Maps of 21st-Century Forest Cover Change." *Science* (November 15, 2013): 850–53.

Helmer, E. H., T. A. Kennaway, D. H. Pedreros, M. L. Clark, H. Marcano-Vega, L. L. Tieszen, T. R. Ruzycki, S. R. Schill, and C. M. S. Carrington. "Land Cover and Forest Formation Distributions for St. Kitts, Nevis, St. Eustatius, Grenada and Barbados from Decision Tree Classification of Cloud-Cleared Satellite Imagery." *Caribbean Journal of Science* 44, no. 2 (2008): 175–98.

Klak, T., J. Wiley, E. Mullaney, S. Peteru, S. Regan, and J. Merilus. "Inclusive Neoliberalism? Perspectives from Eastern Caribbean Farmers." *Progress in Development Studies* 1, no. 1 (2011): 33–61.

Klein, N. *The Shock Doctrine: The Rise of Disaster Capitalism*. New York: Picador, 2007.

Mann, C. "Ancient Earthmovers of the Amazon." *Science* 29 (August 2008): 1148–52.

Moran, E. *Developing the Amazon*. Bloomington: Indiana University Press, 1981.

Olson, D. M., E. Dinerstein, E. D. Wikramanayake, N. D. Burgess, G. V. N. Powell, E. C. Underwood, J. A. D'Amico, I. Itoua, H. E. Strand, J. C. Morrison, C. J. Loucks, T. F. Allnutt, T. H. Ricketts, Y. Kura, J. F. Lamoreux, W. W. Wettengel, P. Hedao, and K. R. Kassem. "Terrestrial Ecoregions of the World: A New Map of Life on Earth" *BioScience* 51 (2004): 933–38.

Stonich, S. "International Tourism and Disaster Capitalism: The Case of Hurricane Mitch in Honduras." In *Capitalizing on Catastrophe: Neoliberal Strategies in Disaster Reconstruction*, edited by N. Gunewardena and M. Schuller, 47–68. Lanham, MD: Altamira Press, 2008.

Swenson, J. J., C. E. Carter, J. Domec, and C. I. Delgado. "Gold Mining in the Peruvian Amazon: Global Prices, Deforestation, and Mercury Imports." *PLoS ONE* 6, no. 4 (2011): e18875. DOI:10.1371/journal.pone.0018875.

Timms, B. F. "Development Theory and Domestic Agriculture in the Caribbean: Recurring Crises and Missed Opportunities." *Caribbean Geography* 15, no. 2 (2009): 101–17.

———. "The (Mis)Use of Disaster as Opportunity: Coerced Relocation from Celaque National Park, Honduras." *Antipode* 43, no. 4 (2011): 1357–79.

Timms, B. F., J. Hayes, and M. McCracken. "From Deforestation to Reforestation: Applying the Forest Transition to the Cockpit Country of Jamaica." *Area* 45, no. 1 (2013): 77–87.

Chapter 2

The Making of a Region

Five Hundred Years of Change from Within and Without

Edward L. Jackiewicz and Fernando J. Bosco

THE MAJOR THRUST of this book is on contemporary themes in Latin America and the Caribbean (LAC); however, it is important to set both a physical geography and human-environment relations context (see chapter 1) as well as a geo-historical background to better understand the major issues confronting the region today. The purpose of this chapter is to provide that historical context, highlighting socio-spatial inequalities. The emphasis will be on the territorial evolution of the region from pre-Columbian times, to colonialism, to independence, to neocolonialism and other forms of continuing foreign influence, and concluding with current efforts to form a more united region through trade blocs and political alliances.

Covering more than five hundred years in this short chapter is an arduous task, but efforts are made to highlight historical themes related to geographical transformations that help contextualize the remainder of the book. Also, since chapter 3 highlights economic issues in the modern era, there is a concerted effort here to avoid redundancies and focus primarily on cultural and political issues.

An Etymology of a Cultural Region

The term "Latin America" is an invention by a French geographer for the nations that had been under the yoke of Europe's Latin countries (Spain, Portugal, and France), those whose languages derive from Latin. Thus, Latin America is a cultural region with a Eurocentric moniker that obscures its indigenous past and sheds some light on its troubled history. The Caribbean, which is often lumped together with Latin America and is included in many parts of this book, is named after the sea that surrounds the islands and the now nearly extinct Carib Indians. The early European influences in that region include Spain and France as well as the British and Dutch. The region was later populated with migrants from Africa, China, and India who were relocated to replace the decimated native population.

The countries of LAC were forcibly brought into the European realm of global domination with dramatic consequences in all spheres of life. When the Industrial Revolution began, the LAC countries' role in the global economy deepened as they became key exporters of raw materials and consumers of products manufactured in the global North, so when discussing the term "globalization," the LAC countries are well versed, with over five hundred years of exposure (see chapters 3, 5, and 7).

The Pre-Columbian Americas: What's It Like to Be Discovered?

While estimates as to how many people populated Latin America and the Caribbean at the time of conquest range from approximately twelve million to more than one hundred million, there is no doubt that most of the societies were highly advanced, comparable to or even more advanced than those of Europe. The most advanced, and thus best known, of these civilizations are the Incans of Andean South America, Mayans of lowland Central America including the Yucatán Peninsula, and Aztecs (or Mexica, as they called themselves) of highland Mexico. Highlighting these three is not to diminish the influence of other groups, such as the Arawaks, Chibchas, Caribs, Araucanians, and other peoples, who have all made important cultural footprints on the region. The achievements of all of the region's indigenous groups are well documented elsewhere and are beyond the scope of this chapter. Suffice it to say that all had food production systems that supported large and concentrated populations (see chapters 1 and 8) and road networks that facilitated military movement and trade—the Inca highway network reached from what is today central Ecuador to present-day central Chile and northern Argentina. In addition, all these civilizations established large urban centers and ceremonial sites with impressive architecture, such as Tenochtitlán in Mexico or Machu Picchu in Perú (see chapter 4). Communal living was common, and while warfare between groups was widespread, there was no way for them to anticipate what was about to happen during the next 150 years.

The following quote by sixteenth-century Spanish priest and historian Bartolomé de las Casas succinctly summarizes the early interactions between the Spaniards and the indigenous folks:

> The reason the Christians have murdered on such a vast scale and killed anyone and everyone in their way is purely and simply greed. . . . Their insatiable greed and overweening ambition know no bounds; the land is fertile and rich, the inhabitants simple, forbearing and submissive. The Spaniards have shown not the slightest consideration for these people, treating them (and I speak from first-hand experience, having been there from the outset) not as brute animals—indeed, I would to God they had done and had shown them the consideration they afford their animals—so much as piles of dung in the middle of the road. They have had as little concern for their souls as for their bodies, all the millions that perished having gone to their deaths with no knowledge of God and without the benefit of the Sacraments. One fact in all this is widely known and beyond dispute, for even the tyrannical murderers themselves acknowledge the truth of it: the indigenous peoples never did the Europeans any harm whatever; on the contrary, they believed them to have descended from the heavens, at least until they or their fellow citizens had tasted, at the hands of these oppressors, a diet of robbery, murder, violence, and all other manner of trials and tribulations. (de las Casas 1542, preface)

Indeed, it is estimated that as much as 95 percent of the indigenous population was decimated at the hands of the Europeans through warfare, imported diseases (especially smallpox), and slavery, leading to what many scholars have described as the worst demographic calamity in recorded history (Mann, 2005) or what is also known as a *demographic collapse*. The map of the so-called New World was then to be reconfigured by outsiders and the locals and imported slave workers subjected to nearly three long centuries of colonial rule. In sum, the highly advanced societies of the Americas were to be almost entirely remade in a relatively short period of time, retaining only small remnants of what took centuries to establish.

Carving Up the New World: The Treaty of Tordesillas and Colonial Strategies

Treaty of Tordesillas

The geopolitical transformation of the region began almost immediately after Columbus first made contact, with the Treaty of Tordesillas in 1494. The treaty was designed to divide trading and colonial rights of the newly discovered lands between Spain and Portugal, to the exclusion of other European countries. The dividing line was a meridian 370 leagues (typically, one league was the distance a human or horse could walk in one hour) west of the Cape Verde Islands, already in Portugal's possession. The division gave a chunk of the eastern part of South America, the bulge that sticks out into the Atlantic Ocean, to the Portuguese and the rest to Spain. The initial boundaries were not heavily enforced at the time, and the Spanish gave little to no objection to Portugal's expansion to the west, ultimately resulting in the formation of Brazil's current boundaries. In 1750, the Treaty of Madrid officially granted Brazil the territory that it now has.

Spain and Portugal followed different colonial and territorial strategies in different places. Portugal focused primarily on plantation economies in Brazil, with an emphasis on sugar. Brazil became the largest producer of sugar by the early 1600s, creating a large coastal economy that also relied on the transatlantic slave trade for labor (see chapter 8). On the other hand, Spain's focus was mostly on mineral exploitation, agricultural settlements, and ranch economies in the interior of the continent. As time went by, Spaniards developed more settlements, began living alongside indigenous populations, and pushed territorial frontiers farther and farther, beginning in the Caribbean in the very early 1500s, founding cities and ports such as Lima and Callao in Perú in 1535 and achieving a permanent settlement in Buenos Aires (current Argentina) by 1580, after earlier failed attempts. Spanish colonialism in Latin America also changed over time. In the sixteenth century, Spain was driven by both economic and religious motives. This is the period that coincides with the "Black Legend" of Spanish colonialism in Latin America (i.e., the "conquistadores" annihilating native populations and leading to their demographic and cultural collapse, the attempts to spread a more pure and strict form of Catholicism among the natives, and so on). But these economic and religious motives were often in tension. While the devastating effects on the native population are undeniable, conflicting and complementary intentions created divergent colonial experiences in different places. Colonial power was contested among dominant elites and also by the popular classes (Adelman 1999). By the eighteenth century, the Spanish religious goals were almost abandoned and replaced with imperial (and much more secular) objectives. At this point in time, Spain was competing fiercely with other European powers for colonial domination and expansion, and the imperial objectives of Spain in Latin America were clashing with those of Portugal, England, and other European powers (Difrieri 1980).

Organizing the Territory: Audiencias and the Viceroyalty System

Once the conquest was under way, Spanish America needed a system to govern Spain's new territories. The Council of the Indies was established in 1524 as the supreme executive, legislative, and judicial bodies of the regional government. The council had as its agents an overlapping system of viceroyalties and and *audiencias* (the territories assigned to specific royal courts), governed by viceroy, captain general, or governor. Even though the council was marked by increasing levels of ineptitude during its tenure, it did provide the most authoritative records on the colonial history of the region (Keen and Haynes 2004).

Viceroys, governors, and captain generals had essentially the same function: responsibility for overseeing the civic and military functions in their respective realms. One difference is that viceroys typically were given the larger and more important territories to govern (Keen and Haynes 2004). While the administrative leaders of audiencias often worked in collaboration with their viceroyalty counterparts, these overlapping jurisdictions, not surprisingly, were the source of frequent conflict. The first audiencia was established in Santo Domingo in 1511, and although this one only lasted until 1526, at the time of independence in the early nineteenth century, there were twelve audiencias active in Spanish America, which closely resemble some of the borders we know today (figure 2.1).

The viceroyalty system essentially oversaw the lands that were heavily populated and wealthy, creating a great opportunity for these representatives of the monarchy (figure 2.2). The first of the four was New Spain, created after the conquest of the Aztecs in 1521. Its capital was located in Mexico City, although its territory was quite expansive, including the Pacific islands of Guam and the Philippines as well as Cuba, Puerto Rico, much of the United States west of the Mississippi as well as what we now know as Florida, and the area south to, but not including, Panama.

The Viceroyalty of Perú was the second to be established (1542), after the conquest of the Inca Empire. Their capital was in Lima, from which they governed much of South America at the time. The viceroys were responsible for governing the economic system, which was based primarily on the extraction of mineral resources, and protecting against invaders from other European countries, namely, England, France, and the Netherlands. In the 1600s, Potosí, at more than thirteen thousand feet above sea level and rich in silver, became the largest city in South America, despite being too high for any agriculture. All provisions to support the population were brought to the area by mules (Chasteen 2006).

The third of the viceroyalties, New Granada, was not established until 1717. This territory in northern South America includes the countries we now know as Ecuador, Colombia, Venezuela, and Panama, as well as Guyana and parts of northwestern Brazil, northern Perú, Costa Rica, and Nicaragua. Its capital was in Bogotá, but difficult terrain in this region made it a challenge to govern effectively and inhibited travel and communications. Therefore, the autonomous administrative units known as *audiencias* were established in peripheral areas, exacerbating the political and cultural differences found throughout the viceroyalty and hindering Simón Bolívar's (more on him later) attempts at unification.

The fourth and shortest lived of the viceroyalties was Río de la Plata, founded in 1776 in a territory that was formerly part of the Viceroyalty of Perú and one of the late Bourbon Reforms (see below). Its capital was in Buenos Aires and was formed largely for trade. Buenos Aires was a major center of illegal trade and security as Great Britain and Portugal both had a growing interest in the region, roughly the area of what is now Argentina, Uruguay, Bolivia, and Paraguay.

During the colonial period, there was a need to deepen and enhance control over the new territories. The most significant of these were the Bourbon Reforms (named for Spain's House of Bourbon) throughout the eighteenth century. The reforms were intended to stimulate technological and economic growth in order to enrich Spain so that Spain could better compete

Figure 2.1. Audiencias and their date of origin. Map by David Deis.

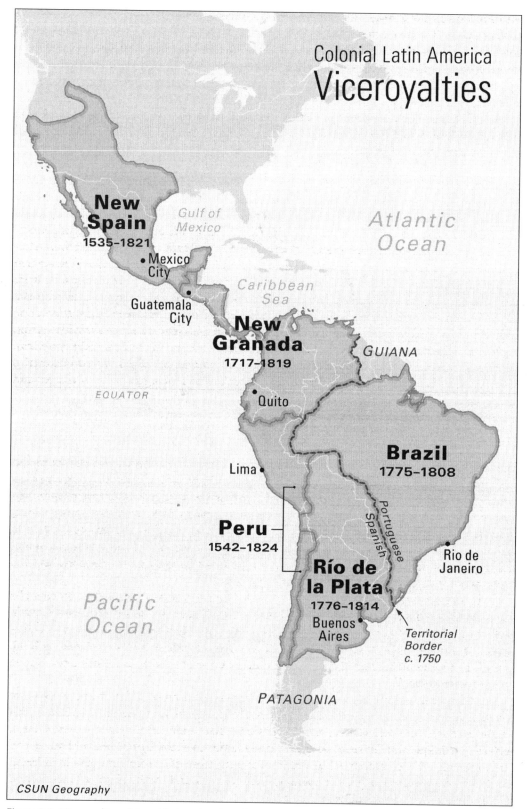

Figure 2.2. Viceroyalties of Spanish America. Map by David Deis.

with England in the struggle for empire that dominated the eighteenth century (Keen and Haynes 2004). These reforms were typically brought over by peninsular Spaniards, that is, those from Spain, increasingly fostering resentment among the locals, including the *criollos* (those born in the Americas). On the ground, taxes were raised, ports were opened for trade exclusively with Spain, agriculture was modernized, and state monopolies were established. In effect, these reforms inflamed the growing resentment in the colonies, planting the seeds for revolt and ultimately independence. Perhaps the culmination of the growing dissatisfaction with the colonists was the Rebellion of Tupac Amarú II (1780–1782), which was an uprising of both native and mestizo peasants.

Brazil

The colonial experience in Brazil was quite different from what occurred in Spanish America, due largely to the limited resources of the Portuguese. Much of the colonial administration was given over to private individuals in a captaincy system, a combination of feudalism and commercialism in which captains answered to the king but also generated profits from their territory (Keen and Haynes 2004). The introduction of sugarcane to Brazil's coastal areas, particularly in the northeast, led to a major transformation in the colony, generating large amounts of wealth derived from monoculture and the introduction of slave labor from West Africa (see chapter 8 for a discussion of the role of sugar in colonial Latin America). When sugar became less profitable, gold and diamond mining became important extractive activities, shifting economic activity to interior locations and giving rise to new villages and towns, such as Ouro Prêto.

Central America

The countries of Central America had a somewhat different path toward independence and as Eakin (2007) notes had "one of the least dramatic and least violent episodes" of the revolutionary period (193). During the colonial period, the Central American states were within the territory of New Spain. At the time, all of Central America as we know it today (sans Panama, which was part of the Viceroy of Gran Colombia) was known as the Kingdom of Guatemala and governed by a captaincy general in Guatemala City. It was one of the most isolated and least significant areas of the Spanish Empire, as it did not have abundant resources and the majority of the native population lived in the highlands.

When Mexico declared independence in 1821, Central America followed on its coattails (Chasteen 2006) but separated itself from Mexico. By 1823, the United Provinces of Central America was formed, joining together the five republics of Guatemala, Honduras, El Salvador, Costa Rica, and Nicaragua. However, this was not a marriage built to last, and by 1840, four of the five countries had declared their independence, resulting in the countries we see on the current map.

The Caribbean islands' move to independence was even more different and a bit more complex. Indeed, even today some islands are not independent, for example, Anguilla, British Virgin Islands, Turks and Caicos, and the Cayman Islands are still British colonies. Others, such as Martinique and Guadeloupe, are officially in the Overseas Department of France, and Puerto Rico is a US commonwealth. The islands were more of a crossroads, and each island has its own unique story to tell. The Spanish, British, Dutch, and French all played a significant role, as did the United States later on.

The Caribbean was perhaps the region most completely annihilated as a result of colonization. Like in Brazil, the introduction of sugarcane in the mid-seventeenth century precipitated a massive clearing of the land for plantation sugar, coinciding with the introduction of West African slaves (Richardson 1992).

Land Grabs and the Control of Space at a Local Level

When it came to daily existence in colonial Latin America, indigenous folks and slave labor were most affected by the highly unequal restructuring and subsequent redistribution of the land system at a more local or regional level. Even today, Latin America has the most unequal distribution of land on the planet—a direct legacy of colonial rule, when a small number of people owned large swaths of land—and large numbers of people squeezed into small land areas, in many cases land they do not own. The invaders' control of the land was part and parcel of their control of the economy, politics, and culture, resulting in a complete domination of the region. The ability to export LAC's natural resources was the driving force behind controlling the land. It began with control over the mines and the development of sugar plantations, where darker-skinned natives, soon replaced by slaves, would do the manual labor.

The transformation of the region's land took on several forms. The *encomienda* was introduced by Queen Isabella in 1503, granting land and labor to the conquistadores in exchange (in theory) for the protection of the Indians as well as their being taught the Spanish language and indoctrinated into the Catholic faith. In reality, this turned into a feudal system where the natives were exploited and often worked to death. Witnessing the maltreatment of natives on these lands inspired Bartolomé de las Casas to abandon his own encomienda to become an advocate for the indigenous population.

Haciendas were one form of large landholding where conquistadores were the beneficiaries. These parcels of land became an important status symbol in the region, and their output was mostly used for subsistence and distribution to those close to the *patrón*. Haciendas typically included mines and agriculture, or some combination, and the workers were known as *peones* or *campesinos*. The dissolution of haciendas spurred the Mexican Revolution of 1917, leading to their demise, although remnants of them still remain today.

Plantations were another of the earliest forms of land control and exploitation of local resources. Again, local labor was used to produce a single crop for the global market—beginning with sugar. Sugar plantations transformed the landscape of first the Caribbean and later the mainland, and their labor-intensive practices and soon to be decimated native workforce provided the impetus to import slaves from Africa. Bananas and coffee later became important plantation crops in the region. When these large pieces of land were transformed into plantations, they often replaced subsistence agricultural areas, creating challenges for the locals in feeding themselves from their own land.

A fourth form of landholding during the colonial period was the cattle and sheep ranches common in southern South America, known as *estancias*. Estancias remained an important symbol of wealth and social standing after the colonial period, all the way to the present. Cattle were introduced to the region by the Spanish and became an important part of the cultural and economic character of the region. Now, some of the estancias have been converted to guesthouses accommodating tourists trying to recall some notion of romanticism associated with this period.

Change in the Air

Latin American liberals (not to be confused with contemporary liberals in the United States), who were predominantly criollo urban dwellers and, according to Arias (2003), often more ruthless than the conquistadores, rose to positions of prominence in the latter half of the nineteenth century. Their ambition was to promote a free market and greater individual liberties, following European and US models, which were seen as becoming more "liberal" or "modern" (see chapters 3 and 7). There are two significant aspects of this transformation worth mentioning. First, this new "freedom" really only pertained to urban areas, as the rural areas were still dominated by haciendas and plantations where the indigenous people and mestizos worked in slave-like conditions under their criollo masters on land that was largely owned by the church, which typically supported these conservative landowners. Second, because Europe's success had harsh racial overtones, that is, the "superiority" of whiteness, an accepted explanation for Latin America's lack of development or modernity was its darker skin color. Numerous countries began to encourage immigration from Europe to "whiten" their populations (see Chasteen 2006). These policies were widespread throughout the region, but were most prevalent in the Southern Cone countries, which received nearly 90 percent of this migrant stream. Specifically, southern Brazil, Argentina, and Uruguay were the largest recipients, perhaps because the climate was more conducive to their needs, that is, not tropical and similar to the migrants' countries of origin. In Argentina, the leading destination, a full 30 percent of its population was foreign-born by 1914. As Chasteen (2006) notes, the size and impact of this European migration was comparable to that of the earlier forced migration of Africans to the region.

Another aspect of the colonial period that warrants mention is that Spain deliberately did not manufacture products in the Americas, preferring to do so at home and then export, which meant that once independence arrived there was no manufacturing infrastructure in place, nor were there individuals with factory experience or expertise, which burdened the region with a technological lag when compared to countries of the global North—a disparity that still has some resonance (see chapters 3 and 5).

Simón Bolívar, Independence

The independence movement in the Americas began with Haiti breaking free from France in 1804. On the mainland, it was the May Revolution of 1810 in Argentina that was credited with starting the wars of independence throughout the region. Two of the most influential figures in the independence movement were Simón Bolívar and José de San Martín. By 1822, Bolívar's forces were controlling much of northern South America, sowing the seeds for independence. In 1830, Bolívar helped found the first union of independent nations in South America, known as Gran Colombia. The influence of Bolívar is relevant today: the former and recently deceased president of Venezuela, Hugo Chavez, dubbed his early twenty-first-century efforts to unite Latin America as a "Bolivarian" revolution (see chapter 3). Bolívar himself was a liberal white criollo but one who had plenty of support from the nonwhite majority in the northern part of South America. While Bolívar was instrumental in the liberation movement in northern and western South America, San Martín was making waves against the Spanish in the south. Between 1814 and 1817, the general began his military campaign in Argentina, then crossed the Andes into Chile, defeating the Spanish there. Three years later, San Martín led Perú's independence movement against Spain. The two leaders later met in Guayaquil, where San Martín unexpectedly decided to return to Argentina, leaving the final battles of independence to the leadership of Bolívar.

Brazil's path to independence was not marked by violence, as were those of the rest of the region. Its independence was officially declared in 1822, but it was a monarchy until that was overthrown in 1889. More startling perhaps is that slavery was not abolished in Brazil until 1888, even though the number of slaves in the country had been in decline since the 1820s.

It is important to note, as Chasteen (2006) claims, that the criollos had tired of rule by the *peninsulares* (those born in Spain) and had initiated the revolts, not to create a more egalitarian society and embrace the masses, but rather because they wanted to rule themselves. Also, the rebellions had greater gravity in fringe areas such as Venezuela and Argentina than in prime economic centers such as Mexico and Perú, and as a result they were the first to break free from colonial control.

Arias (2003) points out that Latin America has been plagued by a "spatial asymmetry" at the global, national, and regional scales, something that is still highly evident today (see chapter 4). This unevenness has its origins in precolonial times and has been perpetuated and exploited throughout the region's history by actors at all of these geographic scales, including the church, *caudillos* (strongman who held power locally or regionally), dictators, the World Bank/IMF, the United States and other foreign countries, local politicians, and many more. One of the repercussions of this socio-spatial divide is recurrent revolutions and uprisings and ongoing resentment of those with more by those with less (see chapter 10 for examples of popular and peasant movements in the region).

Battle Lines

Latin America has been the stage for several wars that have also contributed to the shaping of national boundaries. The most familiar is perhaps the vast amount of land lost by Mexico in its war with the United States between 1846 and 1848, following the United States' annexation of Texas. The result was that Mexico lost a large amount of territory in the southwestern United States, including California (see chapter 13).

The War of the Triple Alliance (1864–1870) pitted Paraguay against its three neighbors: Brazil, Argentina, and Uruguay. There are several versions of why the war began, but the result was that Paraguay lost many lives as well as nearly half its territory to Argentina and Brazil. Less than a decade later, the War of the Pacific commenced, which was a battle of Chile versus an alliance of Bolivia and Perú. The cause of the war is attributed to competing claims for the mineral-rich lands of the Atacama Desert in what is now northern Chile and one of the driest spots on the planet. Bolivia suffered the most as a result of this war by losing its coastal access as well as some mineral-rich lands. Bolivia is still today trying to regain its access to the Pacific Ocean. It should be mentioned that Bolivia and Paraguay are the only two landlocked countries in South America and the two poorest. These two countries went to war in the 1930s over an area known as the Gran Chaco, a dry area thought to be rich in oil. Paraguay emerged as the victor in this very bloody war between two poor countries. The boundary lines resulting from this war were not made official until 2009. Other more recent territorial disputes include the conflicts between Chile and Argentina over several islands along the Beagle Channel in the southernmost section of the continent beginning in the 1970s but with origins going back to the uncertain boundaries of colonial times. This dispute was ultimately settled after the findings of an international tribunal and by papal intervention, narrowly avoiding an armed conflict between the two countries in 1978.

The Colossus to the North

A chapter on the geographical formation of Latin America and the Caribbean would be remiss without some discussion of the role of the United States in shaping this region (see chapter 3). While the United States did not have any direct role in drawing lines on the map, except of course for the infamous takeover of parts of Mexico discussed above, this final section of this chapter illustrates the significant influence the United States has had in "filling in" those places on the map.

A fitting place to begin is with the passing of the Monroe Doctrine in 1823. The doctrine, originally drawn up to protect the region against potential attempts by European countries to establish or reestablish new colonies in the region, opened the door for now nearly two centuries of controversial US involvement in the region's domestic affairs. By the 1890s, the United States began to supplant Great Britain as the most significant foreign influence in Latin America. The involvement became more official with the Roosevelt Corollary of 1904, an amendment to the Monroe Doctrine, which allowed the United States to intervene whenever LAC nations "seemed unstable"—subjective terminology that was certainly open to abuse and paved the way for economic and political interventions, which would later be referred to as *neocolonialism*. The exertion of this power was in play almost immediately when the United States helped organize a revolt in Panama, with very strategic objectives (see textbox 2.1).

The twentieth century is littered with a series of United States–initiated overt and covert military interventions, particularly in places of strategic importance, igniting an anti-American

---

Textbox 2.1. The Panama Canal as an Example of US Domination

At the turn of the twentieth century, the idea of building a canal linking the Atlantic and Pacific Oceans was gaining momentum. The French had tried in the 1880s but were unsuccessful, but this did not deter the United States. The immediate problem was that Colombia, which controlled Panama, would not sell the land to the United States. This inspired Theodore Roosevelt to organize a revolt in Panama with US assistance, enabling Panama to overthrow the Colombian rulers and set up its own government. In short order, this new Panamanian government signed a canal treaty with the United States, which included granting them control of the land where the canal was to be built. The US paid Panama $10 million for sovereign control of the land in exchange for its protection by the US Marines. The canal was completed by 1914 at which time the United States established a near-permanent presence in the Canal Zone with a post office, commissary, and customhouses.

The construction of the canal required lots of technical expertise as well as cheap imported labor from the West Indies. As many as 75,000 people worked on the project and nearly 6,000 of them died as a result of tropical diseases and accidents.

Interestingly, control of the canal was administered by the United States until President Jimmy Carter decided in 1977 to turn the canal over to Panama. This became official in 1999, and the canal is now run by the Panama Canal Authority, and it is a great source of revenue.

sentiment in several countries. Of course, this is counterbalanced with the ongoing love affair with many things American, such as music, film, television, cuisine, and so on. (The term "American" is used here as it is throughout the Western Hemisphere to refer to people from the United States, even though it is recognized that all people of the hemisphere are Americans as well.) The target of many of these interventions has been in Central America and the Caribbean, most likely because they are geographically closer, relatively small and easier to manage (Clawson 1997), and of strategic importance.

Keen and Haynes (2004) note that between 1898 and 1932, the United States intervened militarily in nine Caribbean nations on thirty-four different occasions and ran the governments of Panama, Nicaragua, the Dominican Republic, Cuba, and Haiti for long periods (528). Most observers agree that this involvement and control undermined these countries' ability to develop and chart their own economic and political courses. This political involvement, not surprisingly, was accompanied by substantial economic investment. By the 1930s, a full 35 percent of US foreign investment was funneled into Latin America, much of it in oil. This was the early stage in the evolution of multinational corporations (MNCs). Much of the policy that followed was to protect these economic interests.

Tensions mounted in the region with the onset of the Cold War, when US leaders tended to view the world as divided into two camps: their own, which was committed to free enterprise, and the other, communist (Keen and Haynes 2004). Countries of the global South were viewed as places that could go either way and were thus places of strategic importance, a situation sometimes resulting in protracted and deadly wars (think Korea and Vietnam). Of course, viewing all of these countries through a black-and-white lens is a highly limiting view of a diverse range of political and economic experiences across the globe, arguably a way of thinking that fogs our geopolitical views even today.

Not surprisingly, tensions escalated following the Cuban Revolution of 1959 and the US fear that more countries would follow. The protection of US economic interests and/or the Cold War's geopolitical lines led to controversial engagements with several Latin American countries, including Guatemala (1954), Cuba (1961), Brazil (1964), Chile (1973), El Salvador (1980), Nicaragua (1981), Grenada (1983), Panama (1989), and others. With the end of the Cold War, US involvement in the region began to focus more on trade, in which debt was the coercive tool used against the region to impose an economic system based on free trade and privatization (see chapters 3 and 5).

Current US involvement in the region is not just limited to economic reform, as overt and covert involvement continues, as evidenced by recent affairs in Venezuela (see chapter 3) and the tacit support of the drug war in Colombia (see chapter 7) for the past twenty-plus years. On a more positive note, US relations with Cuba seem to be softening. In 2014, President Obama and Raul Castro announced that the two countries would restore diplomatic ties for the first time since 1961. As of this writing, US travelers are now able to visit the island without a government license and can spend money and use credit cards there. The trade embargo, however, still remains. It is hard to say whether progress with Cuba is indicative of a renewed US interest in the region as a whole.

Conclusion

Again, it is worth reiterating that this chapter is in no way comprehensive in its coverage of Latin American history (how could it be?), and many aspects have been glossed over or omitted. But it does provide a historical context with which to view contemporary issues, especially from a geographic perspective. It also offers up a conceptual foundation as a means to contextualize issues such as globalization and neocolonialism and to show the formation of the various nation-states as we know them today.

Foreign intervention is one of the enduring characteristics of this region, even though the players and stakes have changed over time. As chapters 5 and 7 explain in more detail, China is now a key player in terms of foreign influence and intervention in Latin America and the Caribbean, fueled by a booming demand for natural resources from across the Pacific Ocean. Just a few decades ago, this scenario would have been unthinkable. Chinese influence is not limited to the economic realm. For example, the Chinese government is building a controversial military installation in Argentina's Patagonia region (with cooperation from the current Argentine government) to expand its space exploration and satellite programs. Sovereignty thus remains elusive even in the twenty-first century, as external as well as internal forces combine to place the region in newer states of dependency.

Key Terms

criollo: People of Spanish descent born in the Americas.

encomienda: A system of tributary labor in Spanish America whereby indigenous people were granted "protection," payment, and instruction in the Christian faith in exchange for their labor.

hacienda: A large landholding, often combining subsistence farming, mining, and other activities, where indigenous people often lived and worked the land. An important status symbol in Spanish America.

peninsulares: Spanish people born in Spain and residing in the New World.

plantation: A large land-holding organized to produce a cash crop for export.

Suggested Readings

Castaneda, Jorge G. *Mañana Forever? Mexico and the Mexicans.* New York: Knopf, 2011.

Galeano, Eduardo, Isabel Allende, and Cedric Belfrage. *Open Veins of Latin America: Five Centuries of the Pillage of a Continent.* New York: Monthly Review Press, 1998.

Mann, C. C. *1491: New Revelations of the Americas before Columbus.* New York, Knopf, 2005.

Schlesinger, Stephen, Stephen Kinzer, John H. Coatsworth, and Richard A. Nuccio. *Bitter Fruit: The Story of the American Coup in Guatemala, Revised and Expanded.* Cambridge, MA: Harvard University David Rockefeller Center for Latin American Studies, 2005.

References

Adelman, J., (Ed.). *Colonial Legacies: The Problem of Persistence in Latin American History.* New York: Routledge, 1999.

Arias, Arturo. "Politics and Society." In *The Companion to Latin American Studies*, edited by P. Swanson. London: Oxford University Press, 2003.

Chasteen, John Charles. *Born in Blood and Fire: A Concise History of Latin America.* 2nd ed. New York: W. W. Norton, 2006.

Clawson, David. *Latin America and the Caribbean: Lands and Peoples.* Chicago: William C. Brown Publishers, 1997.

de las Casas, Bartolemé. *A Short Account of the Destruction of the Indies.* Taken from www.thelatinli brary.com/. Originally published 1542.

Difrieri, Horacio. *El virreinato del Río de la Plata: Ensayo de geografía histórica.* Buenos Aires: Ediciones Universidad del Salvador, 1980.

Eakin, Marshall C. *The History of Latin America: Collision of Cultures.* New York: Palgrave Macmillan, 2007.

Keen, Benjamin, and Keith Haynes. *A History of Latin America.* 7th ed. New York: Houghton Mifflin, 2004.

Mann, C. C. *1491: New Revelations of the Americas before Columbus.* New York, Knopf, 2005.

Richardson, Bonham. *The Caribbean in the Wider World, 1492–1992.* New York: Cambridge University Press, 1992.

Chapter 3

Cycles of Economic Change

Political Economy from Neocolonialism to the Bolivarian Revolution

Edward L. Jackiewicz and Linda Quiquivix

In this chapter, we trace the evolution of Latin America's economic and political development over the past century, highlighting key characteristics of four dominant phases: modern/liberal, import substitution, neoliberal, and post-neoliberal. We focus on the respective policies of each era, the crises that provided the impetus for change, and how policies impacted the region's landscape in highly uneven ways. The greatest emphasis, as a prelude to the rest of the book, is placed on the last years of the twentieth century and the first decade-plus of the twenty-first century, as significant events such as the economic crisis in Argentina, elections of leftist leaders, reelections, and the endurance and support of and challenges to several antineoliberal presidents are illustrative of a region in flux.

The chapter builds a conceptual framework for understanding Latin America's developmental trajectory and illustrates the dynamic nature of such policies over time. For example, this chapter argues that, especially as Latin America and the Caribbean are concerned, today's dominating presence of foreign capital and ideas is nothing new. Paul Streeten (2001) points out that the world economy was actually more integrated at the end of the nineteenth century than it is today (see chapter 2). Further, the region's own history shows that economic policies are not permanent. Placing the neoliberal period that dominated from the 1980s into the new millennium in context, we illustrate that this political and economic transformation was just the latest episode in Latin America's developmental history. Similarly, there is no reason to believe that this most recent post-neoliberalism will last any longer than the others. Indeed, since the late nineteenth century, the region's economic policy has gone through (at least) four phases, all but the latest leaving a similar pattern of, first, growth and then collapse—and always the miserable footprint of inequality. Each phase has been characterized by significant policy changes driven by the current dominant paradigm: the transition to each new phase has been signaled by some type of economic, social, and/or political crisis. It is also important to remember the role of *agency* in this process—that is, how individuals are responding to macro-level changes and how the interaction between the global and the local alters the landscape of the region. The theme of agency resurfaces in many other chapters throughout this volume.

Before we discuss the various eras, it is necessary to outline the parameters and limitations of this chapter. The dates used here to delineate the various eras are intended to provide a general time reference and not precise points in time when one period ends and another begins.

Also worth mentioning is that all countries throughout the region did not embrace policies at the same time or in the same way. Some were much more aggressive in their adherence to certain policies, while others approached them more cautiously. It is beyond the scope of this chapter to illustrate the range of experiences in all of Latin America and the Caribbean; rather, we draw on specific examples from around the region to illustrate the major points.

The Modern/Liberal Period in Latin America (1880s–1930s)

The modern/liberal period in Latin America emerged after independence and, in some ways, marked a significant break with the region's colonial history. This period quickly saw an expansion of world trade dominated by primary product exports such as coffee, bananas, sugar, and beef (see also chapters 5 and 7). These products, among many others, were the entry point into the global economy and in some cases provided handsome returns. Indeed, Argentina entered the twentieth century as one of the richest countries in the world, ranking ahead of the United States and Great Britain and only slightly behind France in terms of per capita gold reserves in 1910.

In other cases, however, export gains were less than adequate, in many ways determined by geographic factors. Countries blessed with the right climate, soils, natural resources, ports, and/or proximity to chief trading partners fared well in their abilities to produce primary products. Brazil and Colombia saw success in coffee, Cuba in sugar, Argentina in wheat and livestock, Mexico in minerals, and Venezuela in oil. The majority of the small, "geographically challenged" countries, however, struggled to find a niche in the increasingly globalized and competitive economy. One notable exception was Panama—although it was too small to export substantial quantities of primary goods, its tiny size became its greatest asset during the construction of its canal, a precious trading route between the Atlantic and Pacific oceans, in the first decade of the twentieth century.

The export-led model was supposed to expand domestic economies by creating jobs not directly related to exports—the "commodity lottery" deciding which countries fared well. Products like Argentinean beef, for example, required many separate processes and linkages (e.g., pasture, fencing, fattening, slaughtering, and packing), making this type of growth possible, illustrating that the export-led model could work well as a stimulus for development. Conversely, those countries in Central America and the Caribbean exporting bananas did so in enclaves, separating industry from the rest of the internal economy, thus giving these countries little chance of growth (Bulmer-Thomas and Knight 2003, 83).

While securing their interests in these primary products, countries from the global North, most notably the United States and Great Britain, would invest in infrastructure in these countries (see also chapter 4). Direct foreign investment (DFI) was substantial not only in those regions that held vested economic interests but also in those that had diplomatic ties and were deemed politically stable (Thorp 1998, 51). It was Argentina, Brazil, Uruguay, Cuba, and Chile that ranked the highest in DFI at this time (Bulmer-Thomas and Knight 2003), reaping many benefits such as the construction of railroads, designed primarily to transport export products to the port city and out into the global economy.

Latin America's break from colonialism allowed the region to enter the global marketplace. However, fundamental aspects of the colonial economy remained in place. While foreigners came to invest, they did not do so as simple gestures of goodwill. Many of the foreign corporations dependent on Latin America's exports would come to buy the large amounts of land and infrastructure they relied on so heavily, oftentimes via government occupation or through backroom deals that cut or even abolished taxes and duties. Land was sold to them at bargain prices, and workers' rights were almost nonexistent. These conditions were ideal for foreign domination, allowing the previous attitudes of colonialism to permeate, spurring an era of neocolonialism. One of the most notorious examples is the United Fruit Company. In 1899, the banana exporter and US multinational (the predecessor of Chiquita Brands International) came to own 112 miles of Central America's railroad and well over 212,000 acres of land throughout the Caribbean and Central America (Schlesinger and Kinzer 1999, 67), initiating decades of corruption and exploitation (see chapter 5). By 1913, the British were a dominant presence in the region, British investors owning approximately two-thirds of the total foreign investment in Latin America (Skidmore and Smith 2001, 44). In Cuba, where sugar dominated the country's exports, United States–owned sugar mills occupied 22 percent of Cuban national territory (Thorp 1998, 78), and in Puerto Rico, the country's three main exports—coffee, sugar, and tobacco—became dominated by US corporations (Thorp 1998, 80). While some owner-ship patterns may have changed, the region still remains heavily reliant on the export of pri-mary products, with many countries having dominated their respective export industries for more than a century (see table 3.1).

Another legacy from the colonial period that was perpetuated was the highly uneven pat-tern of development, which persists even today. Most of this economic growth was occurring in coastal areas, or major cities near coastal areas (see chapter 4), except for situations where it was necessary to develop other parts of the country (for example, the extraction of minerals). These economic enclaves were designed to export products as quickly and cheaply as possible and did little to develop the vast hinterlands of the region. Even though all Latin American countries were politically independent, they were still tied economically to countries of the

Table 3.1. Latin America's Leading Exports, 1913 and 2005

Country	1913	2005
Argentina	maize, wheat	edible oils, fuels/energy
Bolivia	tin, silver	natural gas, soy products
Brazil	coffee, rubber	transport equipment, iron ore
Chile	nitrates, copper	copper, fruit
Colombia	coffee, gold	petroleum, coffee
Costa Rica	bananas, coffee	coffee, bananas
Cuba	sugar, tobacco	sugar, nickel
Dominican Rep.	cacao, sugar	nickel, sugar
Ecuador	cacao, coffee	petroleum, bananas
El Salvador	coffee, precious metals	offshore assembly exports, coffee
Guatemala	coffee, bananas	coffee, sugar
Haiti	coffee, cacao	manufactures, coffee
Honduras	bananas, precious metals	coffee, shrimp
Mexico	silver, copper	manufactured goods, oil
Nicaragua	coffee, precious metals	coffee, beef
Panama	bananas, coconuts	bananas, shrimp
Paraguay	yerba mate, tobacco	soybeans, feed
Perú	copper, sugar	copper, gold
Puerto Rico	sugar, coffee	chemicals, electronics
Uruguay	wool, meat	meat, rice
Venezuela	coffee, cacao	petroleum, bauxite/aluminum

Sources: Bulmer-Thomas and Knight (2003, 58); www.cia.gov/cia/publications/factbook

North Atlantic, and most important was the increasing influence of the United States within the region (see chapter 2). Perhaps this is best illustrated by the presence of the aforementioned American-based United Fruit Company, which proved to have not only a strong economic impact but also a vigorous political might. This US multinational would come to successfully request that the CIA overthrow Guatemala's democratically elected government in the 1950s due to policy differences, in turn sparking a bloody civil war that lasted over thirty years (see Schlesinger and Kinzer 1999).

This vulnerability of economic and political dependency became increasingly evident in World War I and then more fatally during the Great Depression and World War II, pushing Latin America toward a new internally driven paradigm.

The Period of Import Substitution Industrialization (1940s–1970s)

The crash of the New York Stock Exchange in 1929 underscored Latin America's dependency on, and vulnerability to, an economic system heavily reliant on the exportation of primary products. The crash, the subsequent depression, and, later, World War II, proved to be *global* economic disturbances reducing the North's demand for nonessential primary products such as cacao, bananas, and coffee (Thorp 1998, 97–98). With this drop in foreign exchange, Latin America's capacity to buy imports decreased by approximately half (Kay 1989, 36). As Cardoso and Helwege (1992, 84) state, this crisis backed Latin America by default into its second significant economic era, import substitution industrialization (ISI).

ISI held the guiding principle that a developing country should stop relying on imported manufactured goods and should produce substitutes at home. The ISI movement, seeking to grow national industry and offer protection from foreign competition as a means to reduce external dependencies and improve local economies, involved considerable state intervention—starting with government subsidies and high tariffs and quotas on imported goods. The motivations behind ISI were the perceived flaws of the previous period. Chief among these was the economic asymmetry between the global North and Latin America, whereby primary goods were exported to developed countries that would then transform them into finished goods (i.e., value added) and then sell them back to Latin America.

At the United Nation's Economic Commission for Latin America and the Caribbean (ECLAC, originally ECLA), Argentine economist Raúl Prebisch became ISI's primary champion by concluding that it was to Latin America's advantage to isolate itself from the global economy until it could build a strong domestic economy. While serving as ECLAC's executive secretary from 1949 to 1963, Prebisch argued that domestic industrialization would foster the spread of technology, increase employment, enhance the productivity of the labor force, and reduce the region's vulnerability to the international economic system (Birdsall and Lozada 1998).

ISI proved to be most successful in the largest countries with the highest populations (notably Brazil, but also Argentina and Mexico), primarily because they had the greatest growth potential, the most resources, and relatively diversified economies and were thus able to borrow start-up funds to expand their industrial capacity. Moreover, these countries with large consumer bases and bigger markets were able to sell their manufactured goods to their domestic markets. Yet while these countries experienced greater economic growth than their smaller regional counterparts, they also took greater risks: the money borrowed to start these industries, a large portion of which came from private lenders, that is, banks in the global North, and ultimately could not be repaid from the revenues received, thus setting the stage for the debt crises.

Despite the success in certain countries, the inherent flaws in these policies were soon exposed. The demise of ISI was attributable to ill-conceived policies with regard to both the production and consumption of domestic goods. First, because Latin America did not possess the necessary financial resources or the technological capabilities to implement a vast industrial program, the region was still reliant on foreign assistance. Thus, it was not possible for it to entirely break away from the burdens of dependency that characterized the previous period. The success of ISI was also hindered by the poor quality of products produced in the region, arguably because of the lack of competition in the state-run sectors. This generated little demand, as elites preferred and could afford imported products, even if they had to leave the region to buy them. A substantial middle class never materialized, and the poor could not afford to buy much, thereby limiting consumption and stunting the success of local industry. ISI's problems were further exacerbated by the lack of cooperation within the region, a legacy from the colonial period and something that has only been remedied slightly since then. Limited transportation linkages, historical rivalries between countries, and vast natural barriers all contributed to the limited interaction among the region's countries. This meant, to a large extent, that all countries were experimenting with ISI independently. This was especially detrimental to the smaller Latin American countries.

Industrialization programs focused on the largest cities, making these places magnets for employment as great emphasis was put on the industrial sector at the expense of the agricultural region. Not surprisingly, a mass rural-to-urban migration ensued as ISI's new factories promised the opportunity for many to move away from the exploitative rural working conditions to higher wages and a more modern lifestyle in the city. Soon the cities were overrun with would-be workers, and even when the factories could no longer absorb the workers, the rural refugees continued to come. This was the onset of "overurbanization" putting a strain on the urban infrastructure (housing and schools as well as jobs), leading to the informal city, where many found work and housing outside of the formal sector. This fundamental shift in the region's social and economic geography led to a highly urbanized Latin America (see chapter 4) without the concomitant industrialization to achieve stable economic growth (as had previously occurred in the United States, for example).

These flaws would become evident in the 1960s and manifest in greater social unrest, which opened the door for the period's first military dictatorship, in Brazil, in 1964. By the mid-1970s, military rule was commonplace throughout the region, and economies were stagnating. ISI did little to eliminate regional and class disparities in the region, and the now increasingly urban population began to voice its dissatisfaction.

Although the ISI period was a protectionist one, it was still heavily dependent on foreign investment. This was highlighted when the region's economic instability led foreign investors and many international banks to reduce their presence in Latin America. Between 1980 and 1986, net capital inflows to the region dropped by 40 percent, and private net flows from international banks declined a whopping 80 percent (Gwynne, Klak, and Shaw 2003), forcing governments to borrow monies from international lenders, most notably the World Bank and the International Monetary Fund (IMF). The World Bank, whose original undertaking was to aid in the recovery of World War II–ravaged countries in Europe, later modified its mission into working for "a world free of poverty" by injecting money into less developed countries to help expand their economies (see chapter 5). Because the World Bank was under the marked political influence of free-market countries like the United States, these loans often imposed strict conditionalities, broadly known as structural adjustment programs (SAPs), that reinstated the liberal economic policies and reduced role of the state, reminiscent of the modern/liberal period.

Perhaps the death knell for ISI was in 1982, when Mexico declared that it was no longer able to service its debt and the peso was devalued. The country's debt crisis had a contagion effect throughout Latin America, triggering a crisis. The last years of ISI were plagued by military regimes and highly unstable economies characterized by large debts and hyperinflation. Subsequently, an alternative model was sought to alleviate the region's economic woes, although this time the policies came from abroad. However, in retrospect, this period should be remembered as a relative bright spot in the region's development, with Brazil leading the way with an average growth rate during the period of 8.5 percent. According to Grandin (2007, 198), per capita income grew 73 percent between 1947 and 1973, further illustrating that this period was not as dire as some observers suggest.

The Neoliberal Period (1980s–2000s)

ISI's failure allowed advocates of free trade to reintroduce their agenda into Latin America. The model was first implemented in the region under the military rule of Augusto Pinochet in Chile. Pinochet took office after the bloody CIA-sponsored coup and bombing of the presidential palace of Salvador Allende on September 11, 1973. Two years later, Pinochet hired the "Chicago Boys" to restructure the economy. Dubbed so because of their postgraduate education at the University of Chicago, this group of economists called for the privatization of the country's state-owned enterprises as well as the tearing down of any trade barriers put up during ISI. As journalist Greg Palast (1998) outlines, Pinochet came to "abolish the minimum wage, outlaw trade union bargaining rights, privatize the pension system, abolish all taxes on wealth and on business profits, slash public employment, and privatize 212 state industries and 66 banks." Silva (2004) points out that it is important to remember that this economic project was first introduced to the region under the context of an American-backed military coup (158), casting further doubt (and perhaps resulting in limited support) among the region's residents as well as outside observers to its legitimacy, also suggesting that it probably could not have been done in an openly democratic environment.

Neoliberalism was in many ways a return to the pre-ISI, modern/liberal period. Neoliberalism nearly eliminates state intervention in the economy and forces markets to be left unregulated and freely open to global capital (see chapter 5). During this period, the state apparatus was determined to be at the center of ISI's failure and therefore needed to be relegated to a less important role in economic development. Any impediments to trade (i.e., tariffs, quotas) were anathema to the development strategy and were quickly scrapped. The hyperinflation of the previous period scared off many investors and greatly reduced the purchasing power of many residents. By the mid- to late 1980s, nearly all countries were on board, mostly because high debt had greatly reduced their economic sovereignty within the increasingly globalized economic system, and the region had entered into a new development paradigm despite the obvious (yet rarely mentioned) parallels to an earlier failed era. Controversial policies such as privatization (the selling off of state-owned industries) and trade liberalization (the elimination of tariffs and other trade barriers) were paramount throughout the region. Latin America was advised (some would say coerced) to integrate into the global economy as quickly as possible. Neoliberalism's proponents in the global North were led by a supranational triumvirate comprised primarily of technocrats from the world's wealthiest countries: the World Bank, the IMF, and the World Trade Organization (WTO). This collection of powerful decision makers insists that the fall of the Soviet Union in the late 1980s signaled that conservative ideals had triumphed over the socialist endeavors of communism and should be interpreted as "capitalism is here to stay."

By 1989, the ideas of these supranational organizations came to be known as the Washington Consensus, a recipe for stimulating economic growth and development in Latin America that included reforms like cutting public spending, lowering tariffs, decreasing regulation, promoting privatization, and opening up to foreign investment and trade (see chapter 5). This cadre of individuals both within and outside of the region, believing these methods of "globalization" (a term that was not used prior to the 1980s) to be original, was instead committing itself to a set of principles and guidelines that already had a history of failing in Latin America and elsewhere. Countries of the region were now subordinate to supranational organizations that forced them to swallow some bitter pills to reduce the ills that plagued the region. Of course, some countries were more aggressive than others in their implementation of these policies, but it was not really a question of whether to adopt these policies or not, but rather how deeply to embrace them.

The success of neoliberalism was to be based primarily on the notion of efficiency. States were seen as inefficient while the profit-seeking private sector was not and thus could rectify the inefficiencies and excesses of ISI. Proponents of these policies viewed any short-term hardships as necessary growing pains, while critics saw them as fundamental flaws that would have adverse effects on an increasing number of people. Privatization was one of the most controversial aspects of these reforms. The selling off of state industries allowed the state to quickly receive a significant amount of capital while at the same time relieving it of the responsibility of operating a diverse array of industries. It was expected that the private sector would come in and manage these enterprises more efficiently and profitably. In order to sell off these industries, the state had to find buyers/investors, who, not surprisingly, were mostly based in the global North. Inflation was indeed curtailed by these austerity measures concomitant with the neoliberal paradigm, and the trade-oriented policy adjustments once again began to lure investors. Giant US and European corporations soon had critical links into the region: between 1990 and 2001, Latin America received private investment in infrastructure amounting to $360.5 billion, mainly in telecommunications (44 percent), energy (33 percent), and transport (18 percent) (Campos and Jiménez 2003).

But the pitfalls associated with privatization proved to be more than growing pains. Local populations felt the sting as soon as they found themselves without employment, as one of the quickest and easiest ways to make these industries more efficient was to cut costs, often achieved by the laying off or firing of workers. Privatization and the subsequent layoffs occurred at a time when many social subsidies were being cut as well, also to become more efficient, placing an added burden on the already marginalized populations. Proponents of neoliberal policies frequently point to how these policies lowered the hyperinflation of the 1980s, yet there was little else to illustrate their success, particularly as the century came to a close.

Although adhering to the neoliberal prescription, Latin America had not reaped the benefits long overdue. In the 1980s, Latin America's income per person, the most basic measure of economic well-being, actually shrank by 3.1 percent, and by 1996 one-third of the population was classified as destitute, compared with 11 percent in the late 1960s (Grandin 2007). Inflation was rampant throughout the region during neoliberalism's early years, peaking at over 7,000 percent annually in Bolivia (1985), Nicaragua (1990), and Perú (1990) and exceeding

2,000 percent in both Argentina and Brazil. In fact, Bolivia and Perú both *averaged* an inflation rate of more than 1,000 percent between 1984 and 1993 (see Franko 1999; Gwynne, Klak, and Shaw 2003). While the deeper implementation of neoliberalism ultimately lowered inflation rates, one of the few benefits to the masses, the hardships that befell the local citizens during the 1980s resulted in the moniker "the lost decade." ECLAC (2000) goes further to point out that the term "lost decade" falls short. At the end of 1989, the real per capita product stood at the level not of ten but of thirteen years earlier, and even earlier in some economies. While the 1990s saw some growth, it "was accompanied by negative characteristics from unemployment to volatility" (Grynspan 2004), leaving the latter part of the decade to witness an increase in poverty and growing inequality, enough so that it was christened the "lost half decade" of 1997–2002 (Grynspan 2004). Much of the crisis was evident in urban areas, creating what Grandin (2007) refers to as "feral cities." Food shortages became commonplace, and, in fact, there were more than one hundred food riots in major cities since the 1970s, mainly in protest of IMF-imposed reductions in state subsidies. In line with each period's history of growth and then collapse, these distress signals were loud enough to encourage a new breed of leader touting new policies that would champion in a new era.

The Post-Neoliberal Era

During the neoliberal period, much of the power within the global economy shifted from the nation-state to transnational corporations (TNCs). The neoliberal prescription, with promises of improving the standard of living among the masses, echoed facets of the liberal period and even the colonial era. During this era, the influence of transnational corporations and global capitalists escalated throughout the region. Increases in poverty and inequality led to widespread dissatisfaction among residents with political ramifications, opening the door for left-leaning politicians.

In 1998, Venezuela elected left-wing populist Hugo Chávez as president. Soon after Chávez's election, leading US newspapers such as the *New York Times* and the *Washington Post* referred to Chávez as "Venezuela's rambunctious president" and a "firebrand," and to his movement as containing "anti-American elements" (Ellner 2001, 6). The strong backing by Venezuela's impoverished majority helped Chávez survive a failed coup attempt in 2002 and a United States–backed recall referendum in 2004. While Chávez accused the Bush administration of aiding in his removal, reminiscent of Chile's socialist president Salvador Allende in 1973, the United States claimed at the time to have had neither participation in nor knowledge of the incident. This would later be proven false when CIA documents were uncovered in late 2004 showing that, in fact, the United States had knowledge of the coup days before the attempt.

Chávez was quickly joined by other Latin American leaders in his antiglobalization and more regionally focused stance, an important aspect of his Bolivarianismo plan. One of the most vocal and powerful neoliberal antagonists at the time was Brazilian Luiz Inácio "Lula" da Silva, who was elected president in 2002 and served from 2003 to 2010. Lula presented himself as a genuine alternative to neoliberalism. Once in office, Lula was more of a moderate than many had predicted but nonetheless was reelected in 2006, the first time a Brazilian was successfully reelected, and left office as one of Brazil's most popular presidents ever. Lula proved to be a key challenger to globalization's unfair playing field and instituted some key social programs, such as the Bolsa Família program (see textbox 3.1), that lifted thirty-eight million people out of poverty and reduced extreme poverty by 70 percent. Of equal significance was

---

Textbox 3.1. Brazil's Bolsa Família

According to Morais and Saad-Filho (2011), the Brazilian government has improved the social welfare in their country in three important ways: (1) increase in the minimum wage, which increased 67 percent in real terms between 2003 and 2010; (2) an expansion of social security coverage which now reaches 51 percent of the population, compared to 45 percent earlier in the decade; and (3) Bolsa Família, a social program that now reaches more than 11 million families. The Bolsa Família, aided by financial and technical support from the World Bank, is a quite simple program. In exchange for keeping their children in school and taking their children in for regular health checks, families below the poverty level (monthly income less than 140 reais, or approximately US$75) receive a direct cash payment of approximately 22 reais (US$12) monthly for each child attending school. Studies have shown that most of this money is used to buy food, school supplies, and clothes for the children. Historically, Brazil has had some of the worst economic inequality in the world, and this program is helping to slowly lessen the gap. Of course, the program has its critics suggesting that these direct cash handouts are a crutch and create a dependency or that the money would be used inappropriately (e.g., on alcohol, drugs) but it is hard to argue with the results from such a relatively small investment (2.5 percent of total government expenditure). Also, on the plus side is that there is a strong incentive for families to keep their children in school and healthy, which can lead to generational improvements in the country's human capital. This program has spread to other LAC countries, as well as outside the region.

---

the election of his handpicked successor, Dilma Vana Rousseff, who promised to continue with many of Lula's programs, in 2010. In addition to Brazil and Venezuela, the first decade and a half of the twenty-first century witnessed the election of leftist leaders in Argentina, Uruguay, Chile, Bolivia, Ecuador, Guatemala, Nicaragua, and Paraguay. A commonality among all of these presidents is their disdain for many aspects of globalization and their desire to have more national control over strategic natural resources such as oil and gas, thus, in many ways, revisiting aspects of ISI. They also tend to emphasize a progressive social agenda (increase public expenditures to help poor and marginalized populations), which has earned them widespread support in these highly unequal societies. It should also be noted that despite all of these leaders' leftist leanings, they are still quite diverse; for example, Ansell (2011) refers to Lula as a "left-wing neoliberal," so we should be careful not to view this ideological shift in stark black-and-white terms nor clump all of these leaders together.

While there is not the space here to discuss the nuances of each leader's policies, it is important to note that all appeal, at some level, to members of the political left. Some of the key dividing points among the leaders are: relations with the United States, the role of the private sector compared to the government's, and protectionism versus free trade. The more left-leaning administrations, such as those of Argentina, Bolivia, Ecuador, Nicaragua, and of course, Venezuela, are distancing themselves from the United States and want the government to have a more involved role with the economy including protectionist policies, but these views are not commonly shared throughout the region. For example, Chile, Mexico, Perú, and Colombia are less protectionist and promote free trade and are more receptive to economic ties with the United States.

Reflecting back, perhaps the bell tolled for neoliberalism when its most obvious failure materialized at the turn of this century in Argentina, which exploded into a massive uprising leaving thirty-six dead (North and Huber 2004, 1). In late 2001 to early 2002, the country spiraled into an economic meltdown after declaring a record default of $140 billion in public debt, resulting in massive unemployment and a poverty rate of greater than 50 percent (Hershberg 2002). It is important to note that not all of Argentina's (or any country's in the region, for that matter) ills are attributable solely to external factors, as corruption and mismanagement have been endemic to Latin America and a significant contributor to most if not all crises that have plagued the region. While Argentina had long supported the United States in global politics, it hardly received the concern it warranted from its northerly neighbor during its suffocating downturn, as the United States' attention became concentrated in the Middle East and on the global "war on terror." A stunned Argentinean body politic, experiencing the worst depression in its history, went through four presidents in just a few weeks in December 2001 and opted for policies that defied the Washington Consensus. By stimulating internal consumption and ignoring IMF recommendations to pay its creditors first, Argentina's economy has remained relatively stable over the past decade-plus. Moreover, its exports zoomed, its currency stabilized, unemployment rates dropped, and investors gradually returned (Rother 2004).

If we look at the region as a whole, we see that economic growth during the first decade of the twenty-first century outpaced both the United States and Europe. Moreover, it is important to note that while being largely ignored by the United States, Asian countries, with China and South Korea in the lead, have now begun to move into the region. During a state visit in November 2004, the Chinese president, Hu Jintao, announced that his country plans to invest $20 billion in Argentina over the next decade (Rother 2004). Indeed, China has now replaced the United States as the leading importer of Latin American goods, and there is an accelerated increase in "South-South" relations with India, South Africa, and other non-northern countries.

Shades of Bolívar

Another important regional development is the 2008 formation of a regional alliance known as the Union of South American Nations (USAN), which is a merger of two former trade blocs, Mercosur and the Andean Community of Nations, plus the inclusion of several other countries. Based largely on the European Union model, the program has the goals of a common currency, passport, and parliament by 2019. The objective is to have greater regional cooperation, improved infrastructure connecting countries, and greater ease of movement of people and goods within the region. In other words, it is addressing many of the problems that hindered the success of import substitution programs.

The first two decades of the twenty-first century in Latin America have been eventful, beginning with Chávez and his promotion of the "Bolivarian Revolution" (see chapter 2). Chávez won two elections and paved the way for Nicolás Maduro's election upon his death in 2013. The drop in oil prices has hurt Venezuela, and Maduro does not enjoy nearly the same level of popularity and support as did Chávez, and many feel his hold on the leadership of the country is in jeopardy. The rise of China's presence in the region is significant. We must not forget that most of Latin America still relies on the export of commodities such as oil, minerals, and other non-manufactured materials and is thus highly vulnerable to price fluctuations. In order to offset price plunges of certain commodities, China has loaned $118 million to the region to help stabilize the economy; nearly half of this amount went to oil-dependent Venezuela. Much of this money is going to infrastructure improvements; often overseeing these projects are Chinese companies hiring Chinese workers. Also noteworthy is that these loans do not come with the same "strings attached" as did loans from the World Bank/IMF during the previous period.

As a closing note, we should also keep in mind that many elements of the neoliberal doctrine remain in place throughout the region, such as free trade, widespread foreign investment, and so on. We suggest that Latin America has indeed moved into a new era beyond the austere days of neoliberalism; but as with many of the preceding eras, there are challenges and uneven implementation and results, and events on the ground continuously unfold.

Conclusion

The dominating presence of foreign capital and ideas in Latin America is nothing new and is here to stay. The neoliberal transformation has mostly diminished, although remnants, such as some of the manifestations of globalization, remain in place. If there is one lesson here, it's that none of these political-economic systems are permanent. When the theory hits the ground, the results are not always easy to predict.

This new era raises a whole new set of questions for its citizens and observers. What will the role of the United States in this region be in the future? Are there significant resources and political will to make this new alliance, USAN, work for the betterment of the region and its people? Are these gestures toward regional cohesion viable enough to change the development trajectory?

Key Terms

Bolívarianismo: A set of ideas based on the principles of Simón Bolívar, including the creation of a united South America, provision of public education, and protection from foreign powers in political affairs.

import substitution industrialization (ISI): A trade and economic policy that favors replacing imported products with domestic production in an effort to reduce foreign dependency.

neoliberalism: A market-driven approach to economic and social policy that stresses the efficiency of the private enterprise, free trade and open markets, and a decreased role of the government and subsequently increased role of the private sector in economic affairs.

privatization: The selling off of public assets to private parties.

Suggested Readings

Bulmer-Thomas, Victor, and Alan Knight. *The Economic History of Latin America since Independence.* 2nd ed. Cambridge: Cambridge University Press, 2003.

Cardoso, Eliana, and Ann Helwege. *Latin America's Economy: Diversity, Trends, and Conflicts.* Cambridge, MA: MIT Press, 1992.

Gwynne, Robert, and Cristóbal Kay. *Latin America Transformed: Globalization and Modernity.* 2nd ed. New York: Oxford University Press, 2004.

Schlesinger, Stephen, and Stephen Kinzer. *Bitter Fruit: The Story of the American Coup in Guatemala.* Cambridge, MA: Harvard University Press, 1999.

Thorp, Rosemary. *Progress, Poverty, and Exclusion: An Economic History of Latin America in the Twentieth Century.* Baltimore: Johns Hopkins University Press, 1998.

Suggested Films

Lewis, Ari, director, and Klein, Naomi, writer. *The Take*. 2004. Icarus Films.
Walker, Christopher, director and writer. *Trinkets and Beads*. 1996. Icarus Films.

References

Ansell, Aaron. "Brazil's Social Safety Net under Lula." *NACLA Report on the Americas*, March/April 2011.

Birdsall, Nancy, and Carlos Lozada. "Prebisch Reconsidered: Coping with External Shocks in Vulnerable Economies." *CEPAL Review*, October 1998.

Bulmer-Thomas, Victor, and Alan Knight. *The Economic History of Latin America since Independence*. 2nd ed. Cambridge: Cambridge University Press, 2003.

Campos, Javier, and Juan Luis Jiménez. "Evaluating Rail Reform in Latin America: Competition and Investment Effects." Conference on Railroad Industry Structure, Competition and Investment, Toulouse, France, November 2003.

Cardoso, Eliana, and Ann Helwege. *Latin America's Economy: Diversity, Trends, and Conflicts*. Cambridge, MA: MIT Press, 1992.

Domínguez, Jorge I. "Grading the President: A View from Latin America." *Foreign Policy*, July/August 2003.

ECLAC. "Changing Production Patterns with Social Equity." November 2000.

Ellner, Steve. "Hugo Chavez: Radical Populist or Neopopulist?" Prepared for delivery at the 2001 meeting of the Latin American Studies Association, Washington, DC, September 6–8, 2001.

Franko, Patrice. *The Puzzle of Latin American Economic Development*. Lanham, MD: Rowman & Littlefield, 1999.

Grandin, Greg. *Empire's Workshop: Latin America, the United States, and the Rise of the New Imperialism*. New York: Henry Holt and Company, 2007.

Grynspan, Rebecca. "Economic and Social Trends in Latin America: The Bases for Social Discontent." *International Review of Administrative Sciences* 70, no. 4 (2004): 693–709.

Gwynne, Robert N., Thomas Klak, and Dennis J. B. Shaw. *Alternative Capitalisms*. London: Edward Arnold Publishers, 2003.

Hershberg, Eric. "Why Argentina Crashed—And Is Still Crashing." *NACLA Report on the Americas* 36, no. 1 (2002): 30–33.

Kay, Cristóbal. *Latin American Theories of Development and Underdevelopment*. New York: Routledge, 1989.

Morais, L., and A. Saad-Filho. "Brazil beyond Lula: Forging Ahead or Pausing for Breath?" *Latin American Perspectives* 38, no. 2 (2011): 31–44.

North, Peter, and Ulli Huber. "Alternative Spaces of the 'Argentinazo.'" *Antipode* 36, no. 5 (2004): 963–84.

Palast, Greg. "Tinker Bell Pinochet and the Fairy Tale Miracle of Chile." *London Observer*, November 22, 1998.

Rother, Larry. "Argentina's Economic Rally Defies Forecasts." *New York Times*, December 26, 2004.

Scheman, L. Ronald. "Reform US Neighborhood Bully Image." Commentary. *Christian Science Monitor*, December 29, 2004.

Schlesinger, Stephen, and Stephen Kinzer. *Bitter Fruit: The Story of the American Coup in Guatemala*. Cambridge, MA: Harvard University Press, 1999.

Silva, Patricio. "The New Political Order: Toward Technocratic Democracies?" In *Latin America Transformed: Globalization and Modernity*, edited by R. N. Gwynne and C. Kay. 2nd ed. New York: Oxford University Press, 2004.

Skidmore, Thomas E., and Peter H. Smith. *Modern Latin America*. 5th ed. New York: Oxford University Press, 2001.

Streeten, Paul. "Integration, Interdependence, and Globalization." *Finance and Development: The Quarterly Magazine of the IMF* 38, no. 2 (2001).

Thorp, Rosemary. *Progress, Poverty, and Exclusion: An Economic History of Latin America in the Twentieth Century*. Baltimore: Johns Hopkins University Press, 1998.

Tucker, Calvin. "US Fingerprints on Venezuelan Coup." Trinicenter.com, April 22, 2002.

Webb-Vidal, Andy, and Doug Cameron. "US Investigates Risk of Losing Oil Supplies from Venezuela." *Financial Times*, January 13, 2005.

Chapter 4

Urban Latin America

Evolving Forms and Functions

Zia Salim and Fernando J. Bosco

LATIN AMERICA IS HOME to some of the world's most beautiful cities, such as Rio de Janeiro (Brazil), Cartagena (Colombia), and Granada (Nicaragua), and to some of the largest, such as São Paulo (Brazil), Mexico City (Mexico), and Buenos Aires (Argentina). Several demographic and economic shifts have propelled rapid urbanization in the region, creating a diverse urban geography characterized by urban primacy, the presence of megacities, and the more recent rapid growth of midsize cities (see figures 4.1 and 4.2 for the location of the main cities mentioned in this chapter). Many Latin American cities have experienced great architectural, design, and planning improvements in recent years, resulting in higher quality of urban life for many residents. For example, in the last twenty years, Buenos Aires has gained an entirely new and heavily residential neighborhood (Puerto Madero) teeming with glass and steel office and condominium towers, lofts and businesses occupying converted industrial buildings, and public parks and recreational facilities, all as a result of the urban redevelopment of its traditional waterfront commercial port. Similarly, Medellín (Colombia), a city plagued by drug violence and crime less than two decades ago, is now again a thriving metropolis containing some of the best examples of contemporary civic and public architecture in Latin America. Moreover, Latin American cities are increasingly integrated with international circuits of tourism, with urban heritage and cultural tourism playing a large role (see chapter 6). This type of tourism and a growing interest in historic preservation have contributed to the protection of many buildings and districts in cities across the region, such as Havana (Cuba), Cuenca (Ecuador), and Montevideo (Uruguay), to name a few (Scarpaci 2005).

All Latin American cities share some general urban features, but historical and contemporary variations are also found in different parts of the region. For example, there are notable differences between cities in the Caribbean, colonial cities (both Spanish and Portuguese), and the cities in the Andean highlands and the Southern Cone. Latin American cities are incredibly dynamic and vibrant places, but they also exhibit high degrees of social inequality, socioeconomic polarization, stark differences in housing quality, and problems of infrastructure provision. The intensity of these problems also varies significantly *across* and *within* the region. For example, despite the improvements that it brought to the city, the redevelopment of Puerto Madero in Buenos Aires, mentioned above, illustrates the increasing privatization of public space and services in some Latin American cities. Similarly, the favelas (informal housing districts) of Rio de Janeiro are known worldwide as dangerous and marginal slums, characterized by rampant poverty and crime. But some favela neighborhoods such as Rocinha have gradually become integral parts of the city, with marked improvements in housing and services for their inhabitants, while other favelas not too far away remain places of urban marginality and concentrated poverty. On the other hand, Curitiba, another city in Brazil, is known as one of the most livable cities in the world, with a progressive and participatory approach to urban governance (see chapter 11 and textbox 4.2 in this chapter). This diversity of urban experiences illustrates the difficulty of generalizing about Latin American cities.

Latin America: An Urbanized Region

While the definition of an "urban" area has changed over time and varies by country, Latin America as a whole has experienced *high levels of urban growth* since World War II. In 1900, most of the region's population lived in the countryside, and urban populations exceeded five hundred thousand in only three cities, but subsequent city growth was rapid and unparalleled (Gilbert 1994, 25). According to the UN's 2014 World Urbanization Prospects report, there were 115 cities in Latin America and the Caribbean with populations over 300,000 in 2015, and the average proportion of the population that lived in cities had nearly doubled from 41.3 percent in 1950 to 79.8 percent in 2015. In comparison, global urbanization in 2015 was at 54.0 percent. In terms of urbanization percentages, the only regions in the world that surpass Latin America and the Caribbean are Australia/New Zealand and North America. Even Western Europe, the modern urban and industrial hearth, has a lower urbanization rate. Similarly, urbanization trends in Latin America have shown strong growth and have outpaced those in both Western Europe and North America for every five-year block from 1950 to 2000, a trend that is projected to continue until 2025.

Urbanization's pace has become more varied as cities in the region mature. In most countries, this indicator has generally decreased, mirroring demographic trends of decreased migration and natural increase. For example, Brazil's urbanization rate changed from 5.6 percent between 1950 and 1955 to 1.52 percent in the period from 2005 to 2010, a decrease of 4.08 percent. When comparing urbanization rates for the same time period, we see that Jamaica's decreased by 4.94 percent, Mexico's experienced a drop of 3.44 percent, and Nicaragua's decreased by 2.45 percent.

But Latin America is extraordinarily diverse, and the percentage of the population that is already urbanized varies significantly. Argentina and Uruguay had urbanization rates in excess of 90 percent in 2015, while urbanization in Haiti, Jamaica, Guatemala, and Honduras was in the area of 50 percent. Projections indicate that the region will continue to urbanize at varying rates across subregions, with urban population growth likely to be highest in the less urbanized countries such as Bolivia (Fay and Laderchi 2005). Also, a comparison of urban growth rates between the periods of 1950–1955 and 2005–2010 shows that the rate of urban growth in the region as a whole has slowed and urbanization has decreased in three-fifths of the region's countries, while about a fifth of the region's countries have experienced minor changes in urbanization (e.g., Belize, Paraguay), and a fifth of the countries saw increases in their rates of urbanization in the same time period (e.g., Trinidad and Tobago). The variations in percent of urbanization, both current and projected, and the rate of urbanization reinforces an important point about Latin America—it is challenging to make generalized statements about such a diverse region.

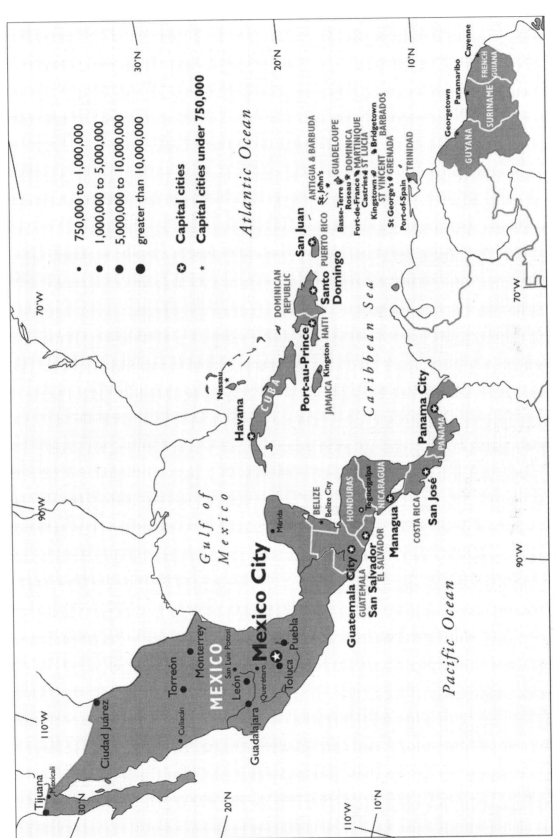

Figure 4.1. Major cities of Middle America and the Caribbean.

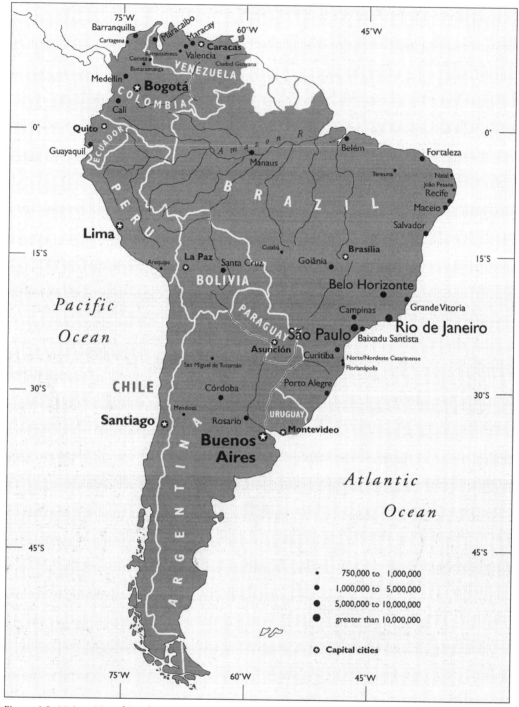

Figure 4.2. Major cities of South America.

Pre-Columbian, Colonial, and Neocolonial Influences in Urbanization

Mesoamerica is recognized as one of the five original urban hearths, the first regions where ancient civilizations settled and where power and social organization were centered. At its peak, the city of Teotihuacán, in the central Mexican highlands, was one of the largest cities in the world, with a population of about two hundred thousand in an area of about twenty square kilometers (eight square miles). The city was elaborately planned, with blocks of apartments, wide streets oriented to the cardinal directions, and large ceremonial structures that included pyramids. Similarly, Tenochtitlán, the capital of the Aztec Empire, is estimated to have been as large as thirteen square kilometers (five square miles). The city was built on an island in Lake Texcoco, and some of its notable features included causeways that connected it to the mainland, wooden bridges that could be raised as a defensive feature, floating gardens, and a zoo. Cortez's conquistadores describe how the Spaniards could not believe their eyes when they entered the valley and first looked down upon a large, well-organized capital city whose monumental temples and palaces seemed to rise out of the lake. In South America, cities of the Incan Empire in the Andean highlands, notably Cuzco and Machu Picchu (figure 4.3), were important centers of indigenous population and development. Thus, Latin American urbanization predates the arrival of colonial powers; in some cases (such as Cuzco and Mexico City) the conquistadores built their cities on preexisting settlements to take advantage of existent infrastructure and population concentrations.

The conquest that began in the Caribbean and spread throughout Latin America dramatically shifted urban systems and layout, with results that are still clearly visible to this day in some places. In the Caribbean, cities developed around colonial ports and convoy routes

Figure 4.3. Machu Picchu, iconic and relatively intact, spectacularly showcases pre-Columbian architecture and craftsmanship.

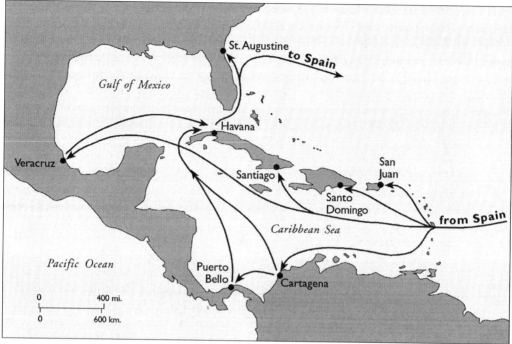

Figure 4.4. Spanish ports and convoy routes in the Colonial Era.

(figure 4.4). Whereas cities in the Caribbean experienced the influences of a number of European colonial powers over several centuries, colonial urban influences in mainland Latin America were mainly the results of control by Spain and Portugal. The Treaty of Tordesillas (1494) divided the mainland between these two powers, with Portugal controlling present-day Brazil and Spain claiming the rest of the region (see chapter 2). As the presence of colonial powers increased, they established gateway cities that fulfilled several interrelated functions: the cities served as focal points for the extraction and preparation of raw goods for export and the distribution of manufactured goods imported from the home country and centers for civilian and military administration and control. Colonial cities were cultural, political, and economic nodes. Smaller cities served more specialized economic functions, such as controlling mining and other extractive industries from a specific hinterland, or serving as ports from which raw materials were exported.

Colonial urbanization also relates to the *layout* of Spanish cities in Latin America. Characteristic features included a gridiron street pattern, with square or rectangular blocks and streets at right angles to each other. Streets were usually oriented in north-south, east-west directions, although some cities that fronted water bodies were aligned with the waterfront. The city's focal point was a main plaza or square, known by various names throughout the region (depending on the location, the plaza was referred to as El Zócalo, the Plaza Mayor, or the Plaza de Armas, among others). Plazas usually served important social functions. Buildings such as churches and, in larger cities, cathedrals, were situated on and near the plaza to reflect their symbolic importance. Administrative offices of the local government and representatives of the Crown, as well as elite residences, were also located on or near the plaza, while middle-class residences were located farther from the plaza, and the remnants of the indigenous population lived on the city's edges.

The Spanish *Laws of the Indies* (1573) are commonly understood as the foundation for the regularized layout of Spanish colonial cities, but cities that predate 1573 (such as Santa Cruz in Bolivia, founded in 1560) follow the same guidelines, indicating that the 1573 regulations merely formalized standardized structural guidelines that had already been in practice.

In contemporary Latin American cities with Spanish colonial heritage, the city's core often reflects standardized patterns of layout, form, and function. The persistence of elements of colonial urban design through the centuries is tangible evidence of how the colonial past undergirds the present. The central plazas in particular remain a key feature. Sometimes the plazas serve open-air commercial functions such as transportation nodes or temporary weekend markets. They also continue to provide important public and social space. On a daily basis, residents of all ages can be seen in plazas across the region, taking part in the social interactions that characterize Latin American cities (figure 4.5). Plazas have also been important political sites in Latin America; contemporary social and political movements typically utilize the centrality and visibility of plazas to make their claims public (see chapter 10).

Figure 4.5. The *Plaza de Armas* in Cuzco, Perú (top half of picture) shows colonial influences in what used to be an Inca capital, while more eclectic modern symbols and architecture occupy and surround the *Plaza de Mayo* in Buenos Aires, Argentina (bottom half of picture). Photographs by Zia Salim and Fernando J. Bosco.

As the colonies in mainland Latin America began to gain independence in the nineteenth century, new foreign influences affected urban landscapes and regional urban structures. Spanish and Portuguese colonial influences gave way to American and British neocolonialism (see chapter 3). The economic power of Great Britain and the United States led to the expansion of railroads across the region and the construction of newer port facilities and other commercial and industrial infrastructure in many cities. For example, in Argentina, the economic importance of the pampas in an export-oriented economy led to the expansion and modernization of the port in Buenos Aires. British engineering and construction firms took the lead in the project, importing from England (and other parts of Europe) everything from the overall industrial design aesthetic to the red bricks used to build the docks and warehouses (figure 4.6). Neocolonialism similarly influenced urban design and urban growth elsewhere in Latin America, from the creation of company towns in Central America to the development of railroads and port cities in Andean nations such as Chile, usually in response to US commercial interests.

Scholars have argued that, in general, urbanism in Latin America has been influenced by (and borrowed from) architectural design and urban planning principles from almost every industrialized nation in the world at different points in time, whether European countries, the United States, or even the former Soviet Union. These influences and "imported modernities" (see figure 4.7), coupled with Latin America's own development trajectories, historical circumstances, and nascent national and hemispheric urban styles, help explain the region's diversity of cityscapes today (Whitehead 2006).

Figure 4.6. New condominium and office towers surround the old docks in Puerto Madero, Buenos Aires. Photograph by Fernando J. Bosco.

Figure 4.7. Two architectural imports in Mexico City: The Torre *Latinoamericana* and the *Palacio de Bellas Artes*. Photograph by Larry Ford.

Urban Primacy and Megacities

Urban primacy refers to the situation in which a particular country's largest city has a population at least double that of the next largest city. These largest cities, known as primate cities, generally act as the hubs of social, economic, and political life. The prevalence and intensity of urban primacy in Latin America is a unique characteristic that sets the region apart from the rest of the world. For example, the population of Lima (Perú) in 2014 was more than

---

Textbox 4.1. Caribbean Cities

Colonial urbanization in the New World began in the Caribbean: Santo Domingo in the Dominican Republic, settled in 1496, has the distinction of being the longest continuously occupied European city in the Americas. The legacy of export-oriented plantation agriculture and colonial economic, administrative, and social needs had particular consequences for urban development in the Caribbean. The earliest colonial Caribbean cities were small in population and size and served plantation economies and were often the sites from which cash crops were exported. They also bore distinct cultural imprints of the colonial powers (from forts and city walls to the appearance of the built environment) and exhibited weak intraregional urban connections (because a variety of European countries colonized the region, connections with distant Europe were often stronger than with nearby islands).

Contemporary Caribbean cities are characterized by urban primacy and have been affected by rural-to-urban migration and high levels of population growth. The region's average urbanization in 2010 was 67 percent, although urbanization varies from highs of 100 percent in Anguilla and Guadeloupe to lows of 36 percent in Haiti and Jamaica. Caribbean cities are still small; only four have one million or more residents: Havana, Santo Domingo, Port-au-Prince, and San Juan. Regardless of city size, the Caribbean faces problems of urbanization, including inequality, infrastructure, and informal housing. Economic inequality is high—Haiti is tied with Colombia for the highest levels of inequality in Latin America and the world. The widespread devastation caused by the January 2010 earthquake in Port-au-Prince brought entrenched issues of poverty and poor infrastructure to the world's attention. Large sections of informal housing exist in cities such as Port-au-Prince and Santo Domingo, and responses to inequality have not always been positive. For example, from the mid-1980s to the early 1990s, Dominican president Juan Balaguer mandated a program of slum clearance that involved widespread paramilitary and police intimidation and violence.

---

eleven times that of Arequipa, the next largest city (9.9 million compared to 850,000). Many important institutions are found in Lima, including governmental buildings and offices, museums, and universities. Primacy means that the largest cities have disproportionately large shares of the total national population. For example, Santiago contains approximately 35 percent of Chile's total population, and just over 30 percent of Paraguay's total population resides in its capital, Asunción.

One of the ways in which urban primacy is measured (the four-city primacy index) calculates the ratio of the population of the largest city to the populations of the next three largest cities combined. Following this index of urban primacy, Argentina's capital, Buenos Aires, is more than three and a half times larger than the total of the next three agglomerations (13,361,000 compared to a combined total of 3,661,000). Similarly, Montevideo is almost five times larger than the next three cities in Uruguay combined (1,269,552 compared to 255,743), and Port-au-Prince is 3.8 times larger than the next three cities in Haiti (2,296,386 compared to 596,132). There are a few notable exceptions to the tendency toward primacy in Latin America. For example, São Paulo and Rio de Janeiro (Brazil) are much nearer in size to each other; in Bolivia, the two main urban agglomerations (Santa Cruz and La Paz) are nearly equal; and in Colombia, there is a relatively less skewed system of cities. Some of the patterns discussed above can be seen in figures 4.1 and 4.2, which show the largest metropolitan areas in the region.

Table 4.1. National Rate of Urbanization and Population in Selected Main Metropolitan Areas (Both as a Percentage of Total Population)

Country	Rate of Urbanization[a]				Main Metropolitan Area[b]	Percentage of Total Population			
	1955[c]	1975[c]	1995[c]	2015[c]		1955[c]	1975[c]	1995[c]	2005[c]
Argentina	69.6	81	88.2	91.8	Greater Buenos Aires	30.6	33.5	32.7	36
Bolivia	35.3	41.3	59.4	68.5	La Paz	12.4	14.7	16.6	16.5
Brazil	41.1	60.8	77.6	85.7	São Paulo	4.8	8.9	9.8	10.3
Chile	63.3	78.4	84.5	89.5	Santiago	23.9	30.1	35.3	36.3
Columbia	38.7	58.5	70.5	76.4	Bogotá	6.5	12.7	15	19.7
Costa Rica	33.9	41.3	54.6	76.8	San José	16.3	21.4	25.1	23.4
Cuba	57.5	64.2	74.3	77.1	Havana	19.7	19.6	19.7	19
Dominican Republic	26.9	47.5	57.6	79	Santo Domingo	9.2	17.6	21.3	27.7
Ecuador	31	42.4	57.8	63.7	Guayaquil	8.7	12.9	16	16.7
El Salvador	37.4	41.5	54	66.7	San Salvador	10.1	14.1	18.3	17.1
Guatemala	28	36.7	43.1	51.6	Guatemala City	12.9	17	16.5	18
Haiti	13.8	20.4	32.6	58.6	Port-au-Prince	5.2	11.2	18.2	23
Honduras	20	32.1	42.9	54.7	Tegucigalpa	5.6	9.4	11.7	13.3
Jamaica	28.7	44	50.6	54.8	Kingston	22.3	24.6	23.2	20.9
Mexico	46.7	62.8	73.4	79.2	Mexico City	13	17.4	17.8	16.8
Nicaragua	37.4	48.7	53.5	58.8	Managua	9.8	15.8	18.6	15.3
Panama	38.5	49	58.1	66.6	Panama City	22.4	30.1	36.9	41.9
Paraguay	35.1	39	52.1	59.7	Asunción	18.7	23.3	26.8	33.5
Perú	43.9	61.5	71	78.6	Lima	15.8	24.4	27.5	31.8
Uruguay	79.1	83.4	90.5	95.3	Montevideo	52.6	49.6	49.3	49.8
Venezuela	54.6	75.8	86.2	89	Caracas	15.3	18.4	12.7	9.3

Source: World Urbanization Prospects, the 2014 Revision (United Nations 2014)

[a] Percentage of total population. The definition of the term "urban" corresponds to that used in each country.
[b] Metropolitan area refers to the city in question and the high-density zones in its vicinity.
[c] The data refer to the years in which population and housing censuses were conducted in each country, that is, around the year at the top of the column.

A final point to make about primacy relates to the relative slowing of growth in primate cities. Between 1970 and 2000, data on thirty-three major cities provided by the UN's Economic Commission for Latin America showed that about a third of the main metropolitan areas (including Buenos Aires, Montevideo, Caracas, and Mexico City) declined in their share of the total national populations, whereas the other two-thirds of the main metropolitan areas grew, albeit at varying paces (table 4.1). A recent trend in the largest Latin American cities seems to be a gradual reduction in the individual cities' measures of primacy (such as the index of primacy and the percent of the population that lives in primate cities). Mid-sized cities have experienced population growth for a variety of reasons, including return migration from the larger cities due to economic turmoil, reduced attraction of urban areas due to environmental and social urban problems, improved intraurban communication, and changing industrialization patterns.

Although the exact number used in the definition has changed over time, metropolitan areas with populations of ten million or more are termed *megacities*. Latin America contains four of the world's twenty-one megacities: São Paulo (number three, population 20,262,493), Mexico City (number five, population 19,460,212), Buenos Aires (number eleven, population 13,074,389), and Rio de Janeiro (number fourteen, population 11,949,619). The expansion of these cities has been rapid, and growth rates remain high. Both urban primacy and the growth of megacities have the potential to cause urban problems: from environmental degradation (see chapter 11), to poor infrastructure, to high population density, to uneven access to resources, to serious social issues, to the need for effective urban planning, these cities face particularly pressing challenges.

Demographic and Economic Drivers of Urban Growth

A combination of historic, demographic, economic, and social factors have come together to contribute to city growth in Latin America. These factors are complex and interact with each other, but untangling them illuminates how parts of Latin America have become some of the most urbanized areas in the world and how some of the region's cities have grown into megacities.

A sustained pattern of rural-to-urban migration was a key factor in the early growth of Latin American cities in the twentieth century. Rural decline, combined with urban industrialization, led to a sustained process of migration from rural to urban areas that started in the 1940s and accelerated in the 1950s. A combination of push (e.g., lack of employment opportunities, rural poverty) and pull (e.g., higher quality of life, more or better job opportunities) factors drove segments of the population to the cities. Communication and transportation infrastructure aided the process: the media portrayed cities as locations of prosperity and well-being, and paved highways and new bus and railroad routes provided networks that were focused on the main cities. In the post–World War II period, young adults and their children tended to out-migrate from the rural areas (Villa and Rodriguez 1996), and women had high rates of internal migration (Singelmann 1993).

By the 1960s, natural increase had become a more significant component of metropolitan growth than migration (Gilbert 1996, 34). Natural increase is a demographic measure that refers to the difference between the number of births and deaths, expressed as a percentage. It does not directly include the role of migration. However, since young adults were more likely to migrate, when they arrived in the cities they made disproportionately large contributions to birth rates and disproportionately small contributions to death rates, and the numbers of their children born in the cities allowed natural increase to overtake migration.

A variety of economic factors have also contributed to urbanization; one of these factors was industrialization, which took place in a number of stages in Latin America (see chapter 3). The earliest nations to industrialize (Argentina, Brazil, and Mexico) did so in the 1930s and 1940s due to global economic dislocations prompted by the Great Depression and World War II (Hirschman 1968). As opportunities declined in rural areas after World War II, capital cities and ports became the locations of manufacturing and industry, and governmental policies promoted the creation of new cities to act as administrative capitals or to promote regional economic development. Industrialization and rural-to-urban migration worked in tandem to propel rapid urban growth and bolster the concentration of urban activity in the region (see chapter 3). These trends led to overurbanization, first defined as an imbalance between high numbers of urban residents and low numbers of available jobs (Germani 1973), later defined as urbanization occurring without sufficient levels of industrialization to support it, and finally defined more broadly as the condition whereby jobs and housing do not keep pace with the rapid growth of cities and their populations With the decline of import substitution industrialization and the beginning of the debt crises in the 1970s, Latin American governments were forced to implement free-market policies under the direction of international lending organizations, including the World Bank, the IMF, and the Inter-American Development Bank (IDB) (see chapters 3 and 5). The institution of structural adjustment programs (SAPs) directly affected Latin American cities. Deindustrialization, particularly in cities where manufacturing was concentrated, and skyrocketing inflation contributed to the growth of the informal economy and an increase in urban poverty. Additionally, urban growth shifted from large cities to urban areas that were more competitive in the global economy. For example, the growth of towns along the US-Mexico border (such as Tijuana and Ciudad Juarez) paralleled the growth of maquiladoras (see chapters 5 and 13), while cities such as Acapulco and Cancún (Mexico) or Cartagena (where the fortress and old walled city were designated a UNESCO World Heritage Site in the mid-1980s) have become important tourist destinations (see chapter 6). The diffusion of growth to these smaller and intermediate-sized towns has, in some cases, deconcentrated patterns of economic development, reduced the extremes of urban primacy, and led to more balanced urban systems.

The *informal sector* refers to economic activities that are not part of the officially recorded economy and, as such, are unregulated. The informal sector's growth corresponds to the rise of neoliberal policies that minimize the state's role and emphasize the private sector's role (see chapter 3). Other factors related to the growth of informality include more flexible work regimes, and social and cultural preferences. In Latin America, both adults and children are key parts of the informal economy (see chapter 12). The urban informal economy has many faces, from teenage boys shining shoes in La Paz (Bolivia), to women selling goods in the streets of Quito (Ecuador), to dentists and doctors working as informal taxi drivers in Havana, to people of various ages engaging in criminal activities, such as drug dealing and prostitution, in Rio de Janeiro. The urban informal sector is also multifaceted. In research in urban Argentina, informal sector employment was shown to have persisted years after the 2002 peak of the debt crisis, even after the country's strong economic recovery. Workers simultaneously participated in both the informal and formal sectors; instead of understanding informality as a mere subsistence strategy aligned in opposition to the formal sector, or as a response to failures in the formal economy, the informal sector can be viewed as a complementary sector that directly contributes to the formal sector (Whitson 2007).

Urban Forms in Latin America

A city model describes urban forms and outlines general zones and spatial land use patterns. Models of city forms are sometimes criticized for being static ideal types that neglect each city's local context and specificity. However simplistic, urban models help illuminate urban processes and dynamics. For example, geographer Larry Ford's Latin American city model (1996) illustrates *centripetal* or centralizing tendencies, while newer illustrations of cities in Latin America tend to highlight extended metropolitan regions, indicating newer *centrifugal* or decentralizing tendencies.

Ford's Latin American city model (figure 4.8) divides urban areas into several zones, beginning with a strong central business district (CBD) featuring mixed land uses and centered on the traditional plaza. In many Latin American cities, such as Buenos Aires and Santiago, the contemporary CBD includes modern offices, government buildings, and commercial areas as well as more traditional districts containing older churches and historic buildings—many of them going back to colonial times or the nineteenth century. This eclectic mix of buildings

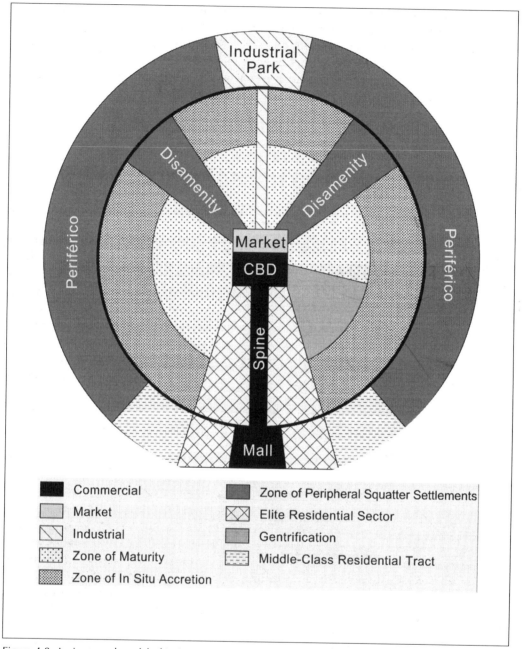

Figure 4.8. An improved model of Latin American city structure.

and land uses occupies spaces on the original city grid. In these areas, most housing once occupied by European colonial (and later criollo) elites has been converted to commercial space, although some housing still remains in the form of apartments. In general, the Latin American city's CBD is flourishing: government and business functions bring thousands of people to the district daily, transportation hubs are often located in or near it, and amenities that attract visitors and tourists are abundant. Additionally, many cities have gentrifying neighborhoods close to the city center that attract new investments and residents, such as the neighborhood of San Telmo in the historic core of Buenos Aires or La Candelaria in the heart of Bogotá.

The Latin American city model also includes an "elite spine" (a corridor of upscale office and retail establishments) that emanates outward from the CBD. The spine contains upscale residential housing, including old mansions and newer condominium towers. Café districts, such as Mexico City's Zona Rosa and Buenos Aires's Recoleta and Barrio Norte, are also found along the spine. Attractive residential districts closer to the spine offer very good quality housing options and easy access to urban amenities such as restaurants, bars, and recreational and entertainment facilities.

Farther out from the CBD and the spine sector one can find most of the traditional housing and commercial structures, located in a series of concentric zones that decline in status with distance from the city core. Even farther away from the core, areas of self-built housing or squatter settlements become prevalent. One of the main problems of Latin American urban areas is the inability to provide sufficient, adequate housing for low-income populations. However, most studies of Latin American urbanism indicate that, over time, precarious housing improves as residents gradually build up their homes, so what looks like a squatter settlement today might become a more established neighborhood with better services and residences. The favela neighborhood of Rocinha in Rio de Janeiro mentioned at the beginning of this chapter is a case in point. Additionally, because large metropolitan areas in Latin America often exceed the jurisdictional boundaries of the main city, outer residential rings can vary in terms of infrastructure and improvements since different municipal governments are in charge. Some outer-ring neighborhoods are more established, with residents enjoying paved streets, electricity, and water, and others are not. Industrial areas tend to be located along peripheral highways radiating away from the core, and industrial parks are more common in the outer residential rings, since industrialization occurred relatively recently in Latin America and land was more readily available in the periphery. An exception can be seen in cities that exhibited early industrialization or that were historically export oriented, such as Buenos Aires and São Paulo, where some industry is located near inner-city rail yards. Most new or larger-scale industrial activity, however, tends to be deconcentrated and in suburban locations.

The basic model of urban form and functions outlined above has been enhanced by more recent research that highlights the development of new urban forms in Latin America that mirror urban forms elsewhere, but in particular those in the United States. Newer or larger urban areas have developed into sprawling polycentric regions with multiple "nodes," as opposed to the traditional monocentric model described above. Within these polycentric or polynuclear metropolitan areas, land uses abut each other, sometimes abruptly: a certain area may join housing, light or heavy industry, and agriculture. These new urban forms grow along transportation corridors that radiate from the central city core. Thus, urban areas are beginning to develop new spatial configurations that include urban corridors, which are elongated zones dedicated to a single land use, and peripheral urban subcenters, which join several smaller developments on the edges of larger cities. More broadly, some urban nodes are beginning to coalesce into larger regions. For example, the so-called Rio/São Paulo Extended Metropolitan Region (RSPER) includes Brazil's two largest cities and the medium-sized cities along the three-hundred-mile transportation corridor that joins them (Tolosa 2003). Similarly, the polynuclear megalopolis centered on Mexico City contains at least 23.6 million people and is projected to expand gradually over time. These newer urban forms align with conceptual work on what Brenner and Schmid term "planetary urbanization" (2011), which posits that contemporary economic processes are concentrating increasing numbers of people in dense, complex agglomerations; these novel types of agglomerations are rendering conventional understandings of the city obsolete. Further, they argue, the impact of urbanization extends far from urban centers, blurring the boundaries between urban and rural.

Neither of these two representations is a singular explanation for the urban and regional form in contemporary Latin America. Each place's particularities (location; size; history; economic, political, and social background; and so forth) play a role. Centralizing and decentralizing tendencies are influenced by external forces. For example, gentrification and revitalization, increased energy costs, and the inertia of large institutions contribute to centralization, while the suburbanization of housing and employment, the deterioration of central cities, and preferences for low-density or gated housing induce decentralization. Cities will exhibit centralizing or decentralizing tendencies depending on which of these sets of combined forces acts with more intensity at a particular time. The social norms and preferences of residents also play an important role in determining the form of the Latin American city.

Socioeconomic Polarization, Residential Segregation, and Urban Poverty

Cities across the world were historically segregated based on class and ethnic differences, and Latin America is no exception. However, the contemporary suburbanization of the middle and upper classes has implications in terms of social polarization and exclusion in Latin America. In the past, cities in the region had relatively straightforward patterns of segregation at the neighborhood scale. For example, in Lima, the district of Miraflores is commonly understood by residents as being in a "good" part of the city, while La Victoria is similarly known to be a disadvantaged central city neighborhood. Similarly, Jardims is regarded as a nice neighborhood in São Paolo and Diadema as a not-as-nice neighborhood.

The inherent spatiality of socioeconomic segregation makes it amenable to geographical analyses (Luco and Vignoli 2003; Peters and Skop 2007) even as segregation patterns have become more complex. Gilbert (1996, 93) identifies three reasons for these more complicated patterns of segregation in Latin America. First, the spatial expansion of urban areas has brought lower income zones into contact with more affluent areas. For example, elite suburbs now adjoin working-class areas that had been a distance away. Second, the growth of the middle class has changed residential segregation patterns as middle-class suburbs now occupy land that is not used due to proximity to low-income areas. Third, topography brings high-, middle-, and low-income areas into closer contact with each other. For example, low-income groups may claim slopes that were previously considered too steep to build upon.

Interestingly, settlement size affects poverty and socioeconomic inequality in different ways (Fay and Laderchi 2005). As settlement size goes up, overall poverty rates decrease—larger cities present opportunities that smaller cities lack. However, inequality rates increase with settlement size—while there are more opportunities in larger cities, the gap between the rich and the poor is wider, sometimes glaringly so. Inequality is most obvious when manifested across very small spatial gradients, as figure 4.9 illustrates. On the left of the image, taken from Google Earth, is Paraisopolis, a favela in São Paulo. On the right of the image is the gated Paço dos Reis luxury development, which features individual swimming pools and patios in addition to the common pools and tennis courts. The difference between the two areas is almost as massive as the distance between them is minute. As socioeconomic polarization increases and the gap between rich and poor widens, gated communities that provide exclusionary housing and reinforce social stratification become more common.

Figure 4.9. Stark contrasts in São Paulo: the boundary between the *Paco dos Reis* gated development and the *Paraisopolis* favela marks a pronounced difference in urban landscapes and lifestyles. Screenshot from Google Earth.

Latin America and the Caribbean have made impressive strides in reducing the proportion of the population in extreme poverty, which the World Bank defines as living on less than $1.25 a day. The World Bank estimates that the proportion of the population in extreme poverty decreased from 12 percent in 1990 to 6 percent in 2010 in Latin America and the Caribbean. However, poverty is a notable facet of urban life in Latin America. The urbanization of poverty can be seen in statistics that indicate that 60 percent of the region's poor and 50 percent of its extremely poor (corresponding to approximately 113 million and 46 million people, respectively) lived in cities in 2005. This urbanization of poverty can also be seen in the immense shift in the proportion of the poor living in cities, which soared from 44 percent in 1959 to 78 percent in 2000 (Brandolini and Cipollone 2003). However, improved access to employment opportunities, particularly in the informal sector, means that poverty rates in cities are lower than the corresponding rates in rural areas and that urbanization tends to lower overall national poverty rates. Key issues facing the urban poor include limited access to formal housing, inadequate service provision, and exposure to violence and crime. Poor service provision by the public sector forces the urban poor to turn to private providers or to improvise informal arrangements. Infrastructure is generally overwhelmed rather than being completely absent, but levels of service quality and reliability are problematic and uneven. Even if poverty rates remain stable and do not increase, the mere phenomenon of growth in Latin American urban populations will lead to increases in the absolute numbers of urban poor.

Urban Housing and Infrastructure

Closely connected to the processes of residential segregation discussed above are the changing shape of housing and the distinct housing trends that are emerging for urban elites and for the urban poor in Latin American cities. *Gated communities* have sprouted up worldwide, including in Latin America: cities as different as São Paulo, Santiago, Trinidad, and Buenos Aires have become sites for various forms of these communities (Coy 2006; Caldeira 2000; Borsdorf, Hidalgo, and Sanchez 2007; Mycoo 2006; Thuillier 2005), and gated developments can be found in smaller cities in the urban system (Klaufus 2010). These gated communities can be understood as a new manifestation of historic processes of social segregation mentioned earlier. Already-cleaved cities become even more polarized as upper-class (and increasingly, middle-class) groups move away from the cities or wall themselves off. Regional variations characterize elite urban gating in Latin America, from (less common) horizontal complexes, to vertical towers with a walled development at ground level (as seen in São Paulo and Rio de Janeiro), to enclosed neighborhoods resembling private country clubs (as seen in the outskirts of Buenos Aires, well outside the formal boundaries of the city).

Although various political, social, and economic factors have contributed to the development of gated communities in Latin American cities, an examination of São Paulo (Caldeira 2000) illustrates how fear of crime is a dominant trope connected to residential segregation. In the 1980s and 1990s Brazil experienced a publicized discussion about crime and urban disorder, partly motivated by political, social, and economic changes. As violent crime increased in the mid-1980s, patterns of abuse by the police forces, coupled with mistrust of the judicial system and an ever-increasing privatization of security, led to an erosion of the rule of law, which prompted urban elites to segregate themselves in fortified enclaves. These gated communities are affected by, and have effects on, the urban fabric that surrounds them.

The growth of *informal housing* is another modern trend, driven by population growth, economic conditions, and rural-to-urban migration. The form of informal housing ranges widely, from deteriorated neighborhoods within the central city, to shacks on the roofs of buildings, to unauthorized structures on private land. As the discussion of the Latin American city model indicates, informal settlements are most prevalent on the urban periphery. Informal housing sectors are known as *pueblos jóvenes* ("young towns") in Lima, *bidonvilles* (tin or can towns) in Port-au-Prince, *favelas* in Rio de Janeiro, *conventillos* in Quito, *poblaciones callampas* ("mushroom populations") in Chile, and *villas miseria* ("towns of misery") in Buenos Aires (Gilbert 2007).

The problems of informal housing are many, and while the scale varies by city, informal housing is widespread and can encompass large numbers of urban dwellers. For example, according to the UN's 2009 *World Urbanization Prospects* report, Mexico City's population was approximately 19.4 million in 2005, and at that time 4.6 million people were estimated to be living in substandard conditions in and around the city—informal zones housed just over one in five people in Mexico City. Table 4.2 provides an overview of so-called megaslums in Latin America. Conditions in informal areas vary but can be very poor—inadequate infrastructure for water, electricity, and sewage, combined with crowded conditions and reduced access to education, health care, and other important governmental services, can cause negative social and environmental consequences. However, stereotypical views of informal urbanization are not necessarily accurate—not all shantytowns are spatially disorganized and socially ungoverned, nor are all residents recent migrants who are criminals, unproductive, or unemployed (Perlman 1976; Lobo 1982; Stokes 1991).

Urban Environments

Cities are closely connected to their physical environments at various scales; the original locations of cities were often in relation to natural features, contemporary cities act as ecosystems

Table 4.2. Megaslums in Latin America and the Caribbean

Global Rank	Name	Location	Population
1	Neza/Chalco/Izta	Mexico City	4,000,000
2	Libertador	Caracas	2,200,000
3	El Sur/Ciudad Bolívar	Bogotá	2,000,000
4	San Juan de Lurigancho	Lima	1,500,000
5	Cono Sur	Lima	1,500,000
18	El Alto	La Paz	800,000
20	Sucre	Caracas	600,000
22	Tlalpan	Mexico City	600,000
27	Aguas Blancas	Cali	500,000
29	Cite-Soleil	Port-au-Prince	500,000

Source: Adapted from Davis (2006, 28)

in their own right, and complex relationships link urban residents and their environmental contexts. Latin American cities have contexts and particularities that create a unique set of environmental impacts. Issues such as pollution and environmental hazards are closely related to the aspects of urbanization discussed earlier in this chapter, including urban primacy, socioeconomic polarization, and informal housing. For example, while their high densities make them more sustainable, primate cities cause concentrated human impacts in terms of traffic, air and water pollution, and waste (see chapter 11). Further, these environmental issues are affected by larger structural issues, including economic development and urban governance.

A variety of sources contribute to urban pollution. For example, for decades, significant economic and public health impacts in Mexico City could be traced to the city's notoriously poor air quality, which was driven by the use of motor vehicles, sprawl, and a large population. These impacts were magnified by the city's physical geography; Mexico City sits in a valley, trapping air pollutants in an unhealthy cauldron of smog. Similarly, impacts on water quality are attributed to aspects of urbanization. Sprawl, the growth of informal housing, and the varying quality of urban infrastructure pose specific challenges with respect to wastewater treatment and, more broadly, to water quality and availability. For example, water services have been found to be worse in Lima's poorer areas than they are in richer areas of the city, despite years of investments in water and sewerage projects. Against the backdrop of larger issues of population growth and an increasingly sprawling city, the varying levels of water availability and service in Lima indicate that spatial inequality in implementation is the issue, rather than lack of finances or the absolute scarcity of water (Ioris 2015).

Environmental hazards, while not unique to Latin America, are worth noting. The region's unique physical geography and climate (see chapter 1) have dynamic impacts on cities. For example, prolonged rainy seasons in 2010 and 2011 in Medellín created rivers in the center of the city and caused catastrophic mudslides (Spanne 2012). Changes in urban land use and land cover, such as the conversion of vegetated areas into settlements, can amplify the risk of hazards. For example, as urbanization reduces water infiltration by increasing impervious surface, it increases the potential for surface runoff and flooding. Urbanization can also put more residents in harm's way. For example, construction on steep slopes puts residents at risk when landslides occur as a result of extreme rainfall events. Unsurprisingly, socioeconomic inequality exacerbates these issues, as the poorest residents tend to live in the most polluted or hazardous areas. Poor residents are often disproportionately exposed to environmental disamenities (e.g., health is impacted by industrial air and water pollution) and hazards (e.g., houses are destroyed and lives lost when landslides destroy informal housing constructed on steep slopes).

Cities across the region differ in their environmental contexts and their ability to respond to environmental issues. For example, Mexico City implemented a series of policy responses that greatly improved air quality. Other cities, such as Curitiba and Bogotá, have used progressive planning to increase urban sustainability (see textbox 4.2). An assessment of how residents of Latin American cities are impacted by their urban environments and how they, in turn, impact their urban environments, connects to broader questions around the long-term ecological sustainability of urbanization.

Textbox 4.2. Planning for Urban Sustainability

While Latin American cities face a variety of significant issues, many cities in the region have implemented unique solutions. The city of Curitiba in southeast Brazil has been internationally recognized as a model for progressive urban planning, receiving numerous awards, including the Globe Sustainable City Award in 2010. Since the adoption of a master plan in 1965, a series of technocratic mayors and planners have collaborated to develop a holistic series of measures to increase Curitiba's ecological, economic, and social sustainability. Although the city experienced rapid population growth, the adoption of a forward-thinking comprehensive approach resulted in impressive sustainability outcomes. Highlights include the widespread establishment of parks, the development of an integrated transportation system that includes extensive Bus Rapid Transit (figure 4.10), the creation of pedestrian malls (in which streets were permanently closed to automobile traffic), the implementation of

Figure 4.10. Curitiba's innovative Bus Rapid Transit system features dedicated bus lanes, high capacity bi-articulated buses, and elevated "tube" stops designed to speed passenger boarding by providing pre-boarding fare payment and same-level boarding through multiple doors. At peak times, some buses run as frequently as every 90 seconds. Photograph by Mario Roberto Duran Ortiz.

innovative recycling programs, the support for historic preservation and social housing, and the decentralization of some government offices. Many of these efforts integrated public input in the planning process. Taken together, these measures have increased recycling, minimized pollution, decreased fuel consumption and carbon emissions, and improved the overall quality of life in Curitiba. The case of Curitiba is also noteworthy because the city's economy has long depended on industrial manufacturing; urban sustainability is seen as being compatible with economic development. This progressive approach to urban planning in Latin America, and the tactics and strategies that accompany it, are hardly unique to Curitiba. For example, in the late 1990s, Bogotá implemented an event known as Ciclovía, in which certain streets were closed to motor vehicles on Sundays and holidays in order to attract runners, pedestrians, and bicyclists. Ciclovía opened streets to pedestrians and cyclists, restricted automobiles, and integrated other events and programming; the concept has been a great success and has since diffused from Bogotá to cities all over the world, including London and New York. The types of innovative urban planning ideas and implementation seen in Curitiba and Bogotá can help Latin American cities, both across the region and down the urban hierarchy, to increase their urban sustainability.

Conclusion: Urban Futures

Increased economic opportunities, hemispheric economic and political integration, and broader globalization trends are bringing about rapid changes to Latin American cities. While common dimensions of urban structure such as centralization and social polarization persist, the region's urban future seems increasingly diverse, as indicated by the slower growth of megacities and the increased vitality of medium-sized cities where new forms of urbanism and urban governance are being tried.

The future of Latin American cities is intertwined with the larger economic and political contexts of the region's countries. A recent study ranked Santiago, Lima, Monterrey, Bogotá, and San José as the "top five Latin American cities of the future" (fDiIntelligence 2011). This ranking reflected the increased ascendancy of these cities' home countries in the current Latin American economic order and the cities' prospects for foreign investment, economic development, and job creation. Yet, a study on the environmental performance of Latin America's major cities (Siemens AG 2011) found no clear relationship between a city's overall urban environmental quality and its income. Curitiba, with incomes about 15 percent above the average relative to other Latin American cities, was the region's urban sustainability leader (see chapter 11 and textbox 4.2). But cities such as Guadalajara and Buenos Aires, which also had above-average incomes, did not fare well in terms of environmental performance. Buenos Aires, the city with the highest gross domestic product (GDP) per capita in the study, ranked well below the average of other Latin American cities in terms of many environmental metrics, from waste management to sanitation to air quality. On the other hand, cities such as Belo Horizonte and Quito were ranked above many other cities in terms of environmental quality, even though their GDP per capita was one of the lowest in the region. These results suggest that urban economic indicators (such as GDP, foreign direct investment, and so on) cannot be relied on to predict improvements in urban conditions (such as environmental quality, sustainability, and so on). The rapid urbanization still taking place in Latin America will require creative and inclusionary urban planning and governance practices, along the lines of what Curitiba has done so far, but tailored to each city's local, regional, and national contexts.

From infrastructure issues to public transportation to waste collection to housing to air and water quality to social justice, a variety of pressing social, economic, and environmental challenges face Latin American cities. An understanding of the region's urban geographies informs the policy responses that will be needed to respond to these challenges. Further, as calls to theorize urbanization in non-Eurocentric and non–US-centric ways gain more prominence (see, for example, Robinson 2006; Sheppard, Leitner, and Maringanti 2013), focusing and expanding research on Latin American cities, across the region and down the urban hierarchy, promises to shed light on urban issues in other contexts around the world.

Key Terms

gated community: A residential area that uses defensive measures such as walls, fences, and access codes to exclude undesirable groups.

informal housing: Housing that is self-constructed by residents, sometimes lacking infrastructure and formalized land tenure.

megacities: Cities with populations of ten million and more.

overurbanization: The condition in lesser developed countries in which jobs and housing cannot keep pace with urban population growth.

rural-to-urban migration: The movement of rural residents to urban areas, usually in search of better opportunities or services.

urban primacy: A condition wherein the largest city in a country is disproportionately larger in size and political, social, and economic influence compared to the second- and third-largest cities.

urban system: An interdependent group of urban places (of a variety of sizes) within a particular region.

Suggested Readings

Bolay, Jean-Claude, and Adriana Rabinovich. "Intermediate Cities in Latin America: Risk and Opportunities of Coherent Urban Development." *Cities* 21, no. 5 (2004): 407–421.

Biron, Rebecca (Ed.). *City/Art: The Urban Scene in Latin America*. Durham, NC: Duke University Press, 2009.

del Rio, Vicente, and William Siembeida (Eds.). *Contemporary Urbanism in Brazil: Beyond Brasilia*. Gainesville, FL: University Press of Florida, 2009.

Gilbert, Alan (Ed.). *The Mega-City in Latin America*. Tokyo: United Nations University Press, 1996.

Hernandez, Felipe, Peter Kellett, and Lea Allen (Eds.). *Rethinking the Informal City: Critical Perspectives from Latin America*. New York: Berghahn Books, 2010.

Irazábal, Clara (Ed.). *Ordinary Places, Extraordinary Events: Citizenship, Democracy and Public Space in Latin America*. London: Routledge, 2008.

Koonings, Kees, and Dirk Kruijy (Eds.). *Fractured Cities: Social Exclusion, Urban Violence and Contested Spaces in Latin America*. New York: Zed Books, 2007.

Suggested Websites

United Nations. *World Urbanization Prospects, the 2014 Revision.* esa.un.org/unpd/wup/index.htm
United Nations Economic Commission for Latin America (ECLAC). www.eclac.org/
Emporis.com. www.emporis.com/application/?nav=worldmap

References

Borsdorf, Axel, Rodrigo Hidalgo, and Rafael Sanchez. "A New Model of Urban Development in Latin America: The Gated Communities and Fenced Cities in the Metropolitan Areas of Santiago de Chile and Valparaiso." *Cities* 24, no. 5 (2007): 365–78.

Brandolini, Andrea, and Piero Cipollone. "Urban Poverty in Developed Countries." In *Inequality, Welfare, and Poverty: Theory and Measurement*, edited by John A. Bishop and Yoram Amiel, 309–43. Philadelphia: Elsevier, 2003.

Brenner, Neil, and Christian Schmid. "Planetary Urbanization." In *Urban Constellations: An Overview of Contemporary Urban Discourse*, edited by Matthew Gandy, 10–13. Berlin: Jovis Verlag, 2011.

Caldeira, Teresa. *City of Walls: Crime, Segregation, and Citizenship in São Paulo.* Berkeley: University of California Press, 2000.

Coy, Martin. "Gated Communities and Urban Fragmentation in Latin America: The Brazilian Experience." *GeoJournal* 66, nos. 1–2 (2006): 121–32.

Davis, Mike. *Planet of Slums.* London: Verso, 2006.

Fay, Marianne, and Caterina Ruggeri Laderchi. "Urban Poverty in Latin America and the Caribbean: Setting the Stage." In *The Urban Poor in Latin America*, edited by Marianne Fay. Directions in Development Series. Washington, DC: The World Bank, 2005.

fDiIntellingence. "American Cities of the Future 2011–2012." Last accessed July 11, 2011. http://www.fdiintelligence.com/index.php/Locations/Americas/American-Cities-of-the-Future-2011-12

Ford, Larry. "A New and Improved Model of Latin American City Structure." *Geographical Review* 86, no. 3 (1996): 437–40.

Germani, Gino. "Urbanization, Social Change, and the Great Transformation." In *Modernization, Urbanization, and the Urban Crises*, edited by Gino Germani. New York: Little Brown and Co., 1973.

Gilbert, Alan. *The Latin American City.* London: Latin American Bureau, 1994.

———. "Land, Housing, and Infrastructure in Latin America's Major Cities." In *The Mega-City in Latin America*, edited by Alan Gilbert, 1–24. Tokyo: United Nations University Press, 1996.

———. "The Return of the Slum: Does Language Matter?" *International Journal of Urban and Regional Research* 31, no. 4 (2007): 697–713.

Hirschmann, Albert. "The Political Economy of Import-Substituting Industrialization in Latin America." *Quarterly Journal of Economics* 82 (1968): 2–32.

Ioris, A. "Water Services in Lima, Peru: Understanding the Linkages Between Urban Development, Social Inequality, and Water." In *Water and Cities in Latin America: Challenges for Sustainable Development*, edited by Ismael Aguilar-Barajas, Jürgen Mahlknecht, Jonathan Kaledin, Marianne Kjellén, and Abel Mejía-Betancourt, 89–101. New York: Routledge, 2015.

Klaufus, Christien. "Watching the City Grow: Remittances and Sprawl in Intermediate Central American Cities." *Environment and Urbanization* 22, no. 1 (2010): 125–37.

Lobo, Susan. *A House of My Own: Social Organization in the Squatter Settlements of Lima, Peru.* Tucson: University of Arizona Press, 1982.

Luco, Camilo Arriagada, and Jorge Rodriguez Vignoli. *Segregación residencial en areas metropolitanas de América Latina: Magnitud, características, evolución e implicaciones de política.* Serie Población y Desarrollo 47. Santiago, Chile: Centro Latinoamericano y Caribeño de Demografía (CELADE)—División de Población, 2003.

Moser, Caroline, and Ailsa Winton. *Violence in the Central American Region: Towards an Integrated Framework for Violence Reduction.* ODI Working Paper 171. London: Overseas Development Institute, 2002.

Moser, Caroline, Ailsa Winton, and Annalise Moser. "Violence, Fear, and Insecurity among the Urban Poor in Latin America." In *The Urban Poor in Latin America,* edited by Marianne Fay. Directions in Development Series. Washington, DC: The World Bank, 2005.

Mycoo, Michelle. "The Retreat of the Upper and Middle Classes to Gated Communities in the Poststructural Adjustment Period: The Case of Trinidad." *Environment and Planning A* 38, no. 1 (2006): 131–48.

Perlman, Janice. *The Myth of Marginality: Urban Poverty and Politics in Rio de Janeiro.* Berkeley: University of California Press, 1976.

Peters, Paul, and Emily Skop. "Socio-Spatial Segregation in Metropolitan Lima, Peru." *Journal of Latin American Geography* 6, no. 1 (2007): 149–71.

Robinson, Jennifer. *Ordinary Cities: Between Modernity and Development.* New York: Routledge, 2006.

Scarpaci, Joseph. *Plazas and Barrios: Heritage Tourism and Globalization in the Latin American Centro Histórico.* Tucson: University of Arizona Press, 2005.

Sheppard, Eric, Helga Leitner, and Anant Maringanti. "Provincializing Global Urbanism: A Manifesto." *Urban Geography* 34, no. 7 (2013): 893–900.

Siemens AG. *Latin American Green City Index: Assessing the Environmental Performance of Latin America's Major Cities.* 2011. Last accessed January 6, 2015. www.siemens.com/entry/cc/features/greencityindex_international/all/en/pdf/report_latam_en.pdf

Singelmann, Joachim. "Levels and Trends of Female Internal Migration in Developing Countries, 1960–1980." In *Internal Migration of Women in Developing Countries,* edited by United Nations Department for Economic and Social Information and Policy Analysis. New York: United Nations, 1993.

Spanne, Autumn. "South American Cities Face Flood Risk Due to Andes Meltdown." 2012. Last accessed January 6, 2015. http://www.scientificamerican.com/article/south-american-cities-face-flood-risk -due-to-andes-meltdown/

Stokes, Susan. "Politics and Latin America's Urban Poor: Reflections from a Lima Shantytown." *Latin America Research Review* 26, no. 2 (1991): 75–101.

Thuillier, Guy. "Gated Communities in the Metropolitan Area of Buenos Aires, Argentina: A Challenge for Town Planning." *Housing Studies* 20, no. 2 (2005): 255–71.

Tolosa, Hamilton. "The Rio/São Paulo Extended Metropolitan Region: A Quest for Global Integration." *Globalization and Urban Development* 3 (2003): 125–46.

United Nations. "World Urbanization Prospects: The 2014 Revision." Last accessed January 6, 2015. http://esa.un.org/unpd/wup/

Villa, Miguel, and Jorge Rodriguez. "Demographic Trends in the Metropolises." In *The Mega-City in Latin America,* edited by Alan Gilbert. Tokyo: United Nations University Press, 1996.

Whitehead, Laurence. *Latin America: A New Interpretation.* New York: Palgrave Macmillan, 2006.

Whitson, Risa. "Beyond the Crisis: Economic Globalization and Informal Work in Urban Argentina." *Journal of Latin American Geography* 6, no. 2 (2007): 121–36.

Chapter 5

Economic and Geopolitical Vulnerabilities and Opportunities

Thomas Klak

Shifting Regional Power Dynamics: The United States, Venezuela, and China

For many decades, Latin America and the Caribbean (LAC) has been depicted as the "United States' backyard," much to the consternation of its southern neighbors. This refers to the way that the United States uncontestably dominated economic and geopolitical relationships throughout the region during the twentieth century (see chapters 2 and 3). One illustration of this regional dominance was that the United States was able to enforce its will, from 1962 until 2009, to exclude socialist Cuba from the thirty-four-member Organization of American States (OAS). The United States' many overt or covert military interventions in LAC throughout the century provide another (Blum 2003). A third illustration of the United States' regional dominance is its long-term trade surplus with most of the region. In 2014, only seven of the thirty-three LAC countries exported more to the United States than they imported from it, and those exports were primarily petroleum. The main exception to this rule of US trade surplus is Mexico's automobile and electronic exports to the United States. Many of those factories produce for United States–based multinational firms. In contrast with the United States' overall trade surplus with LAC, the United States runs a trade deficit with most other countries in the world (ITC 2015). However, international economics and geopolitics have reshaped the region's vulnerabilities and opportunities over the last two decades, owing principally to three factors.

First, as a declining superpower stretched by costly military activity from the Middle East to Afghanistan, the United States has disengaged from and neglected hemispheric relationships (Castañeda 2009). This should not suggest that the United States has entirely ignored Latin America, but instead that it has been focused primarily on promoting free trade. Indeed, the United States secured nine free trade agreements with Latin American countries in the period 2005–2011. However, the United States has failed to adequately consider and address the socioeconomic impacts on the region of its self-advantageous free trade policies and of globalization more broadly. America's preoccupation elsewhere and its socioeconomic neglect has led LAC countries to pursue other political and economic alliances, with Venezuela, other countries in the region, and even beyond the region. One example is CELAC (Community of Latin American and Caribbean States; Comunidad de Estados Latinoamericanos y Caribeños) that thirty-three countries formed in 2011 to strengthen regional unity and common purpose while excluding the United States and Canada (see chapter 3). Further, the larger countries of South America, led by Brazil, now trade substantially more with both Asia and Europe. They have greater economic capacity to seize new trade opportunities. The smaller and weaker countries of Central America and the Caribbean, in contrast, have unfortunately been floundering and drifting without direction with regard to development policy (more on this below).

Second, and relatedly, Venezuela, under the late Hugo Chávez and then Nicolás Maduro, has championed a new hemispheric bloc. Funded by Venezuelan oil, the bloc was conceived by close allies Venezuela and Cuba in 2004 and strategically named Alianza Bolivariana para los Pueblos de Nuestra América (ALBA), or Bolivarian Alliance for the Peoples of Our America. The nine smaller countries that then joined ALBA have obtained Venezuelan aid and technical assistance to upgrade such essentials as airports, schools, hospitals, and telecommunications. These ten ALBA members, including Cuba, plus an additional eight other small LAC countries that belong only to PetroCaribe, obtain Venezuelan oil at deep discounts through long-term low-interest loans. This alliance, while still small-scale by global standards and controversial even within the bloc (Klak 2009), provides large subsidies to member governments and a partial regional reorientation southward toward Venezuela and away from the United States. Venezuelan oil-generated subsidies have propped up fiscally strained member governments with billions of subsidy dollars that they use to pay civil servants, fix roads, and provide minimal social services.

Third, and even more significantly, China's unprecedented rise in power has had massive impacts in LAC, as it has throughout the world. China's trade relationship with the region mirrors the classical pattern of core-periphery flows famously outlined decades ago by Andre Gunder Frank (1967) when describing Latin American underdevelopment: China has increasingly exported a diversity of manufactured goods throughout the region, while it has particularly desired a select few raw materials (see chapter 2). These are mainly South America's iron ore, copper, soybeans, and petroleum, in which China has also invested (Ray and Gallagher 2013). China has made major inroads against the United States in supplying low-cost consumer goods throughout LAC. China has also expanded its regional influence by awarding development loans at a scale greater than the World Bank and other western sources. Venezuela has been by far the region's largest beneficiary of Chinese loans. But Venezuela's over-reliance on oil exports and its generous social subsidies at home and abroad have contributed to stagnation in other economic sectors, high inflation, and the "resource curse" (see chapter 7). China also offers development aid to countries agreeing to its "One China" policy against Taiwan. As of 2015, twelve LAC countries still had full diplomatic relations with Taiwan, but the other twenty-one had switched over sometime since 1970 to recognize only China. Considerable foreign aid from either China or Taiwan has fixed roads and bridges and built sports facilities throughout LAC.

While China's impacts on the American hemisphere are so far impressive, its regional ambitions appear to be at an early stage. As of early 2015, China was in the final stages of buying or leasing two "Goat Islands" off Jamaica's southern coast. The plan is to in-fill them and create a transshipment port and manufacturing platform to greatly expand China's regional exports. Then there is the related work begun on the Nicaraguan Canal, which when completed would connect the Atlantic and Pacific oceans for the world's largest container ships that the Panama Canal cannot handle. Ostensibly financed by a private-sector Chinese billionaire with close ties to his government, the Nicaraguan Canal is among the world's most ambitious engineering undertakings. The predicted ecological impacts of this project on jaguars, harpy eagles, and much else are of grave concern (Meyer and Huete-Pérez 2014).

Figure 5.1. A 2014 Summit of Latin American and Caribbean leaders with China's President Xi Jinping (front, fourth from left). Source: WikiMedia Commons.

The three shifting dynamics just outlined have led to considerable rethinking of development directions in LAC. Many have called for the region to abandon the US neoliberal free trade path, which has swollen imports from the United States, China, and elsewhere, while crippling manufacturing and traditional agriculture in much of LAC. There is considerable favor in the region toward China's development approach, with its gradual, domestically controlled and strategic opening to international trade (Gallagher and Porzecanski 2010).

These introductory points frame the chapter's ensuing discussion, which focuses most attention on the vulnerabilities and opportunities for the fragile Central America and Caribbean (CAC) countries. The three changes in international dynamics outlined above do not alter the historical fact that CAC is a region of small, economically and politically vulnerable, and trade-dependent countries. The region is sandwiched between larger and more industrialized and economically diversified countries to the north and south. Since the 1980s, neoliberalism, that free trade and private sector–focused approach to development, has dominated globally (Harvey 2005). CAC's long-term high levels of trade dependency distinguish the impacts of neoliberalism there compared to most of South America. Namely, neoliberalism puts pressure on these already highly trade-dependent countries to open their economies further and to import and export more. These countries have always had relatively weak private sectors and few products that are competitive internationally. The greater exposure to international competition forced by neoliberalism puts CAC in an especially precarious position.

Under neoliberalism, the international financial institutions (IFIs) and national governments from the region have pursued policies that have introduced development schemes to generate new sources of foreign exchange and employment. These include maquiladoras and free zones, export market niche agriculture, offshore services, and tourism. The chapter reviews the experience with neoliberalism and these targeted sectors to understand why they have not delivered the promised development. The kind of development that should be a goal is sustainable, requiring a strong and secure suite of economic activities in communities that do not degrade the environment. We'll also point out opportunities that are emerging that hold greater promise for a more sustainable development path.

The Historical Roots of Vulnerability and the Rise of Neoliberalism

Whatever the theoretical paradigm adopted to examine the development conditions in CAC countries, their position as colonial, neocolonial, dependent, peripheral, or "price takers" within the international political and economic communities is a necessary point of departure. This chapter employs a theoretical perspective that extends from the dependency theory tradition and that is informed by contemporary world-systems theory (Klak 2014). This perspective takes seriously the range of constraints on development policy options and the vulnerability to exogenous factors in CAC due to the region's position in the global economic periphery (Potter et al. 2004).

The United States is both the largest importer and exporter for virtually every CAC country, with the obvious exception of Cuba, against which the United States has had a trade embargo since the 1960s. (The beginning of a thaw in United States-Cuba relations in 2015 is widely welcomed throughout the region and felt to be long overdue.) While the region's small countries are heavily trade dependent on the United States, it is among the world's least trade-dependent countries. This extreme contrast in the account ledgers, and therefore at the negotiating table, has enormous implications in the neoliberal "free trade" era. Trade is not really free unless all participants can choose *not* to trade (Ikerd 2002). When one side at the table holds the vast majority of the economic and geopolitical power, "coerced trade" might be a more apt descriptor than "free trade."

The historical basis of contemporary vulnerability in CAC is the colonial era, when outside powers established plantations to extract maximum wealth for Europe from these small places (Richardson 1992; McNeill 2009; see also chapters 2 and 7). Political independence did little to alter the colonially established economic and class structures focused on agricultural exports, favoring the elite, and underdeveloped by any standard (Thomas 1988; see also chapter 3). The post–World War II era was one of optimism about development in poorer regions such as CAC. The United States and the IFIs encouraged the region to take foreign loans as a way to speed up the development process. While the loans generated little development, they did contribute to the region's vulnerability in the form of a foreign debt crisis beginning in the early 1980s. The debt crisis has by now subsided because loans have been restructured to make interest payments more manageable. However, whereas LAC owed foreign creditors $497 billion in 2000, that debt increased to $1.4 trillion by 2012 (World Bank 2014). Whatever the terms of debt, the smaller countries of CAC do not have the economic capacity to repay their loans.

Neoliberalism was instituted by the governments of Ronald Reagan in the United States and of Margaret Thatcher in the UK and then spread globally through the IFIs (Harvey 2005). It was originally proposed internationally as a solution to the debt crisis (Klak 2004). Dick Peet aptly summarizes the neoliberal paradigm in a critical review of the work of Jeffrey Sachs, the world's most influential development economist: "Under all existing aid and debt relief schemes, to get their money poor countries have to agree to open their markets to foreign competition, privatize public enterprises, withdraw the state from service provision, reduce state budget deficits, reorient their economies to export orientation, flexibilize their labor markets, and so on down a list written under the belief that markets and free competition can guide any economy into the magic realm of growth, up the ladder of development" (Peet 2006, 452).

The US economic and political elite like how neoliberalism opens new markets for US goods and services, including globally advertised brands that out-compete domestic alternatives. As the IMF's Stanley Fischer rhetorically asked: "Why shouldn't Jamaicans be able to buy all

Figure 5.2. When KFC, followed by Subway and Pizza Hut, arrived in Dominica in 2006, it illustrated the reach of fast food chains to what are otherwise very peripheral locales. Both old and young, tourists and locals are drawn to fast food's seductive combination of salt, sugar, and fat, just as in the United States (Pollan 2006). According to Dominica's national epidemiologist, citizens are now suffering from diseases long associated with poor diets in the United States, such as diabetes, hypertension, coronary heart disease, stroke, high cholesterol, and colorectal cancer (Ricketts 2011). Further, whereas money spent on international fast food largely goes abroad, money spent at the fresh fruit and vegetable market at right supports local farmers and vendors.

the things the rest of the world has available to them?" (*Life and Debt* 2001). The answer is that Jamaica (and all of CAC) must balance the cost of these consumer imports against their primarily raw material and low value exports, for which prices have fallen and markets in the global North are stagnant (figure 5.2). This arrangement furthers the pattern of additional trade deficit, great economic weakness, and therefore more reliance on the IFIs.

Since the 1980s, representatives of the IFIs have regularly visited the capital cities not only of CAC but also of the larger countries of Latin America. During these visits, financial aid and debt restructuring are exchanged for commitments to the neoliberal transition, which in the process has moved slowly, incrementally, but irreversibly along. Since the 1980s Latin American policymakers have placed great emphasis on attracting foreign investors, especially ones proposing to earn foreign exchange (see chapter 3). Luring foreign investors requires reducing government spending and rewriting laws to euphemistically "enhance flexibility in the labour market" (that is, make it more favorable to employers) (Dominica 2006, 45).

The Latin American state's role has therefore shifted away from direct ownership, production, and the provision of social services and toward subsidizing export-oriented investors. The state's new role under neoliberalism is sometimes portrayed as one of downsizing, if not retrenchment, but it is more accurately viewed as a qualitatively different relation between the state, investors, popular classes, and territories (Robinson 2008). For some neoliberal activities, such as promoting exports, creating and managing free zones, and competing to attract investment, the Latin American state's role has actually expanded considerably (Peck 2004).

The main point of this section is to place the region's contemporary development policy and vulnerability in a historical context. The debt crisis that began around 1980 opened the way for a new era of development policy called "neoliberalism," which, despite justifiable misgivings throughout LAC, continues to the present. Neoliberalism, judged to be "the most successful ideology in world history" (Anderson 2000, 17), has profoundly shaped the role of states and the organization of societies throughout LAC, and indeed the world. However, because they were already economically weak and trade dependent, CAC countries have experienced the greatest challenges from neoliberalism in the Western Hemisphere.

The Banana War

Bananas are the world's most traded fruit (UNCTAD 2011). Their export was economically important for many LAC countries during the twentieth century and led to a banana war beginning in 1996. The history of bananas speaks volumes regarding the region's vulnerability and underdevelopment. Beginning in 1899, the United Fruit Company (called Chiquita since 1968) amassed more than 3.4 million acres of rain forest in Central America and the Colombian Caribbean coastal region. It cleared large sections of these exceptionally biodiverse regions and created plantations and vertically integrated production systems that brought bananas to stores in the United States and worldwide. After 1958, Standard Fruit (Dole) and Del Monte joined Chiquita to become the world's three major banana suppliers (Wiley 2008).

The origin of banana exports from the Caribbean was different. Caribbean countries exported bananas prior to World War II, but they became the eastern Caribbean's economic centerpiece in the 1950s. That was when Britain instructed small farmers in what were still its Caribbean colonies, such as St. Lucia, Dominica, and St. Vincent, to plant bananas and to export them to a guaranteed market in the United Kingdom through the British company Geest. Britain also provided farmers interest-free loans and production assistance. This British policy was part of a series of international trade agreements, the name of which changed over time. Europe's Banana Protocols began in 1957 and were followed by four successive Lomé conventions and one Cotonou agreement. France, Greece, Italy, Portugal, and Spain have also provided protected markets to former or current colonies (Gonzalez-Perez and McDonough 2006). Taken together, these policies provided special market access to more than seventy former European colonies, which are now called the ACP (Africa-Caribbean-Pacific) countries. The special market access applies mainly to commodities such as coffee, sugar, and bananas. Only twelve ACP countries export bananas to Europe, and seven of these are in the Caribbean.

The guaranteed British/European Union (EU) market for bananas from its former colonies created one of the few exceptions in the Western Hemisphere to the rule of US trade dependency. For years, St. Lucia, Dominica, and St. Vincent each earned more than half of all their foreign exchange from bananas, which placed them among the countries of the world most dependent on the export of a single cash crop. Perhaps even more telling of banana dependence, in 1993 banana farmers in Dominica were 20 percent of the entire workforce (Wiley 1998). In addition to bananas, agricultural products that generate foreign exchange for these eastern Caribbean countries and that are also grown by small farmers include coffee, cocoa, vanilla beans, citrus fruit, soap, and bay oil. These same farmers have also grown a host of traditional Caribbean subsistence crops that are staples of local consumption.

Europe's guaranteed import of eastern Caribbean bananas made the policy an advantageous form of trade dependency, at least in the medium term. Although farmers have felt powerless against Geest (and, since 1996, against Fyffes and WIBDECO [Windward Islands Banana Development and Exporting Company], which acquired its Caribbean operations), bananas fueled significant growth in middle-class prosperity on the islands. Gains were especially solid for the three islands' fifty thousand banana farmers, whose prominence and vitality are unusual in LAC otherwise dominated by large landholdings. Banana exports helped Dominica, St. Vincent, and St. Lucia climb to the top half of countries of the world as ranked by the Human Development Index. In addition, the public educational systems of these three Caribbean islands, among others in the region, have long been national assets. This reservoir of human capital offers opportunities when looking toward a future that is uncertain but is hopefully one featuring a more sustainable development.

The British banana trade arrangement, by creating conditions for thousands of smallholders to earn steady livable incomes by farming in ways that did not severely degrade the land, contributed to social development. It could have contributed to longer-term national sustainable development, but it came under scrutiny in light of the global neoliberal paradigm mentioned earlier. The implementation of the Single European Market in 1993 and the creation in 1995 of the World Trade Organization (WTO) were institutional manifestations of a global trend toward neoliberalism. Managed trade arrangements like those offered by Lomé/Cotonou essentially violated WTO principles. Unfortunately for the eastern Caribbean islands, their lack of trade dependency on the United States created a bigger problem. The United States successfully argued to the WTO on behalf of Central America and Ecuador that the guaranteed banana market in the EU is illegal and must be terminated (Klak et al. 2011).

European Union trade preferences for bananas expired on January 1, 2006, and were replaced by a tariff system that offers just a 176-euro per ton preference for Windward Islands bananas. This is insufficient to preserve the islands' banana industries. Preferences on their other agricultural exports to the EU expired at the end of 2008. Thanks to the WTO ruling against the EU, the eastern Caribbean banana sector has collapsed and unemployment has risen. The number of banana-exporting farmers in Dominica fell from 6,555 in 1992 to 3,533 in 1998, 767 in 2008 (Klak et al. 2011), to fewer than 300 in 2015. Eastern Caribbean countries have lost a key middle-class sector in the form of small banana farmers that worked the land in relatively benign ways compared to the large-scale Central American, Colombian, and Ecuadoran banana plantations that have usurped most of their European market share (Wiley 2008).

Central America, Colombia, and Ecuador are on the "winning" side in this banana war, and therefore now benefit from strong global demand for their bananas. However, unlike the "losing" side that includes the former British colonies, Central American, Colombian, and Ecuadoran banana workers generally do not own their own small farms. Instead, they toil for low wages on huge plantations that sell their product to the world's largest and oligopolistic fruit companies (Chiquita, Dole, and Del Monte). Throughout the twentieth century, these workers' collective actions to improve their conditions have met serious resistance from owners supported by the state. Pesticide dangers and poisonings have also been well documented (Gallagher and McWhirter 1998; Gonzalez-Perez and McDonough 2006). Thus, judged in terms of sustainable development, both sides of the dispute in Latin America are losers. US banana corporations have won greater access to the EU, and EU consumers have won cheaper bananas. Neither of these victories advances sustainable development in LAC or in the core countries. For LAC, the banana war richly illustrates the region's many vulnerabilities.

The banana war did not end the region's troubles. The most recent setback to LAC bananas is the now widespread black sigatoka disease, which withers leaves and keeps the fruit from fully ripening. Only frequent application of a cocktail of expensive fungicides can keep black sigatoka in check. This again favors the bigger banana exporting countries, but it does not favor their wage workers nor the local environment, which are regularly exposed to the pesticides, applied by aircraft on larger plantations (Ploetz 2015).

The eastern Caribbean region in particular now needs to vigorously expand other sources of foreign exchange, but these remain elusive. One opportunity emerging since 2000 has been to export bananas to the UK under the "fair trade" label. But the incomes farmers earn from fair trade are lower than incomes in the 1980s because prices are pegged to those of the plantation bananas originating in mainland Latin America that have flooded the market. For the eastern Caribbean, fair trade is a small-scale niche market strategy applied to bananas, hardly a substitute for what had long been the region's principal export commodity (Klak et al. 2011). Another potentially more promising opportunity now underway is to put sustained effort into exporting agricultural products within the region, to places such as Antigua, St. Martin, and the US Virgin Islands, which have focused so heavily on mass tourism as to require substantial food imports.

Neoliberalism and Nontraditional Exports

Neoliberal policies have had many impacts on agricultural products besides bananas, and also on a range of urban economic sectors. Since the 1980s, most CAC countries have shifted their economies away from traditional agriculture toward the export of higher value manufactured and "market niche" agricultural products, including winter fruits and vegetables and traditional tropical staples, catering to their substantial and expanding diaspora communities in North America and Europe. They have also subsidized foreign investors so that they establish or subcontract to maquiladoras (Robinson 2008; see also chapter 13). By the 1990s, there was another economic shift toward international services, including tourism (already central to many economies) but also offshore financial services and other telecommunications-based services.

Through these shifts, the region faces a monumental challenge. CAC needs to replace traditional income sources with new ones suitable to the present neoliberal era of more open trade relationships, while protecting itself from the vulnerability associated with relying on a relatively few products sold to North Atlantic countries. At the same time, imports from these same rich countries, driven by lowered protective barriers and demand-inducing advertising, continue to grow.

These nontraditional export efforts can be seen as a "scattershot" approach to new sources of foreign exchange earnings. Even in the smallest countries, policymakers have been actively promoting investment in a host of nontraditional activities. In tiny Dominica, for example, these range from tourism, assembly operations, financial services, and data processing to vegetables, fruits, seafood, and cut flowers (Wiley 1998). Such experimentation raises the question of whether product niches with considerable foreign exchange earning power and stability can be secured or whether they are simply replacing monocrop and single-market dependence with new forms of neoliberal vulnerability. In other words, are exporters and the state behind them trying to do too many extremely challenging things at once while doing little to build toward a sustainable future?

Under neoliberalism, food imports are also increasing and undermining food security and self-sufficiency. Food production for domestic consumption has historically been an important source of employment, but farmers are being outcompeted by US imports (*Life and Debt* 2001; Weis 2007). US crops are produced on a larger scale, with more chemical inputs, and are underwritten with federal subsidies (Ikerd 2002).

Nontraditional agricultural exports such as fruits, vegetables, and flowers have high value by volume and area under cultivation. Central America has been more successful than the Caribbean in selling them in the United States and other North Atlantic markets. However, these exports have had several problems that have restricted benefits, even in Central America. The sector is characterized by dominance by firms from the United States and other core countries, and there has been inadequate state support to develop the sector; overproduction and oversupply from multiple sources, which decreases income; shaky performance and low to no growth for small-scale local producers; and poor working conditions for the employees (Robinson 2008).

The Rise and Fall of Maquiladoras

Over recent decades, the IFIs and national governments have also promoted many nonagricultural exports for the purpose of earning foreign exchange and generating employment. These include the products of maquiladoras whose sites are called "free zones" or "export processing zones" (EPZs), many of which are state subsidized (see also chapter 13 on the US-Mexico borderlands).

Haiti introduced maquiladoras early on. Employment expanded between 1970 and 1984 under the Duvalier dictatorship, after which jobs began to move elsewhere as Haiti became less stable and other countries opened EPZs. Even during peak maquiladora employment, however, Haiti was a net exporter of capital: that is, foreign investors and their Haitian managers moved most of their profits abroad, and more consumer and producer goods came in than were exported as manufactured products. Since the 1990s Haiti's political instability has repelled more maquiladora investment than its sub-fifty-cents-an-hour wages can attract (Dupuy 2005). Today, despite paying subpoverty wages, apparel factories survive only because of special access to the US market granted in 2006 (the Haitian Hemispheric Opportunity through Partnership Encouragement [HOPE] Act). Apparel is two-thirds of Haiti's exports, but exports are less than half of what Haiti receives in remittances, which is discussed further below (see chapter 14 on transnational Latin America).

Elsewhere in CAC, maquiladora employment peaked in the early 1990s. Tens of thousands of mainly young females were employed in factories in Jamaica and all five Central American countries. Most of the eastern Caribbean countries had more than a thousand workers each. The Dominican Republic attracted the most assembly operations and had over 160,000 factory workers. But even there, the assembly plants were low-paying economic enclaves with minimal positive impact on the Dominican economy. Since the mid-1990s, maquiladora employment has declined throughout the region. More and more noncore countries, particularly in Asia led by China, have sought assembly operations and lured investors away from the region with promises of state support, lower wages, and more abundant nonunion workers. Here is one illustration of this massive global shift: In 2001 China and Central America each held a 12 percent share of the US apparel market. By 2009, despite a new free trade agreement between the United States and Central America (CAFTA), the region's share of the US market had fallen to 8.7 percent, while China's had increased to 38 percent (Gallagher and Porzecanski 2010). The largest apparel suppliers to the United States (in order) are now China, Vietnam, Indonesia, and Honduras; Mexico is seventh. Governments compete among each other to attract investors by offering a range of subsidies. To some extent the ubiquitous subsidies simply cancel each other out and undermine efforts to generate foreign exchange.

Even in Mexico's maquiladoras, with their special access to US markets through NAFTA, a predominantly male workforce, and focus on the automobile and electronic industries, maquiladora employment peaked at over 1.5 million in 2000. Since then, hundreds of thousands of jobs have moved to China and elsewhere in Asia, where there is a vastly greater supply of laborers paid well under one dollar an hour.

One comparative study of export processing zones in China, Honduras, and Nicaragua commissioned by the International Labor Organization (ILO) revealed some fundamental problems with the remaining Central American EPZs. Factories pay at or even below the paltry minimum wage, labor organizing has been repressed, and the wages have recently declined further because of the reduced US demand triggered by global economic downturn. Further, Central American EPZs are vulnerable to complete collapse due to China's virtually limitless labor supply: "Today the Honduran and Nicaraguan maquiladoras survive primarily as a result of preferential US trade relations which impose relatively high import taxes on Chinese goods" (McCallum 2011, 17). The ILO report concludes that EPZs' impacts on workers and national development are bleak everywhere, even in China: "While EPZs have flourished as a vehicle for globalized production, as an employer strategy for low-cost exports, and (on occasion) as a governmental strategy to absorb surplus labour and attract FDI, they have failed to create *decent* jobs. In other words, we can usefully view the EPZ strategy as a low-road job creation model by promoting a race to the bottom" (McCallum 2011, 16).

Post-9/11 Vulnerabilities and Offshore Services

In the mid-1990s, the World Bank recommended that Caribbean governments promote international service industries such as tourism, offshore banking, data processing, and offshore services as alternative foreign exchange–earning activities to the failed ones discussed above. Offshore services have taken many forms, ranging from insurance and ship registration to psychic healers, phone sex, and Internet gambling. CAC countries established some of the world's first offshore regulatory environments for Internet gambling. By the early 2000s, Costa Rica hosted about 15 percent of the world's 2,500 gambling sites. Antigua has also been prominent. In Costa Rica, about 3,000 workers, mostly college students and foreigners staying on after teaching English, earned four to five US dollars per hour taking bets or answering customer queries over the phone. Worldwide, online wagers were around $2 billion in 2000, rising to nearly $30 billion in 2010 (H2 Gambling Capital 2011). Note that no US law explicitly prohibits gambling over the Internet inside the United States. But a 1961 US law called the Interstate Wire Act prohibited gambling operations from using interstate telephone lines, and that is generally understood to include the Internet.

The offshore gambling business in CAC countries is probably past its modest peak. A 2011 US Department of Justice ruling restricted the interpretation of the Wire Act to prohibit only sports betting. Since then, some US states have legalized online poker and other gambling, in direct competition with CAC. Then a 2013 film *Runner Runner: A Cautionary Tale for Americans* depicted Costa Rica's online poker as lawless and unethical, which observers thought was fairly accurate. The movie reinforced fears in the United States that offshore gambling is a risky bet. In these ways, CAC's new economic ventures are vulnerable to rulings or perceptions beyond the region.

The events of 9/11 and US policy responses to it have revealed additional aspects of regional vulnerability, including the fragility of other offshore services such as tourism (see chapter 6). The attack occurred as the US economy was beginning a downturn after nearly eight years of sustained growth. The convergence of economic slump and the fear of terrorism in the United States created a heightened sense of socioeconomic, as well as strategic, insecurity. Then President Bush's call to American citizens to go on with their lives, travel, and spend translated into more domestic travel and spending, rather than foreign travel and spending. The reduction of US international travel after 9/11 followed a pattern seen after the first war with Iraq in 1991. US citizens became fearful of flying abroad, and the Caribbean's vulnerable tourism sector, otherwise unrelated to the problem, suffered. Similarly, an immediate effect of 9/11 was a generalized fear of flying internationally among citizens of the United States and also some parts of the EU. The stricter security measures adopted after 9/11 may also have discouraged leisure travel. Caribbean tourism contracted even in locations where Europeans outnumber Americans, such as Barbados, the Dominican Republic, and Cuba.

The second war with Iraq in 2003 worsened the contraction in Caribbean tourism. Air Jamaica, after surviving an $80 million financial loss in 2002, saw reservations fall by almost 40 percent during the first two weeks of hostilities. This decline forced Air Jamaica to reduce flights to some US cities it regularly serviced, thereby worsening the decline in passengers. The Caribbean's regional airlines that serve the smaller islands went even further into arrears and required additional state subsidies to continue operating. Tourism reservations for Mexico similarly declined by 17.1 percent overall and by more than 30 percent for reservations from the United States. One needs to pause and consider the reverberating impacts of sudden exogenous-induced declines of this magnitude, even though they were temporary, throughout societies dependent on tourism revenue. Not until early in 2005 did international travel finally rebound to its pre-9/11 level. For the Caribbean region, so reliant on international tourism, this represents a three-and-a-half-year setback. The more recent global recession reduced tourism again, extending its rollercoaster revenue pattern (see chapter 6).

Since 9/11, the US government, in concert with the OECD (Organization for Economic Cooperation and Development), has sought and achieved greater regulatory oversight of offshore financial centers (OFCs), a large portion of which are in CAC. A major component of these efforts is directed at disclosing sources of money laundering. They include blacklisting suspected individuals and organizations, freezing assets, and investigating the internal records of US banks and their foreign affiliates. The United States, using bank secrecy laws, has been pressuring OFCs to cooperate with the FBI and other US government agencies by providing information on depositors. Nearly all governments hosting OFCs have cooperated and some, such as Grenada, shut down most of these banks. One consequence is a reduction of capital flows through, and therefore revenues going to, the offshore centers, particularly the smaller, poorer, and less regulated ones.

These post-9/11 vulnerabilities have not dissipated with time. Airport and shipping port security costs are now higher throughout CAC. The long-term impacts of 9/11 and the international campaign in response to it reveal how global priorities are set. The antiterrorism campaign demonstrates how a critical event in core countries can quickly and decisively shift global priorities, marginalize and effectively discredit other concerns, and dominate the global agenda.

Remittance Economies and Phantom Landscapes

Having reviewed the fragility of CAC as agricultural exporters, manufacturing export platforms, and international service centers, the obvious questions are: What can people do to make a sustainable living? and How can these countries generate much-needed foreign exchange?

Take the example of Guatemala, which has one of the strongest natural resource bases and economic profiles in the region (Klak 2004). The civil war that killed over one hundred thousand people finally ended in 1996. The peace opened previously remote and dangerous parts of the country for increased settlement. The huge and ecologically precious Petén rain forest region of northern Guatemala has received thousands of peasant migrants who have come to clear and burn land for farming. The Petén also contains oil, and exploration has opened more of the region to environmental harm and settlement. But the supportive infrastructure needed to make small farms viable, such as agricultural extension services, loans, and transportation to get products to market, has been inadequate. Peasants therefore fail as farmers and sell their recently cleared parcels, which are now worth more on the market than when they grew trees, to cattle ranchers, who consolidate them. The peasants then move on to clear more forest. This process has accelerated over time and has cleared hundreds of thousands of acres of rain forest since the late 1990s (figure 5.3).

Figure 5.3. Peasants who clear Guatemala's Petén rainforest have difficulty making a living off the land, so they sell their cleared land to ranchers. Massive inequalities and inadequate state support for sustainable agriculture results in environmental destruction and land use inefficiencies. Guatemala has vast natural resources but also massive problems of hunger.

There is an emerging opportunity for Guatemala and the many other LAC countries with rain forests that are still standing or could be restored. If they commit to protect and rejuvenate their rain forests, wealthier countries will compensate them. At the 2014 UN Climate Summit, the United States and other rich countries followed Germany's lead to pledge funds for rain forest protection worldwide. Guatemala committed to restoring three million acres (Hance 2014). Perhaps the most ambitious of these funds-for-rain-forest programs in LAC has been playing out over recent years between Norway and Guyana; results thus far are mixed but the arrangement holds considerable promise (Lang 2103).

Because most agricultural and industrial sectors have declined in CAC countries, their economies are now heavily reliant on services, remittances, and, as we've discussed, various forms and sources of foreign aid. Services that are growing as a result of tourism promotion include the hotel and restaurant sectors, formal and informal vendors, and taxi and tour drivers. Tourists from core countries also inadvertently bring with them the "demonstration effect," whereby locals are exposed to and grow accustomed to an affluent consumer lifestyle (Pattullo 2006). The dominance of US television and films similarly carries with it this demonstration effect (Potter et al. 2004). Other services that have expanded in recent years include the selling of passports. They also include a standard array of items associated with global consumer culture, such as cable and satellite TV, shopping malls, US-style subdivisions, and fast-food chains (figure 5.2).

Across Central America, the Caribbean, and Mexico as well, the principal export for many years has been workers who migrate legally or illegally to the United States and other core countries. By 2010, CAC countries were ten of the world's top twenty-nine countries of emigration when measured as a share of population. For example, 21 and 39 percent of El Salvador's and Suriname's populations, respectively, live abroad, a figure that soars to 65 percent for Grenada. The associated "brain drain" is also massive: CAC include the world's top seven countries in terms of the number of university-educated emigrants, a particularly jarring statistic considering the countries' relatively small populations (World Bank 2011).

By far the world's greatest international migration flow is from Mexico to the United States. Mexico's former president Vicente Fox noted already in 2003 that remittances were Mexico's "biggest source of foreign income, bigger than oil, tourism or foreign investment." He added this striking statistic: "the 20 million Mexicans in the United States generate a gross product that is slightly higher than the $600 billion generated by [the 90 million] Mexicans in Mexico" (Alonso Lugo 2003). Note, however, that the volume of legal and illegal migration to the United States has slowed in recent years, owing to stricter laws and enhanced enforcement but owing more to the economic downturn, which has reduced income opportunities in the United States.

Back in LAC, the service economy has been stimulated by the remittance-receiving family members who can consume near a middle-class level despite the paucity of gainful employment in their homelands. Their purchasing power is demonstrated by new homes and home additions, trendy clothes and electronic goods, high-tech appliances, fancy vehicles, and domestic service workers. These landscapes and their inhabitants convey the false impression that there is local economic vibrancy, stability, and productivity, and hence earn the label "phantom landscapes."

Beneath the visual prosperity is economic malaise, or worse. In Jamaica, for example, neoliberalism has cut deep into public resources, so that the state is no longer financially capable of maintaining clientelistic relationships with constituents. In poorer parts of Kingston, Jamaica, the state has been upstaged by drug dons who now control neighborhoods and protect and provide for residents better than the state can. The emergent wealth from drug trafficking, indeed a nefarious income-generating opportunity for LAC, also distorts societies and their landscapes throughout the hemisphere (see chapter 8).

Conclusion

Sustainable development has become a universal goal in recent years. It requires a strong and secure set of economic activities in well-remunerated communities that do not degrade the environment. With this goal in mind, the chapter has examined a variety of export sectors and international alliances that have been pursued before and since the neoliberal policy transition. The small countries of CAC have been particularly hard hit by the global shift toward free trade that has restricted their ability to generate foreign exchange through exports, while it has flooded their markets with cheaper imports. Cheap consumer goods help citizens in the short term, but they need good jobs to pay for everything. Those jobs have been in short supply. It can be viewed as ironic that the most successful recent export from the region is their work-forces, which have gone to the United States and other core countries to earn and remit money home. The neoliberal transition has been incompatible with sustainable development because it has undermined autonomy and empowerment at the national and local scales. Neoliberal-ism has created additional problems by pressuring already highly trade-dependent countries to trade more, thereby decreasing their self-sufficiency and self-determination.

From the perspective of world-systems theory, these results are unsurprising (Klak 2014). Sustainable development policies are unlikely to be delivered by indebted, neoliberalizing, peripheral states with so little maneuvering room and so narrowly tied to powerful economic interests at home and abroad. CAC countries are therefore facing major challenges regarding how to cope with their new economic realities. Their ability to replace failed exports with more productive activities will determine the stability of those societies in the years ahead.

World-systems theory also stresses that even the most peripheral countries have some op-tions they can pursue. In the current environment, options have emerged particularly because, as we've noted, the United States has loosened its ties with Latin America and the Caribbean while other countries have stepped up to play a more active regional role. Latin American and Caribbean countries, especially the smaller ones, have needed to search far and wide to cobble together development assistance from China, Venezuela, Canada, the EU, and other prosperous countries in Europe and Asia. This aid provides a wide range of societal needs from telecommunications, public facilities, and transportation to education, health care, and environmental protection. The emerging regional reorientation away from the United States and toward China, in terms of trade, aid, investment, and development mindset, is the most significant of these geopolitical shifts.

With so few economic options, governments have also felt compelled in recent years to embrace the "last resorts" (Pattullo 2006), that is, various forms of tourism development. Chapter 6 examines both mass tourism and ecotourism-related sustainable development. The latter opportunity holds more promise, particularly if ecotourism connects with a range of local productive activities such as small-scale agriculture, fishing, and forestry. These sectors can provide desirable jobs while maintaining some local autonomy from neoliberalism and globalization (Peteru et al. 2010).

Key Terms

IFIs: Refers primarily to the International Monetary Fund (IMF) and the World Bank, which provide countries with financial assistance and recommendations on ways to open their econo-mies to foreign competition while reducing government intervention and spending (Peet 2006).

LAC; CAC: Latin America and the Caribbean (33 countries including Mexico and the 12 in South America); Central America and the Caribbean (the mostly smaller 21 countries between North and South America).

maquiladoras: Factories in LAC employing mainly women to assemble clothing and other consumer nondurables (electronics, plastic goods, shoes, and sporting goods) for export.

remittances: Money or goods sent by workers living abroad to relatives back home.

trade dependency: Measured as the share of a country's economic activity that is international as opposed to domestic, it increases the local impacts of global changes (Gwynne et al. 2003).

Suggested Readings

Desai, Vandana, and Robert Potter (Eds.). *The Companion to Development Studies*. 3rd ed. New York: Routledge, 2014.

Gallagher, Kevin and Roberto Porzecanski. *The Dragon in the Room: China and the Future of Latin American Industrialization*. Stanford: Stanford University Press, 2010.

McNeill, J. R. *Mosquito Empires: Ecology and War in the Greater Caribbean, 1620–1914*. New York: Cambridge University Press, 2009.

Meyer, Axel, and Jorge Huete-Pérez. "Conservation: Nicaragua Canal Could Wreak Environmental Ruin." *Nature* 506, (February 20, 2014): 287–89.

Robinson, William I. *Latin America and Global Capitalism: A Critical Globalization Perspective*. Baltimore: Johns Hopkins University Press, 2008.

References

Alonso Lugo, Luis. "Remittances Are Mexico's Biggest Source of Income, Says Fox." *Associated Press*. 2003. Accessed May 14, 2007. www.signonsandiego.com/news/mexico/20030924-2051-us-mexico.html

Anderson, Perry. "Renewals." *New Left Review* 1 (2000): 5–24.

Blum, William. *Killing Hope: US Military and CIA Interventions Since World War II*. Monroe, ME: Common Courage Press, 2003.

Castañeda, Jorge G. "Adios, Monroe Doctrine: When the Yanquis Go Home." *New Republic*, December 28, 2009. Accessed July 12, 2011. www.tnr.com/article/world/adios-monroe-doctrine

Dominica (Government of the Commonwealth of Dominica). *2006: Medium-Term Growth and Social Protection Strategy, Roseau*. 2006. Accessed September 16, 2009. siteresources.worldbank.org/INTPRS1/Resources/Dominica_PRSP(April2006).pdf

Dupuy, Alex. "Globalization, the World Bank, and the Haitian Economy." In *Contemporary Caribbean Cultures and Societies in a Global Context*, edited by Franklin W. Knight and Teresita Martínez-Vergne, 43–70. Chapel Hill: University of North Carolina Press, 2005.

Frank, Andre Gunder. *Capitalism and Underdevelopment in Latin America*. New York: Monthly Review Press, 1967.

Gallagher, Mike, and Cameron McWhirter. "Chiquita: An Empire Built on Controversy." *Cincinnati Enquirer*, May 3, 1998. Accessed May 14, 2007. www.mindfully.org/Pesticide/chiquita/

Gonzalez-Perez, Maria-Alejandra, and Terence McDonough. "Chiquita Brands and the Banana Business: Brands and Labour Relations Transformations." CISC (Centre for Innovation and Structural Change, National University of Ireland) Working Paper 23, January 2006, at www.cisc.ie/publications/detail.php?publication_code=7544

Gwynne, Robert, Thomas Klak, and Dennis J. B. Shaw. *Alternative Capitalisms: Geographies of Emerging Regions*. New York: Oxford University Press, 2003.

H2 Gambling Capital. "H2 Publishes Preliminary eGaming Data for 2010 and Extends Forecasts to 2015." 2011. Accessed July 16, 2011. www.h2gc.com/news.php?article=H2+publishes+preliminary+eGaming+Data+for+2010+and+extends+forecasts+to+2015

Hance, Jeremy. "Four countries pledge to restore 30 million hectares of degraded lands at UN Summit." mongabay.com. September 25, 2014.

Harvey, David. *A Brief History of Neoliberalism*. Oxford, UK: Oxford University Press, 2005.

Ikerd, John. "The Real Costs of Globalization to Farmers, Consumers and Our Food System." 2002. Accessed May 14, 2007. www.ssu.missouri.edu/faculty/jikerd/papers/Globalization.html

ITC (US International Trade Commission). "U.S. Merchandise Trade Balance, by Partner Country 2014." Accessed March 19, 2015. http://dataweb.usitc.gov/scripts/cy_m3_run.asp

Life and Debt. Stephanie Black, producer and writer. A Tuff Gong Pictures Production. 2001. Accessed December 2008. www.lifeanddebt.org/

Klak, Thomas. "Globalization, Neoliberalism and Economic Change in Central America and the Caribbean." In *Latin America Transformed: Globalization and Modernity*, edited by Robert N. Gwynne and Cristóbal Kay, 67–92. 2nd ed. London: Edward Arnold Publishers; New York: Oxford University Press, 2004.

———. "Development Policy Drift in Central America and the Caribbean." *Singapore Journal of Tropical Geography* 30 (2009): 2–17.

———. "World Systems Theory." In *The Companion to Development Studies*, edited by Vandana Desai and Robert Potter, 121–27. 3rd ed. New York: Routledge, 2014.

Klak, Thomas, James Wiley, Emma Mullaney, Swetha Peteru, Sean Regan, and Jean-Yves Merilus. "Inclusive Neoliberalism?: Perspectives from Eastern Caribbean Farmers." *Progress in Development Studies* 11, no. 1 (2011): 33–61.

Lang, Chris. "Why Is Norway Paying Guyana for REDD?" REDD-Monitor.org. January 17, 2013.

McCallum, Jamie K. "Export Processing Zones: Comparative Data from China, Honduras, Nicaragua, and South Africa." International Labour Office, Industrial and Employment Relations Department. Working paper 21. Geneva: ILO. 2011. Accessed July 12, 2011. www.ilo.org/public/libdoc/ilo/2011/111B09_41_engl.pdf

Pattullo, Polly. *Last Resorts: The Cost of Tourism in the Caribbean*. 2nd ed. New York: Monthly Review Press, 2006.

Peck, Jamie. "Geography and Public Policy: Constructions of Neoliberalism." *Progress in Human Geography* 28 (2004): 392–405.

Peet, Richard. "Review of *End of Poverty: Economic Possibilities for Our Time* by Jeffrey Sachs." *Annals of the Association of American Geographers* 96 (2006): 450–53.

Peteru, Swetha, Seann Regan, and Thomas Klak. "Local Vibrancy in a Globalizing World: Evidence from Dominica, Eastern Caribbean." *Focus on Geography* 53, no. 4 (Winter 2010): 124–33.

Ploetz, Randy. "Black Sigatoka of Banana: The Most Important Disease of a Most Important Fruit" *The American Phytopathological Society*. Accessed March 21, 2015. http://www.apsnet.org/publications/apsnetfeatures/Pages/blacksigatoka.aspx

Pollan, Michael. *The Omnivore's Dilemma: A Natural History of Four Meals*. New York: Penguin Press, 2006.

Potter, Robert, David Barker, Dennis Conway, and Thomas Klak. *The Contemporary Caribbean*. Essex, UK: Addison Wesley Longman and Prentice Hall, 2004.

Ray, Rebecca, and Kevin P. Gallagher. *China-Latin America Economic Bulletin*. Global Economic Governance Initiative, Boston University, 2013.

Richardson, Bonham. *The Caribbean in the Wider World, 1492–1992*. Cambridge: Cambridge University Press, 1992.

Ricketts, Paul (Dominica's national epidemiologist). Personal communication, 2011.

Robotham, Don. "Crime and Public Policy in Jamaica." In *Understanding Crime in Jamaica: New Challenges for Public Policy*, edited by Anthony Harriott, 197–238. Mona, Jamaica: University of West Indies Press, 2005.

Thomas, C. Y. *The Poor and the Powerless: Economic Policy and Change in the Caribbean*. New York: Monthly Review Press, 1988.

UNCTAD. *World Investment Directory*, vol. 9, *Latin America and the Caribbean 2004*. Parts 1 and 2. New York: United Nations, 2004.

UNCTAD. "Banana." *Info Comm*. 2011. Accessed July 13, 2011. www.unctad.org/infocomm/anglais/banana/market.htm

Weis, Tony. "Small Farming and Radical Imaginations in the Caribbean Today." *Race and Class* 49, no. 2 (2007): 112–17.

Wiley, James. "Dominica's Economic Diversification: Microstates in a Neoliberal Era?" In *Globalization and Neoliberalism*, edited by T. Klak, 155–78. Lanham, MD: Rowman & Littlefield, 1998.

———. *From Banana Empire to Banana Split: Globalization and the Banana Industries of the Western Hemisphere*. Lincoln: University of Nebraska Press, 2008.

World Bank. *International Debt Statistics 2014*. Washington, DC: World Bank, 2014.

World Bank. *Migration and Remittances: Top Countries*. Accessed July 12, 2011. siteresources.worldbank.org/INTPROSPECTS/Resources/334934-1199807908806/Top10.pdf

World Bank, Caribbean Division. *Coping with Changes in the External Environment*. World Bank Report 12821 LAC. Washington, DC: World Bank, 1994.

WTO. *International Trade Statistics*. 2013. Accessed March 17, 2015. https://www.wto.org/english/res_e/statis_e/its2013_e/its13_appendix_e.htm

Chapter 6

Mass and Alternative Tourisms in Latin America and the Caribbean

Edward L. Jackiewicz and Thomas Klak

SIMILAR TO MANY WORLD REGIONS, Latin America has embraced tourism to lure in money from beyond the region, provide jobs, and stimulate local economies. Latin America offers a bevy of resources that appeal to potential tourists from around the world but is burdened by negative stereotypes and images of violence, corruption, and so on (some more real than others) that discourage some potential visitors.

Before discussing Latin American versions of tourism and their challenges, it is important to contextualize tourism as a global phenomenon. The World Tourism Organization (WTO) 2013 Annual Report shows that international tourist arrivals exceeded one billion travelers in 2012 and continued the momentum with 5 percent growth in 2013 (WTO 2014). From international tourism that was restricted to the elite a century ago, to about one out of every seven people on the planet being an international tourist by 2013, a democratization of tourism is apparent. The biggest growth in LAC in 2013 was in Central America (4 percent), while South America (2 percent) and the Caribbean (2 percent) both showed slower growth than in 2012. Note the potential cultural learning opportunity that global tourism represents, as "the single largest peaceful movement of people across cultural boundaries in the history of the world" (Stronza 2001, 264).

So what does all this tourism mean at the regional or local level in LAC? More specifically, to what extent can tourism contribute to sustainable development at the regional or local level? We examine these questions by holding tourism examples up against a definition of sustainable development (see chapter 5) represented by a three-legged stool. The stool requires all three legs to be strong: sustainable tourism must be simultaneously economically viable and inclusive, socially and culturally positive for both hosts and visitors, and environmentally positive (Klak 2007). What effects do tens of millions of visitors have on working people, struggling businesses and communities, and fragile environments?

This chapter begins with a discussion of tourism generally, followed by a brief presentation of its evolution in LAC, highlighting its increasing importance to many countries of the region. We will then discuss various types of tourism and offer several case studies. Last, in light of recent trends, we comment on the potential of tourism to contribute to sustainable development in LAC in the twenty-first century.

What Is Tourism, Who Are the Tourists, and Why Are They So Fickle?

It is first important to understand tourism as an export industry, albeit an atypical one. Consumption occurs at the site of production as an experience, rather than as a tangible product that is manufactured and sent abroad (Davenport and Jackiewicz 2008). Tourism is best conceived of as an export because it brings in revenue from beyond national borders, thereby helping to pay for imports or allowing economies to expand.

It is often difficult to identify what is or is not a tourist activity. For example, when someone from an inland village makes a day trip to the beach, is that person a tourist or local? Outsiders might view this person as a local, but nearby residents might not. If someone from the United States owns a condo in Costa Rica where she or he lives four months a year, is she or he a tourist when in Costa Rica? Further, the fifty-two million visitors to LAC in 2010 included not only those traveling for leisure on foreign passports, but also members of the vast LAC diaspora who return to visit relatives or participate in cultural events. Also included in the total are students like you studying abroad. Are they all international tourists, as the United Nations World Tourism Organization (UNWTO) classifies them? Is it more important how this person is viewed by others or how they view themselves, that is, does that person *feel* like a tourist? Similarly, if someone works as a bartender in a restaurant that caters both to tourists and to locals, would you classify that person as working in the tourism sector?

These questions highlight challenges associated with measuring and analyzing tourism and its impacts. Regardless of these complexities, tourism's significance throughout the world is without doubt. As the industry continues to grow, research in this area has expanded as well and encompasses the economic, cultural, social, political, and environmental impacts of this form of mobility. Geography, with its interdisciplinary approach, is well poised to tackle these issues.

Tourism and traveling have become a source of cultural capital, and some people now "collect" tourist experiences as they would more material or tangible items and constantly seek new or more exotic experiences to tell their friends about. Similarly, new destinations frequently emerge to lure tourists to their "unique" experience, whether it be in the rainforest, a mountain resort, a small village, or an undiscovered beach town. Adventurous tourists and exotic destinations seeking alternate sources of income are finding each other, creating new spaces of tourism.

Relatedly, tourism destinations often have a brief heyday after which they lose their allure. In Jamaica, for example, decades ago Montego Bay was the tourism mecca, but that focus shifted to Ocho Rios, then to Negril, and now to other more remote parts of the island. As St. Lucian Nobel Laureate Derek Walcott (1997, 274) described the transformation, a remote and still authentic place in LAC gets written about and read about by international audiences, or in other words: "a backward place, unimportant, and one now being corrupted into significance by these prose." In this way, a place can be quickly discovered and tourism-colonized, only to be abandoned in favor of the next "hot" destination. The built environment that tourism requires is left behind as empty hotel rooms and shells of abandoned restaurants and bars that previously replaced mangrove forests and coastal lagoons. This sequence of places paving over nature only to be abandoned for greener pastures suggests another geographical pattern of "development as destruction" (Smith 2008).

The impacts of this geographical fickleness are grave for locals relying on tourism for income. Indeed, tourism flows can change rapidly due to forces occurring in the source or the host countries or, as the negative impact of 9/11 on LAC tourism demonstrated, even beyond them. These changes, known as "demand shifters" (Ioannides and Timothy 2010), have many origins. Demand shifters can rather suddenly increase or decrease tourist flows. They include demographic changes, for example, as with the emergence of a relatively healthy and affluent baby boomer crowd with the time and resources to travel; special draws such as international sporting events; natural disasters; political or economic turmoil; other safety concerns (either perceived or real); and currency exchange rates. Places can come in and out of favor among would-be tourists based on outside judgments. If a country winds up on the US State Department's travel warning list, then tourism may contract (as of this writing, Haiti, Mexico, and Colombia are the only LAC countries on the list, but also worth noting is that Cuba is not even mentioned because it has been for decades illegal for most US citizens to travel there). Despite these warnings, Colombia has experienced rapid tourism growth and Mexico remains the runaway leader in number of visitors. In these two countries, there are obviously other factors at play that supersede the State Department's warning. Most demand shifters are not so formally institutionalized, but they nonetheless can turn tourists away and disrupt economic well-being in the host countries unless other factors intervene.

Tourism's Bundled Complexity: Case Study of Cancún, Mexico

Tourism can be understood as a complex set or bundle of economic, political, sociocultural, and environmental activities and impacts (Shaw and Williams 2004). Thus, when analyzing the tourism industry or tourism destinations, one must be cognizant of the diversity and multiple ingredients and impacts. The development of Cancún into Mexico's most popular resort illustrates this bundled complexity. In the mid-1970s, long-famous but rapidly aging Acapulco still received 21 percent of international tourists to Mexico, and Cancún was a sleepy beach town. Then the national government decided Cancún would be an ideal location for an international resort, accessible to the many Caribbean cruise lines, whereas Acapulco is not. The government also decided that tourism would be central to its modernization project and Cancún would be central to these plans. At the time, the state of Quintana Roo where Cancún is located (see figure 6.1) was struggling economically, and there was growing concern about indigenous uprisings in this area, partly because it bordered then-turbulent Central America (Hiernaux-Nicolas 1999). The Inter-American Development Bank (IDB) along with the Mexican government approved project financing, and construction was soon under way. The development plan created a strict divide between the tourist zone and the urban zone where most of the workers would live, creating Cancún's distinctive "tourist bubble" segregated from locals. Cancún's lavish resorts contrast with unserviced squatter settlements and, farther out, rural poverty. By 1995, Cancún was Mexico's largest hotel resort city, receiving 20 percent of international visitors, while Acapulco's share had fallen to a mere 4 percent (Hiernaux-Nicolas 1999). Acapulco and Cancún highlight tourism's competitive nature, whereby one locale's gains may be at another's expense—and these shifts happen at all geographical scales from local to international.

In addition to the dramatic economic change brought about by tourism, it has demographic, cultural, and environmental impacts. Not surprisingly, many poor Mexicans migrated to Cancún seeking employment in tourism, construction, and related industries. The region also became a magnet for transnational tourism-related investment that accelerated regional growth, spreading down the Yucatán Peninsula into cities such as Playa del Carmen and the neighboring islands of Cozumel and Isla de Mujeres.

Moreover, the local Mayan culture has been commodified to suit American tourist demands and curiosities, resulting in an extravagant and overbuilt mass tourism that locals call Gringolandia (Torres and Momsen 2005). Cancún features jet ski "jungle" tours in the local mangrove lagoons, Maya waiters dressed in "authentic" dress, caged tigers, and a crocodile park, among many other spectacles—all neatly packaged for American tourists (Torres and Momsen 2005, 316). Native American culture is on display in places like Cancún in a form of "mock authenticity," packaged and sold to tourists in forms they expect and can handle (Urry 1990). Merrill (2009) similarly notes that in Teotihuacán, Mexico, as in many other indigenous regions, residents have resurrected traditional folk dances as tourist entertainment. Observers debate whether such acts preserve or commodify and destroy cultures. Would these performances be happening if not for the tourists? Do tourists provide a necessary economic incentive to preserve cultural traditions?

The environmental impacts on the Cancún region have been severe. Prior to becoming a tourism mecca, Cancún was a barrier island. Land has been extended for resorts, golf courses, and amusement parks, thereby disrupting important nesting sites for sea birds and turtles, as well as the world's second-longest coral reef system. Furthermore, Cancún now has more than seven hundred thousand permanent residents and receives approximately five million international tourists annually, creating massive demands for water and sewage disposal—a seemingly unsustainable path.

Tourism Trends in Latin America: Change and Continuity

Table 6.1 shows the number of international visitors arriving to various LAC countries in the years 2005, 2010, and 2012 (the latest available year). The first thing to notice is the great disparity in the number of visitors to the various countries, for which geographical size provides only a partial explanation. Not surprisingly, Mexico's proximity to the United States makes it the runaway leader in the region, but also notice that the number of international tourists to Mexico has not shown significant recent growth, despite continued marketing efforts. Also notable is that many of the Caribbean islands have seen little growth, while many countries in Central and South America are experiencing rapid increases in the number of international tourists. Tourism to LAC countries also seems to be increasingly on the radar of more international travelers, as the overall numbers increased significantly between 2010 and 2012. Take note of the rapid rise in several Central American countries, that is, Guatemala, Panama, and Nicaragua, perhaps indicating that they have shed their image as war zones and danger areas, thus appealing to a wider range of tourists.

Arguably more important than tourist numbers are revenues, because it matters little if tourists visit a country if they do not put money in locals' pockets (cruise passengers are notorious for visiting a port of call for a day without spending any money there). Table 6.2 presents tourism receipts for three recent years and, for comparison, each country's population. Comparing receipts to population provides a way to gauge the countries for which tourism has national economic impacts. For example, Mexico's eleven billion dollars in tourism revenues by far tops the region, but the revenues amount to under one hundred dollars per Mexican per year, and are flat over time. Of course, in a country as large and diverse as Mexico, the impact of tourism and spending is wildly diverse throughout; for example, the impact and spending in Cancún is much greater than in rural areas not receiving many visitors. Also, worth noting is that Mexico and several other countries have many other sources of export revenue, unlike a country like the Bahamas, which is much more heavily reliant on the approximately $5000 per capita annual tourism earnings (in itself an impressive number, although recently in decline).

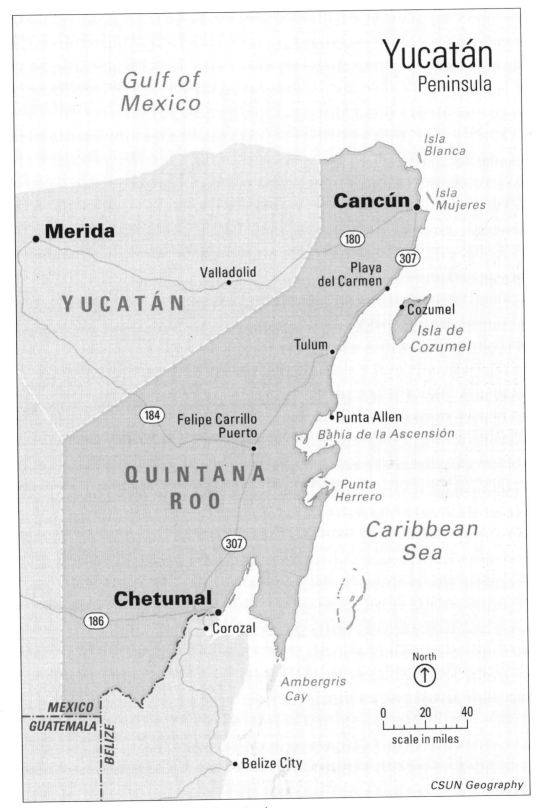

Figure 6.1. Quintana Roo and the Yucatán Peninsula.

Table 6.1. International Tourist Arrivals (000's)

Country	2005	2010	2012
Mexico	21,915	22,395	23,403
Caribbean			
Bahamas	1,608	1,368	1,422
Barbados	548	532	
Cuba	2,261	2,507	2,815
Dominica	86	67	79
Dominican Rep.	3,691	4,125	4,563
Jamaica	1,479	1,922	1,986
Saint Lucia	318	306	307
Central America			
Belize	237	238	277
Costa Rica	1,679	2,100	2,343
El Salvador	1,127	1,150	1,255
Guatemala	1,316	1,219	1,951
Honduras	673	896	895
Nicaragua	712	1,011	1,180
Panama	702	1,317	1,606
South America			
Argentina	3,823	5,288	5,585
Bolivia	524	807	1,114
Brazil	5,358	5,161	5,677
Chile	2,027	2,766	3,554
Colombia	933	1,405	2,175
Ecuador	860	1,047	1,272
Guyana	117	150	177
Paraguay	341	465	579
Perú	1,571	2,299	2,846
Uruguay	1,808	2,352	2,711
Venezuela	706	526	710
TOTAL	56,420	63,419	70,482

Source: World Bank (2015)

Barbados earns nearly as much as the Bahamas per capita but is economically stronger because it has a few other export earners. The Dominican Republic has recently emerged as an important mass tourism destination, but it still earns under $500 annually per capita, nonetheless earnings it desperately needs. In Central America, Belize's receipts are the smallest. But because of its relatively small population, Belize earns the most per person (over $800 per year, compared to less than fifty dollars annually for El Salvador). In comparison, Panama's tourism revenue gains over the last five years are the most impressive in LAC. South American countries have also registered recent receipt gains, but on a per capita basis, they are still relatively small (e.g., Perú's annual tourism revenues are under one hundred dollars per person). Fortunately South America is more economically diversified than Central America or the Caribbean, where the concept of tourism as the "last resort" more aptly applies.

Table 6.2. International Tourism Receipts and Population

Country	Pop (000s) 2010	Tourism Receipts (US$ mil)		
		2005	2010	2012
Mexico	113,423	11,803	11,872	13,320
Caribbean:				
Bahamas	343	2,069	2,223	2,415
Barbados	273	896	1,105	na
Cuba	11,258	2,150	2,503	2,614
Dominica	68	57	87	110
Dominican Rep.	9,927	3,518	4,240	4,736
Jamaica	2,741	1,545	1,986	2,070
Puerto Rico	3,749	3,239	3,211	3,193
Saint Lucia	174	369	326	
Central America:				
Belize	312	214	264	299
Costa Rica	4,659	1,671	2,111	2,544
El Salvador	6,193	361	390	894
Guatemala	14,389	791	1,378	1,419
Honduras	7,601	463	650	666
Nicaragua	5,788	206	309	422
Panama	3,517	780	1,676	3,784
South America:				
Argentina	40,412	2,729	4,930	5,655
Bolivia	9,930	239	499	581
Brazil	194,946	3,861	5,919	6,890
Chile	17,114	1,109	1,636	3,180
Colombia	46,295	1,222	2,083	3,257
Ecuador	14,465	486	781	1,039
Paraguay	6,455	78	217	265
Perú	29,077	1,308	2,274	3,288
Uruguay	3,369	594	1,496	2,222
Venezuela	28,980	650	794	904

Source: World Bank (2015)
na=data not available

The Insidious Nature of Tourism: Soft Power, Agency, and Cultural Exchanges

Tourism has many cultural impacts, some of which can be understood through the concept of soft power, or getting others to want what you want. This concept was first applied to describe how the United States exerted cultural influence on Eastern Europe during the Cold War. In this context, US ideals such as consumerism were believed by US policymakers to have a transformative power on these cultures. Understanding how US soft power has been expressed through tourism is important. According to Merrill (2009), the hemisphere's first foray into mass tourism occurred in Mexico in the 1920s. During this time, a wide range of characters, including drunkards, poets, artists, college students, adventurers, and vacationers, fled US Prohibition and took their money south of the border, seeking excitement and adventure. What ensued was a transformation of both locals and tourists. Largely driven by economic needs, locals began to cater to the tourists' demands. Soft power, as Merrill describes it, is not as blatant as political/economic or military imperialism, which is why it has been absent from many discussions of both tourism and imperialism. Rather, soft power shows up in travel narratives, guidebooks, postcards, works of film, and literature. These media forms can be powerful and persuasive. For example, think of postcards, television commercials, billboards, Internet ads, and so on, for Mexico and how they convey images of exoticism, hedonism, paradise, and so on, which in turn encourage a certain type of behavior that often objectifies local populations.

Also important to this discussion is the role of agency among the hosts. While many locals are greatly influenced by the increasing presence of relatively well-to-do tourists and try to mimic their behavior and attitudes as representative of some type of modernity, there is another side to these cross-cultural exchanges. Tourists, while exerting their economic and cultural power, can also be quite vulnerable. Many tourists have been swindled or coerced into doing things that they end up regretting by savvy locals experienced in and comfortable navigating the contested terrain where tourists and locals meet. This tourism dance, or interaction between tourist and host, can range from buying trinkets on street corners to getting your picture taken with the zebra-striped donkey in Tijuana, engaging in prostitution (which is rampant in many LAC countries), and many other tourism-centered activities.

Although under different circumstances than in Mexico, Cuba during the pre-Castro era experienced similar events. To US tourists, Cuba was theirs for the taking. US culture during the 1950s was relatively conservative, but a Cuban vacation offered a highly sexualized atmosphere where gambling, drinking, and philandering were the norm, earning Cuba the nickname the "playground of the Caribbean." This all came to a grinding halt in 1959 when Castro came to power and succeeded in cleansing Havana of this debauchery. It is worth noting, however, that Cuba's resurgence as an exotic tropical tourism locale since the 1990s has resurrected much of the illicit, sexualized, prerevolutionary tourism.

In Cuba and Mexico (and indeed the rest of LAC), cultures were and are being commodified to meet the entertainment desires of foreigners. Decades ago, many traveled south to satisfy their thirst for alcohol and combined it with gambling and prostitution for an unholy triumvirate of vices. Tijuana and other border cities were, not surprisingly, major beneficiaries during Prohibition. These cross-national relationships continued on after Prohibition ended in 1933 and still exist today in Mexico and are being rekindled in the new Cuba. Both Mexicans and Cubans were the "other" and were there to be "consumed." Merrill (2009) argues, with regard to tourism, that the influence of US tourists abroad throughout the twentieth century was instrumental in the growing US hegemony in this hemisphere. His research focused on US tourist impacts in Mexico, Cuba, and Puerto Rico, and illustrates the not-so-benign nature of tourism. From Merrill's research, travel writers, entertainers, hoteliers, and advertisers, as well as travelers, have all had a great influence (intentional or not) on host cultures.

The Many Forms of Tourism

To begin distinguishing the many current forms of tourism in LAC, it is useful to contrast the typical features of mass tourism with the emerging alternative forms. The former is typically beach and/or shopping focused, dominated by large global chains and franchises and set to North Atlantic standards of comfort and overconsumption; it often centers on culturally isolated resorts or cruise ships (figure 6.2) (Mowforth and Munt 2003). The Mexican and Caribbean island mass-tourist sector is highly globalized, has high leakage rates averaging over 50 percent, and depends on imports for food, beverages, and equipment, most of which come from large-scale, nonlocal (if not US) suppliers (Jules 2005; Torres and Momsen 2011). Fur-

Figure 6.2. A cruise ship docks for the day at the port of St. John's, the capital of Antigua and Barbuda.

thermore, the environmental impacts of both large-scale resort and cruise tourism are often severe (Johnson 2002; Jules 2005). The conclusion of one long-term study of cruise tourism in the eastern Caribbean is that, rather than bridging the cultural divide, it "is creating an ever-wider chasm between the tourist and the islander and contributing to misperceptions and disappointments on the part of both hosts and guests" (Pulsipher and Holderfield 2006, 299). Therefore, mass tourism, as it is typically practiced, does not meet our three-legged-stool criteria for sustainable tourism.

Alternative tourisms, by contrast, hold more promise for sustainable development, but it is still an unfulfilled goal or aspiration. Alternative tourisms take many forms, all of which can be generally characterized by their smaller scale, more local cultural emphases, and greater environmental sensitivities (table 6.3). Alternative tourisms are more likely to promote healthy local farming, land, and diets; local artisanry; professional skills development; employment diversification; and community solidarity and pride. Indeed, a major motivation behind the development of alternative tourisms has been to bring tourist dollars, which have been monopolized by big hotels, cruise lines, and travel services with high leakage rates, to smaller-scale players and locales and more local control. Alternative tourists tend to engage in more physical

Table 6.3. Modifiers Used to Describe Alternative Tourisms

academic	eco-	new
adventure	ecological	organic
agro-	educational	people-to-people
anthro-	environmentally friendly	pro-poor
appropriate	ethical	responsible
archaeo-	ethnic	safari
birding	fair trade	scientific
bottom-up	green	soft
community	heritage	sustainable
contact	historical	trekking
cottage	indigenous	wilderness
cultural	nature	wildlife

Source: Klak (2007, 1044)

activity, interact more with the local culture on its own terms, and consume more modestly and context appropriately than in mass tourism.

The various forms of alternative tourism in table 6.3 are best conceptualized and operationalized as an interconnected cluster, not as a buffet from which to pick and choose. Alternative tourism experiences on the ground regularly integrate many of these themes (Fennell 2003). One is rarely doing just one—say agro-tourism—without some of the others—for example, community, historical, green, or bottom-up tourism. The various types of alternative tourism should be considered complementary, overlapping, and synergistic components of sustainable local tourism ensembles.

An important point is that the alternative forms of tourisms are considerably more diverse and multifaceted than the most well-known one, that is, ecotourism. Indeed, ecotourism is so widely proclaimed as to be of little analytical value—nowadays nearly every tourism outlet claims to be ecofriendly. The dichotomy between mass and alternative tourisms present in this section is best thought of as a heuristic. We've defined the ends of a conceptual continuum against which real-world examples can be assessed. Empirical reality typically falls between the extremes. Furthermore, a case can be made that the two types of tourism have things to teach each other: mass tourism needs to learn how to operate more sustainably; alternative tourism needs to learn how to better market its product, reach customers, and generate greater earnings (Hawkes and Kwortnik 2006).

Case Studies of Emerging Alternative Forms of Tourism

This section presents examples of tourism activities in various regional locales. It will serve to illustrate how wide ranging tourism activities have become. As we review these examples, we keep in mind our priority of sustainable development, and use that to evaluate the trends.

Case Study: Retirement Tourism in Corozal, Belize

As US baby boomers (i.e., those born between 1946 and 1964) head into retirement age, they are increasing demand for retirement properties, especially in warm-weather areas. In the United States, rapid population growth has driven real estate prices up in many traditional retirement states such as Florida and Arizona, encouraging potential retirees to seek out alternative destinations. Many Latin American nations have been working to fill this void. While US citizens have been moving to certain Mexican locales for decades, it has become a region-wide phenomenon at a greater scale, with active recruitment by receiving destinations.

Belize has emerged as a popular destination for several reasons: (1) proximity to the United States, (2) a pleasant, tropical climate, (3) low cost of living, (4) English speaking, (5) generous government incentives on owning real estate, and (6) relative safety. One place in Belize that is on the radar of lifestyle/retirement migrants is the small mainland town of Corozal. The population of the town is less than ten thousand. Its appeal to tourists is that it is only nine miles from the Mexican border and typically less expensive than nearby island destinations. More than forty years ago, a Canadian developer built a community just north of Corozal called Consejo Shores. The development is on the coast and has approximately 350 residential lots with eighty-five homes catering primarily to the United States and Canadian market (as of this writing, the cost for a vacant lot begins around US$10,000 while a four-bedroom, two and a half-bath home was selling for US$295,000). The community is not unlike one you would find in the US Sunbelt, complete with golf course, satellite television, biking trails, parks, and so on. While many retirees prefer living in the gated community with all of the amenities of home, others choose to live in town with the locals, where their presence is more conspicuous. Interviews conducted in this area suggest that while many of the retirees feel they fit in well and are welcomed by the residents, the local Belizeans tell a different story, suggesting that the foreigners are "arrogant" and "act like they're rich even though they are not." There is certainly some conflict and mixed emotions about the increasing presence of foreigners, specifically Americans, in this small town (see Jackiewicz and Govdyak 2015).

Additionally, the Belize government offers retirees incentives to relocate there, including tax breaks on land purchases. Registered retirees can buy a discount card for a small fee to cross the border into Mexico and buy less expensive gas, shop at Costco, and see English-language movies, as the closest theaters are there. Without doubt, these migrating retirees are altering the landscape, and as more countries compete for these migrants, one must question its prospects for long-term, sustainable development, primarily from an environmental and economic perspective.

Case Study: Viejo San Juan, Puerto Rico: Whose Old City?

The history of Puerto Rican development illustrates Pattullo's (2005) concept of "last resorts." Earlier economic mainstays such as sugarcane and other tropical crops during past centuries, or pharmaceutical manufacturing during the twentieth century, have collapsed after losing their preferential markets. As a US possession since 1898, Puerto Rico richly illustrates how, when the US mainland takes an economic downturn, the dependent periphery feels the economic brunt many times over and longer (Pantojas-García and Klak 2004). Such is currently the case, with Puerto Rican unemployment nearly double the national average, in addition to substantial underemployment.

Tourism is now Puerto Rico's main source of income, generating nearly $1000 in annual per capita revenue (table 6.2). Because of its colonial architecture and geographically advantageous location between the US mainland and the rest of the Caribbean, Old San Juan is one of the most frequented ports of call for US cruise ships and the most visited place in Puerto Rico (figure 6.3). Bars, restaurants, souvenir shops, and historical sites cater to cruise tourists, their main source of income. Some bars and restaurants charge naive tourists, who are there for no more than a day, prices for food and drink that are exorbitant by Caribbean standards. Signs of lingering recession are apparent throughout San Juan, including its tourism gem, the old city. Many buildings are abandoned, for sale, or for rent, partly a ramification of the collapse of the housing bubble on the mainland. Below the elevated old city, the drug economy leads those involved, when tourists peer down from atop the old city wall, to scream "move on" and hurl objects at them. All this illustrates elements of social breakdown, with tourists unwelcomed by some who are excluded from tourism's benefits, indeed excluded from the legal economy as a whole. There is remarkably little in this description that accords with the three-legged stool of sustainable tourism.

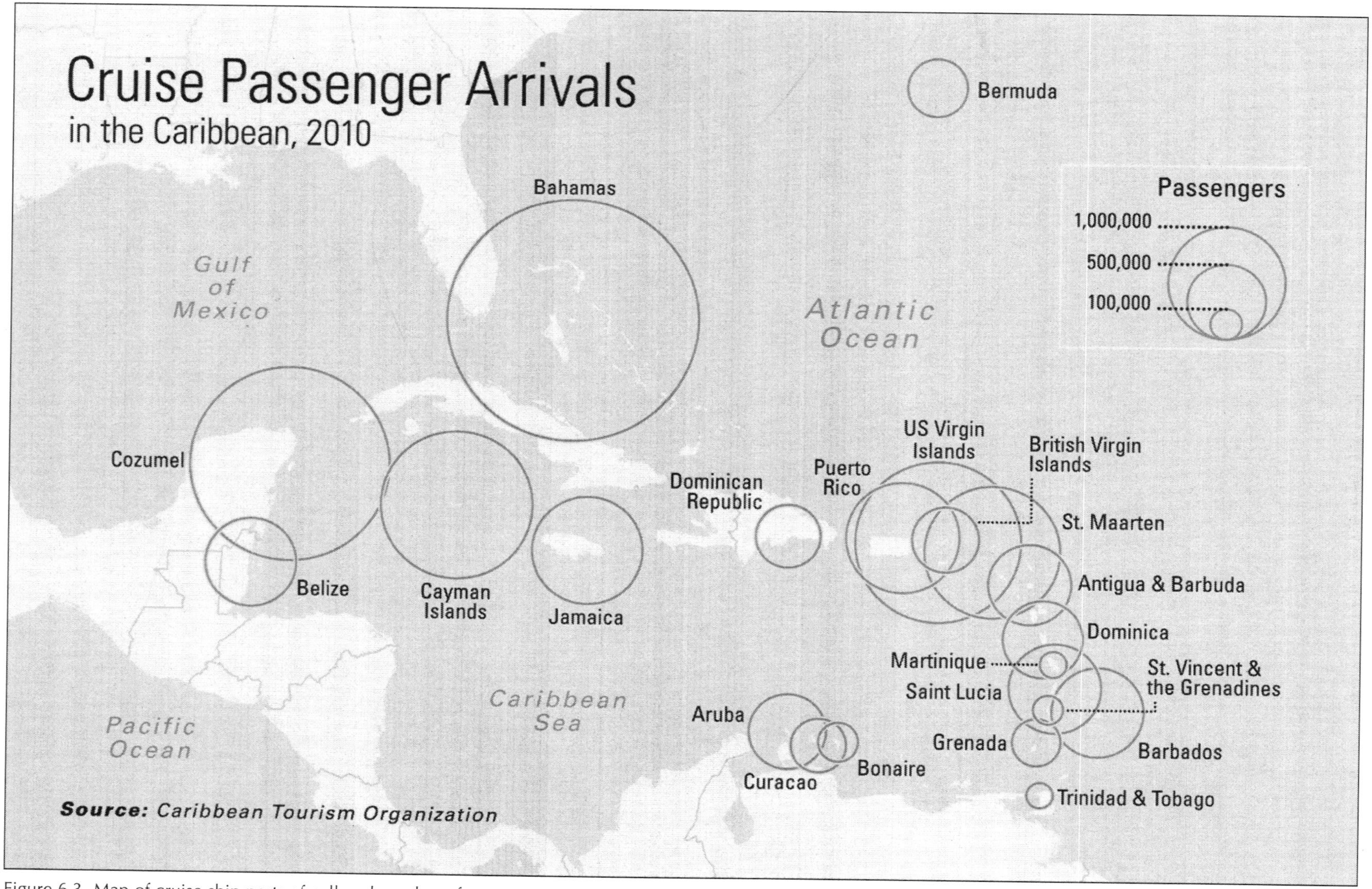

Figure 6.3. Map of cruise ship ports of call and number of passengers.

Case Study: Campeche, Mexico: Mock Authenticity or Local Economic Development?

The interconnected themes of alternative tourisms are woven into many of the advertisements for tourist lodges. Websites for tourism sites often note that they offer a combination of natural, historical, and cultural attractions. A lodge near the Calakmul Biosphere Reserve in Campeche state, southeastern Mexico, illustrates what are often hyperbolic claims. The first sentence on the lodge's website states that "Chicanna Ecovillage Resort, in Xpujil, Campeche, is an ecological, self-sufficient resort, where nature remains untouched" (www.chicannaeco villageresort.com/). Prospective visitors would need to reconcile how a forty-two-room hotel manages to leave the local environment undisturbed. The lodge does take advantage of ample sunlight to heat water in the forty-two rooms. However, this is water-intensive tourism, including a pool, in a region of water scarcity. The lodge also features elements of Mayan architectural style, including thatched roofs, albeit supported by conventional construction materials. Similar tourist *palapas* in the Cancún region through the so-called Riviera Maya to its south are frequently thatched with grass rather than the traditional palm leaves. Pastures are expanding in the region's southern *ejidos* in part to meet the growing demand for the grass, with negative environmental impacts (Roy Chowdhury, personal communication).

Case Study: Ghetto Tours: Voyeurism or Cultural Engagement?

As tourists continuously seek out experiences that are more "real," "authentic," or "off the beaten path," certain common or everyday and even dangerous places have become attractions. Tough urban neighborhoods have become more familiar to a global audience, especially through movies such as *The Harder They Come*, *City of God*, and *Man on Fire*, which portray them as violent, drug infested, and crime ridden. Nonetheless, they appeal to some travelers' curiosity, if not voyeurism. Given the stereotypes, these places feel dangerous (and therefore perhaps alluring) to the tourist who is escorted and protected by professional tour guides.

One example of such ghetto tours is that of Kingston, Jamaica's Trenchtown district, where reggae originated and Bob Marley held court in the 1970s. Safely under supervision by recognized tour operators, Trenchtown visitors witness the vagaries of daily street life. Tours can include a museum, a library, a recording studio, and school and religious activities. Interaction with locals is encouraged. One comes away with a more nuanced and optimistic view of Trenchtown than the stereotypical image of drugs, violence, and desperation.

Rio's favelas offer another example of unorthodox tourism (*favela* is the common name for Brazilian shantytowns). Favela tours begin with taxi service from the tourist hotel to the favela's gate. It is important to point out that not any favela (or squatter settlement) is open for tourism. Rio de Janeiro has more than five hundred favelas but only a few (those that are considered the safest or most established) offer tours, Rocinha being the most popular. Guides, residents of the favela with bright-colored shirts, then escort visitors into the favela, thereby signifying they are on an official tour and not just wandering, thereby securing their safety. Once inside the favela, it is clear that the labyrinthine streets would not be navigable by an outsider. The tour then proceeds deep into the favela and the tourist gets to see firsthand the daily existence of low-income residents (you might ask why this is appealing), and some residents even manufacture souvenirs for the tourists to purchase. In addition to seeing the homes, tourists also get a glimpse of the favela's schools, nurseries, and local markets. These tours appeal to a small number of visitors; that is, you do not see hundreds of foreigners trekking through these neighborhoods. The cost for this approximately two-hour trip is twenty US dollars per person, although it is not clear how revenues are distributed.

Figure 6.4. Author with his two "bodyguards" entering the Rocinha favela, Rio de Janeiro.

While ghetto tours appeal to more adventurous tourists, they are part of a growing number of touristic forays into the everyday experiences of Latin American and Caribbean people. Many hotels and cruise lines now routinely offer side trips into communities and villages where tourists learn about local customs, social services such as schools and health care, and agricultural or fishing livelihoods. How to assess the impacts of such "everyday experience" tourism? If these tours feature mock cultural performances for tourists, while outside organizers appropriate the lion's share of income, then they can be seen as replicating tourism's historically worst features. If, on the other hand, tours help to valorize community or village work and life, create positive cross-cultural exchanges, and bring income where it is desperately needed, they can be seen as contributing to sustainable development (Klak 2007).

Case Study: Argentine Estancia Tours

One of the enduring images of Argentina's past is that of the *gaucho*, or Argentine cowboy. Visits to an estancia provide (mostly) tourists with a glimpse of this way of life and are included in the itinerary of most visitors. These trips can easily be done on a day trip from Buenos Aires, though many offer the option to stay overnight. Either way, tour vans or buses pick up visitors at their hotel in the capital city (or elsewhere) and drive them to the estancia as part of the overall fee. The day typically consists of a tour of the estancia property, including a house decorated with period pieces, horseback riding, a barbecue lunch with a music and dance performance, and a gaucho show on horseback. The cost of a day trip begins at approximately one hundred dollars per person, so it has indeed become a lucrative practice allowing the gauchos to maintain their way of life, or at least some semblance of it, by catering to tourists. On my visit, there were nearly one hundred visitors in attendance, and it is important to point out that there are quite a few estancias within a days' drive of Buenos Aires. These tours are family friendly and transport tourists back in time to a romanticized version of rural Argentina in a very encapsulated and serene way. Tourists enjoy the escape from the large metropolis of Buenos Aires and the taste of the authentic lifestyle. The revenue generated from these activities seemingly provides a good standard of living for the modern-day gauchos as well as helping to maintain the ranch in a way that offers tourists a glimpse into what life in rural Argentina was like in days past.

Tourism scholars wrestle with these types of activities, vacillating between whether they feel these tourist experiences help preserve a culture that would otherwise be lost or commodify a culture in a way that voids it of meaning and significance, simply to earn an income. It is not an easy issue to resolve, but reveals another aspect of the tourism landscape in all its complex nuances.

Conclusion and Tourism Futures

This chapter has highlighted the importance of tourism as, in effect, an export industry and a possible vehicle for future economic growth in Latin America and the Caribbean. Tourism will continue to be a prominent feature in LAC (like in most of the world) and will incorporate a wider array of activities and locales. Value-oriented cruise tourism, with its limited trickle-down into local economies, will continue to account for the great majority of tourist numbers. Pre-packaged, all-inclusive stay-over tourism is not much better than cruise tourism in terms of the leakage rate. More promising than either cruise or mass tourism for contributing to sustainable development are the various forms of alternative tourism. As we have stressed, alternative tourisms can contribute to sustainable development if they are economically viable and inclusive, socially and culturally positive for both hosts and visitors, and environmentally supportive.

Tourism in LAC has historically been an evolving enterprise. The top destinations have changed over time, as have the activities tourists engage in. Locales have quickly risen in prominence, but for most places, the attraction to tourists has been fickle and relatively short-lived. Given this turbulent history, it should come as no surprise that the global recession beginning in 2008 had negative impacts on LAC tourism. For most LAC countries, the number of tourists and tourism revenue has rebounded to pre-recessionary levels, buoyed by discounts offered to fill hotel rooms and tours. But lingering recessionary impacts raise the question of whether the tourism democratization trend of the twentieth century will continue. The tightening, or complete and permanent loss, of the discretionary income for middle-class people in the global North is likely to constrain LAC tourism for the longer term. Here, *longer term* means too long for the current providers of tourism products to wait out the recession in anticipation of another period of relative abundance in the future.

Instead, providers have experienced demand contraction and therefore must attempt to attract tourists in new ways. Among the many forms these recent efforts take are such things as wedding tourism, health spa tourism, or corporate tourism (for retreats and getaways for employees and clients). Others are seeking to sell off tourism assets. Many properties in tourist zones are now for sale, for rent, or foreclosed, a trend paralleling the housing market slump in the United States. Latin American and Caribbean assets for sale include both existing tourism sites and so much previously agricultural land, which amounts to the only real asset in aging farming communities. Much of the land and property is being sold off to foreign tourism interests, both individual and corporate. Most people seeking to sell, even at the current bargain prices, will not find buyers. For the many small, rural places for which tourism dollars are the "last resort," there is mostly disappointment. Ironically, that can be seen as a good thing (although not for the individual seller), before vast swaths of rural land are hastily sold off abroad.

For most of Latin America and the Caribbean, the hope for tourism's economic vitality needs to be reassessed. It is unlikely that even tourism, with all of its limitations regarding sustainable inclusivity, will be able to provide an economic foundation in the foreseeable future. Costa Rica during the 1980s began a government-led program that held out hope for others to utilize tourism in a beneficial way. However, given the region's historical development patterns (Kay 1989), it is unreasonable to assume that governments will be able to lead in forging an integrated regional development that incorporates tourism in a way that will benefit local cultures, economies, and environments.

Indeed, sustainable tourism development is exceedingly difficult to achieve. Historically tourism has had limited trickle-down to communities and villages, and therefore has not been sustainable. In response, alternative tourisms have proliferated but are challenged to deliver substantial and longer-term economic benefits to communities and villages. Today LAC countries are ill prepared for the sustainability challenge because they are saddled by trade dependency, foreign debt, economic weakness, and long-term and even heightened vulnerabilities (see chapter 5). The global recession during recent years demonstrates LAC tourism's vulnerabilities to exogenous changes.

Sustainability requires that change come from the tourists themselves, not just from the tourism sites and hosts. In an ideal scenario, tourists would be cognizant of each country's resources and limitations and behave in appropriate ways, such as limited water use in areas that have shortages, eating local food rather than "American" food coming off a ship from Miami, and respecting and engaging local cultures. Like sustainability in general, sustainable tourism development should be seen as a goal toward which to purposefully commit, take action, and make incremental progress. The three-legged stool of sustainable tourism development and the promise of alternative tourisms can help practitioners to assess their operations and researchers to evaluate LAC tourism in context.

Key Terms

demand shifters: Forces causing the demand for tourism to fluctuate up or down.

democratization of tourism: International tourism's century-long trend, in which it has evolved from being a purely elite leisure activity to one now more accessible to lower income groups and typified by value-focused family cruise packages.

last resorts: A concept coined by Pattullo (2005) referring to the fact that Caribbean countries have exhausted all other economic pillars, leaving only tourism as a hope for generating significant foreign exchange.

leakage rate: The share of tourist spending appropriated by interests outside of the host community in which the tourism takes place.

mock authenticity: Displays, performances, and artifacts for tourists that present local culture in forms modified to suit tourists' expectations, desires, and appetites (Richardson 1992).

soft power: Getting others to want what you want. With regard to tourism, this concept refers to how the increasing presence of US tourists in Latin America created demand among locals for the US consumer-driven lifestyle.

Suggested Readings

Boniface, Brian and Chris Cooper. *Worldwide Destinations: The Geography of Travel and Tourism.* 4th ed. Elsevier. 2005.

Merrill, Dennis. *Negotiating Paradise: US Tourism and Empire in Twentieth-Century Latin America.* Chapel Hill: University of North Carolina Press, 2009.

Pattullo, Polly. *Last Resorts: The Cost of Tourism in the Caribbean.* 2nd ed. London: Cassell Books. 2005.

Shaw, Gareth, and Alan M. Williams. *Tourism and Tourism Spaces.* Thousand Oaks, CA: Sage, 2004.

References

Davenport, J., and E. Jackiewicz. "Spaces of Tourism." In *Placing Latin America: Contemporary Themes in Human Geography,* edited by E. Jackiewicz and F. Bosco, 111–25. Boulder, CO: Rowman & Littlefield, 2008.

Fennell, D. *Ecotourism.* 2nd ed. New York: Routledge, 2003.

Hawkes, E., and R. Kwortnik. "Connecting with the Culture: A Case Study in Sustainable Tourism." *Cornell Hotel and Restaurant Administration Quarterly* 47 (2006): 369–81.

Hiernaux-Nicolas, D. "Cancun Bliss." In *The Tourist City,* edited by D. R. Judd and S. S. Fainstein. New Haven, CT: Yale University Press, 1999.

Ioannides, D., and D. J. Timothy. *Tourism in the USA: A Spatial and Social Synthesis.* New York: Routledge, 2010.

Jackiewicz, E., and O. Govdyak. "Diversity of Lifestyle Migration: A View from Belize." *Association of Pacific Coast Geographers Yearbook* 77 (2015): 18–39.

Johnson, D. "Environmentally Sustainable Cruise Tourism: A Reality Check." *Marine Policy* 26 (2002): 261–70.

Jules, S. *Sustainable Tourism in St. Lucia: A Sustainability Assessment of Trade and Liberalization in Tourism-Services.* Winnipeg, Manitoba, Canada: International Institute for Sustainable Development, 2005.

Kay, Cristóbal. *Latin American Theories of Development and Underdevelopment.* New York: Routledge, 1989.

Klak, Thomas. "Sustainable Ecotourism Development in Central America and the Caribbean: Review of Debates and Conceptual Reformulation." *Geography Compass* 1, no. 5 (September 2007): 1037–57.

Merrill, D. *Negotiating Paradise: US Tourism and Empire in Twentieth-Century Latin America.* Chapel Hill: University of North Carolina Press, 2009.

Mowforth, M., and I. Munt. *Tourism and Sustainability: Development and Tourism in the Third World.* 2nd ed. New York: Routledge, 2003.

Pantojas-García, E., and T. Klak. "Globalization and Economic Vulnerability: The Caribbean and the 'Post-9/11 Shift.'" In *Caribbean Security in the Age of Terror: Challenge and Change,* edited by I. Griffith, 176–98. Kingston, Jamaica: Ian Randle Publishers, 2004.

Pulsipher, L., and L. Holderfield. "Cruise Tourism in the Eastern Caribbean: An Anachronism in the Post-Colonial Era?" In *Cruise Ship Tourism,* edited by R. Dowling, 299–314. Cambridge, MA: CABI Publishing, 2006.

Richardson, Bonham. *The Caribbean in the Wider World, 1492–1992.* New York: Cambridge University Press, 1992.

Shaw, G., and A. M. Williams. *Tourism and Tourism Spaces.* Thousand Oaks, CA: Sage Publications, 2004.

Smith, Neil. *Uneven Development: Nature, Capital, and the Production of Space.* 3rd ed. Athens: University of Georgia Press, 2008.

Stronza, A. "Anthropology of Tourism: Forging New Ground for Ecotourism and other Alternatives." *Annual Review of Anthropology* 30 (2001): 261–83.

Torres, R. M., and J. D. Momsen. "Gringolandia: The Construction of a New Tourist Space in Mexico." *Annals of the Association of American Geographers* 95, no. 2 (2005): 314–35.

——— (Eds.). *Tourism and Agriculture: New Geographies of Consumption, Production and Rural Restructuring.* New York: Routledge, 2011.

UNESA (United Nations Department of Economic and Social Affairs). 2011. *World Population Prospects,* esa.un.org/unpd/wpp/Excel-Data/population.htm

UNWTO (United Nations World Tourism Organization). Annual Report 2013. http://dtxtq4w60xqpw .cloudfront.net/sites/all/files/pdf/unwto_annual_report_2013_0.pdf

Urry, J. *The Tourist Gaze.* London: Sage, 1990.

Walcott, Derek. "The Antilles: Fragments of Epic Memory." In *Traveller's Literary Companion: Caribbean,* edited by James Ferguson, 274. Chicago: Passport Books, 1997.

World Tourism Organization. "International Tourism 2010: Multi-Speed Recovery." Press release, January 17, 2011.

Chapter 7

Natural Resources

Christian Brannstrom

L ATIN AMERICA'S NATURAL RESOURCES—hydrocarbons, minerals, fisheries, forests, and croplands—have been globalized commodities for more than five hundred years. The establishment of Spanish and Portuguese colonies relied on forced labor, including slavery, to produce sugar and silver for export (see chapter 2). The export of natural resources such as coffee, copper, and rubber supported the growth of independent nation-states in the 1800s, helping fund legislative assemblies, prisons, and railroads. Technological innovations, industrialization, and consumption patterns created strong demand for natural resources in the 1900s—although the Great Depression of the 1920s and 1930s punctured global demand for more than a decade—that motivated extraction of mineral, petroleum, and agricultural resources. These booms supported economic growth and industrialization strategies that were partly successful in Argentina, Brazil, and Mexico (see chapter 3). In other countries, such as Nicaragua and Bolivia, agricultural and mineral resource booms consolidated the grip of a small group of elites on land and power.

A new resource boom, led by the rise in demand from Chinese industries, began in the late 1990s. Some observers use the term "China Effect" or "China Cycle" to describe the effect of booming Chinese demand, which appeared to stabilize in 2011 and 2012, on a renewed cycle of investment in mineral and agricultural resources that Latin American countries have been eager to supply. Rhys Jenkins (2010) argued that the global expansion of China negatively affects some industrial sectors in Latin America and promoted excessive specialization in natural resource exports. Latin America's exports to China shifted from mainly manufactured goods to primary products or natural resources, which comprise nearly three-quarters of Latin America's exports to China (Gallagher and Porzecanski 2010). As Asian industrialization slowed around 2012, the "great commodity boom" was over (*The Economist* 2014).

This chapter defines natural resources, characterizes their geographical distribution, emphasizes current and past importance of those resource systems, and summarizes key cases in Brazil and Mexico. This chapter emphasizes contemporary natural resources; readers interested in earlier periods are directed to other studies on pre-1500 resource uses by indigenous peoples (Denevan 2001; Whitmore and Turner 2001) and works covering the colonial period and "long" nineteenth century (Topik, Marichal, and Frank 2006; Brannstrom 2004).

Political Economy of Latin America's Natural Resources

Renewable natural resources include water, fisheries, forests, and cropland. Non-renewable resources are fossil energy (petroleum, natural gas, and coal) and minerals such as iron ore, silver, and copper. Natural resources require labor, capital (finance), and technology to be transformed into commodities, defined as tradable items that may be graded and mixed according to objective standard type such as "gold" and "soybeans" in markets, such as the Chicago Board of Trade, for future delivery or speculation. Transnational corporations (TNCs) often dominate production and trade in these globalized commodities. Even in domestic markets, commodities rely on financial and logistical connections among consumer, producer, and intermediary.

Commodity chains describe connections between places of production and places of consumption. Each "link" is, potentially, a site of specialized labor, application of technology, wealth accumulation, environmental degradation, and state intervention. Material characteristics of resources—such as growth period, perishability, or location in geological strata—present obstacles or challenges to capital investment. These obstacles often generate new networks and strategies that become part of commodity chains. For example, petroleum extraction depends on a long chain of relations extending from knowledge-intensive exploration, drilling, transport, and refining before it reaches consumers as gasoline. Although coffee requires less capital, it takes years for shrubs to mature and, once productive, the harvest season is confined to only a few weeks.

Decision makers have used two competing political economies to manage the extraction of natural resources and influence the distribution of economic benefits. Resource nationalism relies on state ownership or control of natural resources to advance political, social, and industrial objectives. This political economy emphasizes that resources, especially hydrocarbons and minerals, belong to the "people" and that state employees, not foreign investors, are the best managers of resources. Nationalism orients policies such as establishment of state ownership of resources and creation of state-owned companies (see chapter 3), such as Petróleos de Venezuela S.A. (PDVSA).

By contrast, neoliberalism and economic liberalism, its nineteenth-century predecessor, rely on the market to determine the extraction of natural resources. These policies involve privatization of state-owned resources to the highest (or best connected) bidder and TNCs or domestic firms to extract natural resources according to market imperatives. In this view, state ownership of resources creates inefficiencies, bloated bureaucracy, and corrupt practices. Supporters of this view believe that the proper role of government is to regulate resource extraction and invest tax or royalty revenues in support of social policies, infrastructure, and other sectors of the economy.

All Latin American countries except Cuba have privatized agricultural natural resources, meaning that landowners make decisions about what to produce, although they often respond to market signals that governments influence. Agrarian policies in Latin America range from land reforms that redistributed large landholdings to peasants and, on the other extreme, policies that favored large export-oriented farms. In addition, agricultural political economy includes government influence in transport, irrigation water, prices for inputs and crops, land tenure, and worker well-being, among others.

Resource nationalism and neoliberalism have different conceptual underpinnings. The definition of resources as "natural" endowments that countries must exploit according to their "comparative advantage" in specific mineral or agricultural resources supports neoliberalism. In this view, countries should concentrate on exporting resources with which they are naturally "endowed." Belief that economic growth is strongest in conditions of low barriers to movement of capital and goods across borders, and minimal state involvement also align with the conceptual underpinnings of a neoliberal political economy. By contrast, resource nationalism relies on dependency theory and the "resource curse," which emphasize negative consequences of high reliance on resource exports leading to geographically uneven development, such as stunted industrialization and creation of enclaves. The critique of Latin American resources as a story of plunder, with riches flowing from "open veins" to "distant centers of power" (Galeano 1973, 12), supports resource nationalism.

Regardless of which political economic model orients resource use, environmental, social, and political conflicts are inevitable because of the many stakeholders involved in trying to determine the proper use of resources. For example, users of irrigation water argue among each other and with government officials over the volume and price of water. TNCs disagree with the state about the terms of mining concessions, and communities affected by the numerous negative consequences of mining argue with TNCs and the state regarding compensation and remediation. In Ecuador and Bolivia, protests led by unionized workers and the urban poor opposed attempts at privatization of hydrocarbons, while earlier economic crises and foreign intervention had pushed policymakers from nationalism to neoliberalism (Perreault and Valdivia 2010). Many of these conflicts, such as the case of a Guatemalan community opposing a Canadian mining company (Pederson 2014), attract relatively little media attention, but they are hugely significant in the lives of millions of ordinary people in Latin America who live near sites of natural resource extraction.

Geographical Distribution of Resources

Renewable Natural Resources

Agricultural land, often augmented by irrigation water and fertilizer, is the most geographically widespread natural resource. Checking labels on fruit and vegetables in the produce section of grocery stores helps us appreciate this fact. To take the case of Mexico, its farm exports to the United States were valued at $7.6 billion in 2013. Nearly half of the tomatoes sold in the United States originate in Mexico, where they are picked by hand from vines more than ten feet tall. Recruited by contractors promising good wages, approximately 150,000 workers seasonally move to labor camps near farms.

Mexico has two globally significant clusters of export-oriented cropland. An irrigated complex in the northwestern state of Sonora has become a major supplier of fruits and vegetables to US grocery stores and restaurants. The *Los Angeles Times* reported in December 2014 that a tomato, bell pepper, and cucumber farm near Culiacan, Sonora, relied on one thousand workers housed in squalid conditions, earning eight to twelve dollars per day but often indebted to company stores. The Bajío, located between Guadalajara and Mexico City at approximately 1,500 to 2,000 meters in elevation, has been known as *el granero de México* (Mexico's granary) since it emerged as an important agricultural region in the middle 1500s. Farmers there rely on irrigated cropland for high-tech vegetable farms and greenhouses that supply US and Mexican markets (figure 7.1).

Figure 7.1. Tying up bell peppers destined for US markets in a greenhouse in the Bajío. Courtesy Heather Lee Brown.

Coffee in the southern Mexican and Central American highlands, the premier agricultural resource in the mid-1800s, continues to be a widespread means to sustain livelihoods. Elites created vast estates in Guatemala and El Salvador, exacerbating land-tenure inequalities, while mainly family-scale holdings predominated in Costa Rica. Some former coffee lands in Costa Rica now grow mini-squashes, vegetables, and other produce, making the country the third-leading supplier of vegetables to the US market. However, Costa Rica is also the most intensive user of pesticides on per-hectare basis (Galt 2014).

Topographical and climatological characteristics favorable to coffee extend into the Colombian Andes, where coffee supported industrialization and state institutions at a much larger scale than Central America. Colombia's National Federation of Coffee Growers promotes its Juan Valdez coffees and coffee shops globally, building on the marketing icon originally created in 1959. Latin American countries are among the world's top producers of fair trade and organic, bird-friendly and shade-grown coffees in the world. These specialized coffees command higher prices, but farmers absorb certification costs and report delays in receiving payment (Tellman, Gray, and Bacon 2011).

On the Caribbean coast of Central America, banana TNCs, headquartered in the United States, took advantage of abundant rainfall, proximity to ports and US markets, a relatively pliant and spatially fixed labor force, and favorable land policies to establish vast plantations starting in the 1880s and persisting to the present (figure 7.2). Banana TNCs, in collaboration with US authorities, exerted quasi-colonial influence over governments, while quickly shifting

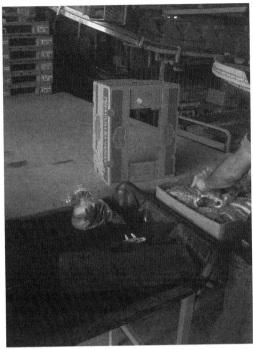

Figure 7.2. Bananas in Sixaola, Costa Rica, being readied for export. Note the calipers for measuring bananas to export criteria. Photograph by Christian Brannstrom.

production to new sites when pathogens threatened their plantations, as John Soluri showed in his book *Banana Cultures* (2005). Banana firms could move, but the fixed work force, often dominated by Afro-Caribbean people, were stuck in the Caribbean Coast, unable to follow banana plantations because of segregationist state policies. Abuses of pesticides were also common. For example, the film *Bananas!* shows the plight of sterile Nicaraguan male banana plantation workers who were exposed to chemicals that were banned in the United States after sterility impacts were known. When US and European consumers developed a taste for fresh pineapple, firms such as Del Monte established vast plantations on Caribbean slopes, taking advantage of high rainfall and proximity to ports, such as Limón, where trucks hauling pineapples for export are ubiquitous on the highway leading to the city's port.

On Caribbean islands, US sugarcane growers created what César Ayala (1999) called the "American Sugar Kingdom" after the 1898 war in which the United States dislodged Spain and became the imperial power in Cuba, Puerto Rico, and the Dominican Republic. Their modern mills were on a vastly larger scale compared to the sugar plantations that the Spanish, French, British, and Dutch colonialists established beginning in the seventeenth century with four to five million imported African slaves. The Cuban sugar industry survived the longest in the Caribbean. After Cuba expropriated US firms in the early 1960s, sugarcane farms became state property supported by subsidies from the former Soviet Union, which supplied cheap credit, mechanization, and fuel in exchange for Cuban sugar. The demise of the Soviet Union has meant disarray for the Cuban sugarcane industry. Today, nowhere in the Caribbean can sugarcane farms compete with Brazilian sugarcane converted to sugar and ethanol.

In South America, agricultural natural resources occupy numerous locations and support significant economies. Flower production in greenhouses in the Andean highlands around

Figure 7.3. Irrigated grape plantation in Petrolina, Brazil. Photograph by Christian Brannstrom.

Quito and Bogotá take advantage of climate at high elevation (approximately 2,000 meters) and proximity to international airports that connect flower growers to Valentine's Day (February 14) and Mother's Day (second Sunday in May in the United States), two days around which the floricultural cycle rotates. Irrigated lands in Perú's coastal desert produce fresh asparagus for winter markets eager for a taste of summer. Chile's arid coastal lands rely on irrigation water for avocado and apple orchards and vineyards that produce crops for consumers in Asia, North America, and Europe. In Brazil's semi-arid northeast, a center of irrigated fruit production around Petrolina and Juazeiro relies on government-built irrigation works tapping the São Francisco River to grow mangos and grapes for Northern Hemisphere markets (figure 7.3).

Vast soy, corn, sugar, wheat, and cotton fields extend across the central and southern sections of Brazil and northern Argentina, continuing into portions of Bolivia, Paraguay, and Uruguay. In Brazil, these agricultural lands are located partly in the Cerrado, a woodland-shrubland nearly 60 percent cleared for crops and cattle, and Atlantic Forest, nearly 90 percent deforested for crops, pasture, and cities. Brazil's status as "agricultural superpower," in the words of former US Secretary of State Colin Powell, owes to its world-leading production of coffee, citrus, and sugarcane, and top exporter status for animal protein and soybeans. Driving across these vast farming communities, visitors are reminded of the farming landscapes in the United States with enormous expanses of crops, agro-industrial TNCs, and huge tractor dealerships (figure 7.4). In southern Brazilian states, farmers rotate corn or soy with wheat; in tropical latitudes, farmers opt for a soy-corn cycle, although cotton has become more lucrative.

Figure 7.4. John Deere tractor dealership in Luis Eduardo Magalhães, Bahia state, a booming region in Brazil's northeast soy belt. Photograph by Christian Brannstrom.

The Argentine Pampas, a grassland region analogous to the North American prairie, became a major cattle and wheat producer in the late 1800s, which Buenos Aires exported, spurring urban and industrial development that attracted millions of European migrants. In the 1980s, farmers in the Pampas and the Santa Fe regions transitioned into soybeans, which now extend west into the drier Chaco, including provinces such as Córdoba, Santiago del Estero, and Chaco. Farmland in Santiago del Estero, valued at $150–$200 per hectare in 2001, had increased to $7,000 per hectare by 2011 (Leguizamón 2014). Much of the soy harvest is destined for cattle, hog, and chicken feedlot operations.

Forests as natural resources represent livelihood sustenance and timber commodities. The Brazilian Amazon is the site of numerous extractive reserves and indigenous territories that aim to maintain forests as livelihood-sustaining resources. Collectively, these territories amount to nearly 50 percent of the Brazilian Amazon's area (Nepstad et al. 2014). Rubber tappers, who confronted cattle ranchers and their hired gunmen in the 1980s, won the right to use standing forests for their livelihoods, even though their livelihoods increasingly rely on cattle (Vadjunec 2011). Massive forestry projects, nearly exclusively reliant upon fast-growing exotic species, have replaced native species across large areas of southern Chile (Klubock 2014), Brazil, and Uruguay. TNCs, which own land directly or obtain product from landowners through contracts, have planted vast stretches of land with exotic "fast wood" forests that supply paper-pulp mills. Fibria, the world's largest producer of eucalyptus pulp,

Figure 7.5. Fibria barge filled with eucalyptus leaving plantation area. Courtesy of Anna Santos.

has plantations covering over 500,000 hectares in Brazil, feeding three mills that produce personal hygiene products, printing and writing paper, and specialty paper. Figure 7.5 shows a Fibria barge filled with eucalyptus cut in coastal areas of Bahia, bordering a marine extractive reserve, bound for a mill.

Fisheries, a renewable natural resource, are globalized and local. The wild-caught anchoveta fishery in Peruvian waters, dominated by industrial-scale vessels whose catch is destined for fishmeal, exports feed for aquaculture and confined chicken, hogs, and cattle. In southern Chile, farmed and wild salmon supply distant markets, while leaving major challenges for policymakers regarding management of coastal waters and spawning streams. Export-oriented shrimp farms are present all along Latin America's Pacific Coast. In many coastal areas, small-scale fishers confront competing resources uses, such as hotels, marinas, and shrimp farms, that conflict with their livelihoods (Alvarado and Taylor 2014).

Mangroves, the coastal forest often removed to make way for shrimp farms, support hundreds of communities reliant upon shellfish and marine resources. These communities, sometimes composed of ethnic minorities, have sought to develop conservation areas to restrict destructive land uses (García et al. 2014). In El Salvador's Lower Lempa River, poorly (and irregularly) paid forest guards aim to protect mangroves from resource poaching of the many shellfish that rely on mangrove systems, while the government has aimed to restore mangroves for flood protection and carbon sequestration (figure 7.6).

Figure 7.6. Emblem on uniforms of the forest guards of the Lower Lempa in El Salvador, sponsored by a non-governmental organization specializing in mangrove protection, shows the symbolic importance of mangroves to local residents. Photograph by Christian Brannstrom.

Non-Renewable Natural Resources: Hydrocarbons

Latin America's largest petroleum producers, Venezuela, Mexico, and Brazil (figure 7.7), represent different models of nationalism and neoliberalism. Mexico has faced declining output, while Venezuela's oil comprises more than 80 percent of total exports. In Bolivia, Ecuador, and Trinidad and Tobago, hydrocarbons are more than 50 percent of exports. Overall, Latin America produced approximately 12 percent of the world's oil in 2013.

In Venezuela, oil TNCs and the state-owned PDVSA have operated for several decades in and around Lake Maracaibo. In the 1970s, with high oil prices, middle classes of "Venezuela Saudita," as it was known optimistically, went shopping in Miami. But the dream of modernization ended abruptly in the 1980s, culminating in February 1989 riots that killed hundreds in Caracas. The "Caracazo," as the massacre was known, set the stage for the political rise of a career military officer, Hugo Chávez, in the early 1990s (see chapter 3). The Chávez regime (1999–2013) used oil to promote social and geopolitical aims. A slogan emblazoned on PDVSA's headquarters, *Con Chávez, sembramos petróleo en el pueblo* ("With Chávez, we sow petroleum among the people") repeats the *sembramos petróleo* discourse, used in Venezuela since the 1930s, promoting the potentially useful role of oil in Venezuelan modernization. Early in his regime, Chávez created an oil-for-doctors program with Cuba, which sent 30,000 doctors to Venezuela's slums and villages in exchange for oil (Strønen 2012). He also fired 18,000 striking PDVSA workers in 2002 after a long strike; these workers soon found employment among TNCs eager to obtain talented workers in Houston and the Alberta tar sands in Canada. Then, in 2006, Chávez forced contract renegotiations on TNCs operating in the Orinoco oil fields, which hold an estimated 500 billion barrels of crude oil. These events help explain declining oil output after the mid-2000s (figure 7.7).

Brazil's government created Petrobras, its national oil company, in the early 1950s, long before PDVSA existed but before Brazil had discovered sizeable deposits. Nationalization used the "petroleum is ours" discourse, giving making Petrobras a state-owned monopoly for oil production, refining, and distribution. In 1997 the government partly privatized Petrobras and allowed foreign competition in the oil sector, while retaining majority control. Petrobras became a TNC, investing in Bolivia, Argentina, Ecuador, and African countries. Then it discovered the Campos basin off the coast of Rio de Janeiro and São Paulo states, where 8 to 12 billion barrels of oil (known as "pre-salt" because of its geology) are buried under 2,000 meters of water and another 4,000 meters of rock and salt.

A corruption scandal emerged in late 2014 that threw Petrobras into disarray after the admission that 3 percent of the value of refining contracts, already 20 percent overvalued by colluding contractors, sustained a slush fund for the ruling Workers Party (PT). This allegation, apparently, would justify a US$31 billion write-down on its assets. In early 2015, a major accountancy refused

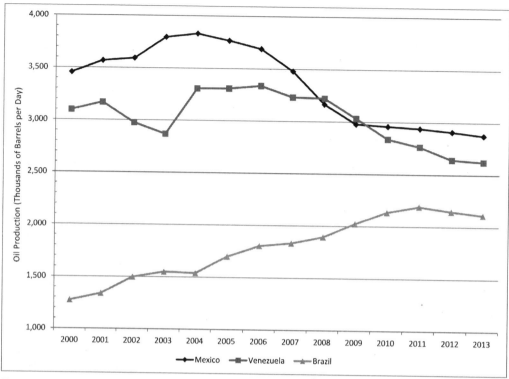

Figure 7.7. Oil production in Venezuela, Mexico, and Brazil (2000–2013, thousand barrels per day). BP Statistical Review of World Energy, June 2014.

to sign a quarterly earnings report, which had an unrealistic write-down, plunging Petrobras into further crisis until it finally secured an audited financial statement. Bondholders, understandably, are furious because they provided capital for Petrobras, which spent funds lavishly on over-inflated contracts. Petrobras is accountable to international investors, who demand audited financial statements, while susceptible to venal and corrupt politicians who see the state-controlled firm as a means to enrichment.

The western Amazon, a lowland region of tropical rainforests, has oil and gas concession and exploration blocks that cover more than 700,000 square kilometers, an area larger than Texas (Finer et al. 2015). Beginning in the 1960s, Chevron developed oilfields in concessions from Ecuador in the eastern (Amazonian) region known as *Oriente*, where a pipeline connects oilfields to a Pacific port. But Chevron spilled approximately seventeen million gallons of oil and left eighteen billion gallons of wastewater, much in unlined pits and sometimes in close proximity to villages. Oil development supported the arrival of thousands of colonists from highland Ecuador and United States–based missionaries, which together introduced clothing, Christianity, and disease to native peoples, as Joe Kane describes in *Savages*. Petroecudor, the Ecuadorian national oil company, took over Chevron's assets in the 1992 and, apparently, exonerated the TNC of environmental damages. In 1993, the *Aguinado v. Texaco* lawsuit began in the United States, then was transferred to Ecuadorian courts, where plaintiffs won a judgment of nearly $9 billion in damages in 2011 against ChevronTexaco, which refused to pay and, at any rate, no longer has assets in Ecuador. The legal work of the plaintiffs is portrayed in the documentary *Crude*, which generated video footage helping implicate the lead US attorney, Jeff Donziger, in his own legal nightmare.

Figure 7.8. Anti-fracking grafitto on a park bench along Avenida Argentina in Neuquén, Argentina. Courtesy of Trey Murphy.

While the case of Ecuador's Oriente attracted much media interest, less heralded developments include the rapid rise of China as a major investor in Ecuador. After Ecuador's $3.2 billion default in 2008, China quickly become Ecuador's main creditor, lending billions of dollars on the basis of nearly 80 percent control of Ecuador's oil exports. Another important aspect is an internal conflict: indigenous people in the *Oriente* try to stop oil production, but workers and settlers from the highlands protest for better management of oil revenues (Valdivia 2008). A similarly poorly reported case is Argentina's massive Vaca Muerta field, which holds approximately 16.2 billion barrels of shale oil and has attracted investments by several oil and gas TNCs and numerous complaints by indigenous groups. These resources would be obtained by hydraulic fracturing, or fracking, which some residents of Neuquén, the main city in the Vaca Muerta, oppose as evidenced by "Fracking: this is not progress" grafitto painted on a park bench (figure 7.8).

In Bolivia, natural gas has played a pivotal role in contemporary politics. Massive protests in 2003, known as the "gas war," erupted after Bolivia's president tried to export natural gas through a Chilean port located in former Bolivian territory, lost in the 1870s. Gas had moved by pipeline to Brazil and Argentina since the late 1990s with no similar controversy, although routing pipelines through indigenous territories remains a source of contention. The political turmoil that ensued set the stage for the election of Evo Morales, who partly nationalized hydrocarbons and minerals in the aim of industrialization and social spending, even if indigenous peoples—who strongly supported his political campaigns—bear the brunt of negative impacts from resource extraction (Hindery 2013; Perreault and Validivia 2010). Autonomy movements in the Chaco region, where gas is produced, focus on changing how natural gas royalties are distributed (Gustafson 2011).

Non-Renewable Natural Resources: Hard Rock and Alluvial Minerals

Latin American and Caribbean countries accounted for nearly one-fifth of global mineral exports by value in 2012. The largest share of mineral exports were primary or unrefined metal ores, such as iron ore, which accounted for nearly $80 billion in export value in 2011, in comparison with $40 billion for refined non-ferrous metals (such as copper and bauxite), and $20 billion for steel and metal products. Latin America produces around 20 percent of all bauxite (primarily Brazil, Jamaica, and Suriname), 45 percent of raw copper (mainly Chile, Perú, and Mexico), 20 percent of the world's gold (mainly Perú, Mexico and Colombia), nearly half of the world's silver (Mexico, Perú, Chile), and one-fifth of the world's iron and molybdenum, which is used for production of steel alloys that withstand high temperatures.

Silver and gold, the literal "open veins" that Eduardo Galeano (1973) described, were a major attraction to Spaniards, Portuguese, and other European powers. In Mexico, Zacatecas was a major silver producer by the mid-1500s, while Potosí, at 4,000 meters elevation in Bolivian Altiplano, had a population of 160,000 in the middle 1600s, the largest city in the Americas, because of the silver in its *Cerro Rico* and the number of workers that were coerced through labor tribute systems, slavery, and wages to work in the mines. Mercury mined at Huancavelica in Perú was used in the amalgamation (patio) process in Zacatecas and Potosí, producing deadly fumes that damaged worker health, as Nicholas Robins describes in *Mercury, Mining, and Empire* (2011). Both mining centers were in decline by the 1800s, eclipsed by other mines. Bolivia is still a large producer of silver, accounting for 5 percent of world output. Government involvement in mining swung from the liberalism (light regulation allowing enrichment of a small number of families who owned tin mines) to nationalization in the 1950s, which created the state-owned COMIBOL. Political economy turned neoliberal, as a condition of policies imposed by the International Monetary Fund in the 1980s, which resulted in stripped assets and laid-off workers from COMIBOL and a new concession model. The partial nationalization in 2009 under Morales gave the Bolivian government a stronger presence in mining, but a neoliberal-nationalist tension persists.

Chile produces one-third of the world's copper, and its mines receive massive investments by the world's largest mining TNCs, such as Rio Tinto, Anglo American, BHP Billiton, and Xstra. Mining began far later than in Mexico or Bolivia, with initial mining of nitrates, used as fertilizer and explosives in Europe in the 1800s. The search for nitrate mines was a critical factor in Chile's northern expansion—with British support—at the expense of Perú and Bolivia, which lost its access to the sea in the 1870s War of the Pacific. Industrialists found nitrates while they were searching for guano, dried bird excrement, that Peruvian islands had exported to North America and Europe for fertilizer since the 1840s (Cushman 2013).

By the 1950s Chile's Atacama Desert and its semi-arid "norte chico" attracted massive investments in enormous open-pit copper mines, such as Chuquicamata, which appeared in *Motorcycle Diaries*, a 2004 film about the early life of Ernesto Ché Guevara. Nationalization of copper mines began in 1971, under Salvador Allende's presidency, and continued under Augusto Pinochet's dictatorship. The state-owned CODELCO, the only significant state-owned mining company in Latin America, is the world's largest copper producer and controls about 30 percent of Chile's copper production but more than 60 percent of Chile's total revenue. CODELCO pays a higher tax rate and dividends to the Chilean state treasury than mining TNCs.

In Perú's highlands, mining between 1990 and 2007 attracted $12.35 billion in investments. Unlike Chile, Perú has no state-owned mining firm and relies on issuing mining concessions or leases to firms. These mining TNCs or domestic firms pay rent and corporate income tax to the state treasury. Most concessions are located at elevations above 3,000 meters, meaning that downstream water users are potentially negatively affected by mining effluent and decreased water quality and quantity. Anthony Bebbington and Jeffrey Bury (2009, 2013) analyze conflicts between communities and mining TNCs, noting that conflicts have encouraged some positive changes, such as changes to tax and royalty policies that favor indigenous communities affected by mining.

The same global processes that encouraged large investments in the highland Andes have motivated thousands of small firms to establish alluvial mining enterprises, which mostly operate illegally, in the lowland Peruvian Amazon. Gregory Asner and co-authors (2013) showed recently that increases in global demand for gold, especially from Asian economies, supported large investments in the mining sector and had major impacts in Amazon forests, where thousands of clandestine gold operations exceed formal gold mines in terms of area deforested in the biodiverse Madre de Dios region. Other scientists have detected high rates of deforestation for gold mining in Guyana and Suriname (Alvarez-Berríos and Aide 2015).

Brazil's massive iron ore exports owe much to the ability of one firm, Vale, to meet rising demand from China's steel industry. Nearly all of Brazil's iron ore originates in two regions: Carajás in Pará and the region known as the Iron Quadrilateral (Quadrilátero Ferrífero) in Minas Gerais state. Iron ore from Carajás, Brazil's largest reserve, reaches foreign markets by a 900-kilometer rail line to São Luis Maranhão. In 1997, Brazil privatized its Companhia do Vale do Rio Doce (CVRD). Reborn as Vale, the firm became a TNC by investing in production of metals and fertilizers in Chile, New Caledonia, Oman, and Indonesia.

Natural Resources: Case Studies

Creating Soylândia in Brazil

Soybean, a versatile oilseed processed into animal feed and household cooking oil, helps feed the world's growing demand for animal protein. In 2013, China purchased 70 percent of Brazil's soybeans, while European Union countries were the main consumer of Brazil's soybean cake for animal feed. Brazil, the world's largest soy exporter, faces many logistical difficulties getting soybeans to ports. More than half of the Brazilian soy harvest arrives in ports by truck, leading to queues extending 25 kilometers in length.

Rapid increases in Latin America's soybean area began first in Brazil, during the 1970s, followed by Argentina (figure 7.9). "Soylândia," the approximately thirty million hectares of soybeans planted in Brazil, approximately equivalent to the area of the US state of Arizona, resulted from numerous processes (Hecht and Mann 2008). Rio Grande do Sul's wheat farmers planted soy as an off-season crop in the early 1970s. Soy expanded into northern Paraná state

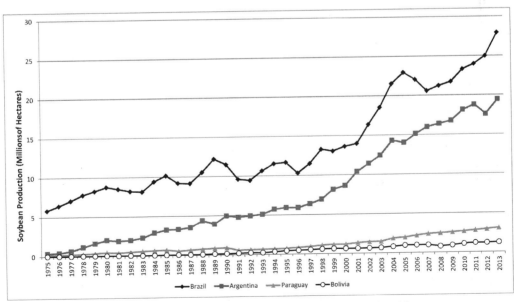

Figure 7.9. Soy production in South America, 1975–2013 (hectares). FAOSTAT 2015.

and São Paulo state when a devastating 1975 freeze killed millions of coffee trees, clearing the way for soy and signaling the demise of the coffee economy that had supported the industrialization of São Paulo in the late 1800s. The frost coincided with the sharp increase in soy prices because of the US soy export embargo and Brazilian subsidies for farm mechanization. Soy expanded into the Cerrado, once considered an infertile wasteland, through the initiative of farmer groups from Rio Grande do Sul, Paraná, and Santa Catarina to purchase and subdivide Cerrado ranches, creating colonization settlements. Private colonization firms settled 3.9 million hectares in Mato Grosso state during the 1970s and 1980s, representing a major force in clearing Cerrado for pasture and crops (Jepson 2006, 2010).

The Brazilian government's subsidies for colonization, partly funded by the Japanese development agency, encouraged further expansion of soy. Soy farmers cleared land with few legal obstacles, but they required agricultural technologies in the form of cultivars adapted to relatively even day lengths and infertile soils. These agronomic challenges were met by Brazil's federal researchers, which *The Economist* praised in 2010 for its role in creating the "miracle" of turning the Cerrado into a breadbasket. Environmentalists see this "miracle" quite differently—as a plague that led to approximately 60 percent of the Cerrado cleared from its initial two million square kilometers (Brannstrom 2009). Expansion of soybeans past the Cerrado and into the Amazon rainforest, where stronger environmental protections exist, is a major debate involving the soy industry, state governments, scientists, and non-governmental organizations. When Greenpeace activists reported in 2006 on how illegally produced soybeans were feeding poultry destined for European fast-food outlets, the industry quickly established a moratorium against purchasing soy from farms established illegally in the Amazon forest region (Brannstrom et al. 2012). Brazil's soy is highly dependent on imported fertilizers. Nearly 90 percent of Brazil's soy crop is bioengineered for resistance to Monsanto's Roundup herbicide. Soy is produced on large farms, commonly over one thousand hectares, exacerbating Brazil's unequal distribution of wealth. Finally, expansion of soybeans at the expense of pasture encourages cattle ranchers to clear forests deeper in the Amazon basin.

Mexico's Oil: From Nationalization to Energy Reform

Oil production in Mexico began during the *Porfiriato* of the late 1800s and early 1900s, which allowed foreign surface owners to control the sub-surface. Mexico began exporting oil in 1911, after US oilmen developed the first productive oilfields in the Gulf Coast region, mainly the 120-mile stretch between Tuxpan and Tampico known as the Huasteca. Foreign oil firms practiced highly racialized and degrading ways to "discipline" the Mexican labor force, ranging from use of the *enganche* or "hook," the use of overstated claims to recruit single male workers to the Huasteca oil fields, to establishing company jails and dispensing demeaning treatment of Mexican subordinates. A case in point is a British oil executive in the Huasteca who refused to deal with Mexican workers face-to-face—he turned his chair to avoid looking at Mexicans in his office (Santiago 2006).

Foreign ownership of oil continued through the outbreak of the Mexican Revolution in 1910 until nationalization on March 19, 1938, one the most important and memorable moments in modern Mexico. The origin of nationalization is found in oil worker demands for a collective agreement across the industry, supported by massive strikes that were on the verge of crippling oil production. After foreign oil firms ignored a Mexican Supreme Court decision supportive of a collective labor agreement, twenty thousand oil workers were about to strike. But then a 10 a.m. radio broadcast by President Lázaro Cárdenas declared that foreign oil assets would become property of the Mexican state by midnight. This created Petróleos de México (PEMEX), which developed into a state-run monopolistic behemoth controlled by the PRI, the political party that maintained control of Mexican politics until Vicente Fox's election in 2000.

PEMEX's greatest technical achievement was the development of Cantarell, the world's largest offshore oilfield, which began producing in 1979. Cantarell, a "city on the sea," as Lisa Breglia (2013) calls it, houses twenty thousand workers—with uniforms from PEMEX, Halliburton, and Schlumberger—in "flotels." Oil production sustains jobs but pollutes water and air for the 150,000 people living fifty miles south, in Ciudad del Carmen. Most of the Cantarell's oil, known as Maya Crude in commodity markets, is sent unrefined to the United States because PEMEX lacks adequate refining capacity. At its peak in 2004, the Cantarell oilfield produced 2.2 million barrels per day, nearly three-quarters of Mexico's oil production, but by 2009 production had fallen to 700,000 barrels per day (figure 7.7). PEMEX has a blemished safety record in the Cantarell. For 290 days during 1979–1980, the Ixtoc I blowout released more than three million barrels into the Gulf. In 2007, an accident on the Kab-101 platform killed twenty-two people.

Cantarell's declining output motivated two parallel developments: one is to search for new oil fields in deeper waters of the Gulf of Mexico, and the other is to push PEMEX from nationalism to neoliberalism. Extending the oil frontier into deeper waters is financially challenging and technologically complex and also requires geopolitical negotiation regarding maritime boundaries with the United States. Specifically, there are two undefined "gaps," creatively named "western" and "eastern," beyond the Exclusive Economic Zones of the United States and Mexico. Both countries believe that hydrocarbons exist beneath the ocean floor in these "gaps."

State-owned PEMEX survived the NAFTA negotiations of the early 1990s. But in 2008 President Felipe Calderón prepared an "energy reform," which opponents labeled as "privatization proposal." This was an auspicious moment, with oil at nearly $150 per barrel and declining oil output from Cantarell. Calderón's predecessor, Vicente Fox, had also attempted an oil reform, but Calderon's was bolder: open PEMEX to private investment and give PEMEX financial autonomy from the Mexican government.

According to Lisa Breglia (2013), the Calderón administration spent $16.5 million on television advertisements arguing for "PEMEX modernization," carefully avoiding the word "privatization." Calderón also promoted product placement mentions of "energy reform" on Mexican chat shows and *telenovelas*. His government created a video arguing for a *tesoro bajo el mar* ("treasure under the sea") that Mexico could exploit best through "reforms." Meanwhile, Calderón's political nemesis, Andrés Manuel López Obrador (AMLO) spearheaded a national movement against Calderón by denouncing privatization of PEMEX, defending the principles of the 1938 nationalization—oil as a public good. AMLO's group countered the "tesoro bajo el mar" video with a parody of *Lord of the Rings: The Two Towers*, by showing US president George W. Bush as Gollum, thanking Calderón for Mexican oil, his "precious treasure."

The ensuing national debate in the Mexican congress and numerous public fora during 2008 ended with no action being taken until Calderón's successor, Enrique Peña Nieto, pushed constitutional changes and a revised *reforma energética* through the Mexican congress in 2013 and 2014. These reforms ended the PEMEX monopoly, gave it first refusal on oil and gas fields, and opened Mexico to direct investment by foreign oil and gas firms. Some observers described the reforms as necessary to turn around declining oil output and increase oil-based revenue, while others saw the reforms as creating fiscal difficulties for Mexico and opportunity for TNCs to profit from Mexico's oil and gas.

Conclusion

What will be the fate of Latin America's natural resources at the end of the commodity boom? Latin America's natural resources show every indication of being central to critical global challenges, such as fossil energy's role in climate change and the ability of agricultural systems to feed a more affluent global population. Conflict seems likely to continue over sites of extraction. Policy may swing between resource nationalism and neoliberalism. We can be sure that emerging resources, such as forests for carbon sequestration, land for biofuel production, and coastal areas for tourism development, will generate new conflicts among people, governments, and TNCs.

Acknowledgments

Funding to the author from the National Science Foundation (BCS-1234156 and BCS-0647249) and the National Geographic Society (7856-05) helped support research summarized in this chapter. Comments from Matt Fry helped sharpen the focus of the chapter.

Key Terms

agricultural superpower: Term used to describe Brazil because of its world-leading production of coffee, citrus, and sugarcane, and top exporter status for animal protein and soybeans.

Aguinado v. Texaco **lawsuit:** Legal complaint dating from 1993 aiming to obtain damages from oil production in eastern Ecuador.

Bajío: Known as Mexico's granary since the 1500s, now site of irrigated cropland for high-tech vegetable farms and greenhouses that supply US and Mexican markets.

Cantarell: Located in Mexico's Gulf area, major oil producer until output declined after 2004 peak of 2.2 million barrels per day.

China Effect: Also known as "China Cycle," describes the impact of increasing Chinese demand for resources from Latin America, spurring new resource booms that ended around 2012.

Cerro Rico: Potosí mountain mined for silver since the 1500s, located in in the high-altitude Bolivian Altiplano.

commodity chains: Links between produces and consumers of commodities (tradable items, usually natural resources, graded and mixed according to objective standard type).

natural resources: Renewable natural resources include water, fisheries, forests, and crop land; non-renewable resources are fossil energy (petroleum, natural gas, and coal) and minerals such as iron ore, silver, and copper.

neoliberalism: Ideology that favors markets to determine the extraction of natural resources; relies on privatization, concessions; also known as economic liberalism, its nineteenth-century predecessor.

open veins: Term used by Eduardo Galeano (1973) to describe the plunder of Latin America's mineral and agricultural resources by Spanish and Portuguese imperial powers.

PDVSA: Petróleos de Venezuela S.A., Venezuela's state-owned oil company.

PEMEX: Mexico's state-owned oil company, created in 1938 and developed into a political behemoth, but was subject of reforms in 2013 and 2014 that will allow foreign participation in hydrocarbons.

Petrobras: Brazil's state-owned oil company created in the early 1950s, but partly privatized in1997, allowing it to develop into a TNC with global presence.

resource nationalism: Ideology that favors state ownership or control of natural resources to advance political, social, and industrial objectives.

*sembramos petróleo***:** Official Venezuelan discourse regarding spreading benefits of petroleum to its people in terms of employment, social programs, and other material benefits.

Soylândia: Brazil's vast soybean area, nearly the size of Arizona, relies on foreign markets that consume soy for animal feed, cooking oil, and processed foods.

Vale: Brazil's massive mining transnational corporation that formerly was the state-owned Companhia do Vale do Rio Doce, until 1997 privatization.

Suggested Readings

Bebbington, Anthony J., and Jeffrey T. Bury (Eds.). *Subterranean Struggles: New Dynamics of Mining, Oil, and Gas in Latin America.* Austin: University of Texas Press, 2013.

Breglia, Lisa. *Living with Oil: Promises, Peaks, and Declines on Mexico's Gulf Coast.* Austin: University of Texas Press, 2013.

Cushman, Gregory T. *Guano and the Opening of the Pacific World: A Global Ecological History.* New York: Cambridge University Press, 2013.

Galeano, Eduardo. *Open Veins of Latin America.* Translated by C. Belfrage. New York: Monthly Review Press, 1973.

Galt, Ryan E. *Food Systems in an Unequal World: Pesticides, Vegetables, and Agrarian Capitalism in Costa Rica.* Tucson: University of Arizona Press, 2014.

Hindery, Derrick. *From Enron to Evo: Pipeline Politics, Global Environmentalism, and Indigenous Rights in Bolivia.* Tucson: University of Arizona Press, 2013.

Kane, Joe. *Savages.* New York: Vintage Books, 1996.

Klubock, Thomas Miller. *La Frontera: Forests and Ecological Conflict in Chile's Frontier Territory.* Durham, NC: Duke University Press, 2014.

References

Alvarado, Nikolai A., and Matthew J. Taylor. "¿Del mar quién es dueño? Artisanal Fisheries, Tourism Development and the Struggles over Access to Marine Resources in Gigante, Nicaragua." *Journal of Latin American Geography* 13 (2014): 37–62.

Alvarez-Berrios, Nora L., and T. Mitchell Aide. "Global Demand for Gold Is Another Threat to Tropical Forests." *Environmental Research Letters* 10, no. 1 (2015): 014006.

Asner, Gregory P., William Llactayo, Raul Tupayachi, and Ernesto Raez Luna. "Elevated Rates of Gold Mining in the Amazon Revealed through High-Resolution Monitoring." *Proceedings of the National Academy of Sciences* 110, no. 46 (2013): 18454–59.

Ayala, César J. *American Sugar Kingdom: The Plantation Economy of the Spanish Caribbean, 1898–1934.* Chapel Hill: University of North Carolina Press, 1999.

Bebbington, Anthony J., and Jeffrey T. Bury. "Institutional Challenges for Mining and Sustainability in Peru." *Proceedings of the National Academy of Sciences* 106, no. 41 (2009): 17296–301.

Bebbington, Anthony J., and Jeffrey T. Bury (Eds.). *Subterranean Struggles: New Dynamics of Mining, Oil, and Gas in Latin America.* Austin: University of Texas Press, 2013.

Brannstrom, Christian (Ed.). *Territories, Commodities and Knowledges: Latin American Environmental History in the Nineteenth and Twentieth Centuries.* London: Institute of Latin American Studies, 2004.

———. "South America's Neoliberal Agricultural Frontiers: Places of Environmental Sacrifice or Conservation Opportunity?" *Ambio* 38, no. 3 (2009): 141–49.

Brannstrom, C., Lisa Raush, J. C. Brown, R. Marson, and A. Miccolis. "Compliance and Market Exclusion in Brazilian Agriculture: Analysis and Implications for 'Soft' Governance." *Land Use Policy* 29 (2012): 357–66.

Breglia, Lisa. *Living with Oil: Promises, Peaks, and Declines on Mexico's Gulf Coast.* Austin: University of Texas Press, 2013.

Cushman, Gregory T. *Guano and the Opening of the Pacific World: A Global Ecological History.* New York: Cambridge University Press, 2013.

Denevan, William M. *Cultivated Landscapes of Native Amazonia and the Andes.* Oxford: Oxford University Press, 2001.

Economist, The. "The Miracle of the Cerrado." August 28, 2010, 58–60.

Economist, The. "Life after the Commodity Boom." March 29, 2014, 35–38.

Finer, Matt, Bruce Babbitt, Sidney Novoa, Francesco Ferrarese, Salvatore Eugenio Pappalardo, Massimo De Marchi, Maria Saucedo, and Anjali Kumar. "Future of Oil and Gas Development in the Western Amazon." *Environmental Research Letters* 10, no. 2 (2015): 024003.

Galeano, Eduardo. *Open Veins of Latin America.* Translated by C. Belfrage. New York: Monthly Review Press, 1973.

Gallagher, Kevin P., and Roberto Porzecanski. 2010. *The Dragon in the Room: China and the Future of Latin American Industrialization.* Stanford, CA: Stanford University Press, 2010.

Galt, Ryan E. *Food Systems in an Unequal World: Pesticides, Vegetables, and Agrarian Capitalism in Costa Rica.* Tucson: University of Arizona Press, 2014.

García, Carolina, Héctor Tavera-Escobar, Carlos Vieira, Carolina Rincón, and Elmer Rentería. "Fostering Ethno-Territorial Autonomy: A Colombian Case Study of Community-Based Conservation of Mangroves." *Journal of Latin American Geography* 13 (2014): 117–52.

Gustafson, Bret "Flashpoints of Sovereignty: Territorial Conflict and Natural Gas in Bolivia." In *Crude Domination: An Anthropology of Oil,* edited by Andrea Behrends, Stephen P. Reyna, and Günther Schlee, 220–40. New York: Berghahn Books, 2011.

Hecht, Susanna B., and Charles C. Mann. "How Brazil Outfarmed the American Farmer. *Fortune Magazine* (January 21, 2008): 92–105.

Hindery, Derrick. *From Enron to Evo: Pipeline Politics, Global Environmentalism, and Indigenous Rights in Boliva.* Tucson: University of Arizona Press, 2013.

Jenkins, Rhys. "China's Global Expansion and Latin America." *Journal of Latin American Studies* 42 (2010): 809–37.

Jepson, Wendy. "Private Colonization on a Brazilian Frontier, 1970–1980. *Journal of Historical Geography* 32 (2006): 839–63.

Jepson, Wendy, C. Brannstrom, and Anthony M. Filippi. "Access Regimes and Regional Land Change in the Brazilian Cerrado, 1972–2002." *Annals of the Association of American Geographers* 100, no. 1 (2010): 87–111.

Kane, Joe. *Savages.* New York: Vintage Books, 1996.

Klubock, Thomas Miller. *La Frontera: Forests and Ecological Conflict in Chile's Frontier Territory.* Durham, NC: Duke University Press, 2014.

Leguizamón, Amalia. "Modifying Argentina: GM Soy and Socio-Environmental Change." *Geoforum* 53 (2014): 149–60.

Nepstad, Daniel, David McGrath, Claudia Stickler, Ane Alencar, Andrea Azevedo, Briana Swette, Tathiana Bezerra, Maria DiGiano, João Shimada, Ronaldo Seroa da Motta, Eric Armijo, Leandro Castello, Paulo Brando, Matt C. Hansen, Max McGrath-Horn, Oswaldo Carvalho, and Laura Hess. "Slowing

Amazon Deforestation through Public Policy and Interventions in Beef and Soy Supply Chains." *Science* 344 no. 6188 (2014): 1118.

Pederson, Alexandra. "Landscapes of Resistance: Community Opposition to Canadian Mining Operations in Guatemala. *Journal of Latin American Geography* 13 (2014): 187–214.

Perreault, Tom, and Gabriela Valdivia. "Hydrocarbons, Popular Protest and National Imaginaries: Ecuador and Bolivia in Comparative Context." *Geoforum* 41 (2010): 689–99.

Robins, Nicholas A. *Mercury, Mining, and Empire: The Human and Ecological Cost of Colonial Silver Mining in the Andes.* Bloomington and Indianapolis: Indiana University Press, 2011.

Santiago, Myrna. *The Ecology of Oil: Environment, Labor, and the Mexican Revolution, 1900–1938.* New York: Cambridge University Press, 2006.

Soluri, John. *Banana Cultures: Agriculture, Consumption, and Environmental Change in Honduras and the United States.* Austin: University of Texas Press, 2005.

Strønen, Iselin Åsedotter. "Development from Below and Oil Money from Above: Popular Organisation in Contemporary Venezuela." In *Flammable Societies: Studies on the Socio-Economics of Oil and Gas,* edited by O. J. Logan and J. A. McNeish. London: Pluto Press, 2012.

Tellman, Beth, Leslie C. Gray, and Christopher M. Bacon. "Not Fair Enough: Historic and Institutional Barriers to Fair Trade Coffee in El Salvador. *Journal of Latin American Geography* 10 (2011): 105–27.

Topik, Steven, Carlos Marichal, and Zephyr L. Frank (Eds.). *From Silver to Cocaine: Latin American Commodity Chains and the Building of the World Economy, 1500–2000.* Durham, NC: Duke University Press, 2006.

Vadjunec, Jacqueline. "Extracting a Livelihood: Institutional and Social Dimensions of Deforestation in the Chico Mendes Extractive Reserve, Acre, Brazil." *Journal of Latin American Geography* 10 (2011): 151–74.

Valdivia, Gabriela. "Governing Relations between People and Things: Citizenship, Territory, and the Political Economy of Petroleum in Ecuador." *Political Geography* 27 (2008): 456–77.

Whitmore, Thomas M., and B. L. Turner II. *Cultivated Landscapes of Middle America on the Eve of Conquest.* Oxford: Oxford University Press, 2001.

Chapter 8

Drug Geographies

A Cultural Historical Profile

Kent Mathewson

Drugs, both illegal and licit, are defining features of much that is written or depicted about contemporary Latin America. Drug reportage has become a staple in popular news media, accentuating the lurid and negative dimensions of drug commerce, trafficking, and consumption. Beyond the headlines, there lies a rich repertoire of drug-related images, lyrics, and commentary woven into Latin American cinematic, musical, and literary productions. Aside from these arenas of cultural production, there is a growing scholarly literature on the place of psychoactive agents in Latin America's varied geographies.

As with the media coverage, much of the recent scholarly work on illicit drugs focuses on the economic and political aspects, especially international trafficking, and increasingly on their imbrication in political processes, from fueling armed insurgencies to oiling the machinery of state in all of its branches (Bagley and Walker 1994; Walker 1996). There is also an established literature that treats drugs and their geographies in a wider scope (Courtwright 2001). Here, the illicit or illegal cultivated substances such as cannabis, coca, and opium, plus their derivatives, are joined by legal but regulated drugs such as alcohol and tobacco (Porter and Teich 1995), as well as an array of plant sources of mild psychoactives such as sugar, coffee, tea, and cacao directed to the world market, along with more locally produced sources of stimulants, depressants, and hallucinogens. Any survey that fails to include these agents risks eliding whole chapters from the complex history of drugs in Latin America and their varied geographies. This expanded view of drugs reveals a historical and cultural record with millennial time depth and nearly universal importance in indigenous societies (Mathewson 2004). It also demonstrates the centrality of drug use, production, and commerce in the building and articulations of colonial economies and societies. As for modern times, drugs in all of their dimensions, at times for better but often for worse, constitute part of what Latin America has come to mean in the eyes of the world and how it is located within various coordinates of our modern and postmodern worlds.

As both a force and factor in the production of Latin America's economic, political, and cultural conditions, drugs offer perhaps the best illustration of the workings of what has come to be called *globalization*. Few would argue that the place of drugs in Latin America's economies has been insignificant (Jankowiak and Bradburd 2003). At times, drugs have seemingly come to dominate a particular nation's economic rhythms and realities (Williams 1994). For example, in Colombia during recent decades, the illicit drug cocaine has stormed the portals and taken over the palace—from currency exchanges and export earnings, to acts of corruption and military expenditures, to clandestine farm and laboratory productions and ultimately the infinite informal economics of street and backroom dealings. No sector of the economy or polity is said to be immune. The metaphors of disease and contagion are often mobilized in the attempt to characterize the danger and dynamics of the drug trade. As with disease, one can identify the etiologies spawning the drug trade, and one can chart its traffic flows along paths or through networks. But little thought goes into uncovering the geographies the trade creates, or locating the geographies in which drug use, production, and commerce take place.

In this chapter, I will draw some of the contours and provide a few datum points to show what a comprehensive geography of drug making, taking, and commerce for Latin America might entail. Not surprisingly, it is an uneven surface, with some places and regions registering intense nodes or zones of activity while other areas scarcely merit marks on the map. The history is not so uneven, but certain periods have pulsated with action, while other phases have been paced with only humdrum movement, involving mostly individuals or local groups pursuing quotidian routines. In addition, definitions need to be examined, and expanded (Lewin 1964). "Drug" in its generic sense refers to "any substance that in small amounts produces significant changes in the body, mind, or both" (Weil and Rosen 1993, 8). But foods and poisons can also fit this description. Sugar is both food and drug, and alcohol can be all three. On a continuum from food to poison, drugs can be described as agents of mind and/or body change that are primarily neither food nor poison. Here, we will limit the discussion to psychoactive substances. Moreover, most usage is outside formal or normal medicinal practice. "Drugs" in the Latin American context usually refers to the three classes of illicit substances (cannabis, coca/cocaine, and opium/heroin) plus lesser quantities of bootlegged pharmaceuticals or confected synthetics such as amphetamines and tranquilizers. There are, however, several dozen other "drugs" that should be not overlooked. These include a range of stimulants, stupefacients, and hallucinogens. In terms of their historical importance to Latin America's interactions with other world regions, and among its inhabitants on a quotidian level, the array and range of drugs that are produced, consumed, or marketed can be arranged hierarchically in five levels.

Hierarchies of Import and Export

If judged on its historical importance, commercial export success, and range of geographical distribution, cane sugar (*Saccarum* sp.) should be considered Latin America's premier drug plant (figure 8.1). Sidney Mintz's *Sweetness and Power* (1985), a brilliant history of cane sugar as a costimulant of both New World slavery and early North Atlantic industrialism, convincingly makes the case that sugar should be seen as both a "food" and a metabolic stimulant. If sugar's derivative drugs—such as rum, *aguardiente*, and *cachaça*—are added to the equation, it is no contest. Following sugar, the ranking of second-order substances such as tobacco (*Nicotiana* sp.), coffee (*Coffee* sp.), cacao (*Theobroma cacao*), and coca (*Erythroxylon* sp.) is not so clear. Each has controlled the economies of single colonies and regions, and even whole nations, at differing times. In aggregate, they have engaged millions of workers and generated billions in revenues. Like sugar, their manufactured products have serviced the habits and provided the pleasures for many millions of consumers, at home but especially abroad. All are domesticated plants with several consumed species (save cacao), though each genus has a dominant commercial species with its own history and geographies (Coe and Coe 1996; Goodman 1993; Gootenberg 1999; Pendergrast 1999).

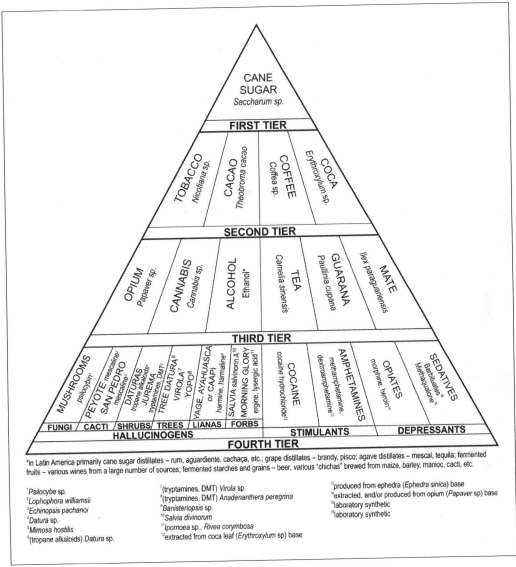

Figure 8.1. Hierarchy of psychoactive substances in Latin America.

The third tier of drugs has a strong local base of consumers, but the drugs also find their way into national and international markets. They include both illicit and licit substances. Alcohol in all its exuberant varieties and cannabis (*Cannabis* sp.), in mainly its marijuana form, are the main controlled or proscribed drugs at this level (Rubin 1975). Native regional stimulants, such as mate (*Ilex paraguariensis*) and guarana (*Paullina cupana*), are culturally and economically important in parts of South America. Mate is the national drink of Argentina and is consumed in neighboring nations. Guarana is consumed mostly in Brazil but is expanding its range and markets. Like sugarcane and the most common species of cannabis, tea (*Camellia sinensis*) and opium (*Papavera somniferum*) are Asian cultivars that were introduced in colonial times to Latin America (Booth 1998). Both are produced for the export market and also have localized distributions.

A fourth tier of drugs can be identified. This group comprises all of the other psychoactive substances collected or cultivated, prepared or manufactured, or consumed in, or exported from, Latin America. Many of these drugs, especially the hallucinogenic plants and their preparations, are not part of normal commercial networks (Emboden 1979). Primarily embedded in indigenous cultural practices, or local rural and urban customs with strong links to indigenous folkways, these substances have only limited articulations with larger economic spheres. Most of the plant-derived drugs at this level are collected from undomesticated plants rather than cultivated ones. The remaining drugs in the fourth tier include refined forms of substances occurring in plants, such as morphine from opium and mescaline from peyote and San Pedro cacti; semisynthetics, such as heroin made from morphine; and pure synthetics, made in laboratories from non–naturally occurring chemicals. Whereas the first group in this tier—naturally occurring collected drugs—has long histories of use and cultural embeddedness, possibly predating agriculture in some cases, the others are artifacts of modernity and have established geographies only in the past half century or so.

Drug Geographies in Historical Perspective

It is quite likely that knowledge of psychotropic drugs was part of the pharmacopoeia and skill kits that Mesolithic hunters and gatherers brought with them from Asia to the late Pleistocene New World some twenty thousand or more years ago (La Barre 1970). It is certain that their descendants uncovered a cornucopia of psychoactive agents in settling the subtropics and tropics. One of the striking anomalies of global-scale biogeography and culture history is the disparity between the number of Old and New World hallucinogenic substances. Of some 120 identified hallucinogenic substances found in nature, fewer than two dozen have Old World origins (La Barre 1970). The rest are found in the New World, most in Latin America. The discovery of drugs from natural sources is one of humanity's great empirical ventures. While no theorist of agricultural origins has proposed a full-blown case for drug plants as the initial focus of the domestication process, tending wild forms of tobacco, coca, cacao, and the myriad fruits and other plant sources of fermentable beverages may have spurred early experiments in genetic modifications (Bruman 2000). Carl Sauer (1952) suggests that it was the nonfood plants important to tropical Mesolithic fisherfolk, such as vines for cordage, gourds for floats, and fish poisons, that led to the first serious manipulations. Psychotropic drugs play roles in many tropical forest agriculturalists' hunting activities. They may have played a role in the transition as well. Whether antecedent, or just part of the larger Neolithic Revolution, drugs continued to play important roles as simple agricultural societies evolved into more complex sociopolitical structures—from tribes, to chiefdoms, to states, and, in a few cases, to empires (Rudgley 1994).

The locus of power in neotropical chiefdoms from Mexico to subtropical South America was refracted and reflected through both material objects and symbolic spheres involving drugs and their ritual consumption. In Andean and Amazonian contexts, the shaman's stool was the literal seat of power. A range of powerful hallucinogens, including San Pedro cactus (*Trichocereus* sp.) (mescaline source), yage or ayahuasca (*Banisteriopsis* sp.) (harmaline source), and yopo or cohoba (*Anadenanthera* sp.) (tryptamine source) were associated with these objects (Furst 1972). One of the diagnostic traits of a chiefdom level of complexity are large earthen mounds, usually at the center of villages or ceremonial precincts. These were often the sites of ritual celebrations involving beers, or *chicha*, made from root crops such as manioc (*Manihot esculenta*) or maize (*Zea mays*), and other drugs such as coca, tobacco, and hallucinogens. Chiefly power was in part demonstrated through such public gatherings. Drugs were a central component in the cultural and sociopolitical cement that went into constructing and maintaining chiefdoms. The geography of chiefdoms in pre-Columbian times varied over time, but the main areas included large parts of Central America, the Caribbean, and northern South America, the so-called Intermediate Area in archaeological terms. To the north were the states and empires of Mesoamerica, and to the south the states and empires of the Andean realm (see chapters 2 and 4).

Expanding Polities, Expanding Trade

With the rise of states and empires in the pre-Columbian world, complex and accumulative trade networks and production and consumption regimes developed (see chapter 2). Cacao, a key component in ritual beverages (often mixed with other drugs and condiments), became the coin of the realm throughout Mesoamerica. Cacao beans were used as specie and were the standard medium of commerce (Coe and Coe 1996). Conflicts among states and empires in Mesoamerica were often over the control of resources and their places of extraction or production. Cacao territories were among the most contested (Bergmann 1969). Tobacco, like cacao, was often state controlled and regulated, and its consumption was associated with ritual practices, but it also was used in quotidian ways. Other Mesoamerican substances with similar production and use patterns include alcoholic beverages made from *Agave* species, especially *pulque*, and chili peppers (*Capsicum* sp.) (Bruman 2000). Today, chili peppers are seen as purely condiments, often the defining element of regional or national cuisines. In pre-Columbian contexts, chili peppers were culinary staples but also admixes for intoxicating and/or hallucinogenic drinks.

The production, consumption, and regulation of drugs in South American states and empires parallel and in some cases duplicate the patterns and practices of the Mesoamerican complex polities. The case of coca is best known and recorded (Mortimer 1974). Even more than cacao in Mesoamerica, it assumed centrality in the Andean culture, society, and, in some regions, economy. It was at once a sacred substance, devotional object, trade item, quotidian staple, and stimulant aid to labor and transport throughout vast portions of western South America. The main producing areas in pre-Columbian times lay along the eastern flanks of the Andean cordillera at intermediate elevations, as they do today. The altitudinal and geographical differentials between zones of coca production and the main higher zones of coca consumption helped develop the vaunted Andean system of ecological and economic "verticality." From colonial times until quite recently, the cultivation and use of coca was largely eliminated from northern and southern Andean districts. Coca's Peruvian and Bolivian hearth and homelands, though beleaguered, have persisted in the face of various campaigns of suppression. It is these famed eastern Andean valley regions, such as the Yungas in Bolivia and the Huallaga in Perú, which provided the geographical base for cocaine's emergence onto and into modern global drug scenes.

In pre-Columbian times, however, these prime producing areas fed a much less expansive trade. Even though Andean states and empires may have attempted to control the cultivation, trade, and consumption of coca, it was a far too important part of both the sacred and profane lives of Andean peoples to allow either local or imperial elites to overly circumscribe it or its use. There is some evidence, on the other hand, that elites had more success in controlling the production and use of maize for ritual *chicha* or "beer" making. The eminent Andean scholar

John Murra (1973) argues that many of the finest stone-faced and irrigated terrace systems in Incaic landscapes were constructed for ritual maize cultivation. The geographical extent of these features is fairly well documented, and many are on spectacular display at renowned ceremonial centers such as Machu Picchu. If Murra is correct about this, then this is an example of drug geography literally encoded in stone and distributed widely throughout the ancient Inca Empire.

One of the universal traits of empires is the dynamics they set in motion with the "barbarians" on their peripheries. Among the routine dynamics are circuits of trade that feed scarce or exotic products from less developed peripheries to civilizational cores. Among the more spectacular features are episodes of invasion and occasionally conquest of imperial centers by "barbarian hordes." The bands and tribes of Chichimeca roaming the arid lands north of the states and empires of central Mexico are a classic example (Sauer 1941). These "barbarians" gathered peyote (*Lophophora williamsii*) and other desert drugs and directed them to the imperial centers to the south. What began as simple trade relations periodically begat invasions. For the Incas, the tropical forest tribes at and beyond their imperial edges were a source of a number of exotic trade goods, including hallucinogenic drugs such as *yage* and *yopo*. From pre-Columbian times until the present, border zones along with remote peripheries have played important roles in the production and transshipment of drugs (Perramond 2004). This is one of the geographical constants in the shifting theaters of drug production and trade throughout Latin America's history. Today, the new barbarians at the empire's gates are often said to be Latin America's footloose migrants, some serving as "drug mules," others following drug trafficking trails past porous borders, while still others finding informal employment in the illegal drug business once they reach their destinations.

Europe's Forced Entry

In a sense, the arrival of Europeans in the New World constitutes an extreme case of assault from a remote periphery (see chapter 2). To Moctezuma and his court at Tenochtitlán, or to Atahualpa and his court at Cuzco, the Spaniards seemed to be barbarians in the extreme. The European invaders initially brought little for exchange save disease, against which the native pharmacopeias were largely ineffectual. Beyond the precious metals, the Europeans found a secondary source of wealth in psychoactive drugs, with tobacco and cacao heading up the list (Bradburd and Jankowiak 2003). With their appropriation, many pre-Columbian patterns and practices of collection, production, and trade were disrupted or redirected (Wolf 1982). Other patterns and processes were reconstituted with their incorporation into the European world imperial system (Wallerstein 1974). Cacao was both desacralized and demonetized but never decommodified. It became the prime export commodity in the colonial economies of coastal Ecuador and Venezuela and later in Bahia, Brazil (see also chapter 3). Tobacco was another drug that in pre-Columbian times was used mostly in ritual contexts, but under European commodity colonialism, it became a staple crop in most of Europe's New World colonies. Cuba's prominence in the cultivation and later the production of tobacco products, especially cigars, did not develop until late in the colonial period. This illustrates yet another principle of the development of drug geographies in Latin America, that is, the uneven and shifting loci of cultivation and production centers over time.

Columbus was sailing, or so he said, for the "East Indies" when he undershot Asia and landed in the "West Indies" (Sauer 1966). Spices, even more than precious metals or fine manufactures of silk and porcelain, were the main objective. Spices common in the West today such as pepper, cinnamon, cloves, nutmeg, mace, ginger, and other, less well-known spices were highly valued in Europe during the Middle Ages (Dalby 2000). Initially, cane sugar, because of its cost and scarcity, fitted the spice mold more than its later role as a food and drink additive. European elites desired Asian spices as luxury commodities, not so much as food condiments, and less as preservatives, but as substances in their own right to be bought, sold, and consumed (Schivelbush 1992). Their cultivation and production was often in clandestine or closely guarded locations. They generated complex trade circuits and immense profits. Their consumption was often ritualized and fetishized. In all of these aspects, spice use and trade in Europe's late Middle Ages anticipated the future waves of drugs to come.

Colonial Patterns

While the roots of the modern drug trade in Latin America may lie with Europe's quest for exotic spices in Asia, the base was laid with Europe's occupation of the Americas. Although Columbus failed to find the fabled spices of the Orient in the Caribbean, he did find conditions suitable for sugar production. He brought sugar from the Canaries to Santo Domingo on his second voyage, in 1493. African slaves quickly followed. From Hispaniola, sugar was diffused to all of Spain's New World colonies. By the 1520s the Portuguese had introduced sugar to Brazil from their successful plantations on Madeira and São Tomé (Galloway 1989).

For the first century, the Iberians had a monopoly on the New World sugar business. Sugar production produced significant landscape change in the regions wherein it prospered (Watts 1987). Not only was it land extensive in its soil needs, but it often required water for irrigation. Processing required abundant power (draft animal or wind) for grinding and fuel (usually wood) for boiling. Landscapes were simultaneously degraded (deforested and soil depleted) and "improved" (plots mounded and/or terraced, irrigation works constructed). Perhaps the single most enduring impact of sugar production on Latin American geographies was the associated implantation of millions of enslaved African laborers. With few exceptions, the regions with the largest African-descended populations even today are those where sugar plantations held sway. Starting in the seventeenth century, northern European powers in-filled areas in the circum-Caribbean basin seized from, abandoned by, or never settled by the Spanish (Richardson 1992). The British, French, and Dutch each occupied a wedge of the Guianas and ultimately all the Lesser Antilles, along with Jamaica and Saint-Domingue (Haiti). The Dutch also occupied prime portions of northeast Brazil between 1630 and 1654. During the eighteenth century, British Barbados and Jamaica and French Saint-Domingue became crown jewels in their respective empires. Sugar provided the luster and lucre, African slaves the labor. The flows of capital and commodities set in motion by these occupations (of land *and* labor) gave rise to the infamous Triangular Trade, wherein Caribbean sugar and molasses were shipped to New England or England and distilled into rum, which was then traded for slaves in West Africa directed back to the Caribbean (figure 8.2). The French and Dutch performed comparable triangulations between their colonies, metropoles, and Africa. On lesser scales and intensities, tobacco, coffee, and cacao followed these geometrics. In more than metaphorical ways, the drug trade circuits established in colonial times between Latin America and the North Atlantic realm pointed the way for new drug commodity flows in postcolonial times.

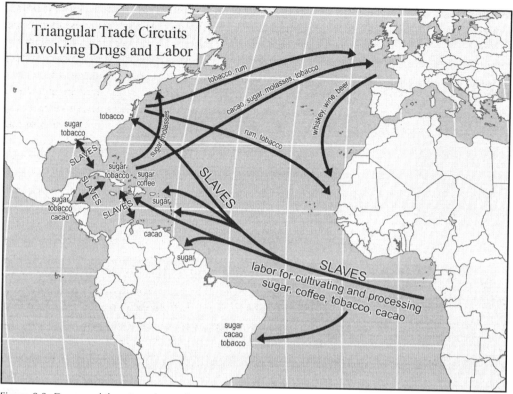

Figure 8.2. Drugs and the triangular trade system.

Modernity's Diffusions and Suffusions

The geographic patterns of precolonial and colonial drug production, trade, and use in Latin America, while not static, generally formed and unfolded at tempos befitting premodern economies and societies. From the mid-nineteenth century onward, nation formation, industrialization, and liberal economics accelerated the circuits of exchange and pathways of change (see chapter 2). New demand and supply regimes developed in both the realm and its North Atlantic extensions. Swiss perfections of chocolate confection led to mass marketing and consumption in the global North (Coe and Coe 1996). Tobacco cigars became an emblem of Victorian sophistication (Corti 1996), while coffee and cane sugar became quotidian necessities of all classes (Mintz 1985; Pendergrast 1999). At the same time, new psychoactive agents—ones that a century or so later would come to both symbolize and constitute the modern drug trade—began to enter the mix. The first was cannabis.

An ancient Old World cultigen of probable central Asian provenance, *Cannabis sativa* used as a drug probably first reached the New World as part of the African diaspora (Rubin 1975; Duvall 2014). An element of slave society in disparate locales throughout Latin America, it apparently diffused selectively into indigenous and local folk usage (namely, *maconha* in Brazil and marijuana in Mexico). A second diaspora brought to it Euro-American attention. South Asian ("East Indian") indentured laborers in the Caribbean, especially Jamaica, are credited with "introducing" ganja, long a popular medicinal and recreational drug in India, to the Caribbean (Rubin 1975). From there, Afro-Caribbean Creoles are said to have introduced it to the Central and South American rimland (Goode 1969). By the mid-twentieth century, potent strains of cannabis were being widely consumed locally and increasingly trafficked to markets in North America and beyond. International prohibitions on cannabis did not take hold until the late 1930s. With usage mostly confined to the rural poor or marginalized urban sectors throughout much of its history, cannabis was largely a local affair. As part of the countercultural currents of the 1960s, vast new transclass markets were opened up, first in the North Atlantic realm and then in Latin America. Various producer regions and districts—especially mountainous zones of difficult access—in a number of countries experienced boom times as a result of the cannabis craze. Mexico's Sierra Madre Occidental, Colombia's Santa Marta, and Jamaica's Blue Mountains all developed into major cannabis-producing areas. During the 1970s national authorities in these countries were prompted and aided by US antidrug policies to launch campaigns of repression and eradication in these and other districts. The effect of this was at least twofold. First, new growing areas were developed within these countries and beyond. These spatial displacements have been characterized as "the balloon effect": put the squeeze on one region and the activity balloons up in another region. Second, many of the trafficking networks formed during the heyday of the cannabis boom—the 1960s and early 1970s—were converted to cocaine networks from the mid-1970s on (Walker 1996).

Like cannabis, the origins of cocaine commerce can be traced to nineteenth-century developments, but its mature articulations were a century in the making. The North Atlantic world discovered coca's stimulating elixir properties in the mid-nineteenth century, and refined cocaine became widely available by the 1880s in tonics, in beverages (such as Coca-Cola), and as a powder for ingesting, inhaling, or injecting (Courtwright 2001). This initial cocaine boom was brought to a halt by legislation and suppression starting in the early 1900s. The second cocaine boom, which began in the 1970s, drew on traditional source areas such as Bolivia's Chapare region and Perú's Huallaga Valley for the raw coca, but increasingly Colombia, particularly Medellín, became the center for processing the finished product. The capital quickly amassed by Colombia's notorious regionally based cocaine cartels variously rippled and rushed out across Latin America, creating an increasingly vertically integrated enterprise. The infrastructure included transportation fleets (vehicles, watercraft, and aircraft), refineries and factories, banks and commercial houses, and archipelagos of producing areas in traditional zones or clandestine narcoplantations in new cultivation territories, chiefly in Colombia's upper Amazonian districts. In some cases the cartels sponsored coca plantations in "liberated" territory in guerrilla zones operated by the Maoist Sendero Luminoso in Perú or the Marxist FARC (Fuerzas Armadas Revolucionarias de Colombia) and ELN (Ejército de Liberación Nacional) in Colombia (Reyes 1994). No nation or dependency and few regions in Latin America or the Caribbean have escaped cocaine's entanglements (Scott and Marshall 1991). Since the 1970s, dozens of Latin American governments have fallen, either directly or indirectly, to "cocaine coups" or scandals involving drug corruption (Steinberg and Mathewson 2005). Yet in an age when neoliberal solutions to Latin America's persistent problems of dependency and underdevelopment have been forced on the region by national elites in concert with international agencies (see chapter 3), cocaine's shortcut receipts for privatized prosperity and entrepreneurial success are hard to refute.

Within the overlapping spaces of cannabis and cocaine trafficking, there are other illicit drugs that have more restricted histories and geographies. Opium poppies came to the New World with the colonial pharmacopoeia, and later were part of the baggage that Chinese coolies brought to western South America and the Caribbean. Since at least the 1960s, opium cultivation for heroin production in Mexico, Colombia, and Guatemala has been the agency of criminal syndicates, often in collusion with local and sometimes national authorities. The opium business generally enjoys the preexisting networks and infrastructure established by the cocaine and/or cannabis trades. Since the 1920s, there have been minor currents in the traffic of psychoactive pharmaceuticals diverted from legitimate channels. Since World War II, various commercially produced drugs (particularly amphetamines, barbiturates, and tranquilizers) have made their way from legitimate channels into the Latin American drug networks. Trafficking scales range from freelance tourists bringing home more than "just for personal use" to truckloads, boatloads, and planeloads smuggled across borders.

Present and Future Trends

Whereas once regions of Latin America would specialize in the production and distribution of one or two illicit drugs, increasingly there is diversification of products. This is most evident in the case of methamphetamine. Starting in the 1980s, major cocaine traffickers such as the Mexican Amezcua cartel began to dabble in the "meth" market as a sideline. By the 1990s the Mexican syndicates realized that manufacture and distribution of meth could be profitable in and of itself. At the same time, small-scale (home or backyard) meth labs experienced explosive growth on the West Coast. In classic innovation diffusion style, the trend spread east, becoming most widely established in the Midwest. In the past decade, official reaction to the epidemic of meth abuse has curbed much local production in the United States. Picking up market slack, the Mexican cartels have greatly increased the purity, potency, and quantity of their product. As of 2005, it was estimated that Mexican superlabs were supplying 60 percent or more of the illegal amphetamine consumed in the United States. Mexican cartels were directly importing tons of ephedrine (the natural precursor drug) from India and China to supply their labs.

Perhaps the most profound and alarming development in Latin American drug geographies in the past two decades has been the rise of various Mexican-based drug cartels to positions of such wealth and power that they now threaten the stability of the Mexican state and society as well as the security of Mexico's Central American neighbors (figure 8.3). Many observers see Mexico as entering a phase of "narcoterrorism" and disruption reminiscent of Colombia in the 1980s. The chaos created may bear similarities, but the geographies are distinct. In Colombia's case, most of the narcoterrorism involved one cartel—the Medellín cartel led by Pablo Escobar—and its efforts to counter the Colombian state's (with robust US aid) campaign to dismantle it. Subsequently, Colombia's cocaine industry and commerce became deeply entangled in that country's decades-long multisided civil war, with both leftist guerrilla armies and right-wing paramilitary groups joining in the bonanza of coca cultivation, refining, and distribution. While the various armed political factions and cartels had definable territories, their ultimate goals were not necessarily tied to territorial defense and/or expansion.

In its current stage, the Mexican situation seems to be a simple, if often horrific, deployment and display of violence for territorial control and expansion by the seven or eight main cartels. The cartel territorial domains were originally established by common agreement in the 1980s. Initially they served to protect production sites (cannabis and opium fields, meth labs), promote links with corrupt local officials, and facilitate drug flows. Over time, however, arrests or deaths of cartel leaders, formation of new cartels, and shifting alliances among the cartels have led to territorial instabilities. This in turn has led to a, if not quite Hobbesian, "war of all against all," then multiplying sites of both quotidian and exemplary forms of violence that have become part of the Mexican national landscape. It is estimated that since the Mexican

Figure 8.3. Mexican drug cartel territories.

government declared "war" on the drug cartels in 2006, as many as one hundred thousand persons have died due to drug violence. Another thirty thousand have "gone missing," most presumably casualties of the drug wars, too. Initially most of the victims were cartel combatants or Mexican police killed in circumstances ranging from sequestrations, to assassinations, to pitched battles. Increasingly, however, journalists, politicians, drug enforcement officials, and innocent bystanders have been killed in the wake of the cartels' internecine warfare. More recently, cartel assassins have turned to mass murder. In 2010 and 2011 the Zeta cartel carried out a series of mass murders of bus passengers in Tamaulipas state, mostly Central American migrants en route to the United States. In 2014 forty-three activist students were abducted by drug gang members in Guerrero state and purportedly executed and incinerated.

As the casualties mount, the Mexican drug war's boundaries also threaten to expand. Several cartels have extended their reach into neighboring Guatemala, Belize, Honduras, and El Salvador. They are not only claiming domains within these national spaces but also enlisting both local and transnational gangs such as Salvatrucha as affiliates. Aside from the spread of violence, both extreme/spectacular forms as well as the quotidian varieties involving graft, corruption, sub-lethal brutality, and generalized fear inculcation, their networks are being greatly expanded. In the past decade the Mexican cartels have not only eclipsed the Colombian cartels' former hegemony over the transnational drug trade in the Americas, but they have established territorial footholds and market control in countries and regions far beyond their Mexican/Central American domains. The West Coast cartels, primarily the Sinaloa cartel, have created extensive trading networks in Asia. Initially this was to facilitate the importation of ephedra, the plant source of ephedrine, a precursor of methamphetamine. Later, other circuits of the drug trade were tapped into, including procuring opium and heroin from Burma and Afghanistan. From their eastern bases, the Zetas and Gulf Coast cartel established ties with the Italian Mafia to traffic cocaine in Europe. The Zetas have also expanded aggressively into the Caribbean, especially the Dominican Republic, but also in a number of the Lesser Antilles, and are poised to force their way into Jamaica, with its long established local drug gangs. At the same time the Mexican cartels were forging beachheads in the Caribbean, they were doing the same on the other side of the Atlantic in West Africa. Weak states, official corruption, and easy air and sea access provided multiple locales for establishing transshipment sites for drugs bound for Europe. Vertical economic and horizontal integration and expansion have gone hand in hand to create Latin American networks of global reach with their proximate geographical groundings in Mexico, but with prior origins in the Colombian regional centers of production and distribution. There seems to be scant cause to see these processes and trends reversed in the near term. What does seem certain is that these geographies and the drugs that generate them will continue to be constructed and shaped by historical contexts, regional laws, consumer preferences, and the entrepreneurial drive of an important segment of Latin America's informal economic actors.

Conclusion

From the initial sedentarism of post-Pleistocene settlers, if not earlier, to the hyperconnectivity and mobility of postmodernity, the procurement and/or production, exchange, and consumption of psychoactive drugs in Latin America has been a constant feature of daily life, providing the material substance for much ceremonialism and significant portions of the realm's economic vitality as well. Entire landscapes have been made and remade in the service of sugar, tobacco, coffee, cacao, coca, cannabis, and opium cultivation. Entire local, regional, and national economies have been created and directed by the imperatives of both licit and illicit drug commerce. Entire communities, ethnic groups, and class strata have been brought into being and organized around the production, circulation, and consumption of psychoactive substances. Each of these patterns and processes is reflected in distinct geographies manifested at differing scales—from the bodies of individuals and their households, to localities and regions, to national states and global transactions. In this chapter, I have not attempted to chart the particulars of the drug trade per se. Nor have I mapped the different drugs' distribution areas or trafficking paths. This information is generally available in the extensive literature, both scholarly and popular, on the topics of both licit and illicit drugs in Latin America. I have included a selection of this literature in the references. Despite the extant scholarship with its voluminous coverage on some topics such as sugar or coca and cocaine, the general topic and most of its particulars have barely been explored from the perspective of geographers and geography. It is a wide-open research frontier that awaits both the curious student and the committed scholar.

Key Terms

Atlantic Triangular Trade: Refers to the colonial trade patterns linking North American and European port cities with Caribbean islands and West African entrepôts. African slaves, Caribbean sugar, and North Atlantic rum were the basic commodities, though other agricultural and manufactured goods complemented and completed the circuits. Secondary circulations included tobacco, coffee, and cacao from the circum-Caribbean/Chesapeake region directed to New England and Europe and metal and textile goods from North Atlantic factories to West African sites for slave trades.

drug: Any substance that in small amounts produces significant changes in the body, mind, or both (Weil and Rosen 1993). Foods and poisons also fit this description. Thus, drugs can be defined as agents of body and/or mind change that are primarily neither food or poison, although some drugs such as alcohol can be all three depending on quantity and context of consumption. In addition, drugs here refer to substances not normally consumed for normal or formal medical practice.

Suggested Readings

Courtwright, D. T. *Forces of Habit: Drugs and the Making of the Modern World.* Cambridge, MA: Harvard University Press, 2001.

Goodman, J., P. E. Lovejoy, and A. Sherratt, eds. *Consuming Habits: Drugs in History and Anthropology.* New York: Routledge, 1995.

Mintz, S. W. *Sweetness and Power: The Place of Sugar in Modern History.* New York: Viking, 1985.

Steinberg, M. K., J. J. Hobbs, and K. Mathewson (Eds.). *Dangerous Harvest: Drug Plants and the Transformation of Indigenous Landscapes.* New York: Oxford University Press, 2004.

References

Bagley, B. M., and W. O. Walker III (Eds.). *Drug Trafficking in the Americas.* New Brunswick, NJ: Transaction Publishers, 1994.

Bergmann, J. F. "The Distribution of Cacao Cultivation in Pre-Columbian America." *Annals of the Association of American Geographers* 59 (1969): 85–96.

Booth, M. *Opium: A History.* New York: St. Martin's Press, 1998.

Bradburd, D., and W. Jankowiak. "Drugs, Desire, and European Expansion." In *Drugs, Labor, and Colonial Expansion,* edited by W. Jankowiak and D. Bradburd, 3–29. Tucson: University of Arizona Press, 2003.

Bruman, H. J. *Alcohol in Ancient Mexico.* Salt Lake City: University of Utah Press, 2000.

Coe, S. D., and M. D. Coe. *The True History of Chocolate.* London: Thames and Hudson, 1996.

Corti, C. *A History of Smoking.* London: Bracken Books, 1996.

Courtwright, D. T. *Forces of Habit: Drugs and the Making of the Modern World.* Cambridge, MA: Harvard University Press, 2001.

Dalby, A. *Dangerous Tastes: The Story of Spices.* Berkeley: University of California Press, 2000.

Duvall, C. *Cannabis.* London: Reaktion Books, 2014.

Emboden, W. *Narcotic Plants: Hallucinogens, Stimulants, Inebriants, and Hypnotics: Their Origins and Uses.* London: Studio Vista, 1979.

Furst, P. T. (Ed.). *Flesh of the Gods: The Ritual Use of Hallucinogens.* London: Allen & Unwin, 1972.

Galloway, J. H. *The Sugar Cane Industry: An Historical Geography from Its Origins to 1914.* Cambridge: Cambridge University Press, 1989.

Goode, E. *Marijuana.* New York: Aldine, 1969.

Goodman, J. *Tobacco in History: The Cultures of Dependence.* London: Routledge, 1993.

Goodman, J., P. E. Lovejoy, and A. Sherratt (Eds.). *Consuming Habits: Drugs in History and Anthropology.* New York: Routledge, 1995.

Gootenberg, P. (Ed.). *Cocaine: Global Histories.* London: Routledge, 1999.

Jankowiak, W., and D. Bradburd. *Drugs, Labor, and Colonial Expansion.* Tucson: University of Arizona Press, 2003.

La Barre, W. "Old and New World Narcotics: A Statistical Question and an Ethnological Reply." *Economic Botany* 24 (1970): 73–80.

Lewin, L. *Phantastica: Narcotic and Stimulating Drugs, Their Use and Abuse.* London: Routledge and Kegan Paul, 1964.

Mathewson, K. "Drugs, Moral Geographies, and Indigenous Peoples: Some Initial Mappings and Central Issues." In *Dangerous Harvest: Drug Plants and the Transformation of Indigenous Landscapes*, edited by M. K. Steinberg, J. J. Hobbs, and K. Mathewson, 11–23. New York: Oxford University Press, 2004.

Mintz, S. W. *Sweetness and Power: The Place of Sugar in Modern History.* New York: Viking, 1985.

Mortimer, W. G. *History of Coca: "The Divine Plant" of the Incas.* San Francisco: And/Or Press, 1974. First published 1901.

Murra, J. V. "Rite and Crop in the Inca State." In *Peoples and Cultures of Native South America*, edited by D. R. Gross, 377–89. Garden City, NY: Doubleday, 1973.

Pendergrast, M. *Uncommon Grounds: The History of Coffee and How It Transformed Our World.* New York: Basic Books, 1999.

Perramond, E. P. "Desert Traffic: The Dynamics of the Drug Trade in Northwestern Mexico." In *Dangerous Harvest: Drug Plants and the Transformation of Indigenous Landscapes*, edited by M. K. Steinberg, J. J. Hobbs, and K. Mathewson, 209–17. New York: Oxford University Press, 2004.

Porter, R., and M. Teich (Eds.). *Drugs and Narcotics in History.* Cambridge: Cambridge University Press, 1995.

Reyes, A. "Drug Trafficking and the Guerilla Movement in Colombia." In *Drug Trafficking in the Americas*, edited by B. M. Bagley and W. O. Walker III, 121–30. New Brunswick, NJ: Transaction Publishers, 1994.

Richardson, B. C. *The Caribbean in the Wider World, 1492–1992: A Regional Geography.* Cambridge: Cambridge University Press, 1992.

Rubin, V. (Ed.). *Cannabis and Culture.* The Hague: Mouton, 1975.

Rudgley, R. *Essential Substances: A Cultural History of Intoxicants in Society.* New York: Kodansha America, 1994.

Sauer, C. O. "The Personality of Mexico." *Geographical Review* 31 (1941): 353–64.

Sauer, C. O. *Agricultural Origins and Dispersals.* New York: American Geographical Society, 1952.

Sauer, C. O. *The Early Spanish Main.* Berkeley: University of California Press, 1966.

Sauer, J. *Historical Geography of Crop Plants: A Select Roster.* Boca Raton, FL: Lewis Publishers, 1993.

Schivelbush, W. *Tastes of Paradise: A Social History of Spices, Stimulants, and Intoxicants.* New York: Pantheon, 1992.

Scott, P. D., and J. Marshall. *Cocaine Politics: Drugs Armies, and the CIA in Central America.* Berkeley: University of California Press, 1991.

Smith, P. H. (Ed.). *Drug Policy in the Americas.* Boulder, CO: Westview Press, 1992.

Steinberg, M. K., J. J. Hobbs, and K. Mathewson (Eds.). *Dangerous Harvest: Drug Plants and the Transformation of Indigenous Landscapes.* New York: Oxford University Press, 2004.

Steinberg, M. K., and K. Mathewson. "Landscapes of Drugs and War: Intersections of Political Ecology and Global Conflict." In *The Geography of War and Peace*, 242–58. Oxford: Oxford University Press, 2005.

Walker, W. O., III (Ed.). *Drugs in the Western Hemisphere: An Odyssey of Cultures in Conflict.* Wilmington, DE: Scholarly Resources, 1996.

Wallerstein, I. *The Modern World-System: Capitalist Agriculture and the Origins of the World-Economy in the Sixteenth Century.* New York: Academic Press, 1974.

Watts, D. *The West Indies: Patterns of Development, Culture and Environmental Change since 1492.* Cambridge: Cambridge University Press, 1987.

Weil, A., and W. Rosen. *From Chocolate to Morphine: Everything You Need to Know about Mind-Altering Drugs.* New York: Houghton Mifflin Company, 1993.

Williams, R. G. *States and Social Evolution: Coffee and the Rise of National Governments in Central America.* Chapel Hill: University of North Carolina Press, 1994.

Wolf, E. R. *Europe and the People without History.* Berkeley: University of California Press, 1982.

Chapter 9

Nongovernmental Organizations

Scale, Society, and Environment

J. Christopher Brown

THIS CHAPTER IS ABOUT NGOs, short for "nongovernmental organizations," in Latin America. NGOs are a whole range of organizations, from an agricultural cooperative of family farmers similar to what one would find in Kansas, to a not-for-profit urban health clinic similar to what one would find in Los Angeles, to a group of environmentalists similar to what one would find lobbying Congress in Washington, D.C. These organizations are ordinary to many of us in the United States. In Latin America, however, they have grown in number and importance only over the last few decades. Understanding NGOs in Latin America, and NGOs throughout the world for that matter, is important because they signal some major societal and even environmental changes in the region, which is why so many scholars study and track them.

Understanding the growth of NGOs and their importance in society must involve comprehension of international political, economic, and even environmental events over the last few decades. One major author has called the worldwide phenomenon of NGO growth and prominence an associational revolution (Salamon 1994, 2010). "Revolutionary" means something that is new and that challenges what existed before. Up until the advent of NGO growth and influence, most people around the world tended to rely on two major institutions to organize, to get things done, and to provide for the needs of themselves and their communities. Those institutions were the market (the economy) and the state (governments). NGOs, then, are institutions that have entered the stage as both alternatives to, and challengers of, the predominance of the market and the state in society.

The "associational" part of this revolution refers to the kind of human organization that NGOs represent. The dominant institutions of the market and the state are often talked about as fairly anonymous entities. Ordinary people often view these institutions as impersonal, indifferent, cold, even abusive. It is no wonder why, considering the market is often likened to an invisible hand, and considering many in charge of government in Latin America have often abused their power to the detriment of people and the environment. NGOs, then, are novel associations of people, often from the lower and middle classes (but not always!), who work outside the state and market to provide the things that people need.

How significant is this associational revolution, and what general types of associations make up this revolution in Latin America in particular? One way to express the global significance of the revolution is to take note of how powerful international organizations like the United

Nations, the World Bank, or the EU, all-important forces in development, interact with NGOs. All these organizations now often channel funds through NGOs to carry out development projects. For example, between 1990 and 1994, the EU increased greatly the amount of foreign aid it gives through NGOs, from 47 to 67 percent of total aid (*The Economist* 2000). More than 70 percent of World Bank–supported projects approved in 1999 involved NGOs in some way (World Bank 2000). More recently, the Organization for Economic Cooperation and Development reported that foreign aid—from the twenty-nine countries that make up OECD's Development Assistance Committee—channeled to and through NGOs increased from $14.5 billion in 2008 to $19.5 billion in 2011 (OECD 2013).[1]

Another indication of the importance of the associational revolution is the fact that many governments are now increasingly concerned about the power that NGOs have in impacting domestic politics and threatening sovereignty. For decades, many governments have feared that international funding of local NGOs represents undue influence within countries. Even democratically elected governments around the world have worked to counteract the associational revolution by passing laws that restrict NGOs in some way. In 1990, less than 10 percent of countries around the world had laws that restricted the work of NGOs. By 2012, 44 percent of countries had such laws (Dupuy et al. 2014). These laws are often designed to limit the types of NGOs that can form and the amount of funds they can receive from international sources. In what appears a never-ending arms race, the United Nations and other global entities like the World Bank have worked to counteract these restrictions by creating specific programs that encourage governments to make it easier for NGOs to work within their borders in partnerships to combat poverty, improve the environment, serve the needs of refugees, and many other efforts related to securing human rights (Reiman 2006).

NGOs and Alphabet Soup

The way NGOs have been classified has changed greatly over the years. In the 1980s, most people thought of NGOs as private, tax-exempt, nonprofit agencies that worked to provide overseas relief and development services. Such a view completely ignores NGO activity in the developing world. Researchers also used the term "PVO" (private voluntary organizations) and began to include organizations based in the developing world that served their own communities. As the associational revolution began to take hold, researchers began using the term "NPO" (nonprofit organization) and used it interchangeably with NGO. By the early 1990s, researchers Salamon and Anheier (1999) theorized that an organization's NPO status could be determined by considering characteristics such as legal status, origin of income, role or function, and structural/operational characteristics. Salamon and Anheier eventually decided that the structural/operational characteristics of NPOs were the most useful in classifying them, and they came up with five major features that make NPOs stand out from other forms of human organization. First, NPOs are formal organizations—they are not based solely on family or kinship ties between people or geographic proximity. There is some officially stated reason why they exist, explanation of who can become members, and so forth. Second, they are private, as opposed to government-sponsored, organizations. Third, they do not operate with the goal of making profits. Fourth, they are autonomous. And fifth, they are voluntary. Even as others started treating NPOs and NGOs as synonymous, Salamon and Anheier stuck to their definition of NPOs because they felt that NGOs were mainly groups whose function was to deal with social and economic development issues.

Other researchers felt that NGOs should be categorized by the relationship they have with civil society and the state in general. This was especially important to researchers seeking to understand the role the organizations played in checking the power of what were, at times, brutal authoritarian regimes. In some cases, NGOs grew out of broader social movements that first defined themselves as they protested the policies of authoritarian governments of the 1960s and 1970s in Latin America and elsewhere (see chapter 10). With respect to the question of the relationship to the state, the picture of what is or is not an NGO is complicated further. That is because states have often involved themselves in NGO activity by creating the NGOs themselves (GONGOs, or government-organized NGOs). The state's strategy here is as follows: state officials realize that more and more foreign aid is being channeled through NGOs, and so to try to gain control over this significant amount of capital, state governments form their own NGOs.

By now it should be clear that no definition of NGOs is likely to satisfy everyone. One does need to settle on a definition, though, so following the lead of a number of scholars, this chapter uses an NGO definition based on structural/organizational terms that includes organizations that are autonomous, private, not for profit, and designed to improve the quality of life for people who are economically or politically disadvantaged or otherwise vulnerable; thus we are leaving out NPOs that might have some type of business/professional focus or NPOs that serve the interests of people in the upper classes of society. This definition, however, is blurred in the second case study of this chapter, which shows how business-oriented NPOs worked with international environmental NGOs to stem deforestation in Brazil.

The practice of trying to classify NGOs is complicated and may seem more geared toward inventing "alphabet soups" of confusing new acronyms that in the end do little to get to the bottom of what NGOs really are (Vakil 1997). If this is all so confusing and involves splitting hairs, then why go through the process of deciding what is or is not an NGO? One reason is simply to recognize the incredible diversity of NGOs around the world. Another is that only by coming up with some type of NGO classification scheme can researchers make within-country and cross-country comparisons in studies on the associational revolution. Finally, if a standard classification of NGOs were developed, it might help NGOs network with similar groups around the world, helping each other by sharing experiences and expertise.

NGOs and the Politics of Scale

NGOs form an extremely diverse set of human organizational forms. One way to understand NGOs is to classify them in terms of the scale of their organization. We commonly use the word "scale" to mean the size or reach of an operation. Calling something large- or small-scale says something about, for example, how many people, how much capital, or how much technology is involved in a given human activity. In common usage, it appears that such language also contains information about the type of people involved in a given human activity. "Small-scale" implies the "little guy," the worker, the family farmer, the members of the family business, and often in the developing world the peasant and the indigenous person—people often viewed as being harmed by globalization. "Large-scale" implies "big-timers," capitalists, big-businessmen, corporations, and rich people—people often viewed as being helped by globalization.

Geographer Mark Purcell and I have argued elsewhere that there are problems with such tendencies to associate certain scales of organization with certain activities and certain people or actors (Brown and Purcell 2005; Purcell and Brown 2005). Such thinking lacks an understanding of two important conclusions from a literature that has developed over the past few decades largely within political economic studies of the urban landscape. As a whole, the literature is given the name "the politics of scale," and its first main finding, simply stated, is that scale is socially constructed. What this means is that people produce scales of human organization as part of their struggle for social and political power in a given situation. An organization of peasants from a particular area might create a *local*-scale organization in order to make demands from the municipal government for better roads, for example. In this sense, the scale of the organization is more a part of a strategy to achieve a goal than anything else. Thus, the scale itself does not lead to a given human or environmental outcome, such as better roads. Rather, it is the increased power of the people—working at a particular scale of organization with a particular agenda—that leads to an outcome, namely, better roads.

Another main finding of the politics of scale literature is that scales are highly dynamic. Recall that people use scale to gain power of some sort. So, as people constantly shift strategies to jockey for power, various scales of human organization are constantly being created, deployed, and dismantled in order to achieve that power. Thus, there is nothing essentially good or bad about any scale of human organization. Scales of organization themselves do not have any predetermined effect on the outcome of any human activity. For example, while we may tend to think that small-scale, family farmers take better care of their land from an environmental standpoint than, say, a large-scale corporate farm, it is not the scale of the organization of the farm that creates the good or bad effect of farming. Rather, the social or environmental outcomes of farming depend on the goals and practices of the people in charge of the farming operation.

Still, many people tend to believe that small-scale, or "local"-organized, human activities are preferable to large-scale or more "global"-organized activities. With respect to Latin Americans, part of that tendency comes from experiences with the spectacular failure of Latin American development programs in the 1970s–1980s that were supposed to make life better for the poor while improving the condition of the environment. There will be more on this later, but suffice it to say that those programs were largely organized as extremely large-scale projects, the vision and financing for which came from centralized, often authoritarian national governments and globally organized financial institutions like the World Bank. If such large-scale projects were so damaging, then conventional wisdom dictated that smaller-scale, decentralized development projects would correct those problems. Local people would be in more control over the development money and decisions that affect their lives.

Taken as a whole, this discussion about scale is a useful guide for a discussion of NGOs in Latin America and how they organize. It also highlights the way people use scale as a tool to challenge the power of other people organized at similar or different scales. Finally, the theory directs us to be aware of romanticizing or giving essential qualities to NGOs in Latin America simply because they are often organized at smaller scales than international corporations and national governments. Rather than expecting to see particular outcomes from the actions of these organizations, the goal is to investigate links between the agendas of NGOs and the outcomes of pursuing those agendas.

The Social and Environmental Context of the Associational Revolution

The associational revolution arose within a context of past political, economic, cultural, and environmental events both in Latin American countries and internationally. The development of NGOs in Latin America can be told as a story of a slowly emerging separate sector in society that arguably was always present in society ever since pre-Columbian times. Then, as the

Catholic church and the modern state impacted those societies with their own forms of human organization, this sector of society would gradually differentiate itself into the more defined sector that it is today. All societies develop forms of human organization that step in and help people in some way when other, often more formal, institutions fail. Before the modern state and the modern market existed, people in Latin America and elsewhere had their own forms of societal and cultural institutions to rely on. Authors who have contributed to Salamon and Anheier's studies on the nonprofit sector in Latin America all mention pre-Columbian societal forms as an important contributor to what would eventually become known as part of the nonprofit sector and NGOs. For example, a principle known today as "Andean reciprocity" was the basis of an organizational system ensuring that hunger and misery among less advantaged groups were addressed through redistribution of excess production from more fortunate groups. This organization was based on kinship ties among different groups of people.

The next important point in this history is the introduction of colonial forms of human organization that would build on pre-Columbian forms. Most importantly, colonization brought the church and its ideals of charity and assistance to the poor. Colonial governments gave the church broad powers for hundreds of years to establish schools, hospitals, asylums, and other "charitable" organizations. The strong relationship between the colonial state and the church would not last, however, and by the 1800s and the independence of Latin American countries from European power, governments wrested from the church much of the power it had in society (see chapter 2). It was during this period that the church independently continued its works by establishing "brotherhoods" and "sisterhoods," private charitable organizations among the elite, which provided assistance to the needy.

Moving into the twentieth century, Latin American societies and economies began to modernize, and with these changes, new groups in civil society began to organize people in much greater numbers than ever before. In Latin America's growing cities and in the countryside, labor unions and peasant groups organized to demand better working and living conditions. Such demands put the state in a difficult political position. It could meet those demands with the power it had to legislate changes to benefit the lower classes. But if it did this, it would alienate the powerful landed elite and emerging entrepreneurial, urban classes that helped keep in power those individuals who controlled government. In some cases, when demands were not met, revolution resulted. In others, military dictatorships took over the state in order to maintain order. In yet other cases, populist governments attempted to please both the elite and the poor by supporting the development of the civil society sector in a way that allowed government to control the demands such groups could make on the state and on the elite. From the Cold War through the early to mid-1980s, many Latin American countries, often with material and ideological support from the US government, were ruled by military dictatorships that brutally repressed any type of non–state-sponsored organizations. Universities, unions, political parties, and other organizations were no longer avenues for people to attempt to work toward change.

During the time of the authoritarian regimes, the only non–state-sponsored organization that continued to develop its works among underprivileged classes was the Catholic church. After having been aligned so often with the interests of the elite and state in Latin America, many in the Catholic church spurred a new movement in the 1960s and 1970s called "liberation theology." This had a profound impact on the subsequent development of NGOs in Latin America because, for the first time, the church worked to organize people outside of the direct control of Rome and even of the diocese and local churches. Liberation theology was a movement to use the teachings of Christ and the Bible to motivate the poor and oppressed of Latin America to rise up, organize, and address their need for basic human rights and a more secure livelihood. Though it was an overarching ideology, it encouraged decentralized action to improve peoples' lives. The ideology itself encouraged local groups, known as Christian Base Communities, to address their problems in their own particular way. Christian Base Communities of that era formed the roots of many of today's local NGOs in Latin America.

Then the failure of massive development projects in the 1980s and 1990s, and democratization of governments in Latin America, all helped lead to the growth of NGOs and the rise of their importance in development. Numerous international government-level meetings had been held beginning in the 1970s to assess the state of the world and proposals for its improvement. Amid the problems of acid rain, global warming, holes in the ozone layer, and extinction crises wherever tropical forests were falling, it became very clear that the forces of "modern" development were actually causing many social and environmental problems. The very scale and intensity of development projects like dam building and agricultural colonization in rainforests sparked an unprecedented campaign by concerned citizens around the world to stop the resulting environmental destruction. One of the most well-publicized and galvanizing development failures was that of a series of colonization projects that took place in the Brazilian Amazon during Brazil's military dictatorship in the 1970s and 1980s. Designed to bring the distant Amazon into the national economic sphere, development projects involving billions of dollars constructed roads through the jungle and settled peasant farmers from more densely populated regions. Tax incentives given to large companies resulted in conversion of enormous areas of rainforest land into cattle ranches. Illegal gold mining, logging, and occupation of indigenous lands resulted as well, leading to high deforestation rates and predictions that the Amazon forest would be destroyed by the year 2000. Civil society organizations (CSOs or nascent NGOs) formed in response to this destruction. For example, rubber tappers of the Amazon began to organize unions to demand their forestlands be protected from development. Their leader, Chico Mendes, was assassinated by cattle ranchers who were threatened by Mendes's successful organizing efforts and the great amount of attention he was drawing frvom Brazilian domestic and international environmental and human rights NGOs.

Democratization in Latin America and around the world in the 1980s and 1990s also opened the political space needed for the participation of ordinary citizens in carrying out processes like development. This democratization gave increased legitimacy to an organized civil society making demands on government, as Chico Mendes had done in Brazil. The problem was that these demands were being made when the state had little revenue to meet those demands. Latin America was in the midst of a serious debt crisis, a situation resulting from the fact that the governments of the past, mostly authoritarian, had borrowed so much money to fund development programs, like the Amazonian development projects, that newly formed democracies were forced to pay out huge percentages of the country's gross domestic product merely to pay the interest on loans. If countries were to spend money to improve the lives of citizens, they would have to borrow more money. Here, the interests of multilateral agencies like the World Bank, the IMF, and governments converged. States needed money, and lending agencies like the World Bank needed a way to increase their legitimacy as organizations concerned about helping the poor directly in a socially and environmentally sound way. A new ideology in development helped provide the final circumstance in Latin America that would help propel NGOs to their level of prominence in society today: neoliberalism (see chapter 3).

The rise of neoliberalism in development theory and policy has had tremendous implications for the formation and strengthening of NGOs. Amid the economic recession and debt crisis of the early 1980s, it was clear to policymakers that the state-directed import substitution industrialization model of development had failed. The state was also seen as an inefficient institution that could not be relied on to raise the capital needed to improve society. As a result, the World Bank and the IMF forced indebted countries wanting to borrow more money to implement structural adjustment programs. These programs embraced a trimmed-down state, privatized industries and services, and established free markets to contribute toward export-oriented economic growth that would generate the income required to pay off debt. Many indebted Third World nations adopted these strategies by the end of the 1980s. With state expenditures slashed, even less money remained in state coffers for social, health, and environmental programs. Some form of human organization had to fill the gap left by the relative weakening of the state and entrance of the logic of global market capitalism to Latin America. NGOs would enter the stage as local, regional, national, and international forms of human organization recognized by the state and the market as independent players that had to be given some level of consideration in development and in efforts to protect the environment.

NGOs, Conservation, and Development in the Brazilian Amazon Part I: Rondônia

As explained in the earlier discussion about the context of the development of the associational revolution in Latin America, the rise of NGOs in the 1980s and 1990s in countries like Brazil had much to do with the democratization of politics, and it was in part a response to the spectacular human and environmental disaster of internationally funded megadevelopment efforts in regions like the Brazilian Amazon. The state of Rondônia, Brazil, in the southwest Brazilian Amazon (figure 9.1), was a place in the Amazon where the settlement of thousands of families

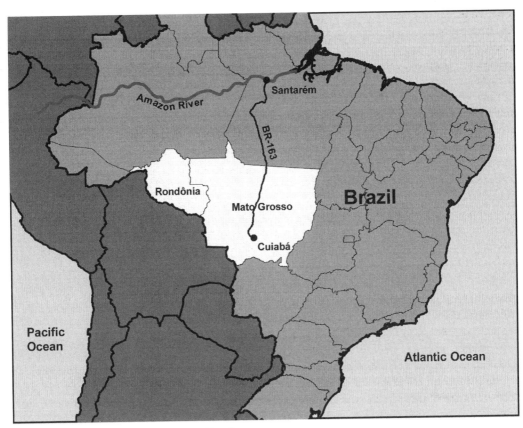

Figure 9.1. Rondonia and Matto Grosso, Brazil.

and the construction of a major dam and roads all led to high deforestation rates, invasion of the lands of indigenous peoples and rubber tappers, and disease suffered by settlers. Development in Rondônia even led some observers to wonder if the entire Amazon would be destroyed by the year 2000. The World Bank, the institution that was a major financier of the development in Rondônia, came under enormous pressure from major international and national-level environmental NGOs in the United States and Europe (like the World Wildlife Fund, the Environmental Defense Fund, and the Sierra Club) to change its development policies. These NGOs made contact with local NGOs in the Amazon to gather information about human and environmental abuses in the development projects and to join in the campaign against the World Bank. Such collaboration was a classic example of what is called "jumping scale," because powerful NGOs in the United States and Europe (organized internationally) teamed up with local NGOs in the Amazon ("jumping" the Brazilian national scale) to pressure the World Bank.

The World Bank responded by announcing a new development project for the state of Rondônia that was designed in large part to promote economic activities among settlers, rubber tappers, and indigenous groups in a way that would help lead to forest conservation. The project was called PLANAFLORO (Plan Agropecuario y Forestal de Rondônia), and it introduced an entirely new way of delivering development assistance: it granted money directly to local NGOs who were then responsible for carrying out development projects in their own communities. This decentralization of development was a major rescaling of the control over development. Much of the rhetoric supporting the plan told the now-familiar story that because local NGOs are most familiar with the social and ecological conditions of their own communities, development would proceed best if the NGOs themselves controlled the process. It is true that the World Bank and the Brazilian national government (very centralized institutions) made major mistakes in how they attempted to develop Rondônia. But the politics of scale literature warns us that simply rescaling development, in this case by decentralizing, does not in and of itself create a better situation for people and the environment. Let's review the environmental and political complexity of what followed as PLANAFLORO was implemented.

The World Bank charged the Rondonian state government with developing a process to distribute millions of dollars in grants to NGOs across the state. The majority of projects ended up funding NGOs representing small-farmer associations and cooperatives; these NGOs most often proposed to develop alternative production activities among their members in a way that led to conservation of tropical forests. Common activities like cattle ranching and the cultivation of coffee and cacao were seen as having little economic future, and cattle ranching, especially, had led to Rondônia's high deforestation rates. So, the cultivation of native fruit and palm trees, fish farming, and beekeeping became some of the most commonly proposed activities. Beekeeping, in particular, was promoted as contributing to productive conservation. Productive conservation is the idea that people need to have an economic incentive to protect forests, so if people can market forest products (things that require the maintenance of forests), they will want to protect forests. Unfortunately, beekeeping as practiced in the projects was not productive conservation. Even though bees are "natural," and though they simply take nectar from flowers to make their honey, the bees used in the development projects were from the species *Apis mellifera*, the honeybee (in this case, the Africanized "killer" bee). These bees do not require forests to survive; they are not even native to the Amazon or to any humid tropical forest. These bees produced a lot of honey in Rondônia *because* of excessive deforestation and the resulting process of ecological succession on abandoned fields. Such environments contain lots of weedy flowers that make excellent bee forage. Now, beekeeping did not *cause* any more deforestation in Rondônia, but NGOs actively promoted it as productive conservation.

In contrast to the view of local NGOs and their members as virtuous ecological stewards, this showed that either NGO leaders and members were not being truthful when promoting their programs or they really were not aware of the ecological conditions of the honey production system itself (Brown 2001).

Through the 1990s, when the NGOs were implementing their PLANAFLORO-funded development projects, I was always concerned that when the development funds dried up, so might the NGOs themselves. I sensed that some NGOs were focusing more and more on how to get additional grant funding (based on the idea of productive conservation) than they were on making their financial operations and the production systems of their clients more sustainable in the long run. Sadly, the farmers' association I worked with closely when I lived in Rondônia in the 1990s closed its doors several years ago for a number of reasons, including political infighting among members, mismanagement and graft of funds, and inability to deliver on contracts made with buyers. Some of the original beekeepers still practice their craft, selling honey to neighbors and at farmers' markets, but the idea of having an organization that builds new production systems that strengthen the economy, conserve forest, and give voice to the collective concerns of now second- and third-generation settlers appears to have been lost along the way. A whole set of research is waiting to be done to see what became of the hundreds of NGOs that received decentralized development assistance and whether PLANAFLORO had measurable, positive social and environmental impacts.

NGOs, Conservation, and Development in the Brazilian Amazon Part II: Mato Grosso

The state of Mato Grosso is to the east and south of Rondônia (figure 9.1). It was also a target of decentralized development funding in the 1990s with its own World Bank–funded project, but I want to use very recent events to show what impact international NGOs in particular are having there related to important economic activity and forest conservation. Mato Grosso has become one of the world's newest and important "breadbaskets" (*The Economist* 2010). The development of highly mechanized, high-input, high-output agriculture there over the last twenty years has helped make Brazil a world agricultural superpower, and one of the main commodities playing a major role in this transformation is soybeans (see chapter 7). As soybean cultivation spread from Brazil's south into areas farther north, into Brazil's vast savanna, or *cerrado*, and into areas of humid tropical forest, international NGOs like Greenpeace and the Nature Conservancy have become involved in developing ways to ensure that soybean cultivation does not threaten humid tropical forest. In addition to being an area of major cropland expansion, Mato Grosso has become a target of international NGO action for a number of reasons. Blairo Maggi, once governor of Mato Grosso, is the world's largest soybean producer, and he has long pushed for the paving of a highway through his state that would allow soybeans to be transported north to ports along the Amazon River where they could be exported directly to foreign buyers in Europe and Asia. Such a route would bring greater profits to soybean farmers in Mato Grosso, who have long been forced to transport their soybeans across a much more costly overland route on highways from Mato Grosso to ports in southern Brazil. Other issues have made agricultural expansion very controversial in Mato Grosso. Soybean producers have been prosecuted for enslaving rural workers on soybean plantations, and Minnesota-based Cargill, which built a soybean port facility on the Amazon River in the town of Santarém for the purpose of exporting soybeans from Mato Grosso, was accused of building its port without following environmental regulations.

All of these issues came to light in a publication produced by Greenpeace, *Eating Up the Amazon* (Greenpeace International 2006). The publication documented social and environmental abuses related to soybean production in the state, and it was accompanied by a sensational protest orchestrated by Greenpeace where the group attempted to blockade the Cargill port in Santarém. Soon after the Greenpeace action, major soybean processing firm associations (nonprofit business-oriented NGOs or NPOs) declared a moratorium on the purchase of soybeans produced on land deforested after July 2006. The moratorium is still in force as of this writing in 2015, and the monitoring of the moratorium has shown that deforestation for the purposes of planting soybeans has decreased to negligible levels.

This story tells us a number of things about NGOs. First of all, it shows that NGOs at the international scale can have a major impact on the actions of local people like soybean farmers who make decisions each year about what and where to plant their crops. Greenpeace marshaled an international scale to put the pressure on the soy purchasers and processors to declare the moratorium, and NGOs like the Nature Conservancy are working with municipal governments and local farmer organizations to develop the kind of mapping and GIS (geographic information system) techniques needed to track the spatial extent of agricultural production, to comply with state and federal environmental regulations, and to comply with new rules like the moratorium. It appears that local and regional farmer NGOs have not been major participants in the planning and execution of the moratorium, so here is a case where international-level NGOs and business-oriented NGOs (or nonprofits) have taken the lead in addressing environmental concerns.

The moratorium also shows that NGOs of different backgrounds and ideals can work together to reach agreements that affect the decisions made by farmers. Given the controversy surrounding soybean production in the Amazon, who would have ever imagined that Greenpeace and the major agricultural industries they were after would end up having their names side by side as official signatories to the moratorium? It also bears mentioning that some observers praise the moratorium as an example of the good that neoliberalism can do for the environment. These observers would say that these private NGOs have done a much more efficient job than any national government would in regulating the environmental impact of farming in the Amazon. It is beyond the scope of this chapter to comment in depth on such views, but suffice it to say that the national government has not been entirely absent from the processes involved in the moratorium (Brown and Koeppe 2013). As just one example, much of the expertise required to monitor the moratorium comes from Brazilian national government agencies specializing in the use of satellites to remotely monitor agricultural activity.

Conclusion

The stories above illustrate the diversity of NGOs, the projects they are involved with, the interests they represent, and the scale at which NGOs can organize themselves to accomplish particular goals. Some observers who focus mainly on NGOs the size of small-farmer organizations in Rondônia, or other economically disadvantaged groups, might argue that Greenpeace and major agricultural trade groups should not even be discussed together in a chapter on NGOs. While it is not always clear what is and what is not considered an NGO, NGOs tend to be institutions that work outside the two dominant institutions that have organized people's lives in recent history, the state and the market. NGOs in Latin America have their roots in pre-Columbian civilizations, before the modern state and market were ever in existence (though they certainly were not called NGOs back then!), and they have evolved and will continue to evolve, as NGOs both create and react to changes in political economic circumstances. NGOs are not always locally organized groups of people, nor are they always large, regional, national, or international groups. That's where scale comes in. People will organize themselves at whatever scale necessary, even a combination of local and global scales, to accomplish their goals and projects. NGOs, as much as state bureaucracies/policies and the market, are exceedingly important institutions in our world today. How they respond to today's human and environmental challenges will have a major impact on how ordinary citizens treat each other and the environment in an age of globalization.

Key Terms

associational revolution: The ongoing process of proliferation and influence of NGOs in development policy and in the delivery of services to particular groups and communities of people.

NGOs (nongovernmental organizations): This term often refers to novel associations of people who work together to provide for their own needs and to meet their own goals, outside of what the market and/or state provide alone.

politics of scale: The recognition that different scales of organization (local, national, international, and so on) do not produce a given result by themselves but rather are produced and constructed by people pursuing particular agendas.

Acknowledgments

My research over the years in Brazil has been supported by grants from Fulbright, the Inter-American Foundation, the Centers of Latin American Studies at the University of Kansas and UCLA, and the National Science Foundation. I am also grateful to all the NGO leaders and members, scholars and government officials, and friends in Brazil who have helped me in my research over the years. Thanks as well to all my graduate students and my coauthors who have helped me make sense of the dynamics of civil society in Brazil. Thanks to Chris Bishop for assembling the map.

Note

1. The OECD identifies NGOs as CSOs (Civil Society Organizations). More about this issue of what to call NGOs and what they are in the next section.

Suggested Websites

Johns Hopkins Center for Civil Society Studies conducts numerous ongoing research projects on the nonprofit sector around the world. Their publications and reports can be browsed at http://ccss.jhu.edu/.
World Bank reports and publications contain a wealth of information on bank involvement with NGOs and civil society. You can browse for publications from the Bank's main page at www.worldbank.org/.
The North American Congress on Latin America publishes articles dealing with a wide variety of political, economic, and ecological issues in Latin America. You can browse through articles and issues at their website at www.nacla.org.

The Organization for Economic Cooperation and Development has extensive data on foreign aid that can be accessed at https://data.oecd.org/.

References and Suggested Readings

Agnew, J. "The Territorial Trap: The Geographical Assumptions of International Relations Theory." *Review of International Political Economy* 1, no. 1 (1994): 53–80.

Avelino, G., D. S. Brown, and W. Hunter. "The Effects of Capital Mobility, Trade Openness, and Democracy on Social Spending in Latin America, 1980–1999." *American Journal of Political Science* 49, no. 3 (2005): 625–41.

Brown, J. C. "Responding to Deforestation: Productive Conservation, the World Bank, and Beekeeping in Rondonia, Brazil." *Professional Geographer* 53, no. 1 (2001): 106–18.

Brown, J. C., and M. Koeppe. "Debates in the Environmentalist Community: The Soy Moratorium and the Construction of Illegal Soybeans in the Brazilian Amazon." In *Environment and the Law in Amazonia: A Plurilateral Encounter*, edited by James M. Cooper and Christine Hunefeldt, 110–26. Sussex: Sussex Academic Press, 2013.

Brown, J. C., and M. Purcell. "There's Nothing Inherent about Scale: Political Ecology, the Local Trap, and the Politics of Development in the Brazilian Amazon." *Geoforum* 36, no. 5 (2005): 607–24.

Davies, T. R. "The Rise and Fall of Transnational Society: The Evolution of International Non-Governmental Organization Since 1839." Working Papers on Transnational Politics. London: City University of London, 2008.

Devine, J. "NGOs, Politics and Grassroots Mobilisation." *Journal of South Asian Development* 1, no. 1 (2006): 77–99.

Dupuy, Kendra E., James Ron, and Aseem Prakash. "Who Survived? Ethiopia's Regulatory Crackdown on Foreign-Funded NGOs." *Review of International Political Economy* (2014): 1–38.

Economist, The. "Sins of the Secular Missionaries." January 27, 2000.

———. "Brazilian Agriculture: The Miracle of the Cerrado." August 26, 2010.

Greenpeace International. *Eating Up the Amazon.* 2006. http://www.greenpeace.org/usa/Global/usa/report/2010/2/eating-up-the-amazon.pdf

Hearn, J. "African NGOs: The New Compradors?" *Development and Change* 38, no. 6 (2007): 1095–110.

Keck, M. E., and K. Sikkink. *Activists beyond Borders: Advocacy Networks in International Politics.* Ithaca, NY: Cornell University Press, 1998.

OECD. *Aid at a Glance. Flows of Official Development Assistance to and through Civil Society Organisations in 2011.* (2013). http://www.oecd.org/dac/peer-reviews/Aid%20for%20CSOs%20Final%20for%20WEB.pdf

Purcell, M., and J. C. Brown. "Against the Local Trap: Scale and the Study of Environment and Development." *Progress in Development Studies* 5, no. 4 (2005): 279–97.

Reimann, K. D. "A View from the Top: International Politics, Norms and the Worldwide Growth of NGOs." *International Studies Quarterly* 50, no. 1 (2006): 45–68.

Salamon, L. M. "The Rise of the Nonprofit Sector." *Foreign Affairs*, July/August 1994, 109–22.

———. "Putting the Civil Society Sector on the Economic Map of the World." *Annals of Public and Cooperative Economics* 81, no. 2 (2010): 167–210.

Salamon, L. M., and H. K. Anheier. *The Emerging Sector Revisited.* Baltimore: Johns Hopkins Center for Civil Society Studies, 1999.

Salamon, L. M., H. K. Anheier, R. List, S. Toepler, and S. Wojciech Sokolowski and Associates. *Global Civil Society: Dimensions of the Nonprofit Sector.* Baltimore: Johns Hopkins Center for Civil Society Studies, 1999.

Vakil, A. C. "Confronting the Classification Problem: Toward a Taxonomy of NGOs." *World Development* 25, no. 12 (1997): 2057–70.

World Bank. *The World Bank, NGOs and Civil Society.* Washington, DC: World Bank Group, 2000.

Chapter 10

Latin American Social Movements

Places, Scales, and Networks of Action

Fernando J. Bosco

FIFTEEN YEARS INTO the twenty-first century, social movements in Latin America continue a long tradition of organizing for social change. Latin America's civil society is dynamic and in a constant state of mobilization, with diverse groups such as human rights and student activists, poor people's and peasant movements, and different ethnic, racial, and cultural minorities challenging the institutions of the nation-state and making claims for economic gains, land and resources redistribution, and cultural and political recognition. This chapter provides an overview of such contemporary Latin American social movements. Though it is not possible to cover in detail all of the social movements in the region, the discussion in this chapter is informed by making reference to practices of some contemporary social movements in Latin America. These include human rights activities in Argentina, El Salvador, and Guatemala; the students' movements and uprisings in Chile, the movements of urban unemployed people in Argentina; the movements of peasants, small landholders and/or rural landless people in Brazil, Bolivia, and Chile; and the indigenous movements of people seeking economic and political recognition in Bolivia, Colombia, Guatemala, Ecuador, and Mexico, as well as several other groups seeking cultural gains and expanded citizenship rights in the largest urban areas in Latin America (table 10.1).

This chapter specifically describes many of the mobilization strategies of activists. "Mobilization" refers to how social movements come and stay together, how social movements organize their activities and their strategies for recognition and visibility, and how social movements connect with each other to build coalitions and networks across space-time. The focus of this chapter is also on the *geographies* of social movements in Latin America. Specific places (cities, neighborhoods, public spaces in cities such as streets and plazas) and events occurring at different geographic scales (local, regional, national, and transnational) play a crucial role in the mobilization of Latin American social movements. Thinking explicitly about place and scale helps us understand the difference that thinking geographically makes in the understanding of social movements, which are often interpreted and analyzed in nongeographic ways. Through some examples of the mobilization practices of the social movements that appear in table 10.1, this chapter works as an analytical tool to help interpret collective action in Latin America from a geographic perspective. The material provided in this chapter complements the other discussions of activism presented in chapters 9 and 11. Together, these chapters provide an overview of the political geographies of civil society in Latin America.

Table 10.1. Some Latin American Social Movements and Their Organizations

Social Movement	Organizations	Country
Indigenous people and peasants	*Ejército Zapatista de Liberación Nacional* http://enlacezapatista.ezln.org.mx	Mexico
	Confederación de las Nacionalidades Indígenas del Ecuador (CONAIE) http://conaie.nativeweb.org	Ecuador
	Confederación de Pueblos Indígenas de Bolivia (CIDOB) http://www.cidob-bo.org	Bolivia
	Coordinación de Organizaciones del Pueblo Maya de Guatemala (COPMG)	Guatemala
	Asociación Nacional de Mujeres Rurales e Indígenas (ANAMURI) http://www.anamuri.cl	Chile
Poor and landless people	*Movimento dos Trabalhadores Rurais Sem Terra (MST)* http://mstbrazil.org	Brazil
	Movimiento Sin Tierra Bolivia (MST) http://mstbolivia.blogspot.com	Bolivia
Relatives of victims of human rights abuses	*Asociación Madres de Plaza de Mayo* http://madres.org/ *Madres de Plaza de Mayo Línea Fundadora* http://www.madresfundadoras.blogspot.com.ar *HIJOS* http://www.hijos-capital.org.ar	Argentina
	Comite de Madres Mons. Romero (CoMadres) http://www.comadres.org/	El Salvador
	HIJOS Guatemala http://hijosguate.blogspot.com	Guatemala

Defining and Contextualizing Latin American Social Movements

As several of the chapters in this volume demonstrate, Latin America as a whole continues to experience economic and social tensions between the included and the excluded, that is, between people who can regularly participate in the formal institutions of society, politics, and the economy and those who are not able to do so (NACLA 2005). The binary of inclusion/exclusion is at the crux of the formation of Latin American social movements. Exclusion is often at the core of what defines social movements because social movements often involve groups of people ("collective actors") who feel they are left outside of formal institutions of government and politics. Participants in social movements often share some common interests and attempt to change their "outsider" or "excluded" status by engaging in collective practices aimed at challenging and changing society.

The definitions above can be interpreted and contextualized in light of the activities of several social movements in Latin America. Excluded and disempowered groups of indigenous peasants in many countries, such as Bolivia, Ecuador, Colombia, Brazil, and Mexico, have been at the forefront of social mobilization and political change in South America. The participants in these movements are attempting to change society because they feel that current economic, social, and political structures in line with neoliberalism (see chapter 3) benefit only a few people at the expense of the majority. For example, the Confederación de las Nacionalidades Indígenas del Ecuador (Confederation of Indigenous Nationalities of Ecuador) has been a very effective organization of indigenous people, a key actor in removing two presidents (in 1997 and 2000) and in the advocacy for a pluricultural and plurinational Ecuador (Jameson 2011). In the Chiapas region of Mexico, the Ejército Zapatista de Liberación Nacional (Zapatista National Liberation Army) emerged as one of the first movements against neoliberalism and globalization in the early 1990s. The Zapatistas first organized landless indigenous peasants locally through a combination of anticapitalist discourses and Mayan cosmology, and over time have become successful in enrolling international political and economic support on their behalf (Andrews 2011). The Zapatistas have become a transnational or global social movement that connects with the struggles of poor people elsewhere, including poor or marginalized people in the so-called global North. For example, the Zapatistas are now connected to Mexican indigenous and peasant migrants working and living in California in the United States.

Similarly, in the case of Bolivian social movements, the struggles of indigenous people and peasants in recent years have been over access to important resources such as natural gas and oil and over the rights to economic benefits that would come out of their sale to foreign multinational corporations. Specifically, activists oppose foreign exploitation of natural resources (see chapter 7) and would prefer that more of the benefits generated by the sale of resources such as natural gas and oil would go toward improving the lives of ordinary Bolivians (see chapter 11). Because activists feel that they have no true representation in the formal institutions of the state, they attempt to bring about change by getting involved in noninstitutionalized practices, such as coordinated blocking of roads and massive mobilizations of peasants in the streets, among other strategies of resistance. Activists hope that these practices will force the government to pay attention to their plight and consider them active participants in economic decisions that shape the future distribution of benefits in the country. The relation between access to natural resources and grassroots mobilizations has become an important part of the landscape of activism in Latin America. This kind of struggle is now often identified as an issue of "resource nationalism" (see chapter 7 for a definition and an expanded discussion).

The different definitions of social movements provided above can be applied and made relevant to several other Latin American social movements beyond the Ecuadorian, Mexican, and Bolivian indigenous organizing. For example, in the twenty-first century, large popular movements and uprisings that span different social and racial formations have mobilized against neoliberal policies (see chapter 3) and government corruption, in Argentina in 2001 and more recently in Brazil, beginning in 2013 and continuing to the present. But the binary of inclusion/exclusion and the noninstitutionalized practices that social movements follow in an attempt to alter their members' livelihoods are not necessarily circumscribed to the economic realm, as might have been implied by the examples mentioned so far. On the contrary, many of the current struggles of social movements in Latin America can be defined also as involving cultural politics. Cultural politics are processes enacted when sets of social actors shaped by, and embodying, different cultural meanings and practices come into conflict with each other. Meanings and practices often considered marginal or residual in relation to a dominant cultural order can become the sources of political processes. For example, social movements that talk about alternative conceptions of democracy, justice, nature, and citizenship enact a cultural politics because the meanings that they attach to those concepts seek to redefine social power in either explicit or implicit ways (Alvarez, Dagnino, and Escobar 1998, 7).

The case of a broad "Pan-Mayan" movement that has operated in Guatemala since the mid-1980s is a good example of a social movement that has organized and mobilized in an attempt to make visible important cultural and ethnic identities. Led by well-educated Mayan people including lawyers, teachers, development workers, linguists, and social scientists, the explicit goal of the movement has been to undermine the authoritativeness of non-Mayan accounts that dominate portrayals of the Mayan culture (Warren 1998). In an attempt to reverse this situation, the movement has concentrated its efforts on the promotion and revitalization of Mayan language, revitalization of chronicles of culture and history of Mayan resistance in school texts, and promotion of Mayan forms of leadership. One of the most interesting dimensions of this cultural politics has been the use of indigenous religion to subvert dominant themes of Catholicism in contemporary Guatemala (Warren 1998).

There are many other cases of Latin American social movements that fit the formal definition provided above and whose struggles also revolve around both issues of distribution/economy and issues of inclusion/cultural politics. Many Latin American social movements that make claims in the economic realm are also involved in cultural politics. The indigenous social movements listed in table 10.1, for example, often struggle for economic resources and cultural recognition simultaneously. The same can be said for many of the human rights organizations in Latin America, since most of them embrace a broad definition of human rights that includes respect for civil liberties as well as economic rights, such as the right for people to work. The protests and activities of the student movement in Chile over the last decade (in 2006 and then again in 2011) are also good examples. Students in Chile have been organizing against the continued privatization of the education system. But their activism and street protests have also been about political and cultural recognition for young people, who are usually excluded from the formal democratic process and politics because of their age (Aitken 2014). In addition, ethnic demands are part of the Chilean student movement, in particular by indigenous Mapuche students who are disproportionately poor in comparison to other mainstream Chilean students and who have been extremely affected by rising prices in education as a result of neoliberal reforms (Webb and Radcliffe 2013).

The remainder of this chapter will focus on explaining how the struggles of social movements in Latin America can be interpreted from a geographic perspective and how their effectiveness and/or failure often also depends on geographic dimensions, such as the way in which activists mobilize in places, build networks across space, and act collectively across many geographic scales simultaneously.

Latin American Social Movements and the Importance of Place

Geographers have long argued that the mobilization of social movements unfolds in places and that, very often, the effectiveness of social movements' public actions depends on their visibility in public space. Meeting points in public spaces in cities (such as parks and streets) provide an arena and stage for organization of activism (Bosco 2001), and social movements can strategically use such spaces to their advantage (Mitchell 2003). The struggles and the identities of resistance also are often borne locally through activists' sense and experience of place (Pile and Keith 1997). Many Latin American social movements mobilize because of attachments to place or territory, in many cases because their existence is tied to their ability to claim land or a place that they can call their own.

One relevant example that illustrates the connection between place and social movement mobilization is the Movement of Rural Landless Workers, or MST (Movimento dos Trabalhadores Rurais Sem Terra), in Brazil. The movement began in the southern Brazilian states of

Rio Grande do Sul and Santa Catarina in 1984 but then expanded to twenty-two of twenty-six Brazilian states (Wolford 2004). Set in the context of poor rural and urban areas, the movement's main strategy has involved the occupation of "unproductive" lands. The explicit goal of the movement is to obtain rights to property and to secure land for those who actually work it. On April 17, 1997, over fifty thousand people loosely affiliated with the MST marched and demonstrated in Brasília, giving visibility to the largest grassroots social movement in Brazil's history (Wolford 2004). Over twenty years later, the movement keeps demanding of the government further rights to property for an increasingly landless population in Brazil. Over the years, the movement has organized 1.5 million landless workers and has been involved in over twenty-five thousand occupations, creating two thousand legal settlements that house 350,000 families and that involve a land area larger than Italy (Starr et al. 2011). A similar movement has emerged in Bolivia, and it is now tied to the Brazilian MST.

The activities of the *piquetero* (picketers') movement in Argentina in the early 2000s or the more recent activities of the student movement in Chile (also known as the *"pinguinos"*) are other examples of the ways in which strategic occupations of places in the city become crucial to the visibility and effectiveness of a nascent social movement. The picketers' movement is an organization of unemployed people that arose in late 1997 in Argentina and became even more significant after the country's economic collapse in the early 2000s. The movement is part of a series of antineoliberal social movements that are active in contemporary Latin America, groups that can also be considered to be a part of (or inspired by) a much broader transnational antiglobalization movement. Activists in the movement blame neoliberal policies for creating the conditions that led to their own present exclusion from society, namely, their condition of being unemployed and poor. Even though they are unemployed, activists in the movement refuse to become invisible to the rest of Argentine society. Their strategies of resistance relied, in part, on becoming more *visible* to the rest of society by creating road and street blockades and cutting highway links, disrupting economic activities (e.g., flows of transportation and merchandise). Their road and street blockades, achieved by putting their own bodies into the struggle, became infamous and were even declared illegal and criminal by the Argentine government. Yet their disruptive use of public space and the identification of the movement with a very specific place-based practice (the street blockade) contributed to the visibility and success of the picketers' movement and forced the government to create transitory employment programs and other forms of social assistance. These forms of assistance for the unemployed were not available prior to the movement's street blockades and other forms of public street protests, and so they were directly linked to the movement's strategies of occupying public space (Medina 2011). Couched in the same antineoliberal framework and countering the privatization of education in the country, the student movement in Chile utilized similar strategies over the last decade. In 2006, students occupied schools nationwide, and then, aided by social media, began massive street demonstrations wearing their black and white school uniforms (hence the name "pinguinos" [penguins] for the movement) and even moving school desks out to the street and public places. The student occupations were effective, catching the government by surprise, and forcing the government to begin meetings with student representatives to come up with ways to meet their demands.

Other Latin American social movements involved in cultural politics (as explained in the previous section) are also involved in a very active politics of place. Often, for social movements, "being" and "having a place to be" are difficult to separate. This is a dimension of activism that demonstrates the intrinsic place-based nature of many social movements' struggles. For example, Colombia's broad black or Afro-Colombian movement (a movement that seeks ethnic recognition and political inclusion for Colombians of African origin) has tied its struggle for inclusion to simultaneous claims for territory. People who live in the forested areas along Colombia's Pacific coast have long been demanding integration into Colombian society *and* recognition as an ethnic group (e.g., the right to be "black") in conjunction with demands for rights to a territory (e.g., right to space for being) (Grueso, Rosero, and Escobar 1998). Recent research on the sociopolitical organizational structure of these communities has also shown that there is an "aquatic space" (as opposed to artificial political boundaries) that is the method of organization for black and indigenous populations living in the river basins and deltas throughout the region. This aquatic space is a set of spatialized social relationships among Afro-Colombians that not only facilitates political organization but is also the foundation for their organization and mobilization through grassroots networks and groups such as the Process of Black Communities and the Peasant Association of the River Atrato (Oslander 2004).

Geographers also have argued that a social movement's sense and experience of place entails much more than location or territoriality. Sense of place is about the complex interplay of processes in a context that may or may not be geographically circumscribed. Especially in the case of social movements that are spread across space, a sense of place can be symbolic. A symbolic sense of place for a social movement refers to its "home," a common meeting ground that is associated with a spatial imaginary.

One of the best documented examples of the relation between a Latin American social movement and a symbolic sense of place is the case of the Madres de Plaza de Mayo in Argentina (Bosco 2001, 2004, 2006). The Madres de Plaza de Mayo groups are part of the human rights movement in Argentina. The movement began as a small group of women began searching for their missing sons and daughters who had been "disappeared" by the military government of Argentina in the late 1970s. The group began meeting in the main square (the Plaza de Mayo) in downtown Buenos Aires (figure 10.1) in 1977 as a small gathering of just a few women. Over time, the women got together with (and actively recruited) more women like them, and by

Figure 10.1. Silhouettes of the "disappeared" are painted on the ground in the Plaza de Mayo in downtown Buenos Aires.

1984, there were twenty-one groups of Madres de Plaza de Mayo across Argentina. The groups of mothers developed a strong connection with the Plaza de Mayo, their gathering place, and over time the movement developed a strong sense of place.

The case of the Madres de Plaza de Mayo in Argentina demonstrates how, for many Latin American social movements, the survival and continuity of activism are inextricably tied to places and to the creation of a sense of place. The practice of collective rituals (routine group activities that reinforce a sense of collective identity) shows that, in the case of the Madres, activist bonds are not encouraged by proximity to one location but rather by a socially constructed symbolic proximity based on the group's identification with a particular place.

The type of activism started by the Madres de Plaza de Mayo in Argentina in the 1970s has been replicated by several other "motherist" movements of people kidnapped and disappeared in Latin America. For example, there has been an active movement of activists' mothers in El Salvador, organized by peasant mothers and wives of people who were targeted for being dissidents during the civil war that engulfed the country between 1979 and 1992 (Bejarano 2002). Similar motherist groups have been organized in the border city of Ciudad Juarez, Mexico, since the late 1990s by women whose daughters (who were mostly maquiladora workers) were kidnapped, raped, killed, and/or disappeared (see chapter 13). Very recently, new groups of mothers of murdered and disappeared people have been gathering in public squares in the Mexican border city of Tijuana, as drug violence has resulted in the disappearance of young people in that area as well. In all these cases, activist mothers have gathered in public squares and conducted silent demonstrations, like the mothers in

---

Textbox 10.1. The Madres de Plaza de Mayo in Argentina

The first group of mothers of the disappeared decided to meet weekly in the Plaza de Mayo in downtown Buenos Aires to exchange information regarding the whereabouts of their missing sons and daughters. The Madres' first meetings were not meant to be public demonstrations, but they began functioning as such once the police threatened the women with arrests for loitering. This forced the Madres to begin walking, many times on the perimeter of the Plaza de Mayo to avoid being arrested. That was the origin of the Madres' weekly marches in the square. Many other mothers of the disappeared started to conduct similar marches in the main squares of their cities at the same day and time as the original group in Buenos Aires. These meetings of women in public squares became a collective ritual that united members and proved important for the survival of the movement. Even today, the Madres' weekly public marches still take place, every Thursday at 3:30 in the Plaza de Mayo and in public squares across Argentina (figure 10.2). Over the years, the Madres' half-hour silent march around the obelisk in the center of the Plaza de Mayo in downtown Buenos Aires has become their signature public display of activism. The Plaza de Mayo remains a central symbolic gathering place for the Madres' movement. Emblems of their movement (white headscarves) are painted on the ground, forming a circle in the center of the square that reminds everyone of the mothers' silent protest even when the women are not present. For the Madres de Plaza de Mayo, being in the square at a specific day and time, knowing that other women like them are doing exactly the same in many other different places, is a way to reinforce their feeling of membership in the social movement. For the Madres de Plaza de Mayo, public squares (irrespective of location, including plazas in other countries and continents) represent sites of resistance, recruitment, solidarity, and conflict resolution.

Figure 10.2. The Madres de Plaza de Mayo in the city of La Plata during one of their weekly marches.

Argentina, and also have taken advantage of their visibility in public space to make their causes known to the wider public and to recruit new members and supporters. All these motherist movements are good examples of social movements that use symbolic places in the city as a strategy for movement visibility and survival.

Latin American Social Movements and Networks across Geographic Scales

The strategic use of place and a sense of place are critical to most social movements in Latin America. But the sense of place that social movements build does not have to be *necessarily* associated with a material place. For example, activists using the Internet to organize might also have a virtual sense of place, since particular locations in cyberspace (websites, for example) often act as homes for networks of activists in different locations. The use of the Internet by social movements also speaks about the mobilization of activists across space. Much like a sense of place, equally important to a social movement is a sense of space, which describes the social movement's spatial arenas of operation or potential operation. Although social movements are often rooted in places, they are not always necessarily local. On the contrary, activists often build networks that transcend formal geographic boundaries and enlarge social movements' spaces of action, enhancing their possibilities for success. For example, activists develop friendships, emotional connections, and strategic alliances with social movement participants in other distant locations, and information technology such as the Internet provides a medium to sustain such networks (Bosco 2007). Thus, social movements can range from the local to the global, and in the context of contemporary globalization, it is very common to talk about transnational or even global social movements.

Social movements and activism in general are seen as "networks of networks" (Diani and McAdam 2003) and as intricate webs of social relations constituted by shared practices between individual activists and formal and informal organizations, embedded in places and also operating across space in "multiscalar" political action. Scholars have already shown that whereas the politics of resistance are often organized around place-specific struggles, what also gets diffused and organized across space is the "common ground" shared by different groups—often the result of groups' entangled interests (Routledge 2000, 27). These entangled interests and common ground are what scholars typically refer to when they talk about transnational social movements that group individuals and groups of activists in many places (across scales) simultaneously. Geographers often pay attention to the effects of geographic scale in the mobilizing strategies of social movements. For example, it is now commonly argued that the effective mobilization of activists often requires "scaling up"—making connections outside of the local, creating transnational webs—or even developing multiscalar strategies of collective action (see chapter 9 for an explanation of the politics of scale).

There are many examples of these strategies of networking across scales and transnationally in Latin American social movements. During the process of Chilean democratization that began in the late twentieth century, the women's movement in Chile was enlarged and supported by activists who formed new networks of nongovernmental organizations (NGOs) and grassroots organizations. The networks were national in scope but transcended the Chilean confines since many of the NGOs obtained funding from European NGOs in countries such as Sweden (Schild 1998). More recently, struggles related to food sovereignty and peasant livelihoods in southern Chile have also involved networked spatial practices that have joined specific actors across spaces and geographic scales. Specifically, peasant women involved with the National Association of Rural and Native Women (also known as ANAMURI) have created a network of seed curators that protect and multiply local seeds in household gardens. Additionally, they have connected with the national and global slow-food movement to bring attention to peasant foods, local flavors, and tourism, effectively linking southern Chile peasants with global food activism (Cid Aguayo and Latta 2015).

The case of the Madres de Plaza de Mayo in Argentina is also relevant here. To enlarge their capacity of mobilization and effectiveness, over the years the Madres expanded their networks across scales to reach the international arena. This geographic strategy to enlarge their networks was based on the Madres' strategic use of emotional bonds and images and discourses of motherhood to reach and connect with distant others. Other human rights activists created support groups for the Madres de Plaza de Mayo both in Argentina and abroad, in Europe, North America, and even Australia (figure 10.3). In most cases, it was other activists who approached the Madres with ideas about the creation of support groups. The support groups, which gave logistical support to the network of Madres and helped disseminate the Madres' goals and message, were created on the basis of feelings of love and admiration for the mothers.

Many of the activists in these support groups explain their devotion to the Madres de Plaza de Mayo in emotional ways, talking about their love for the Madres de Plaza de Mayo as if they were their own biological mothers—perhaps even drawing from a broader cultural template of love for and devotion to mothers that, if not universal, is at least typical in Latin America. The groups abroad maintain and reaffirm the emotional connections with the Madres (which gave rise to the support groups in the first place) by organizing local events

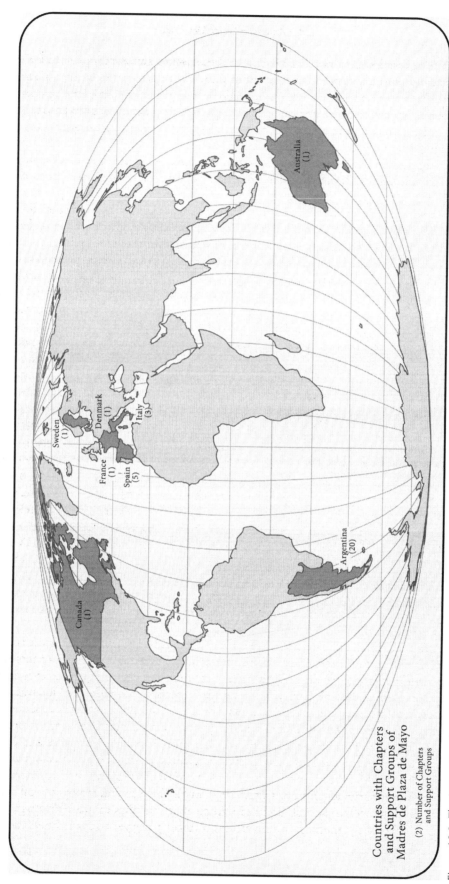

Countries with Chapters
and Support Groups of
Madres de Plaza de Mayo

(2) Number of Chapters
and Support Groups

Sweden
(1)

Denmark
(1)

Italy
(3)

France
(1)

Spain
(5)

Canada
(1)

Argentina
(20)

Australia
(1)

Figure 10.3. The international reach of the Madres de Plaza de Mayo: volunteer support groups are spread out across Argentina, North America, Europe, and Australia.

in which they discuss the Madres' activism. In these events, supporters often talk about the Madres in heroic ways, expressing their admiration for these women and mobilizing local support by framing emotions in ways that resonate with particular audiences. Occasionally, one or more Madres de Plaza de Mayo are able to visit the support groups abroad, and the personal visits cement their emotional connections even further and ensure the continuity of the groups' activities (Bosco 2006).

Other Latin American social movements have also networked across space to enlarge their mobilization potential and relied on the communication and organization capacity provided by new communications technology such as the Internet. The Zapatista movement in southern Mexico has been widely cited as an example of the successful use of the Internet to connect the plight of excluded indigenous peasants to the networks of knowledge and power of academics and activists in the United States and other countries of the industrialized world. The Internet allowed the Zapatistas to gather support for their claims from abroad, thus forcing the government in Mexico (at the national and local level) to begin to seriously consider the movement's demands. Over its fifteen years of activism, the movement has built a movement that scholars today call international Zapatism, a transnational activist network that surrounds the Zapatistas. This transnational social movement includes partnerships with people and organizations from more than seventy countries who provide material or political donations, and it is an example of the way in which social movements from the "global South" actually inspire other activists in the "global North" to take action (Andrews 2011).

Communications technology such as the Internet also has allowed other social movements to come together in the first place. The connections between the geographic arrangements of activism in relation to new communications technology is well represented by a network of human rights activists called HIJOS. The network of HIJOS was first born in Argentina, but it is now transnational in scope, thanks in part to the Internet. HIJOS is a grassroots collective started by the children of people who were "disappeared" (i.e., illegally kidnapped, tortured, and murdered in a systematic plan of state-sponsored terrorism) during Argentina's "dirty war" of the late 1970s (in some cases, the members of HIJOS are grandchildren of members of the Madres de Plaza de Mayo). The name of the network, HIJOS, meaning "children" in Spanish, is also an acronym that stands for Hijos por la Identidad y la Justicia y contra el Olvido y el Silencio (Children for Identity and Justice and against Forgetting and Silence). As a transnational network, HIJOS has evolved to include the sons and daughters, both in Argentina and abroad, of people who were disappeared in Argentina and in some other Latin American countries, as well as children of survivors of imprisonment and of those who fled their countries into exile (Bosco 2007).

In Argentina, HIJOS followed the same trajectory as the movement of the Madres de Plaza de Mayo, forming local groups that gathered in specific places such as plazas and parks and recruiting others who shared the same grievances. Over the years, HIJOS organized over eighteen local chapters throughout Argentina, and the network continues to grow even today. One unanticipated effect of the formation of HIJOS in Argentina was that the network expanded even more with the incorporation of the sons and daughters of disappeared people, who were living in exile in Europe and other countries in Latin America. The same grievances that brought together HIJOS in Argentina also allowed distant activists to begin communicating with one another, giving rise to a broad transnational network of HIJOS, with more than sixteen chapters across Latin America and Europe (figure 10.4). But in the case of the transnational network of HIJOS, coming together at first did not mean meeting in a physical place like the Plaza de Mayo, or in collective gatherings in universities or other places to commemorate the disap-

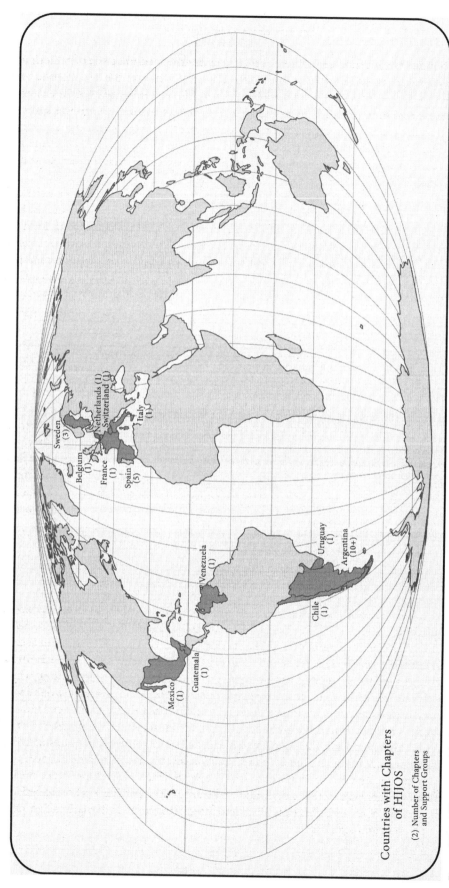

Countries with Chapters of HIJOS

(2) Number of Chapters and Support Groups

Sweden (3)
Netherlands (1)
Switzerland (1)
Belgium (1)
France (1)
Italy (1)
Spain (5)
Mexico (1)
Guatemala (1)
Venezuela (1)
Chile (1)
Uruguay (1)
Argentina (10+)

Figure 10.4. Hijos goes global: countries in Latin America and Europe where groups of sons and daughters of disappeared people have organized.

peared, but rather gathering using the Internet. The Internet became a site of gathering for the network of HIJOS in exile, and what generated that gathering was the need to find an outlet for members' shared past experiences and grievances. For example, on many websites hosted around the world, members of HIJOS (or Hij@s, as they name themselves in cyberspace) began posting narratives describing their experiences of what it felt like to be a son or daughter of a disappeared person—regardless of one's physical location. Soon, through the Internet and personal contacts, the physical network of HIJOS in Argentina became linked to the virtual network of HIJOS around the world.

Interestingly, those participating in the virtual network felt the need to experience their activism in a more direct and personal way. So HIJOS abroad (in cities in Spain, in Sweden, and in Mexico, for example) decided to follow the example of the HIJOS network in Argentina and came together in retreats and gatherings in their respective locations. This was the beginning of the regional gatherings of different local groups of HIJOS in each country, a practice that also continues today. Such regional gatherings have proved to be crucial for furthering the political and activist dimensions of the transnational network of HIJOS. These practices again demonstrate the relation between the transnational dimensions of activism and the importance of place for social movements.

In addition, the sons and daughters of disappeared people in other countries, who had never had an outlet for their grievances, have also used the Internet to get to know each other and form new activist networks. A new group of HIJOS was formed in Guatemala, not by Argentines in exile but rather by sons and daughters of some of the more than two hundred thousand people disappeared in Guatemala during the 1980s. The group in Guatemala adopted the same name as the transnational network of HIJOS formed first in Argentina, giving rise to a truly transnational network of sons and daughters of disappeared people that transcends formal political boundaries and national identities and affiliations. In sum, the case of the transnational network of HIJOS demonstrates how the formation and consolidation of some Latin American social movements have become dependent on the existence of communication technologies that have allowed people separated by large geographic distances to come together and organize collectively around specific goals.

Conclusion

In recent years, geographers interested in the study of activism in Latin America have made significant contributions to more geographic understandings of the activities of social movements and grassroots networks of activists in the region. This chapter has emphasized how geographic dimensions such as place and scale play a role in the mobilization of Latin American social movements. This chapter also highlighted the main dimensions along which one can analyze social movements from a geographic perspective. These two avenues can be summarized as follows: First, to understand the formation and duration of social movements, it is necessary to think of and analyze activism in relation to places, both material and symbolic. Second, to understand the effectiveness and/or failure of mobilization of activists, it is important to pay attention to how social movement and grassroots networks begin to adopt more global perspectives in their actions. This focus informed the last section of the chapter and includes the analysis of the mobilization of transnational activists who are resisting the discourses and practices of global capitalism and attempting to find alternatives they believe to be more just and equitable.

A geographic analysis of Latin American social movements is concerned with understanding the spatialities of mobilization—that is, how social movements come together and how activists organize and build organizations and coalitions in place and across space. The geographic strategies of social movements certainly do not guarantee their success, but it is very difficult to understand how and why social movements fail and/or succeed in their action without paying attention to the role of geographic dimensions, whether these are explicitly part of the mobilization activities of social movements or not.

Key Terms

social movements: Groups of individuals who share common interests and often a common identity, engaged in noninstitutionalized discourses and practices designed to challenge and/or transform society, sometimes even using political means to influence, change, or even dismantle the state.

transnational social movements: Social movements that span, and operate across, several nations and cultures, some of them even at the global scale, helped by common global grievances and held together by shared identities and strategies that bridge cultural and spatial divides among participants.

urban social movements: Social movements that often emerge when urban populations share grievances and problems that are the result of the failure of different levels of government (municipal, provincial or state, or national) to provide them with services and other means of collective consumption.

Suggested Readings

Eckstein, S., and M. Garreton Merino. *Power and Popular Protest: Latin American Social Movements.* Berkeley: University of California Press, 2001.

Johnston, H., and P. Almeida (Eds.). *Latin American Social Movements: Globalization, Democratization, and Transnational Networks.* Lanham, MD: Rowman & Littlefield, 2006.

Maier, E., and N. Lebon (Eds.). *Women's Activism in Latin America and the Caribbean: Engendering Social Justice, Democratizing Citizenship.* Piscataway, NJ: Rutgers University Press, 2010.

Stahler-Sholk, R., H. E. Vanden, and G. D. Kuecker (Eds.). *Latin American Social Movements in the Twenty-First Century: Resistance, Power, and Democracy.* Lanham, MD: Rowman & Littlefield, 2008.

Warren, K., and J. Jackson (Eds.). *Indigenous Movements, Self-Representation, and the State in Latin America.* Austin: University of Texas Press, 2003.

References

Aitken, S. *The Ethnopoetics of Space and Transformation: Young People's Engagement, Activism and Aesthetics.* Burlington, VT: Ashgate, 2014.

Alvarez, S., E. Dagnino, and A. Escobar (Eds.). *Cultures of Politics, Politics of Cultures: Revisioning Latin American Social Movements.* Boulder, CO: Westview Press, 1998.

Andrews, A. "How Activists 'Take Zapatismo Home': South to North Dynamics in Transnational Social Movements." *Latin American Perspectives* 38, no. 1 (2011): 138–52.

Bejarano, C. "Las Super Madres de Latino America: Transforming Motherhood by Challenging Violence in Mexico, Argentina and El Salvador." *Frontiers* 23, no. 1 (2002): 126–50.

Bosco, F. "Place, Space, Networks and the Sustainability of Collective Action: The Madres de Plaza de Mayo." *Global Networks* 1, no. 4 (2001): 307–29.

———. "Human Rights Politics and Scaled Performances of Memory: Conflicts among the Madres de Plaza de Mayo in Argentina." *Social and Cultural Geography* 5, no. 3 (2004): 381–402.

———. "The Madres de Plaza de Mayo and Three Decades of Human Rights Activism: Embeddedness, Emotions and Social Movements." *Annals of the Association of American Geographers* 96, no. 2 (2006): 342–65.

———. "Emotions That Build Networks: Geographies of Two Human Rights Movements in Argentina and Beyond." *Tijdschrift voor Economische en Sociale Geografie* 98, no. 5 (2007): 545–63.

Cid Aguayo, B. and A. Latta. "Agro-Ecology and Food Sovereignty Movements in Chile: Sociospatial Practices for Alternative Peasant Futures." *Annals of the Association of American Geographers* 105, no. 2 (2015): 397–406.

Diani, M., and D. McAdam. *Social Movements and Networks: Relational Approaches to Collective Action.* New York: Oxford University Press, 2003.

Grueso, L., C. Rosero, and A. Escobar. "The Process of Black Community Organizing in the Southern Pacific Coast Region of Colombia." In *Cultures of Politics, Politics of Cultures: Revisioning Latin American Social Movements*, edited by S. Alvarez, E. Dagnino, and A. Escobar, 196–219. Boulder, CO: Westview Press, 1998.

Jameson, K. "The Indigenous Movement in Ecuador: The Struggle for a Plurinational State." *Latin American Perspectives* 38, no. 1 (2011): 63–73.

Medina, P. "Thoughts on the Visual Aspect of the Neoliberal Order and the Piquetero Movement in Argentina." *Latin American Perspectives* 38, no. 1 (2011): 88–101.

Mitchell, D. *The Right to the City: Social Justice and the Fight for Public Space.* New York: Guilford Press, 2003.

NACLA (North American Congress on Latin America). "Social Movements: Building from the Ground Up." *NACLA Report on the Americas* 38 (2005): 5.

Oslander, U. "Fleshing Out the Geographies of Social Movements: Colombia's Pacific Coast Black Communities and the 'Aquatic Space.'" *Political Geography* 23 (2004): 957–85.

Pile, S., and M. Keith. *Geographies of Resistance.* London: Routledge, 1997.

Routledge, P. "'Our Resistance Will Be as Transnational as Capital': Convergence Space and Strategy in Globalizing Resistance." *Geojournal* 52 (2000): 25–33.

Schild, V. "New Subjects of Rights? Women's Movements and the Construction of Citizenship in the 'New Democracies.'" In *Cultures of Politics, Politics of Cultures: Revisioning Latin American Social Movements*, edited by S. Alvarez, E. Dagnino, and A. Escobar, 93–117. Boulder, CO: Westview Press, 1998.

Starr, A., M. E. Martínez Torres, and P. Rosset. "Participatory Democracy in Action: Practices of the Zapatistas and the Movimiento Sem Terra." *Latin American Perspectives* 38, no. 1 (2011): 102–19.

Warren, K. B. "Indigenous Movements as a Challenge to the Unified Social Movement Paradigm for Guatemala." In *Cultures of Politics, Politics of Cultures: Revisioning Latin American Social Movements*, edited by S. Alvarez, E. Dagnino, and A. Escobar, 165–95. Boulder, CO: Westview Press, 1998.

Webb, A. and S. Radcliffe. "Mapuche Demands during Educational Reform, the Penguin Revolution and the Chilean Winter of Discontent." *Studies in Ethnicity and Nationalism* 13, no. 3 (2013): 319–41.

Wolford, W. "This Land Is Ours Now: Spatial Imaginaries and the Struggle for Land in Brazil." *Annals of the Association of American Geographers* 94, no. 2 (2004): 409–24.

Chapter 11

Urban Environmental Politics

Flows, Responsibility, and Citizenship

Sarah A. Moore

THE CHARMING CITY OF Oaxaca de Juarez, in the southern Mexican state of Oaxaca, attracts tourists, language students, and visitors of all ages and nationalities. It is also home to over three hundred thousand people and the center of an urban area whose population is almost seven hundred thousand. In the early 2000s, Oaxaca's dual roles as tourist destination and the site of everyday city life were put into sharp contrast when hundreds of tons of garbage began to pile up on the cobblestone sidewalks, in the urban parks, and against the colonial buildings. The area's one municipal dump had caught fire, prompting nearby residents to block the access road in order to keep city garbage trucks from discharging their loads. These residents were upset at the city's inability to prevent fires at the site and the city's lack of compliance with earlier accords determining how the dump should be managed. The municipal government of Oaxaca was forced to suspend garbage collection, and citizens and tourists alike were made to live with their own waste (see figure 11.1). This event and others like it throughout the first decade of the twenty-first century have forced the city of Oaxaca to negotiate with neighborhood organizations, and with the state and federal governments, to change the way that municipal solid waste (MSW) is managed in the area.

These struggles over the management of MSW in the city of Oaxaca highlight a number of important common themes in urban environmental politics in Latin America. In discussing this and other examples from the region, I will highlight three main points: (1) challenges of urban environmental management often lead to shifts in the responsibilities of governmental and nongovernmental entities, (2) local populations have been able to shape urban ecologies through popular movements and protests, and (3) conflicts over urban environments, in turn, play an important role in shaping local political identities. Before turning to these three points, though, it is necessary to define the major terms used in this chapter.

Defining the Urban Environment

Any discussion of environmental problems in the context of Latin American cities must begin with definitions of the terms "urban" and "environment." Rather than being a static, circumscribed place separate from "rural" areas, it is useful to think of the urban as the result of a set

Figure 11.1. Market area during a garbage crisis in Oaxaca.

of practices that creates recognizable "urban" landscapes (see chapter 4). This more dynamic view focuses on the ways that both institutions and citizens make and remake urban areas continuously. Further, it is important to note that this making and remaking of the city is not separate from the making and remaking of rural areas. The two are tied by the exchange of resources, people, technologies, and environmental goods and "bads," among other things. While most of this chapter will deal with the activities of people and institutions who call the city their home, it must be noted that the flows of cities, particularly those of waste and water, often have a negative impact on surrounding areas and people.

In both the global North and the global South many types of ecological thinking concentrate on the conservation or preservation of what we call nature, often defined as pristine areas separate from human interference. Urban environmental movements, including those for environmental justice, on the other hand, have sought to redefine the environment as where we live, work, and play. Given this definition, there are many urban ecologies. Urban gardening, either for subsistence purposes or to create community spaces, is one practice constituting urban natures. Urban green-space plans, aimed at providing parks and pleasant thoroughfares for residents, are also important parts of Latin American urban ecologies. Though these particular parts of the urban environment are beyond the scope of this chapter, they are important factors in the constitution of urban environments.

This chapter concentrates on the flows of environmental resources and risks in Latin American cities. As Carlos Minc puts it, "Ecology in the Third World begins with water, garbage, and sewage" (Roberts and Thanos 2003, 99). All three issues are tied to the distribution of vital resources (e.g., water) *through* the city or the elimination of wastes *from* the city. These processes of distribution and elimination are essential factors in the health of the populace, which has led observers to describe environmentalism in urban Latin America as "the environmentalization of public health issues" (Roberts and Thanos 2003, 99). The public, though, is not a homogeneous body, but rather a complex and varied group. Therefore, it is important to note that such factors as class, ethnicity, and gender influence access to and use of urban environmental resources as well as exposure to pollution. Some issues, like smog, can be termed relatively "democratic" because they affect people of diverse backgrounds in the same ways, though some people may have more choice in how to react to them. On the other hand, "water, sewer service, and garbage collection are relatively less democratic and therefore, less often solved by the big municipalities" (Roberts and Thanos 2003, 104).

According to recent research, there is no obvious link between the population size, the population growth rate, or the population density of a city and the level of urban environmental problems (Satterthwaite 2003). Rather, the most reliable indicator of environmental problems in Latin American cities and other places in the global South is affluence. The production and accumulation of wealth in urban areas, along with a lack of comprehensive development planning, has had many environmentally damaging effects. While some cities are able to use their economic wealth to attack these externalities, many others cannot. Because municipal governments are often burdened with the responsibility of environmental management in urban areas, their inability to solve such problems has huge implications for urban governance and livelihoods.

Responsibility for the Urban Environment

Many urban residents in Latin America feel that it is the responsibility of the municipal government to ensure a clean and healthy living and working environment (Moore 2008, 2009). This expectation is embedded in the historical relationship between urban centers and citizens' rights. Those people identified by the state as "citizens" have entered into a contract of sorts with the municipal government, which is bound to them by a set of rights and obligations. While it is the responsibility of citizens to participate in the production of the city through their daily activities, it is the responsibility of the city to provide the services necessary for the social reproduction of urban citizens. Historically, the city's responsibility for the public health of citizens can be traced to earlier periods of modernization (Gonzalez Stephan 2003).

In the above example of garbage blockades in Oaxaca, the appropriation of public space through its colonization by garbage upsets the status quo, mainly by denying more powerful citizens the ability to export pollution. It works, in the short term at least, by relying on the fact that citizens hold the municipality responsible for distancing them from their own waste. As McGrannahan and Songsore state, "Many environmental services such as piped water, sewerage connections, electricity, and door to door garbage collection not only export pollution (from the household to the city) but also shift both the intellectual and practical burdens of environmental management for the household to the government or utility" (Satterthwaite 1998, 74).

This relationship between the city and the citizen rarely exists in its ideal form, but the obligations of the municipality to provide sanitation systems, potable water, and solid waste collection have been written into many city ordinances. It is also a part of constitutional law in many places, as well as the subject of newer environmental legislation at state and federal levels. However, the relative obligations of different levels of government as well as the availability of resources to meet those obligations are constantly shifting because of external and internal pressures.

Deregulation in many Latin American countries has left urban environmental problems exclusively in the hands of municipal entities. However, many environmental problems, such as air or water pollution, cross these political lines. This leads to the potential for "joint irresponsibility" (Roberts and Thanos 2003, 108), in which no individual municipality is willing to attend to such collective environmental bads or to the provision of services to avoid these. In many cases, international agencies such as the World Bank (WB) are called on to fund projects dealing with these challenges. Since the early 1990s, when it acknowledged that "health costs resulting from urban water, air and solid waste pollution can reach up to 10 percent of urban income" (Roberts and Thanos 2003, 111), the WB has instituted a number of urban environmental projects in Latin America (see also chapter 9). Many of these projects, due to their technocratic approach, address only short-term needs rather than the deeper social problems at the root of environmental issues (Roberts and Thanos 2003). Instead of concentrating on the political-economic, historical, and social context of particular urban environmental problems, in other words, World Bank loans have traditionally encouraged countries to focus on technological fixes, which may or may not be appropriate to the situation. For example, the WB-funded National Urban Solid Waste Management Project currently under way in Argentina allocates 83 percent of its $54 million budget to building landfills in the country. While this may improve environmental conditions in some areas temporarily, it will do little to address the problems of increased consumption, the spatial inequities of dump location, or the lack of recycling. Similar projects have been undertaken in a range of countries across the globe including India, Sri Lanka, and Tunisia.

External pressure from international organizations such as the World Bank challenges local authority and autonomy. At the same time, the involvement of these institutions in the development of Latin America has led to pressure to "neoliberalize" the economies (and ecologies) of Latin American countries (see chapters 3, 5, and 7). This has also meant shifts in the responsibilities of local, state, and federal governments and the private sector. Privatization of natural resources and environmental management services has been pursued in some areas to increase efficiency and lower costs to the state. As we shall see in the next section, many of these new strategies for managing urban environments in Latin America have engendered significant public opposition (Harris and Roa-Garcia 2013; Perreault 2014; Perreault and Valdivia 2010), some of which has managed to turn the tide against privatization of essential resources, especially water.

Popular Movements and Protests

Oaxaca's Dump and Other Waste Politics in Latin America

Struggles for environmental justice (see Key Terms at the end of this chapter) take many forms in the cities of Latin America. In Oaxaca (see figure 11.2), one of the most visible struggles is that over management of municipal solid waste. The city has, in recent years, pursued programs that have increased the area and frequency of garbage collection. In this way, the municipal government has responded to its mandate from the citizens to keep the city clean. In order to fully make good on that responsibility, though, the city must expel the garbage to outside of its borders. Oaxaca has dumped its garbage in the same sixteen-hectare spot located about eight miles southeast of the city center for over twenty-five years (see figure 11.3). However, the dump was only made official in 1992, when the city used new property laws to take control of

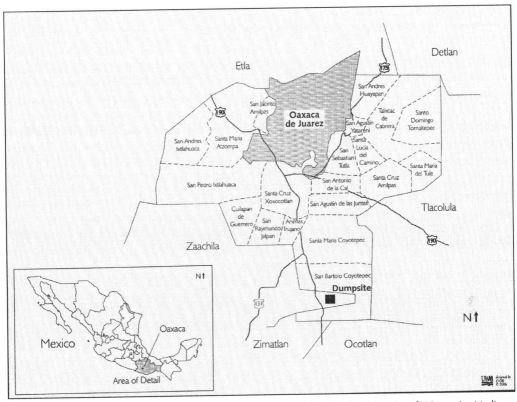

Figure 11.2. City of Oaxaca and surrounding municipalities. Map by C-GIS, University of Wisconsin, Madison.

the area. Since that time, all of the garbage from the city of Oaxaca and its surrounding suburbs has been disposed of in the open-air dump. High rates of rural-to-urban migration, as well as political discrimination and increasing property prices within the city, have led people to settle on the cheap land near the dump. There are also, in fact, communities of people who live on the dump (called *pepenadores*), making their living recycling what they find there.

Residents of communities around the dump have argued with city officials for many years over how the dump is managed. Along with some environmental groups, they have advocated the construction of a sanitary landfill on the site to prevent the spread of much of the air, land, and water pollution that exists in the landfill. The city has responded with rhetoric about its plans to develop a sanitary landfill, but in the end these marginalized communities and groups had very little success in changing management on the ground. Then, in 2000, these communities developed the more successful strategy of blocking the city's access to the dump. This means that the city cannot expel its waste. In addition to logistic difficulties, this disruption in the typical flow of garbage out of the city also puts into question the legitimacy of the municipal government itself. That is to say, if the city cannot get the garbage out of the way of its citizens, then it has failed one of the litmus tests of modern urban competency. This one community's struggle over the dumpsite, therefore, turns into a citywide debate over the management of the site and Oaxaca's environmental situation more broadly. Further, this strains the already difficult relationship between the state and municipal governments, while at the same time putting pressure on local industries and businesses to reduce waste. In this battle, public protest has changed not only the lives of the community members involved but also the city.

Figure 11.3. Oaxaca's dump.

Because waste management is such a key issue in urban environmental issues in Latin America, there are several other examples of public involvement in shaping urban ecologies. While many Latin American countries spend 20–50 percent of municipal revenues on MSW collection and disposal, less than half of municipal solid waste is formally collected and disposed of. Like the pepenadores mentioned above, many people in developing countries, including those in Latin America, generate or supplement their income through informal refuse collection (IRC) (Medina 2005). The people who practice IRC are at risk for physical harm such as punctures from discarded syringes or sharp items and attendant diseases (like hepatitis and tetanus), as well as social marginalization. Being associated with waste marks informal waste collectors and recyclers as less than legitimate modern citizens. An extreme example of the repercussions of this social discrimination comes from Barranquilla, Colombia, where, in 1992, forty "human scavengers" were killed and their organs harvested and sold for transplants. While this "social cleansing" campaign is an extreme example, it illustrates the marginalization and stigmatization experienced by informal waste workers in Mexico, Guatemala, Brazil, and the rest of Latin America (Medina 2000). The precarious nature of the work and the social position of practitioners of IRC, who perform an important service in urban ecologies across Latin America, has led to efforts to extend community-based waste management or to formalize IRC. In São Paulo, Brazil, for example, there are grassroots movements to organize informal collection, including recycling cooperatives. As part of a wider effort to produce sustainable urban ecologies, such movements help to "recover" the social identities and citizenship status of informal waste workers by identifying them with an important environmental service (Gutberlet 2008).

While such grassroots efforts to formalize informal waste labor seek to protect recyclers from social marginalization and physical harm by integrating them into the formal waste management sector and structure of urban environmental management, responsibility for managing urban environments continues to shift from the nation to the city to the individual. These shifts are concomitant with broader neoliberal policies that have also led to privatization of municipal solid waste management in many cities in Latin America, often supported by development institutions like the World Bank. In Belo Horizonte, Brazil's third-largest municipal area, 78 percent of municipal residential collection and 50 percent of recycling is handled by private companies, while in Rio de Janeiro those numbers are 40 percent and 38 percent. In Lima, Perú, 70 percent of residential collection and 100 percent of recycling is done by private firms. Perhaps the most prevalent example of privatization of waste management comes from La Paz, Bolivia, where everything, from residential and commercial collection to recycling and landfilling, has been privatized (Golders Associates 2006). While privatization takes the financial pressure off of some of these municipalities, it also means that waste collection and disposal are in the hands of profit-seeking firms, who may not be interested in environmental sustainability or social justice. Similar issues arise, as discussed in the next section, with neoliberal approaches to water management.

Neoliberal Policies and Opposition Politics

As mentioned above, the adaptation of neoliberal policies by the states of Latin America has meant the following in terms of environmental management. First, at the same time that municipalities are expected to pursue economic growth, they are given less federal and state support to mediate the effects of such growth on urban ecologies. Second, many important services are privatized, either in full or in part, in order to defray costs for urban governments. Additionally, at the same time that urban pollution is increasing and services are becoming affordable for fewer and fewer people, funding for public health services is often reduced. This section focuses on struggles over the privatization of vital resources, though it should be obvious that this has direct implications for the public health issues that are at the center of environmental politics in Latin America. The following cases of water privatization in Ecuador, Bolivia, and Brazil highlight how these practices are contested by local groups and with what effects.

Contests over Water

In his influential study of struggles over access to water resources in Guayaquil, Ecuador, Eric Swyngedouw describes the ways in which a private market for water distribution systems has led to manufactured scarcity, with the result that many people are denied access to potable water. He then describes four basic responses to the limitation of access through these (often corrupt) market distribution systems. They are passive acceptance, individual resistance, self-help (self-constructing and self-financing), and social protest/mobilization (2004, 150).

While some people accept the limited access to water, others act individually by taking advantage of traditional clientelist networks to ensure their personal access to the resource. While such strategies may have positive results for any particular person, they have little effect on the overall system of distribution (Swyngedouw 2004, 151). Alternatively, some community groups organize and pool labor and resources to build their own infrastructure. While these communities are sometimes able to get funding from government aid programs or other groups, they are often limited in scope, scale, and time period.

However, in contrast to these reactions, there are also times when resistance becomes more virulent and effective. In Guayaquil, women's activism has managed to stop the flow of water, at least for short periods (Swyngedouw 2004, 156). The presence of this type of activity, though, does not make Swyngedouw optimistic about the possibility of substantial change through these political actions. Despite his pessimism, though, in part because of struggles like this, the Ecuadorian government has declared water as a human right, and outlawed privatization throughout the country (Harris and Roa-Garcia 2013). On the other hand, despite this legal challenge to privatization, water in Guayaquil is still provided by Interagua, a subsidiary of Bechtel, and no significant change has been made in its distribution. The next section, in contrast, highlights a situation in which social protest was arguably more effective. As we see below, public activism and resistance often significantly impact environmental politics and policies in Latin America (see chapters 9 and 10).

Water in Bolivia

In January 2004, angry residents of El Alto, Bolivia, staged a protest against the high cost of water in that city. They forced the president to cancel the contract of Aguas del Illimani, a subsidiary of the $53 billion French Suez (Forero 2005). This came on the heels of the broadly opposed attempt on the part of now-ousted President Gonzalo Sánchez de Lozada to sell Bolivia's natural gas to multinational companies. This particular incident can be seen as part of a larger anti-privatization backlash that has spread across many of the countries of Latin America. Perú, for example, has experienced a downturn in foreign investment in its oil resources as indigenous peoples and environmental groups have opposed ownership by foreign companies (Forero 2005). Such antiprivatization campaigns have become so prevalent that they have provided the dramatic backdrop for Hollywood blockbusters like *Quantum of Solace*, where James Bond (Daniel Craig) must stop an evil (supposedly green) corporation from taking over large sections of land in Bolivia in order to control the country's water supply. There are also indie films like *Even the Rain*, where clear parallels are drawn between the historical colonialism of Christopher Columbus's encounters with Latin America and the contemporary privatization of water in Cochabamba, Bolivia.

In Cochabamba, the first major public uprisings against privatization came in 2000. The Andean city planned to give the United States–based firm Bechtel a major concession for the city's water services. Rather than accept this, many of the city's six hundred thousand residents took to the streets, forcing the city to back down from its original plan. The oil company, phone company, national airline, electric company, and national train system had all been privatized already, but without the anticipated improvement in services and with increased costs to consumers (Shultz 2003). When Bechtel, just weeks after taking over water services, decided to increase fees 200 percent, the Coalition for the Defense of Water and Life was born. The group managed a three-day, citywide strike and pressured the government to sign an agreement to review water rates. The government did not, however, carry through on this promise. The coalition organized another march, but this time it was violently suppressed with military force. While this quelled some of the protests, it also led to outrage among the public, forcing a rollback in rates. In an effort to cancel the privatization permanently, the coalition organized more actions the following month. The government responded by declaring martial law. Public response to this declaration was further outrage and a large Internet e-mail campaign, which led Bechtel to flee the country (Shultz 2003). The end result was a cancellation of the agreement between the government and Bechtel as well as a shift to broader public support for political candidates who voiced opposition to privatization (Shultz 2003). The success of this protest helped provide fuel to defeat other privatization schemes in Bolivia (Perreault 2005). More than this, the example of Cochabamba has become a rallying cry for further protest movements in Latin America more broadly.

Bolivia continues to be a country in which popular protests over environmental issues drive policy changes and political futures. After ousting two presidents in as many years, on December 18, 2005, the people of Bolivia elected Evo Morales Ayma, an indigenous activist, president. This preceded Bechtel's announcement that it would drop its lawsuit against the government of Bolivia, which was started after the Bolivian government canceled its contract with the corporate giant. Morales's administration has called for continued nationalization of the country's energy sector, particularly in natural gas holdings.

Unlike in the case of Bolivia, activism in São Paulo, Brazil, did not eliminate the privatization of water, but it did impact the way in which privatization was pursued. While this may not be ideal, it does leave room for optimism among researchers like Margaret Keck, who explained,

> During the 1990s, São Paulo, followed by other states and the federal government, passed laws mandating a new regime of water resource management, in which users would pay for what had previously been a free good. The laws called for new institutions (watershed committees and agencies) to manage the complex relationships among producers, consumers and the public. They implicitly understood water issues to involve political problems, rather than strictly technical ones, and thus to require (not simply allow) participation and organizations of civil society. These new institutions are still embryonic, in that parts of the reform still await enabling legislation. . . . Nonetheless, we find some reasons for a bias toward hope in the persistence of the professionals and activists who have long waged the battle for livability. (Keck 2002, 164)

This long-running battle over livability alters relationships between local groups, municipalities, and state and national governments. It also changes the relationship between different groups of people within the city itself. Often, it inspires political action and claims of citizenship from groups previously excluded from the political realm.

Political Identities and Urban Environmental Conflicts

In the above sections, we have seen some of the ways that popular movements have changed urban environments in Latin America. Many of these struggles have also altered the structure of urban citizenship itself. That is to say that they all, in some way, represent the extension or return of rights to important environmental and public health services to groups who had been excluded from these. Here, we discuss how involvement in such environmental struggles becomes an important part of urban citizens' identities.

In the case of Guayaquil, the most effective (though still temporary) actions against water sellers were perpetuated by women. This is significant in that "the right to water is directly related to the right to the city and to the meaning and practice of being an urban citizen" (Swyngedouw 2004, 156). Thus, by participating in social movements to ensure access to this vital resource, women are also insinuating themselves into the role of full and equal citizens. There are many other cases in which women have become public political actors through their association with urban environmental movements (Radcliffe and Westwood 1993).

In Oaxaca, for example, the neighborhood committee of Guillermo Gonzalez Guardado is composed entirely of women who organize the protests and meet with government officials. They use their socially defined roles as mothers and wives to argue for clean environments for their children and families *and* to position themselves as having rights to the city services necessary to guarantee this. At the same time that they are fighting for improved local conditions, they are also arguing for full inclusion in the citizenry (Moore 2008, 2009). While they do so as women, their argument has been generalized to include other marginal groups. It is often the boundary constructed by municipal services that defines the inside and outside of citizenship. That is to say, access to such services is an important part of gaining status and recognition as part of the urban community.

Similar citizenship demands can be seen in the case of struggles over water and gas privatization in Bolivia. Questions of who has the right to water emerged when ownership was to be handed over to foreign companies. An emphasis on water as a collective good meant that even recent migrants to the city were involved in struggles over services that they did not yet possess (Perreault and Valdivia 2010). A sense of entitlement to urban services is one step toward full political participation and urban citizenship. In this way, water projects have the power to designate the inside and outside of urban citizenship, as Swyngedouw observes: "In the end [the problem of water control and access] raises the issue as to who has the right to the city and whose nature is, in the name of progress and modernization, so violently and oppressively appropriated by some at the exclusionary expense of others" (2004, 176). In other words, urban environmental politics in Latin America are not about absolute scarcity of resources or inadequate technology but rather the *distribution* of these resources to all groups through appropriate physical and economic infrastructures. In the last few years, activism against the privatization of water in Latin American countries has led to the legal and political assertion of a "right to water." In July 2010, the United Nations declared access to water and sanitation a universal human right, but this was preceded by constitutional changes in Uruguay, Ecuador, and Bolivia. Argentina, a very early participant in the privatization of water, returned municipal water delivery to state control in 2006. Chile, on the other hand, is still attempting a middle ground where privatization, but with significant state regulation, is the dominant practice.

Conclusion: The Ecotopia of the Americas

The city of Curitiba, located in southern Brazil, is heralded by many scholars as a model of environmental management. The city is broadly thought to provide its citizens with a high quality of life. There are many reasons for this. The transportation system is highly efficient and encourages the use of bicycles and public transportation. The water system works with the ecology of the city to prevent scarcity and to make clean water available. Further, garbage management has been innovative, encouraging high levels of recycling and low levels of informal disposal. As longtime mayor and urban designer Jaime Lerner describes it, "In Curitiba, citizens sort trash into two bins: biodegradable and nonbiodegradable. In the recycling plant . . . , the handicapped, recent immigrants, and the poor are reportedly given work separating materials to be reused and sold to local industries. . . . We transformed the garbage man into an environmental hero" (quoted in Roberts and Thanos 2003, 113).

This ecofriendly solid waste management has counted on two major programs. One is a combination of curbside recycling, which is provided by the city, with an educational component describing "garbage that isn't garbage." The garbage purchase program, on the other hand, gives incentives to people who live outside of the areas that trucks can access (usually poor communities). People can bring their recyclables and trash to designated centers in exchange for eggs, milk, potatoes, bus tickets, and various other goods. The two programs together have helped Curitiba to achieve a recycling rate of almost 70 percent. This was done without high-tech solutions but rather by integrating existing technology with the ecological system.

Given the success of such a program, it is possible to imagine that other Latin American cities, like Oaxaca, as well as cities in other regions of the world, might try to replicate these programs. Indeed, many have tried, but with varying success. To understand why such a system of environmental management might not work in Oaxaca and other cities, I will conclude by considering the *politics* of Curitiba's ecotopia.

As Traicoff points out, "Attributing the successes of Curitiba to the talents of the mayor and the perceptions of the populace towards their city begs the question as to how this culture was created and why it is absent in other Brazilian cities" (quoted in Roberts and Thanos 2003, 114). I would add that the answer to this question is extremely important for the viability of similar programs in other places. One factor in the success of Curitiba is its strong executive, a direct result of its military dictatorship. While this allows for the rapid passage and enforcement of legislation protecting the environment, it diminishes other freedoms. Moreover, rather than continuing public participation in planning, a general boosterism has taken hold, meaning that citizens are expected to extol the city's virtues. Even more importantly, a "belt of noncitizens" composed of poorer and more irregular municipalities surrounds Curitiba. So, while Curitiba is a positive model for environmental management in Latin America, it is "much less so for the consolidation of functional democracy" (Roberts and Thanos 2003, 116). If one judges the success of Curitiba's environmental initiatives purely on measures of ecological health, it is very easy to argue that it should be the model for Latin America to follow into the twenty-first century. On the other hand, if one evaluates Curitiba in terms of the status of the populace, one sees the same problems that still plague many of Latin America's cities. It is the uneven *distribution* of environmental goods and bads (and not the absolute level of these) throughout cities and their hinterlands that endangers the health of urban dwellers. Urban environmental politics aims to do more, therefore, than protect the health of cities. It also aims to empower marginalized groups to claim citizenship and join the political struggle over shaping urban places. In Oaxaca, it is not only the ecological health of the city that is contested through urban environmental politics but also the value placed on the participation of women from the surrounding neighborhoods in determining municipal solid waste policy.

The complexity of this relationship—between urban ecologies and urban politics—illustrates the main point of this chapter. The environments of Latin American cities cannot be evaluated or understood separately from the daily lives of the people who live in them.

Key Terms

ecology: The branch of biology that deals with the relations of living organisms to their surroundings, their habits and modes of life, and so forth.

environmental justice: Both a social movement and an area of research. The social movement in the United States began in protest of the concentration of waste processing and dumping facilities in minority and lower-class communities. Many researchers in this field are concerned with documenting such inequitable spatial phenomena, while others investigate the political economic contexts in which such unequal relationships emerged.

environmental politics: A diverse term that could include conservation and preservationist movements, as well as contests over environmental justice. In short, any power struggle over the distribution of environmental goods and bads could be considered environmental politics.

political ecology: A field of research that explores and explains environmental change and conflict through direct reference to interactions of power between people, institutions, and states.

technocratic: This term refers to solutions to environmental (or other) problems that are driven mostly by technological innovation, rather than resolving social and/or economic disparities at the root of environmental injustices.

Suggested Readings and Films

Even the Rain (*También la Lluvia*). 2010. Morena Films.
Quantum of Solace. 2008. MGM, Columbia, Eon Productions, and B22.
Gutberlet, J. *Recovering Resources—Recycling Citizenship.* Burlington, VT: Ashgate, 2008
Harris, L. M, J. A. Goldin, and C. Sneddon (eds). *Contemporary Water Scarcity in the Global South: Scarcity, Marketization, Participation.* London: Routledge, 2013.

References

"Ecology." *The Oxford English Dictionary Online.* Accessed September 1, 2006. dictionary.oed.com/cgi/entry/50071982?single=1&query_type=word&queryword=ecology&first=1&max_to_show=10
Forero, J. "Latin America Fails to Deliver on Basic Needs." *New York Times,* February 22, 2005, A1.
Golders Associates. "Improving Management and Quality of Municipal Solid Waste Services." Report prepared for Finance, Private Sector, and Infrastructure Unit, Latin America and the Caribbean Region, World Bank, Washington, DC, 2006.
Gonzalez Stephan, B. "On Citizenship: The Grammatology of the Body-Politic." In *Latin American Philosophy: Currents, Issues and Debates,* edited by E. Mendieta, 188–206. Bloomington: Indiana University Press, 2003.
Gutberlet, J. *Recovering Resources—Recycling Citizenship.* Burlington, VT: Ashgate, 2008.
Harris, L. M and M. C. Roa-Garcia. "Recent Waves of Water Governance: Constitutional Reform and Resistance to Neoliberalization in Latin American (1990–2012)." *Geoforum,* 50 (2013): 20–30.
Keck, M. "Water, Water, Everywhere, Nor Any Drop to Drink: Land Use and Water Policy in São Paulo, Brazil." In *Livable Cities? Urban Struggles for Livelihood and Sustainability,* edited by P. Evans, 162–94. Berkeley: University of California Press, 2002.
Medina M. "Scavenger Cooperatives in Asia and Latin America." *Resources, Conservation and Recycling* 31 (2000): 51–69.
Medina M. "Serving the Unserved: Informal Refuse Collection in Mexico." *Waste Management and Research* 23 (2005): 390–97.
Moore, S. A. "The Politics of Garbage in Oaxaca, Mexico." *Society and Natural Resources* 21 no. 7 (2008): 597–610.
———. "The Excess of Modernity: Garbage Politics in Oaxaca Mexico." *The Professional Geographer* 61, no. 4 (2009): 426–37.
Perreault, T. "State Restructuring and the Scale Politics of Rural Water Governance in Bolivia." *Environment and Planning A* 37, no. 2 (2005): 263–84.
———. "What Kind of Governance for What Kind of Equity? Towards a Theorization of Justice in Water Governance." *Water International* 39, no. 2 (2014): 233–45.

Perreault, T. and G. Valdivia. "Hydrocarbons, Popular Protest and National Imaginaries: Ecuador and Bolivia in Comparative Context," *Geoforum* 41, no. 5 (2010): 689–99.

Radcliffe, S., and S. Westwood. "Gender, Racism and the Politics of Identities in Latin America." In *Viva: Women and Popular Protest in Latin America.* London: Routledge, 1993.

Roberts, J. T., and N. D. Thanos. *Trouble in Paradise: Globalization and Environmental Crises in Latin America.* New York: Routledge, 2003.

Satterthwaite, D. "Environmental Problems in Cities in the South: Sharing My Confusions." In *Environmental Strategies for Sustainable Development in Urban Areas: Lessons from Africa and Latin America,* edited by E. Fernandes, 62–83. Aldershot, UK; Brookfield, VT: Ashgate, 1998.

———. "The Links between Poverty and the Environment in Urban Areas of Africa, Asia, and Latin America." *Annals of the American Academy of Political and Social Science* 590 (2003): 73–92.

Shultz, J. "Bolivia: The Water War Widens." *NACLA* 36, no. 3 (2003): 34–38.

Swyngedouw, E. *Social Power and the Urbanization of Water: Flows of Power.* Oxford: Oxford University Press, 2004.

Chapter 12

Children and Young People

Inequality, Rights, and Empowerment

Kate Swanson

Children are dying daily of malnutrition in Argentina as a result of the catastrophic economic crisis in the world's fourth biggest exporter of food. In the past week, images of stunted, emaciated children have scandalised Argentina, long known as the grainstore of the world.

—Baldock 2002

"Women here are too preoccupied with how they look, how thin they are. They all get operations, dye their hair blond—it is excessive," said model Ana Paula Dutil, as sequins pasted at the corner of each eye glimmered under a harsh light. . . . Vain attempts to achieve the perfect figure of an Argentine supermodel are one reason why 1 in 10 Argentine females between 14–18 suffers from an eating disorder, according to a poll of 90,000 teens by the Argentine Association to Fight Bulimia and Anorexia (ALUBA). Both diseases cause sufferers to slowly starve themselves or binge and purge to the point of exhaustion.

—Love 2000

CHILDHOOD IN LATIN AMERICA is a complicated terrain. The disparities between the rich and poor are so vast that children across the region experience very different realities. I begin this chapter with the above quotes to demonstrate how large these chasms can be. In 2002, a severe economic crisis led to a deadly famine in some parts of Argentina. Dozens of children died and thousands were malnourished, while charities rushed in to save hungry children (Bosco 2007). Meanwhile, young women from the wealthier parts of the nation were starving themselves for vanity. These ironies plague Latin America, as it is a region of great contrast both within and between nations. Within any one Latin American country, there are young people who experience childhoods parallel to those of the wealthiest American elite; meanwhile, a much larger number of young people experience childhoods that only the most destitute of American youth could ever imagine. These differences are not only material, but in some cases have deep cultural roots. As discussed earlier in this volume (see chapter 2), Latin America's colonial history created many divides in society based upon socioeconomic status, gender, race, and ethnicity. These divisions continue to play a large role in structuring the fabric of society and, especially, in young people's lives.

As a geographer, I approach this topic through a spatial lens. Scholars interested in the geographies of childhood explore how young people's experiences are socially and spatially structured. Some scholars research how young people are excluded from certain spaces and examine how their gendered, racialized, and aged identities inform this exclusion. Others might explore how young people use, occupy, and experience environments in a way that is different from adults. Still others examine how childhood varies across regions and cultures, demonstrating how childhood is a historically, geographically, and culturally produced construction. In a nutshell, this field of research recognizes that place matters, particularly in the lives of children and young people.

In what follows, I explore some of these themes through case studies on geographic research concerning children and young people in Latin America. I focus on children's rural and urban lives and place particular emphasis on children's work, both in the fields and on the streets. While I recognize that a focus on children's work results in emphasizing the lives of Latin America's poorest citizens, I believe that these lives may represent some of those who face the greatest struggles and most pressing concerns. Before delving into these case studies, however, I first discuss debates surrounding children's rights and childhood and define a few key terms.

Childhood and Children's Rights

To begin, how do we define a "child"? According to the United Nations, a child is an individual between the ages of zero and eighteen. While this may seem straightforward enough, understandings of what constitutes a child vary considerably across space and time. This is because childhood is a social construction; over the last several hundred years, understandings of childhood have changed significantly. In North America and Western Europe, most adhere to the modern construction of childhood, which is perhaps best captured by the following UNICEF (2004) quote: "Childhood is the time for children to be in school and at play, to grow strong and confident with the love and encouragement of their family and an extended community of caring adults. It is a precious time in which children should live free from fear, safe from violence and protected from abuse and exploitation. As such, childhood means much more than just the space between birth and the attainment of adulthood. It refers to the state and condition of a child's life, to the quality of those years."

But this view of childhood has not always been the norm; in fact, this understanding is fairly recent within modern history. French scholar Philippe Ariès (1962) was one of the first to note that in medieval society the idea of childhood did not exist. He argued that prior to the 1700s, children were perceived as miniature adults and treated accordingly.

This becomes evident when one looks through historical laws. For instance, in eighteenth-century England, children were considered adults under law at the age of seven. Children over the age of seven were hanged for trivial offenses, such as stealing a pair of shoes. During the Industrial Revolution, young children were regularly hired to labor in mines and in factories. As reports of child mistreatment and abuse began to filter through the presses, child labor became more of a concern to the bourgeoisie. One of England's first comprehensive child labor laws was the Factory Act of 1833, which banned children from working in factories if they were under the age of nine and limited their working hours (between the ages of nine and thirteen) to forty-eight hours per week. This act also required two hours of daily school attendance for all children under fourteen years of age (Engels 1845 [1987]). Through the 1800s, perspectives on childhood began to change and the place of children switched from one of work to one of school. Gradually, work became perceived as being incompatible with a proper childhood, whereas schooling became perceived as necessary.

Thereafter, children in Western industrializing countries became increasingly protected, sheltered, and financially dependent on their parents and, consequently, children lost considerable status and power. Rather than working to help support their families, as many children elsewhere continue to do, children in the global North have become family welfare recipients. As noted by Scheper-Hughes and Sargent (1998, 12), "Children have become relatively worthless economically to their parents, but priceless in terms of their psychological worth." This modern construction of childhood has also trickled through to families belonging to the upper classes in Latin America. For the elite, children and youth are able to eschew labor in order to enjoy eating at international restaurant chains, shopping at name-brand stores, playing organized sports, attending private schools, and living in gated communities. Yet, for Latin America's poor, their lives may have more in common with the lives of youth in industrializing Britain than those of their wealthy Latin American peers.

Understandings of childhood also vary across cultures, and to this day, many cultures view childhood differently from the modern Western norm. In some Latin American indigenous communities, children's work is perceived as being an important and positive part of rural life. For instance, in highland Ecuador indigenous people joke that children get "four years to live for free." Once children reach the age of four, they have to start working in order to earn their keep. Children are taught how to perform age-appropriate jobs that both build skills and help their families. These jobs begin at the age of four, when children learn how to take animals to pasture. At the age of six, they learn how to cook. Between the ages of eight and ten, they learn how to cultivate crops. By the ages of ten to twelve, they know how to harvest crops. Thus, between the ages of ten and twelve, many children are viewed as competent enough to run a household. Although some might be surprised that children are involved in labor at such at young age, children's work generally integrates many aspects of play. Their labor is also highly valued for its formative contribution to children's social skills, education, identity formation, and recreation (Swanson 2010).

Yet, while children's labor is viewed as essential for skill building and the reproduction of community values in indigenous communities, it is also crucial to economic survival. This economic imperative associated with children's work cannot be overlooked when speaking of "cultural" constructions of childhood. The reality is that in indigenous and Afro-Latino communities, children often work more out of economic necessity than due to cultural preference. The history of colonialism in Latin America put indigenous peoples and Afro-Latinos at significant economic, social, and political disadvantage. For this reason, high poverty and inequality means that these groups are much more likely to labor than other youth in the region.

In order to protect children's rights around the world, in 1989 the United Nations put forth the UN Convention on the Rights of the Child (UNCRC). There are four guiding principles of the UNCRC, including nondiscrimination; adherence to the best interests of the child; the right to life, survival, and development; and the right to participate. Article 32 specifically deals with the complicated issue of child labor. It recognizes the right of the child to be protected from "economic exploitation and from performing any work that is likely to be hazardous or to interfere with the child's education, or to be harmful to the child's health or physical, mental, spiritual, moral or social development." This convention represents a very important global step in protecting children's rights and has now been ratified by every nation in the world, with the exceptions of the United States and South Sudan. Another important measure designed to combat child labor is Convention 182 on the Worst Forms of Child Labor, put forth by the

International Labor Organization (a United Nations agency with 183 member states) in 1999. This convention targets child trafficking, debt peonage, child soldiering, child prostitution, drug trafficking, and other forms of hazardous work. In response to these conventions, nations across Latin America have created their own sophisticated national codes to protect the rights of children and young people in law.

Nevertheless, despite newly enacted laws to protect children's rights, many youths in Latin America continue to work on the streets, labor on farms and plantations, pick garbage on trash heaps, sell their bodies in the sex trade, and work for drug cartels. The International Labor Organization estimates that there are 12.5 million working children in Latin America and the Caribbean, although these types of figures are notoriously difficult to pinpoint with accuracy (Diallo et al. 2013). Some forms of children's work are clearly more hazardous than others. For instance, working as a paid laborer in a small factory or on a banana plantation at the age of twelve is a very different experience from selling handicrafts with your siblings and family members on the streets. Organizations such as MANTHOC (Movimiento de Adolescentes y Niños Trabajadores Hijos de Obreros Cristianos) and its partner organization MNNATSOP (Movimiento Nacional de Niños, Niñas y Adolescentes Trabajadores Organizados del Perú) in Perú fight for children's right to work with dignity and without exploitation. They recognize the important role that children's work can play, not only in terms of socialization and development, but also in terms of maintaining household economies. In fact, many right-to-work organizations argue that if legislation banning child labor was enforced, it would exacerbate conditions of poverty for millions of children and their families.

In the following section, I examine children's rural agrarian lives. This topic is important because within Latin America, the majority of working children labor in the rural agricultural sector (Diallo et al. 2013). Some of this work is on large agricultural plantations, where conditions can be more exploitative, and some is on smaller family farms. As will be discussed, conditions are changing for youth in rural areas, forcing many to leave their villages in search of opportunities elsewhere.

Children's Rural Lives

Samantha Punch (2003) argues that much of the research conducted on children in the global South has focused almost exclusively on the world of children's work. While recognizing that work plays a major role in low-income children's lives, she believes that focusing too much on work obscures some of the more ordinary and everyday aspects of young people's childhoods. Through research in rural Bolivia, she demonstrates that play is an integral part of children's lives. This play is combined with work to help children learn about their environments, homes, and social lives (see also Katz 2004). Distinguishing between work and play can be difficult for rural children as these activities are often intertwined.

The quoted material in textbox 12.1 demonstrates how many household chores this young girl is responsible for at the age of nine (contrast her household responsibilities to those of the typical nine-year-old in the United States, Canada, or the UK for example!). The gendered division of labor in Latin America typically holds girls more responsible for domestic chores than boys, much like how women are typically responsible for a greater percentage of household reproductive work (unpaid work that involves caring for others and maintaining a household). Poverty also dictates that women and girls are often pulled into paid productive labor, such as market vending and petty commodity sales, as well. Beyond this, women and girls are

---

Textbox 12.1. Work and Play

Extract from a nine-year-old girl's diary in rural Bolivia, demonstrating the work children do and how it is integrated with play (Punch 2003, 284):

I got up at 6, combed my hair, washed my face and had my breakfast and pancakes. I went to Felisa's house to look for a goat and afterwards I came home and began to peel potatoes. I put the pot on to cook and made lunch. I went to let the goats out, I milked them and let them out of the enclosure. I went to feed my chicks and then I went to fetch water from the stream, I came home and ate my lunch. My lunch was made of rice. I went to give water and maize to the pigs and from there I fetched water to water my flowers, then I went to harvest potatoes. Then with my sister we went to play with my brother's bicycle and I went to fetch water and my sister saw a little pigeon. We wanted to catch it but we couldn't catch the small pigeon, we fetched water and went to play football. Then I had my tea with bread and then I went to enclose the cows and the goats. I had my supper and went to bed at 8 o'clock.

---

often responsible for community service work, thus increasing demands upon their time. This has been referred to as the "triple burden of women," since women are not only responsible for reproductive work, but also for productive work and community management activities (Moser 1993). However, this unequal gendered division of labor is not universal across Latin America. In some indigenous communities, particularly in the Andes, labor roles are distributed more evenly across genders. This is especially the case among young people. For instance, research that I conducted with children and young people in a rural indigenous community in Andean Ecuador demonstrated that boys and girls are almost equally involved in a range of domestic and agricultural activities (see figure 12.1). Through a survey of forty-three children between the ages of eleven and fourteen, I found that young people worked an average of five to six hours a day. Domestically, children cooked, washed dishes and clothes, cleaned, collected water, collected firewood, and cared for younger siblings. Agriculturally, children helped prepare the land, planted crops, weeded, irrigated, cultivated crops, and applied pesticides. Children were also responsible for bringing animals to pasture, collecting food for animals, fetching water and firewood, and killing guinea pigs, rabbits, and chickens. Due to Andean indigenous gender ideologies that tend toward a more equitable division of labor, there were only slight gender-based variations in the distribution of children's work across domestic, agricultural, and shepherding activities (Swanson 2010).

School is also an important part of children's lives in rural Latin America, but access to education varies across regions. For instance, educational attainment rates are much higher in Argentina, Chile, Uruguay, and Panama than they are in Nicaragua, Honduras, and Haiti (Urquiola and Calderón 2006). Children who live in remote areas have the most difficulty accessing education, as some may have to walk several hours a day to attend the nearest school. Often the nearest school only has primary-level education, making it challenging for young people to educate themselves beyond sixth grade. Lack of resources affects the quality of education, causing infrastructure, supplies, and teacher salaries to remain poor. Although the UNCRC mandates that all states shall "make primary education compulsory and available free to all," the reality is that going to school costs money. Students generally must pay for uniforms, textbooks, transportation, and school lunches, while some are also expected to donate money to support poorly funded schools and teachers. These fees can make education financially inaccessible for many young people.

Figure 12.1. Young children collecting plants and bringing animals to pasture in Andean Ecuador.

In the past, the path to adulthood for many young people involved inheriting or purchasing land, which allowed them to support their own families as agriculturalists. However, over the last several decades, conditions have changed in rural communities. To begin with, populations have grown rapidly, which has put more pressure on land. As health and nutrition improved across Latin America, more children began surviving, thus reducing infant mortality rates. The converse of this is that family sizes began to increase. Across much of Latin America, a demographic shift began in the 1970s wherein fertility rates began to decline. Yet, because of this past fertility bulge, overall numbers of young people will continue to rise well into the future (Carr, Lopez, and Bilsborrow 2009). Furthermore, in some of the more remote parts of Latin America where women's access to birth control remains limited, women continue to have large families, which puts additional pressure on land. In areas where there has been a tradition of land inheritance, many parents' holdings are so small that they cannot divide them into parcels capable of sustaining each of their children's families. In other communities, there simply is not enough land for young people to purchase. As a result, many youths are searching elsewhere for their futures.

Additionally, structural adjustment programs and neoliberal policies introduced since the 1980s have reconfigured smallholder agricultural economies (see chapters 3 and 5). These types of policies have prioritized large-scale farms and plantations, making it difficult for smallholder farms to compete. With the introduction of new agricultural technologies, the costs of agriculture have increased, as farmers are required to mechanize their labor and purchase high-tech seeds, fertilizers, and pesticides if they hope to stay competitive. For many peasant farmers, this simply is not an option.

Cultural globalization has also filtered through to many rural communities in Latin America through television, radio, and other media. As in the global North, television has become part of the nightly ritual in Latin America, as families sit together to watch the latest Mexican, Colombian, or Brazilian telenovelas. Many of the internationally syndicated television programs and Hollywood movies watched in North America and Western Europe are also a key part of Latin American media culture. For young people, this is significant. When they are bombarded with images representing the latest fashions, coolest gadgets, and most important global brands, they respond in the same way as youth elsewhere: they want them.

The difficulty lies in the fact that these types of material commodities and markers of cool are inaccessible and beyond the means of many low-income youth, and this can be very trying. For instance, imagine growing up in a one-room house made of mud and thatch, or poor-quality concrete blocks, watching these advertisements and television programs nightly. As you huddle for warmth on your family's only bed to watch the latest episode of *America's Next Top Model*, you might wonder why these vast inequalities exist, even though you and your family members work so hard to get ahead. For wealthy youth in Latin America, reproducing the modern construction of childhood as seen on television and in movies is not an issue. These young people can have their birthdays at McDonald's and buy the latest fashions and coolest gadgets. But for the poor, watching these programs may enhance their feelings of deprivation and inequality—and understandably so. The unfortunate reality is that as this modern construction of childhood is being exported around the world, the resources needed to reproduce this idealized form of childhood are lacking (see Ruddick 2003). What is happening across Latin American is that young people are becoming acutely aware of their poverty and recognize that youth in wealthier parts of the world—and in wealthier parts of their own countries—are leading lives very different from their own.

In order to overcome some of these problems in rural areas, including poor access to education, limited land opportunities, nonprofitability of agriculture, and cultural globalization, many young people have been migrating to the cities. Some migrate seasonally, whereas some migrate permanently. In 1960, half of Latin America's population lived in rural areas (Fay 2005). This began to change rapidly over the following decades; between 1960 and 1980 Latin America's rural-to-urban migration outpaced that of other regions. Today, 80 percent of South America's residents live in urban areas, whereas 70 percent of Central America's residents do (Carr, Lopez, and Bilsborrow 2009). Thus, the vast majority of Latin America's population is urban, and the youth exodus to the cities is a large contributing factor (see chapter 4).

Street and Street Working Children

While opportunities in cities are better than in rural areas, young people often find themselves working in low-skilled, informal-sector jobs. These types of jobs often have low start-up costs and allow young people to earn some income until better opportunities arise. For anyone who has traveled to large Latin American urban centers, the ubiquitous "street child" is a familiar sight. Stuart Aitken describes a scene in Mexico City's central plaza (2001, 8):

The music they perform is loud, discordant and, if you choose to see and hear them in that way, they are precocious and disrespectful. I can hear them from the other side of Mexico City's central plaza, the Zócalo. They are very loud; they want to be heard. I approach and watch them, listening to their busking through several chaotic, unrecognizable tunes. The oldest boy plays a trumpet while a younger boy and girl thrash a snare and a bass drum respectively. The children seemed intent upon their music rather than the collection bowl in front of a baby who sucks her fingers seemingly oblivious to the cacophony.

Others may have seen children juggling at intersections or singing on buses, sometimes making heartbreaking pitches for a sale. Children and young people are involved in many types of work in cities, but some of their more visible employment activities include shining shoes, guarding cars, working in markets, begging, and selling candies, handicrafts, flowers, and other small goods. Because these children work on the streets in visible public spaces, they are often perceived as "street children," regardless of their situations. Yet, young people have a range of experiences and connections to the streets. In an effort to distinguish between different types of children on the streets, UNICEF popularized the terms "children in the streets" and "children of the streets." They described the former as children who work on the streets but return to their families at night, and the latter as children who make the streets their home and have limited family contact. Others commonly use the terms "street working children" to describe children *in* the streets and "street children" or "street living children" for children *of* the streets. These categories are useful for beginning to make sense of who works and who lives on the streets. Nevertheless, the reality is often more complex, as children maintain varying degrees of contact with their families, which may change over time.

Generally, there are more children working on the streets than living on the streets. Many children work only on weekends or after school in order to earn some money to help their families in their spare time. Others work during school holidays and summer vacations to earn some funds for the following scholastic year. For instance, in my research with child street vendors and beggars in Ecuador, I learned that the primary reason these children work is to pay for their educations. This is corroborated by Bromley and Mackie's (2009) research in Cusco, Perú, where they report that 84 percent of child street traders work to pay for schooling. This is significant as it runs contrary to assumptions that children's involvement in street work causes them to gradually abandon school. While this may be the case in some instances, for many children, street work is an enabling factor for education. Given the many costs associated with schooling (such as uniforms, textbooks, lunches, and transportation) and the difficulties earning income in rural areas, their work on the streets is crucial for continuing with their educations. And by having better educations, children hope that they will also have better and more prosperous futures (Swanson 2010).

Critiques of children's work point to the many hazards associated with working on the streets. As evident in textbox 12.2, street work is difficult and often involves long days under a hot sun while inhaling noxious exhaust fumes and walking great distances to make a sale. Bromley and Mackie (2009) point to some of the risks associated with street work, including accidents, theft and abuse (often at the hands of other children and the police), shortage of time for play, and some disruption to education (as teachers report that students are often too tired to perform well in school). While these risks are real and significant, the authors also point to a number of positives associated with children's work. Although some children reported limited time for play, Bromley and Mackie observed that children's street work was often a hybrid of work and play. For instance, youth would use empty plastic bottles to kick around in a game of *fútbol* (soccer) in between sales pitches to tourists. Other positives include increased self-esteem as children learned new skills and tactics as street traders. In Cusco, some of these skills included being able to converse in a foreign language, manage small budgets, manage time, attract customers, source goods, and negotiate sales. In other

Figure 12.2. Street working children in Quito, Ecuador.

words, children learned how to become young entrepreneurs. Eighty percent of children in Cusco also reported enjoying their work (perhaps reaffirming that their work is often a hybrid of both work and play). Finally, the income that children earn is economically empowering. Children report that while the majority of their income goes toward food and schooling, a smaller portion is kept for personal pocket money to use as they wish (most often on play or consumption). Thus, much like children's rural work, work on the streets can provide young people with important and formative skills.

That being said, another significant concern about children's street work is that some youth become pulled into street life. Whether due to addiction, abuse and neglect at home, enhanced freedom on the streets, incorporation into a street gang, or all of the above, some youth choose or are forced to make the streets their home. Street children are at the most risk on the streets, particularly due to violence. They are a highly stigmatized group who both suffer and perpetrate great violence and raise fundamental questions about constructions of childhood and the ways children are expected to behave. As explained by Jones (1997) in textbox 12.3, children who live and sleep on the streets often behave outside of social norms. These children are con-

Text Box 12.2. Street Working Children

Description of indigenous children's working days in Quito, Ecuador (Swanson 2010, 60-61).

On a typical day, children begin working at seven in the morning. For the most part they work along Quito's two trolley lines. They occupy the narrow spaces surrounding the low concrete dividers that separate traffic from trolley buses. One step to the left or one step to the right at in inopportune time would have dire consequences.

Every time the light turns red, youth upward of ten years old approach cars one by one and say, "compre chicles" (buy gum), with a few packets of gum lodged between their fingers. When they catch a potential customer's eye, some may give a supplicating gesture, while others may point to the babies on their backs and say, "para el wawito" (for the baby). Others may use different tactics and move rapidly down the row of cars until they find a willing customer. For young children the work is similar, yet most beg rather than sell. Children as young as three years old approach cars, extend their hands, and say "regálame" (give me a gift).

From seven to seven, twelve hours a day, women and children spend their days breathing in exhaust fumes under the hot Quiteño sun, walking back and forth along lines of idling cars. At the end of the day, women and children working in the immediate vicinity gather together to take the trolley bus back to their rooms. Before retiring for the night, they purchase the following day's gum supply from a local convenience store . . . [T]hey then crowd into their small rented rooms wherein anywhere from two to ten individuals sleep on flattened cardboard mats on the floor.

Textbox 12.3. Street Children and Public Space

Based upon research in Puebla, Mexico, Gareth Jones (1997, 42) explains how meanings attached to public space have important consequences for perceptions of street children, which he describes as the moral imagination:

The moral imagination produces and reinforces a series of permitted activities and behaviours in public space. The activities of street children challenge what is permissible. Street children present a highly visible aspect of poverty through attempts to gain money from singing on buses or guarding cars. They also break the codes of moral behviour by being dirty or washing in fountains, playing in the main square or sleeping in a shop doorway, being loud, talking slang: and, in Brazil, having a darker skin. . . . The organization of street children into camadas (small gangs) adds menace to this behaviour and reinforces the association of street children with drugs, even if abuse is normally casual and based on so-called 'soft' drugs. . . . Similarly the perception that street children are sexually active and promiscuous constructs a moral imagination. . . . By associating street children with a host of social problems visible to the public, from drug abuse to prostitution and crime, this group is perceived as a threat to society. The most extreme response of 'civilised' society to such a moral threat is the 'social cleansing' offered by the death squads. Rather perversely, malnourished, poorly educated children are perceived to be dangerous by elites and governments.

structed as threats to society, and in some cases, measures to remove them from the streets have been extreme. Brazil is especially notorious for violence perpetrated against street children. The most renowned incident was in 1993 when off-duty police officers massacred a group of eight street children sleeping on the steps of the Candelária Church in Rio de Janeiro (see Jones and Rodgers 2009 for a first-person account from Wagner dos Santos, a survivor). While this happened almost two decades ago, newspaper accounts continue to report abuse at the hands of the police, while youth continue to commit great acts of violence against one another. Much of this violence is highly racialized, disproportionately affecting Afro-Brazilian males (Costa Vargas and Amparo Alves 2010). Young women and girls are also at risk of violence. In her participatory research with young sex workers in Bogotá, Colombia, Ritterbusch (2013) describes a violent social-cleansing campaign designed to rid the streets of undesirable youth. Since the turn of this century, zero-tolerance and *Mano Dura* policing strategies have been used across Latin American cities to cleanse urban streets of unsightly elements, particularly street and working youth (Swanson 2013).

High rates of inequality often correspond to high rates of homicide. Given significant rates of inequality in the region, it is perhaps no surprise that Latin America currently suffers the highest youth homicide rate in the world (Jones and Rodgers 2009). This brutal youth violence has been sensationalized in films like *City of God* in Brazil and *Sin Nombre* in El Salvador. But as many would attest, these film dramatizations are based upon an unfortunate reality in some poor urban communities. In Nicaragua, Dennis Rodgers (2007, 447) describes the situation as the following: "The talk and the fear of crime permeate everyday conversations, particularly regarding the *pandillas*, or youth gangs, that ubiquitously roam the streets of urban neighbourhoods, robbing, beating and frequently killing, transforming large swathes of the country's cities into quasi-war zones, as they fight each other with weapons ranging from sticks, stones and knives to AK-47 assault rifles, fragmentation grenades, and mortars." This constant fear of crime impinges upon spatial freedoms and leads some—particularly the middle and upper classes—to begin building cities of walls represented by a segregated city, as described by Teresa Caldeira's work in Brazil (2000).

Others respond to this violence by fleeing their homelands to travel to *El Norte*. The nations of El Salvador, Honduras, Guatemala, and Mexico are experiencing the largest exodus of young migrants, many of whom present themselves to the US Border Patrol as political refugees who fear for their lives (see chapters 13 and 15). The figures are staggering: over sixty-eight thousand young people were apprehended at the US-Mexico border in 2014 (USCBP 2014). A UNHCR (UN High Commissioner for Refugees) survey of unaccompanied child migrants in US detention centers discovered that 58 percent of children described being forcibly displaced from their homes due to violence. In Central America, gang members often target young teens in order to build their membership base, and refusal isn't an option. As stated by a Honduran teen, "If you don't join, the gang will shoot you. If you do, the rival gang or the cops will shoot you. But if you leave, no one will shoot you" (UNHCR 2014, 10). To escape these personal threats of violence, youth travel thousands of miles on foot and by car, bus, truck, raft, and train at great risk to their safety. But they are willing to take these risks, since the dangers at home are perceived as far worse.

Clearly, experiences of childhood vary across Latin America. For some, particularly the urban poor, violence and poverty have made life exceptionally difficult. While social and economic inequality remains a significant barrier to change, there are a number of programs designed to help children and youth in Latin America and provide them with better life opportunities.

Conclusion

Youth Empowerment

Children's rights and advocacy organizations vary from small grassroots groups working in local communities to larger organizations designed to protect the rights of children and youth on a broader scale. Due to the diversity of issues encountered by young people, organizations focus on a range of overlapping topics, including poverty alleviation, violence prevention, health services, youth activism, education, culture and heritage, and environmental change, among others. Collectively, many of these organizations aim to empower young people to take action in order to effect positive change within their communities.

The Brazilian nongovernmental organization Fundação Casa Grande, for instance, is widely considered to be a model of community and youth empowerment and has won numerous national and international awards (www.fundacaocasagrande.org.br/). Located in Novo Olinda, Ceará, a northeastern state with high levels of poverty and inequality, Casa Grande is led by youth and works for youth. The children who attend this center were once rural agricultural laborers with few prospects for education. Now, poor children from the region have the option to live, study, and work at Casa Grande and run a radio station, a museum, a cultural center, a library, and a theater. Through this process, the organization hopes to empower young people to recapture regional cultural identity, popular folklore, and environmental knowledge. They also hope to provide low-income youth with the same types of opportunities that are provided to more privileged youth elsewhere.

Numerous organizations provide services for street working children, perhaps because these youth are so visible in Latin American cities. Many of these organizations are in line with Bromley and Mackie (2009), who argue that instead of universally condemning children's work, international policy should work toward an approach that provides more recognition of children's right to work under nonexploitative conditions. The authors argue that the benefits of children's work, such as increased income, skills, self-esteem, and socialization, should be viewed positively and that "children should have the option to work, free from the heavy handed interference of officials," as long as their working conditions are protected (2009, 155). The Center for the Working Girl, or El Centro de la Niña Trabajadora (CENIT), in Ecuador is an example of an organization that strives to do just this.

Located in Quito, Ecuador, CENIT is devoted to helping working children, particularly girls (www.cenitecuador.org/). Many of the girls involved in CENIT are first-generation indigenous migrants whose parents moved to the city from rural areas in order to provide their children with better opportunities. Yet due to the high costs of urban living, these children must work to help their families survive. Most end up working in the urban informal sector as street vendors and market vendors. CENIT conducts outreach work to provide low-income families with health and social services, nutrition programs, and job training. It also hosts a school that accommodates the schedule of working children, which makes it easier for parents to enroll their offspring, particularly their daughters (who are often given lowest educational priority). Through CENIT, girls and their siblings have access to quality education and services that they would not otherwise have.

Given high rates of youth violence in the region, organizations such as the Violence Prevention Center or Centro de Prevención de la Violencia (CEPREV) in Managua, Nicaragua, are critical. CEPREV is an organization that has been working with gang members, their families, and the broader community since 1997 (www.ceprev.org/). The organization strives to understand the root causes behind high levels of violence in certain neighborhoods, focusing particularly upon machismo, self-esteem, and interfamilial relations. Through training, outreach, and community programs, CEPREV has reached over thirty thousand people in thirty-six barrios to effect an overall reduction in levels of youth violence as well as increased school attendance and employment for many who have left violence behind.

Finally, youth activism is imperative. Young people in Latin America have a long history of rising up against oppression and inequality and demonstrating publically in the streets. For this reason, organizations such as Mexico's Youth Alternative Resistance or Jóvenes en Resistencia Alternativa (JRA) (espora.org/jra/) represent the radical front of a growing anticapitalist youth activist movement, with links throughout the Americas. JRA stands against the drug war, pushes for demilitarization, and advocates for the rights of indigenous peoples, among other issues. More than anything, the organization uses popular education to mobilize young people to reexamine their world critically and encourage them to fight for equality and justice.

By empowering young people and providing them with better access to education, nutrition, health and social services, and skills training, these organizations hope that young people will have enhanced opportunities in the future. Nevertheless, inequalities within Latin America remain vast; young people must continue the struggle to overcome poverty and marginality, and organizations must support young people along this journey. This generation of global youth may be in a better position than ever to join in this struggle, through the use of new technologies to share knowledge and empower individuals. Collectively and individually, global youth can effect positive change on local and global scales.

Key Terms

social construction of childhood: Recognition that ideas surrounding childhood are not universal, but rather have varied across cultures and throughout history.

street children: Children who work, live, and sleep on the streets and who have limited contact with their families. Sometimes called "children *of* the streets."

street working children: Children who work on the streets but who continue to live with their families. Sometimes referred to as "children *in* the streets."

United Nations Convention on the Rights of the Child (UNCRC): A legally binding international convention that obliges national governments to protect the civil, cultural, economic, political, and social rights of young people under the age of eighteen.

Suggested Readings

Aitken, Stuart, Silvia López Estrada, Joel Jennings, and Lina Maria Aguirre. "Reproducing Life and Labor: Global Processes and Working Children in Tijuana, Mexico." *Childhood* 13 (2006): 365–87.

Punch, Samantha. "Negotiating Migrant Identities: Young People in Bolivia and Argentina." *Children's Geographies* 5 (2007): 95–112.

Radcliffe, Sarah and Andrew Webb. "Mapuche Youth Between Exclusion and the Future: Protest, Civic Society and Participation in Chile." *Children's Geographies* (2014). DOI: 10.1080/14733285.2014.964667.

Schmidt, Leigh Anne and Stephanie Buechler. "Honduran Boys Confronting Adversity: Urban Multilocality and Kin Mobilization." *Children's Geographies* (2014). DOI: 10.1080/14733285.2014.890390.

Swanson, Kate. *Begging as a Path to Progress: Indigenous Women and Children and the Struggle for Ecuador's Urban Spaces.* Athens: University of Georgia Press, 2010.

Organizations Working with Young People (with Volunteer Opportunities)

Casa Xalteva offers Spanish-language training programs for volunteers and education and cultural programs for young people in Granada, Nicaragua: www.casaxalteva.org/.

Centro de la Niña Trabajadora (CENIT) helps working girls and their families by providing educational, vocational, medical, social, and recreational programs in Quito, Ecuador: http://cenitecuador.org/.

Fundación Mariposas Amarillas is a small grassroots organization committed to supporting disadvantaged children and families around Santa Marta, Colombia: http://fmacolombia.weebly.com/.

Mayan Families works with indigenous Mayan families near Lake Atitlan, Guatemala, to provide food, education, shelter, and health services: www.mayanfamilies.org/.

Melel Xojobal works to protect the rights and improve the quality of life of indigenous children and youth in Chiapas, Mexico: http://melelxojobal.org.mx.

References

Aitken, Stuart A. *Geographies of Young People: The Morally Contested Spaces of Identity*. New York: Routledge, 2001.

Ariès, Philippe. *Centuries of Childhood*. New York: Vintage Books, 1962.

Baldock, Hannah. "Child Hunger Deaths Shock Argentina." *Guardian*, November 25, 2002. Retrieved July 22, 2011. www.guardian.co.uk/world/2002/nov/25/famine.argentina.

Bosco, Fernando. "Global Aid Networks and Hungry Children in Argentina: Thinking About Geographies of Responsibility and Care." *Children's Geographies* 5 (2007): 55–76.

Bromley, Rosemary D. F., and Peter K. Mackie. "Child Experiences as Street Traders in Peru: Contributing to a Reappraisal for Working Children." *Children's Geographies* 7 (2009): 141–58.

Caldeira, Teresa. *City of Walls: Crime, Segregation and Citizenship in São Paulo*. Berkeley: University of California Press, 2000.

Carr, David, Anna Carla Lopez, and Richard Bilsborrow. "The Population, Agriculture, and Environment Nexus in Latin America: Country-Level Evidence from the Latter Half of the Twentieth Century." *Population and Environment* 30 (2009): 222–46.

Costa Vargas, João, and Jaime Amparo Alves. "Geographies of Death: An Intersectional Analysis of Police Lethality and the Racialized Regimes of Citizenship in São Paulo." *Ethnic and Racial Studies* 33 (2010): 611–36.

Diallo, Yacouba, Alex Etienne, and Farhad Mehran. *Global Child Labour Trends 2008 to 2012*. Geneva: International Labour Organization (ILO), ILO International Programme on the Elimination of Child Labour, 2013.

Engels, Friedrich. *The Condition of the Working Class in England in 1844*. 1845; New York: Penguin, 1987.

Fay, Marianne (Ed.). *The Urban Poor in Latin America*. Washington, DC: World Bank, 2005.

Jones, Gareth A. "*Junto con los niños*: Street Children in Mexico." *Development in Practice* 7 (1997): 39–49.

Jones, Gareth A., and Dennis Rodgers (Eds.). *Youth Violence in Latin America: Gangs and Juvenile Violence in Perspective*. New York: Palgrave MacMillan, 2009.

Katz, Cindi. *Growing Up Global: Economic Restructuring and Children's Everyday Lives*. Minneapolis: University of Minnesota Press, 2004.

Love, Elizabeth. "Prisoners of Perfection: Countless Argentine Women Suffer from Eating Disorders, and the Psyche of Youth Is Battered by a Cultural Obsession with Appearance." *San Francisco Chronicle*, October 19, 2000. Retrieved July 22, 2011. www.sfgate.com/cgibin/article.cgi?file=/chronicle/archive/2000/10/19/MN1646.DTL.

Moser, Caroline. *Gender Planning and Development: Theory, Practice and Training*. New York: Routledge, 1993.

Punch, Samantha. "Childhoods in the Majority World: Miniature Adults or Tribal Children?" *Sociology* 37 (2003): 277–95.

Ritterbusch, Amy. "From Street Girls to 'VMC' Girls: Empowering Strategies for Representing and Overcoming Place-Memories of Violence in Colombia." *Children, Youth and Environments* 23 (2013): 64–104.

Rodgers, Dennis. "Joining the Gang and Becoming a Broder: The Violence of Ethnography in Contemporary Nicaragua." *Bulletin of Latin American Research* 26 (2007): 444–61.

Ruddick, Sue. "The Politics of Aging: Globalization and the Restructuring of Youth and Childhood." *Antipode* 35 (2003): 334–62.

Scheper-Hughes, Nancy, and Carolyn Sargent. "Introduction: The Cultural Politics of Childhood." In *Small Wars: The Cultural Politics of Childhood*, edited by N. Scheper-Hughes and C. Sargent, 1–33. Berkeley: University of California Press, 1998.

Swanson, Kate. *Begging as a Path to Progress: Indigenous Women and Children and the Struggle for Ecuador's Urban Spaces.* Athens: University of Georgia Press, 2010.

———. "Zero Tolerance in Latin America: Punitive Paradox in Urban Policy Mobilities." *Urban Geography* (2013) 34: 972–88.

UNICEF. "Childhood Defined." *Childhood under Threat. The State of the World's Children 2005* (2004). Retrieved July 22, 2011. www.unicef.org/sowc05/english/childhooddefined.html.

United Nations High Commissioner for Refugees (UNHCR). *Children on the Run.* Washington, DC: UNHCR, 2014.

United States Customs and Border Patrol (USCBP). *Southwest Border Unaccompanied Children (FY2014).* Retrieved April 13, 2014. http://www.cbp.gov/newsroom/stats/southwest-border-unaccompanied-children-2014.

Urquiola, Miguel, and Valentina Calderón. "Apples and Oranges: Educational Enrollment and Attainment across Countries in Latin America and the Caribbean." *International Journal of Educational Development* 26 (2006): 572–90.

Chapter 13

US-Mexico Borderlands

Altha J. Cravey

Every American city is now a border town. If you drive through the Arkansas hills, you will see a single-wide trailer church with a sign that reads *Templo Evangélico*. If you take Interstate 10 through Metairie, Louisiana, and exit north, you will find a Mexican barrio hidden behind a neighborhood of Cajuns. In Naperville, Illinois, Spanish-speaking men in work clothes peruse the abundant "Hispanic foods" aisle, buying corn husks to make their traditional Christmas meal of tamales, but Chicago style—with bratwurst instead of beef.

—Luis Alberto Urrea, 2004

We as Native people, we do not consider you as an immigrant. We believe that the government drew a line and that line—as Native people, there is no line there for us. [. . .] And so we feel that the struggles of the immigrant people as well as the people who live here should be the same. That everybody who's here except the Native people are immigrants and we think you are our Native brothers and sisters.

—Yellow Bird, speaking words of welcome to *Antorcha Guadalupana*
relay runners in central North Carolina in Bishop et al. 2008

THE AREAS OF THE SOUTHWESTERN United States and northern Mexico that are adjacent to the international boundary line are known as the "borderlands" (figure 13.1). It is a place where influences from both nations meet, meld, and are transformed into a unique and distinct cultural identity. Many people live and work in the US-Mexico borderlands, while others travel north through the US-Mexico borderlands en route to US destinations. Many, if not most, northbound migrants traverse a harsh and forbidding natural environment in search of employment and opportunity on "the other side." In recent years, the borderlands region has become so treacherous for migrants that human rights activists call the boundary line the "wall of death." Violence has also spiked in northern Mexico following a 2007 government crackdown on drug cartels. Those who are dying—and confronting diverse forms of violence in the borderlands—are mostly ordinary Mexican citizens. The region's human rights crisis and its complex historical geography are poorly understood, particularly in the United States.

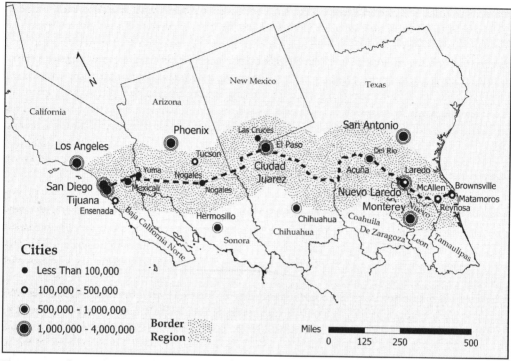

Figure 13.1. The US-Mexico border region. Map by Craig Dalton.

A line two thousand miles long divides the sovereign national territory of Mexico from that of the United States (figure 13.1). On the eastern end, the line follows the Rio Grande River while the western half of the line is purely geometric, cutting through the Sonoran and Mojave deserts and the coastal mountain range. Thousands of newly manufactured television sets, garage-door openers, trucks, and bras and panties move freely across the line every day, while humans are ever more restricted from movement. Why has it become so risky and so costly for human beings to cross this imaginary line in the soil, when regional and national policies increasingly encourage the "opening of the border" to the flows of goods, services, and capital investments? In examining this question, we begin to see why this line in the soil is a potent symbol of conflict, of possible dreams and futures, and of relationships between intimates and strangers. As Gloria Anzaldúa famously wrote in the 1980s, the US-Mexico border is an "open wound" where, "the first world grates against the third world and bleeds" (Anzaldúa 1987).

The Double Life of the Borderline: A Symbol and a Material Reality

The history of the line itself provides insight on relations of domination (power-geometries) that have shaped, and continue to shape, symbolic and material inequities in and between Mexico and the United States. The borderline resulted from a violent conquest, rather than negotiations between two equal states (Limerick 2000, 1987).[1] Mexico lost half of its national territory to the United States with a scant $18 million paid as compensation. Mexican schoolchildren learn about this conquest as the "US Invasion," whereas in the United States, the more neutral sounding "US-Mexico War" is understood as part of the "natural" expansion westward of European settlers who undertook what was seen as a civilizing mission in sparsely populated, underutilized, and well-endowed western territories. Political leaders, as well as adventurers and entrepreneurs, used the idea of Manifest Destiny to legitimize such expansionary conquests. The Treaty of Guadalupe Hidalgo (1848) ended the war and marked out a boundary line in which the United States swallowed some one hundred thousand Mexicans and two hundred thousand Native Americans along with one million square miles of land. The newly established US-Mexico boundary line included deep sea ports on the Pacific Ocean, soon-to-be discovered gold deposits, and all or part of ten new states for the victors: Arizona, California, Colorado, Kansas, Nevada, New Mexico, Oklahoma, Texas, Utah, and Wyoming. A few years later, the Gadsden Treaty (1853) added a portion of southern Arizona and southern New Mexico to the United States and finalized the line we see on contemporary maps.

The line on the map may appear neutral, as does naming the war the "US-Mexico War." For students of Latin American geography, however, it is essential to understand this line as a new kind of land grabbing and new kind of imperialism within the Western Hemisphere. If we can imagine this line as a symbol of US neoimperialism (Gonzalez 2000; Chávez 2008), it is easier to see the way the line is both a symbol of US domination and a concrete physical location. The borderline has a double life.

This chapter begins with a discussion of the historical geography of the US-Mexico line and the US-Mexico border region. The second section explores the rapid urbanization of the borderlands during the Mexican maquiladora expansion. This discussion demonstrates that US and Mexican elites benefitted from a capitalist development project in northern Mexico while families, communities, and individuals suffered social fragmentation and disintegration. At the same time, the *maquila* industry fostered domestic and international migration in Mexico as well as an explosion of informal economic activities. The third section examines the way that informal economic activities, including people smuggling and drug smuggling, gained momentum in recent decades, and how in turn this increase in illegality and informality became a pretext to militarize the Mexican side of the border in a War on Drugs. The final section has some concluding remarks.

Historical Geography of the Borderlands

The harsh natural environment of the borderlands is extremely hot and arid. In both the United States and Mexico, the region was historically a marginal zone, in that it was isolated and distant from centers of cultural, economic, and political influence. Long-distance communication and transportation were only possible through arduous, time-consuming travel across vast open spaces, desert lands, and rugged mountain terrain, with sparse rivers or lakes (Nabhan 1985). These conditions made effective colonization difficult for many years and so the region remained sparsely populated well into the twentieth century.

The experience of Native Americans in the borderlands is a complex and largely tragic narrative. Many diverse Indian groups inhabit the borderlands, which in the eighteenth and nineteenth centuries could be grouped in four categories. Tarahumaras, Yaquis, and Pimas lived simply and settled near their productive farmlands. Zunis, Hopis, Acoma, and others built elaborate pueblo-style compact villages and also farmed the land. Band Indians, such as the Apaches and Navajos, mixed agriculture with hunting and gathering and did not live in permanent settlements. Finally, the nonagricultural Seri Indians formed roving bands and relied on fishing, hunting, and gathering wild foods (Martinez 1988).

The presence of Native people was seen as a "problem" by various interest groups in the United States and Mexico, who felt that native peoples did not adequately exploit the abundant natural resources of the borderlands. At the time of the US-Mexico War, James Polk used this racist mindset to his advantage to argue that the Mexican government was incapable of controlling its territory, particularly the portion inhabited by Indians in northern Mexico.[2] And in spite of winning the war, US victors showed little respect for the new boundary line or for Mexican sovereignty. Indian raiders based in the southeastern United States wreaked death, destruction, and depopulation in northern Mexico throughout the late nineteenth century. People who moved west and settled in Texas and elsewhere in the new territory supported the raiding system and profited by buying goods and captives from the Indian raiders (Martinez, 1988; Stoddard 1983).

The urban, economic, and demographic expansion of the borderlands occurred in spurts that are associated with distinct economic activities. For simplicity, I consider four phases of growth: (1) the development of transportation networks in the nineteenth century and the first decades of the twentieth century; (2) US wartime and post-war recruitment of Mexican laborers during and following World War II; (3) the maquiladoras and urban demographic explosion in northern Mexico, beginning in the mid-1960s; (4) and the recent explosion of informal activities, especially smuggling.

Beginning in the nineteenth century, the international line itself provoked the establishment of small settlement nodes to handle cross-border commerce and traffic. Modern transportation networks, including north-south roadways and railroads, helped to link population centers in the region itself, as well as link these cities and towns with distant national capitals. During the US Prohibition era (the 1920s through 1933), residents in northern Mexico expanded tourism and entertainment industries for a predominately North American clientele. Sex, liquor, drugs, gambling, and other vices were promoted in a variety of ways.

A second growth spurt followed the economic depression of the 1930s and "coincided with a US military buildup during the 1940s and 1950s" (Arreola and Curtis 1993, 26). Military bases were established and expanded quickly in the southwest United States. The manpower shortage in the United States during World War II had a direct impact on the Mexican side of the line as well. Mexican workers were recruited to the United States for seasonal agricultural work and railway construction under the auspices of the binational Bracero Program (1942–1965). In this way, border cities became increasingly important as staging areas for northern-bound migrants.

A third phase of expansion that began in the 1960s was tied to Mexico's maquila experiment, a Mexican development plan that featured electronics and apparel factories—maquilas—along the border. While investment in maquila industrialization quickly overshadowed other economic elements, the Mexican border strategy actually began as set of diverse initiatives including border beautification and tourism promotion. Mexican assembly-plant manufacturing (maquilas) produced a demographic explosion in the northern part of the country and especially along the border.

A proliferation of informal activities at the border has overshadowed the maquila growth spurt and can be considered a fourth wave of expansion. These activities include the highly profitable smuggling of drugs and people along with affiliated services such as safe houses, false documents, and other assistance to undocumented border crossers who want to join the ranks of eleven million (or more!) unauthorized Mexican migrants currently working in the United States.

The third and fourth expansionary waves drove the changes that resulted in the complex contemporary reality of life in the US-Mexico border region. In the next sections of this chapter, I examine in more detail the maquiladora program, followed by a discussion of the wide range of informal activities in the region. Gender dynamics in both expansionary phases helps to highlight the social costs of capitalist expansion, especially on the Mexican side of the line. Gender issues are illustrated and connected to other concerns, such as environmental problems, child rearing, and neighborhood issues.

The Mexican Maquila Program, NAFTA, and Spaces of Neoliberalism

The Mexican maquila program (1965), officially known as the Border Industrialization Program, and the North American Free Trade Agreement (1994) profoundly changed the character of the US-Mexico borderlands. The maquila program began as a massive geographical experiment in which a narrow strip of Mexican territory along the border was carved out as a growth zone, an "export processing zone."[3] The rules of doing business were adapted in specific ways to encourage the expansion of global factories, sometimes referred to worldwide as "the global assembly line." By changing the rules of investment and the norms of labor and business regulation in this zone, Mexico created a neoliberal space and succeeded in capturing a portion of US and global manufacturing investments that were flowing into developing countries in the 1970s and 1980s as part of a global pattern of capitalist restructuring.[4] Industrial sectors that are especially prominent in Mexico's maquilas are textile and apparel, electronics, and automotive parts (Bacon 2004; Fernandez-Kelly 1983).

By creating new factory jobs, the maquila program encouraged urbanization and migration to northern Mexico. Young people poured into the zone from nearby rural areas and from more distant locations in central and southern Mexico. During the 1970s, 1980s, and 1990s, border cities in both countries grew faster than the national averages in their respective countries. Mexican cities with maquila manufacturing grew especially quickly. In his book *Where North Meets South*, Lawrence A. Herzog provides an overview of the expansion of an urban system in the late twentieth century borderlands (Herzog 1990, 48–62). Migrants from the interior of Mexico seek jobs in the maquilas, as well as in the booming informal economy, retail establishments, and family-based micro-enterprises (i.e., fresh tortillas, neighborhood child care, home remedies). Other migrants, sometimes members of the same families, cross the international line and seek better paid opportunities in the United States. Young men tend to cross the border at much higher rates than women, and women are much more likely to work as entry-level laborers in local maquila factories. These transnational flows have had an indelible impact on both countries; long-distance parenting is common among recent Mexican immigrants in the United States, and one in seven Mexicans of working age is estimated to be working in the United States. After the child migration crisis of the summer of 2014, The Center for Migration Policy reported that forty-three thousand unaccompanied minors were released by the Border Patrol to sponsors throughout the states, to varied effects. Although many local governments have risen to the challenge of providing public services to the newly arrived children, many of these children struggle with the emotional burden of adjusting to a new culture and with recovering from the emotional traumas incurred during their journey. For many local governments, budgetary constraints and inadequate training preclude adequate support for these children (Chishti and Hipsman 2014).

The global assembly line (maquila) first emerged in Mexico in 1965 as an ad hoc experiment at isolated sites on the US-Mexico border. The development strategy expanded rapidly into a sophisticated comprehensive federal program to attract export investment. Interestingly, before embracing maquila production, Mexico was already highly industrialized, owing to a long-term government project known as import substitution industrialization (ISI), a centerpiece of Mexico's high growth "miracle" years of the 1940s, 1950s, and 1960s (see chapter 3). In the 1980s, Mexican industrial strategy was transformed and reoriented to foreign investment for export production. Maquila production thus became a symbol of, and a means to, wider philosophical and political transformations guided by *neoliberal principles*—principles that call for less state intervention and the expansion of the "free market." This shift in Mexico's industrial policy was marked by a geographic shift from a centralized industrial core to dispersed northern sites, a transformation in the nature of the state, and a corresponding reorientation of the state's vision for development and for the future. Key aspects of this transformation are listed in table 13.1. A range of inward-oriented development policies was reversed to encourage internationalization, liberalization, and privatization of the economy (see table 13.1). With the implementation of the North American Free Trade Agreement (NAFTA) in 1994, the neoliberal principles enshrined in maquila production were institutionalized and pushed further along the same trajectory (Cravey 1998).

These transformations did not occur in a vacuum: they influenced, and were influenced by, Mexican social structure. Consideration of gender and household relations helps to explain these wider transitions in Mexican history, geography, and development. Industrial workers in northern Mexican factories tend to be young women rather than male bread-

Table 13.1. Comparison of the Old and New Factory Regimes

	Ciudad Madero Old Factory Regime (1930–1978)	Nogales New Factory Regime (1976–present)
Location	Mexico City (and urban central Mexico)	Dispersed sites in northern Mexico along the US border
Strategy	Import Substitution Industrialization	Neoliberal, market-led development
Target Market	Domestic market	Export orientation
Production	• High wages	• Low wages
	• State support for unions	• Unions under attack
	• Subsidy to domestic employers	• Subsidy to transnational employers
	• Regulation of labor-capital relation	• Deregulation of labor-capital relation
Reproduction	• Nuclear household	• (Diverse) extended household
	• Domestic labor done by housewife	• Intense negotiation of domestic labor—labor split between household members
	• Public child care	• Private child care (in household)
	• Worker housing assistance	• Severe housing shortage
	• Public medical care for worker and family members	• Some companies provide medical assistance (i.e., a nurse in the workplace); limited public health provision or clinics

winners. Maquila workers typically pool several incomes and form extended households that include men, women, children, older generations, and sometimes individuals who are unrelated to the family. These households reorganize domestic tasks and incorporate new members as family situations change over time. As wage earners, women maquila workers gain certain improvements in status. Still, women's empowerment entails social costs that are more visible if one compares interior and border locations in Mexico that have been shaped by distinct factory regimes. Below I compare the border city of Nogales, Sonora, with the interior city Ciudad Madero, Tamaulipas, in order to better describe widespread social costs and contradictions in the US-Mexico borderlands.

Nogales, Sonora (population 300,000) represents an entirely different production regime from the import substitution program that shaped Ciudad Madero. In comparing the two Mexican cities, the starkest difference is the lack of state public social programs for workers, families, and communities in Nogales. A casual visitor can observe the distinction in the dearth of clinics, schools, child care centers, public water/sewer infrastructure, and other social goods in this border location. Political economic differences shape the quite different household forms in the two cities, as well as distinct channels of social access (to schools, clinics, clean water, electricity) for urban residents.

The two cities reflect the urban social geographies of different factory regimes. In Ciudad Madero, the neighborhoods where industrial workers live were constructed with wide road-ways, good public water supply, and abundant, well-built schools, clinics, and affordable government housing. In the years between 1940 and 1976, the Mexican government viewed these unionized (and mostly male) factory workers as the cutting edge of its national development strategy. The government worked closely with Mexican employers, union leaders, and workers to ensure stable, healthy neighborhoods. The idea of nurturing domestic capitalists and industrial workers (and unions) in Ciudad Madero was paramount during the ISI years.

This approach was completely revamped in favor of transnational capital accumulation in Nogales in the years of maquila expansion. Social policies in the new neoliberal spaces of Nogales support industrial investment rather than workers and communities. Specifically, state policies and institutions in Nogales are geared toward providing transnational corporations with a dependent and relatively quiescent work force by dismantling, deregulating, and privatizing social provision. In short, the state emerged as a powerful ally of employers by dismantling traditional networks of social provision in new northern transnational production sites, making workers more dependent on their employers than they had been in central Mexico during ISI expansion. Necessary goods, such as health care, child care, and housing, were re-commodified or became available only through the employment relationship. Goods considered social *rights* in Ciudad Madero became social *privileges* in Nogales and in the new factory regime. People who live in the borderlands resist, cope, negotiate, and reshape these processes in multiple and creative ways. However, privatization and private provision of health care, child care, and public housing undermined the system of public goods available to workers in the borderlands.

This makes workers far more vulnerable to the whims of their employers and renders access to social goods (e.g., clean water, health care, education) more insecure. The insecure nature of social goods and the way they are tied to the employment relationship is especially significant given the high turnover rates of maquiladora workers. On average, Nogales maquila workers last fifteen to sixteen months on a particular job.[5] By contrast, workers in Ciudad Madero in the old factory regime considered their jobs to be a lifelong arrangement. The shift in social provision from the state to the employer weakens workers' positions when bargaining over conditions of employment. The geographically uneven nature of social provision reinforces differences in the development of the two industrial regions.

How does all this affect daily life? In what ways are gender and household dynamics caught up in larger globalization processes in northern Mexico? A gender and class perspective helps illuminate survival activities and how the daily struggle to earn a living connects with wider issues. In contrast to workers in earlier high-growth Mexican industrialization zones, maquila workers do not tend to form nuclear households; those who prefer nuclear households find one factory wage to be insufficient. Instead, maquila workers often pool multiple factory incomes in various types of extended household arrangements, sometimes incorporating unrelated individuals (male and female) and expanding and contracting the household as needed over time.

Domestic chores are particularly interesting to consider in these northern Mexican households. In talking with people, I found that mundane household work is a source of intense and ongoing negotiation and conflict in maquila households in Nogales. In contrast to earlier industrial workers, who relied almost exclusively on female domestic labor, these tasks are reorganized. Because the situation is dire and wages are inadequate, men in these maquila households contribute twice as often and in more significant ways to household labor. In fact, some men contribute in regular and systematic fashion. For example, a man who has small children may take the night shift and a woman the day shift, or vice versa, so that one or the other can be home to care for children at any hour of the day or night. Such sequential scheduling is an unusual and creative response to the changing conditions in the new economic areas. As one young mother explained, "My husband takes care of the children. He has to take care of them because I work (in the factory) at night. We take turns with it every day."

In these ways, both paid work and unpaid social reproductive work are reorganized in the context of rapidly globalizing labor markets. (Social reproduction is an idea that creates a more expansive notion of work so as to include all the things we do to restore our health and vitality on a daily and generational basis. It includes biological reproduction—the act of actually giving birth—as well.) A relative dearth of public social programs has shifted a greater burden to individuals and households and, in this way, has intensified conflicts over the division of domestic labor. Gendered negotiations over domestic work influence and are also influenced by gendered negotiations in the (paid) workplace. Maquila workers are burdened by widespread shortages of social goods in their communities as well as insufficient and fluctuating incomes.

A severe housing shortage is also evident to a casual observer in Nogales. Many industrial workers live in rudimentary makeshift housing in squatter areas that are "regularized" over time (see chapter 4). Organizing themselves in large groups and orchestrating "land invasions" is one direct means of providing shelter for oneself in a difficult environment. In the case of land invasions, women are frequently in the forefront of obtaining land and in the long process of gaining title and services (i.e., electricity, water, sewage disposal). In this way, a "politics of place" in Nogales is much more broadly focused than in the old factory regime, encompassing community and neighborhood concerns, and issues of health and social reproduction, as well as identity, gender, and cultural politics (see chapters 10 and 11). Although politics suffuse factory work as well, in the formative years of the new factory regime, Nogales workers consistently lost ground in the workplace, while finding their neighborhoods and households were potential sites for organizing to improve their lives.

An examination of Mexico's transition to a new factory regime suggests that those very pressures that produced nuclear households in the old factory regime in places like Ciudad Madero are causing further fragmentation of industrial households in the new deregulated northern industrial zones. Production in the new factory regime is far less protected from international competition than had been the case in the old factory regime. Near the border, transnational employers lower the cost of doing business by including younger female and male workers, who command lower wages than older, predominantly male workers in the labor market. In this way, employers can lower the costs of social reproduction and retain more profit for themselves. Younger workers find these lower wages to be insufficient for the nuclear family norm of industrial workers elsewhere and therefore develop other household forms. My research suggests that the same forces of fragmentation (and even social disintegration) that created a nuclear family norm in central Mexico now threaten to further shred the social fabric.

The North American Free Trade Agreement built upon the economic success of the maquila experiment. NAFTA locked in many specific maquila practices as well as broader neoliberal practices and "free trade" ideas that made northern Mexico a zone of economic expansion, investment, rapid urbanization, and job growth in recent decades. The United States, Canada, and Mexico signed the treaty as a framework for regional economic cooperation. Some of the immediate and visible social and cultural effects of NAFTA are found in the US-Mexico borderlands, where businesses seek to profit from increased cross-border trade and investments.

The Informal Economy: Drug Smuggling, People Smuggling, and More

Alongside the explosive growth of the maquila industry has been an expansion of informal economic activities in the borderlands, including drug-smuggling and people-smuggling operations that link suppliers in Mexico and Latin America with destinations, employers, and consumers in the United States. These transnational smuggling networks have dense connections to many border communities as well as many small towns and cities throughout the United States and Mexico. The human-smuggling networks are particularly interesting.

The US-Mexico border is a key crossing point for unauthorized migrants to the United States. Human migration across the line, especially but not exclusively from Mexico, has been active since the line was established in the nineteenth century. These migrations were more closely monitored in the twentieth century, especially after the establishment of a United States national police force, the Border Patrol, in 1924. In recent decades, border enforcement and militarization have become even more salient, particularly in urban zones (Dunn 1996; Nevins 2002; Urrea 2004). In the two largest urban areas, San Diego/Tijuana and El Paso/Juarez, fences were reinforced in the 1990s with triple layers of steel, high-tech sensors that can detect movement, and military drones. Border Patrol budgets have skyrocketed and more Border Patrol officers have been hired to guard all sectors of the US side of the line. While migration flows continue apace, these investments in border infrastructure create a highly visual and symbolic demonstration that the United States has "control" of its southern border (Nevins 2002).

Migrants and migrant-smuggling networks that operate in the borderlands have responded to these changes by developing migration pathways that wind through inhospitable rugged desert territory such as the "Devil's Highway" in the rugged dangerous Sonoran desert of central Arizona (Urrea 2004). In this way, tiny border towns such as Sonoita have become busy staging areas and outposts for prospective migrants, *coyotes* (smugglers), and for those who provide rooms, meals, and services to migrants and their guides (see figure 13.2). Migrants thus face increased risk and higher fees in making the journey to interior US locations. Migrants from Guatemala, El Salvador, and other parts of Central America frequently cross this border to enter the United

Figure 13.2. Checkpoint at *El Tortugo,* thirty miles south of the borderline at Sasabe, Sonora. Photograph by Julian Cardona.

States. In recent years, there has also been a markedly increased presence of Mexicans fleeing southern Mexican states such as Oaxaca and Chiapas in an effort to get "to the other side."

The borderlands is a area of extreme violence, and this too provides a means of understanding the region. Violence on the north side of the line is largely directed against migrants from Mexico, Central America, and elsewhere who are trying to enter the United States. Migrants navigate pervasive threats such as petty theft, rape, and deportation (see chapter 15). By contrast, violence in northern Mexico is caught up with everyday traffic in drugs, prostitution, and myriad other informal economic activities. One group of victims who have become well-known are the young women of Ciudad Juarez whose desiccated (and sometimes mutilated) bodies provoke outrage, scholarly investigation, and protest (Portillo 2001; Staudt 2008; Wright 2008; Fregoso and Bejarano 2010; Gaspar de Alba 2010). Hundreds of very young victims, often factory workers of humble origins, have died in the city Charles Bowden (1998) evocatively labeled "the laboratory of the future" for its single-minded focus on neoliberal policies, and simultaneous neglect of social consequences. While the senseless deaths of so many young women increasingly circulates in the press, journalists in Ciudad Juarez suggest that countless young men die in the city as well, with mass graves unearthed from time to time in remote houses that serve as transportation nodes for powerful drug cartels who seek to move their merchandise across the line to the United States. Journalists themselves are now also frequently killed; twenty reporters have died in the country in the four and one-half years since President Calderon declared a War on Drugs.[6] In 2010, the country tied Iraq and was second only to Pakistan in the number of journalists killed. A high-profile appeal for asylum from one journalist of the Ciudad Juarez area is being monitored closely by human rights activists as well as by fellow Mexican journalists.

Violence on the US side of the line takes many forms. It is sometimes official (e.g., Border Patrol) and sometimes not. Smalltime bandits prey upon migrants as they cross the border with perhaps a toothbrush and their life savings. Smugglers, their employees, and others take advantage of the vulnerability of women and commit rape and sexual abuse. Overshadowing these acts is the systemic violence of a contradictory arrangement that recruits workers for many economic sectors in the United States while subjecting would-be job applicants to a terrifying and deadly gauntlet in the borderlands. For over twenty years, Congress has been unable, or unwilling, to craft legislation that would overhaul immigration law. Proposals to do so are quite complex, however, and include longer Berlin Wall–type installations at the border, guest worker programs, lengthy paths to citizenship for "upstanding" migrants, and steep penalties for those who commit the geographical crime of crossing the border without a visa (Nevins 2002). At this time, due to emphatic anti-immigrant rhetoric, it is unlikely that any comprehensive reform proposal will become law. At the same time, it is clear that many sectors of the US economy would grind to a halt if cross-border migration were to slow down. Thus borderland violence, visited upon families and children in the harsh and remote desert, is part and parcel of the dirty, dangerous, difficult underside of the US economy. In a complaint to the officer for civil rights and civil liberties and inspector general of the Department of Homeland Security responding to the child migration crisis of 2014, the National Immigrant Center and American Civil Liberties Union reported that complaints of humiliation, shackling, denial of adequate food or water, long-term separation from parents or other family members, and confiscation of personal belongings in detention centers "reflect longstanding, systemic problems with CBP [Customs and Border Protection] policy and practices" (Ingram 2014).

Demand for Mexican labor in the United States has a long history. In good times, immigrants are recruited for agricultural and other work, whereas in an economic downturn, immigrants are more likely to be deported. Thus, the cycles of the US economy correspond to increased and decreased flows of migrants into the United States, with the Great Depression having spurred dramatic mass deportations. On the other hand, World War II stimulated such a need for short-term workers that the United States and Mexico created the bi-national Bracero Program (1942–1965) in which prospective workers were matched with agricultural employers in the western and southwestern part of the United States. A contemporary program, dubbed H2A for the specific paragraph in immigration law, matches Mexican workers with agricultural employers in the southeastern part of the United States, a region that previously had little Mexican settlement. These government-sanctioned programs have encouraged migration (both official and unofficial) and have deeply influenced the experience of migrants, creating racialized wage scales and distinctly racialized regional formations in the United States.

Another form of violence that illuminates the reality of the borderlands is *discursive violence*. This term refers to visual and rhetorical imagery that can be harmful, painful, and destructive. For example, the term "illegal immigrant" is dehumanizing and pejorative, yet commercial television, daily newspapers, and radio typically use this term to refer to Mexican migrants. In repeated usage, the term denigrates an entire social group regardless of actual immigration status or country of origin. Over time, the term has also become the norm in policy debates and everyday public discourse in the United States, as documented in Joseph Nevins' book *Operation Gatekeeper* (2002). The symbolic imagery of the border fence reinforces an invented notion that people of a certain color and cultural background belong on one side of the line, while people of another skin color and cultural background belong on the other side. Discursive violence and concrete manifestations of violence in the borderlands are destructive and reinforce physical violence on both sides of the border.

Conclusion

By the late twentieth century, approximately ten million people lived in border cities and nearly twenty million lived within a 120-mile zone of either side of the line, creating an immense and complex region. The physical environment is spectacularly harsh and extremely rugged in places. The social and cultural geographies of the borderlands are equally complex and dynamic. In many ways, the region provides a window on the relationship between the United States and Mexico. On a larger scale, a close look at the region reveals some of the contradictory impulses of globalization, neoliberalism, and international development. As the opening quote from Urrea hints, the border has become something larger than life, expanding from its original geographical area around the border to penetrate deep into ordinary places in the United States (and Mexico), and transform everyday activities and places. In all the nooks and crannies where it has penetrated, the border idea is also challenged, contested, and rejected, as evident in the second epigraph at the beginning of the chapter. In spite of the line drawn by the government, Yellow Bird of the North Carolina Lumbee tribe views working-class Mexicans as "our Native brothers and sisters" (Bishop et al. 2008). The US-Mexico border symbolizes and embodies the inextricably close ties that knit together the histories and the future prospects of the two neighboring countries.

No matter what lessons we take from the borderlands, it is important to remember that for many people, the US-Mexico border region is simply a place to live, work, and raise a family.

Key Terms

discursive violence: Visual and/or rhetorical images and ideas that can be harmful, painful, and destructive to individuals or groups.

factory regime: A concept encompassing the apparatus of production regulation (i.e., labor and business law, labor and business bureaucracy, grievance boards) and the organization of the labor process (Burawoy 1985).

informal activities: Legal and illegal ways of making a living, some of which are highly profitable, while others are poorly paid. For example, illegal smuggling of drugs and people is dangerous yet highly profitable. On the other hand, small household enterprises such as those that make and sell tortillas, entertain drivers at busy intersections, and care for neighbor's children may earn essential yet paltry sums.

land invasion: In some parts of Latin America, it is legally permissible to occupy and reside on land that is not being used by its owner. Even where this is legal, there are good and bad outcomes. For this reason, people often plan ahead within a sizeable group before staking a claim in such a "land invasion."

Mexico's sunbelt: Mexico's sunbelt is in the northern part of the country and is thus a mirror image of the US sunbelt (investment moved north instead of moving south).

power-geometries: The systematic and usually highly uneven ways in which different individuals and groups are positioned within networks of time-space flows and connections. These variable subject positions derive from the intimate connections that exist between productions of power and productions of space.

regularize: Over time, groups who claim unused land for their own home sites pressure political parties and urban leaders so as to get electricity services, drainage, water, and even perhaps title to the land.

social disintegration (social fragmentation): The disruption of social relationships and social norms that can occur in the context of war and/or extreme poverty that can lead to a breakdown in the workings of society.

social reproduction: All the tasks we do each day (and each generation) to restore our health and vitality. This concept creates a broader notion of "work" because it includes such things as cooking, cleaning, having children, and teaching values.

Sunbelt: The southern part of the United States in the last few decades became a magnet for investment in contrast to the "Rustbelt" of the northeast.

Notes

1. Historian Patricia Nelson Limerick deliberately uses the word *conquest* to describe the westward expansion of white Europeans who colonized the United States. In doing so, she rejects the view that the United States has a distinctly egalitarian and exceptional history. In highlighting the subjugation of Indians and Mexicans, Limerick's work steers clear of any claim that the United States is naturally benevolent or justice oriented.
2. To learn more about how US westward expansionism fed on racialized ideas of Mexican and Indian people and how this war resulted from the desire to expand slave-holding territories in the United States, see Chávez (2008).
3. The zone only included territory within 20 kilometers of the international border.
4. The central US policy to encourage global manufacturing reorganization was the 1962 changes in the Tariff Code Provisions 806.30 and 807.00.
5. These figures showing high turnover rates are consistent with other maquila research findings.
6. The US War on Drugs dates from Richard Nixon's 1971 campaign of prohibition and foreign military aid and intervention (Webb 1998). Colombia and Central America were drawn into this project long before Mexico.

Suggested Readings

Bowden, Charles. *Down by the River: Drugs, Money, Murder, and Family*. New York: Simon and Schuster, 2002.

Fox, Claire. *The Fence and the River: Culture and Politics at the US-Mexico Border*. Minneapolis: University of Minnesota Press, 1999.

Gómez-Peña, Guillermo. *The New World Border*. San Francisco: City Lights, 1996.

Maciel, David R. and Maria Herrera-Sobek (Eds.). *Culture across Borders: Mexican Immigration and Popular Culture*. Tucson: University of Arizona Press, 1998.

Urrea, Luis Alberto. *By the Lake of Sleeping Children: The Secret Life of the Mexican Border*. New York: Anchor Books, 1996.

References

Anzaldúa, Gloria. *Borderlands/La Frontera: The New Mestiza*. San Francisco: Spinsters/Aunt Lute, 1987.

Arreola, Daniel D. and James R. Curtis. *The Mexican Border Cities: Landscape Anatomy and Place Personality*. Tucson: University of Arizona Press, 1993.

Bacon, David. *The Children of NAFTA: Labor Wars on the US-Mexico Border*. Berkeley: University of California Press, 2004.

Bishop, Elva E., Altha J. Cravey, and Javier Garcia Méndez. *The Virgin Appears in "La Maldita Vecindad."* Versions in Spanish and English. 33 minutes. 2008. virginappears.unc.edu

Bowden, Charles. *Juárez: the Laboratory of Our Future.* New York: Aperture, 1998.

Burawoy, Michael. *The Politics of Production: Factory Regimes Under Capitalism and Socialism.* London: Verso, 1985.

Chávez, Ernesto. *The US War with Mexico: A Brief History with Documents.* Boston: Bedford/St. Martins, 2008.

Chishti, Muzaffar and Faye Hipsman. "Unaccompanied Minors Crisis Has Receded from Headlines but Major Issues Remain." *Migration Policy Institute.* September 25, 2014. Online version: http://www.migrationpolicy.org/article/unaccompanied-minors-crisis-has-receded-headlines-major-issues-remain. Last accessed August 14, 2015.

Cravey, Altha J. *Women and Work in Mexico's Maquiladoras.* Lanham, MD: Rowman & Littlefield, 1998.

Dunn, Timothy, J. *The Militarization of the US-Mexico Border 1978–1992: Low Intensity Conflict Doctrine Comes Home.* Austin: The Center for Mexican American Studies, 1996.

Fernandez-Kelly, Patricia. *For We Are Sold, I and My People: Women and Industry in Mexico's Frontier.* Albany: State University of New York Press, 1983.

Fregoso, Rosa Linda and Cynthia Bejarano (Eds.). *Terrorizing Women: Femicide in the Américas.* Durham, NC: Duke University Press, 2010.

Gaspar de Alba, Alicia with Georgina Gúzman (Eds.). *Making a Killing: Femicide, Free Trade, and La Frontera.* Austin: University of Texas Press, 2010.

Gonzalez, Juan. *Harvest of Empire: A History of Latinos in America.* New York: Peguin Books, 2000.

Herzog, Lawrence A. *Where North Meets South: Cities, Space, and Politics on the U.S.-Mexico Border.* Austin: University of Texas Press, 1990.

Ingram, Paul. "Rights Groups: Border Patrol Abusing Minors Held in Custody." *Tucson Sentinel.* June 11, 2014. Online version: http://www.tucsonsentinel.com/local/report/061114_immigrant_kids/rights-groups-border-patrol-abusing-minors-held-custody/. Last accessed August 14, 2015.

Limerick, Patricia Nelson. *The Legacy of Conquest: The Unbroken Past of the American West.* New York: Norton, 1987.

———. *Something in the Soil: Legacies and Reckonings in the New West.* New York: Norton, 2000.

Martinez, Oscar. J. *Troublesome Border.* Tucson: University of Arizona Press, 1988.

Nabhan, Gary. *The Desert Smells Like Rain: A Naturalist in Papago Indian Country.* Tucson: University of Arizona Press, 1985.

Nevins, Joseph. *Operation Gatekeeper: The Rise of the "Illegal Alien" and the Making of the US-Mexico Boundary.* London: Routledge, 2002.

Portillo, Lourdes, director-producer. *Senorita Extraviada: Missing Young Woman.* Film. 2001. www.lourdesportillo.com

Staudt, Kathleen. *Violence and Activism and the Border: Gender, Fear and Everyday life in Ciudad Juarez.* Austin: University of Texas Press, 2008.

Stoddard, Ellwyn R. *Borderlands Sourcebook: A Guide to the Literature on Northern Mexico and the American Southwest.* Norman: University of Oklahoma Press, 1983. Published under the sponsorship of the Association of Borderlands Scholars.

Urrea, Luis Alberto. *The Devil's Highway: A True Story.* New York: Little, Brown and Company, 2004.

Webb, Gary. *Dark Alliance: The CIA, the Contras, and the Crack Cocaine Explosion.* New York: Seven Stories Press, 1998.

Wright, Melissa. *Disposable Women and Other Myths of Global Capitalism.* New York: Routledge, 2006.

Wright, Melissa. "El Lucro, La Democracia y la Mujer Pública: Haciendo las Conexiones," ("Profit, Democracy and Public Women: Making the Connections"). In *Bordeando La Violencia Contra Las Mujeres en la Frontera Norte de México,* edited by S. Tabuenca and J. Monárrez, 49–81. Tijuana: El Colegio de la Frontera Norte, 2008.

Chapter 14

Transnational Latin America

Movements, Places, and Displacements

Araceli Masterson-Algar

PREVIOUS CHAPTERS DESCRIBED THE flows and connections between specific Latin American locations and regional, national, and international processes and ideas. "Placing" Latin America thus means that we work through a multiplicity of scales. In fact, we can assume that any place is tied to spaces and processes that extend well beyond it (see Introduction). This chapter will examine precisely that "openness" of place by explaining what scholars mean when they address Latin America as a "transnational" space, as well as by offering some examples of transnational processes as lived and imagined by moving populations.

The chapter first outlines some of the theoretical discussions surrounding the term "transnationalism," exploring its prevalence in Latin American intellectual thought and its transdisciplinary reach. The second section addresses Latin American migrations as intrinsically transnational and central to Latin America's historical processes. The last section includes two case studies of transnational Latin American communities, Mexicans in the United States and Ecuadorians in Spain.

Transnationalism in Latin American Thought

In *The Dream of the Celt* (2010), Nobel Laureate in literature Mario Vargas Llosa combines historical research, fiction, and journalism to tell the story of Roger Casement (1864–1916), an Anglo-Irish diplomat, and later Irish nationalist, who denounced the systematic terror and torture of colonial projects in Congo and in the Peruvian Amazon at the turn of the twentieth century. Casement's reports showed the barbaric nature of so-called civilizing entrepreneurships in the African and Latin American regions, a realization that ultimately intensified his advocacy for Ireland's independence. Picking up the transnational lens, how do the contexts of Congo, Perú, and Ireland intertwine? Roger Casement's journey in *The Dream of the Celt* shows the all-encompassing nature of colonialism, which takes differentiated local forms while resting on similar hierarchies that are indeed transnational. Thus, blacks in Congo, indigenous populations in the Amazon, and Irish in Great Britain all share experiences that rest on their position as "inferior" in the racial hierarchies of the time.

In the novel, the local implementation of different forms of slavery, as well as the attempts to denounce them, presents a world of networks and flows. As a British consul, Casement interacts with politicians, businessmen, missionaries, intellectuals, and artists worldwide. As they travel, so do their work and ideas. The publication of the Blue Book in 1912, where Casement denounced the atrocities of the rubber-gathering operations of London-based Peruvian Amazon Company on the Río Putumayo, "generated a commotion that, with London at its center, spread in concentric waves throughout Europe, the United States, and many parts of the world" (Vargas Llosa 2010, 324).[1]

Maintaining the focus on human movements, Vargas Llosa's novel shows the displacements of large populations, some impelled by economic need or political persecution (for example, Irish in the United States) and others forced into servitude or slavery. Thus, blacks in Congo are removed from their communities, as are the indigenous in the Amazonian region. Supervising the "disposable labor" of the Peruvian Amazon Company are large numbers of Barbadians hired to enforce production efficiency under inhuman labor conditions. The Barbadians in turn respond to local businessmen, who work under the directives of the company's powerful stakeholders, both within the region and in the centers of colonial power—England in this case. The worldwide flow of products, people, and ideas in this century-old story warns us against characterizations of globalization as a new development in the age of modern technology and illustrates two of the key features of the transnational lens. First, countering celebrations of "globalization," transnationalism shows its ties to colonial processes at play since the fifteenth century (see chapters 2 and 3). Second, transnationalism unveils the local and global processes integral to people's everyday lives. In other words, the transnational lens attunes us to a global cartography of power, whereby local actors engage, consciously or not, in practices that extend well beyond their local spaces of influence.

Latin America's colonial experience is the backdrop of a long list of Latin American intellectuals who, like Vargas Llosa, have explored the entanglement of local and global processes in the formation of Latin American regional and national identities. Thus, while the word "transnational" might be relatively new in US academia, Latin American intellectual thought has a long tradition of "placing Latin America" at the crossroads of local and global processes. In "Nuestra América" (1891/2005), Cuban independence leader José Martí called for the unity of the Latin American region vis-à-vis colonial powers, formerly Spain, but increasingly the United States. Following Cuban independence, Fernando Ortiz's concept of "transculturación" (transculturation) addressed the cultural outcomes of the coexistence of the local with the global conditions associated with colonial powers: "Men, economies, cultures, ambitions were all foreigners here, provisional, changing, 'birds of passage' over the country, at its cost, against its wishes, and without its approval. All those above and those below living together in the same atmosphere of terror and oppression, the oppressed in terror of punishment, the oppressor in terror or reprisals, all beside justice, beside adjustment, beside themselves. And all in the painful process of transculturation" (Ortiz 1995, 98–102).

In other words, Latin America emerges from the dynamics at play in the encounters between "local histories and global designs" (Mignolo 2000), from the colonial period to present-day mass globalization.

In the mid- and late 1960s, dependency theory became the theoretical model for understanding Latin America's position in the world economy. Fueled by the pitfalls of import substitution industrialization (see chapters 3 and 13)—including the increasing gaps between rich and poor—and a new atmosphere of possibility emerging from the Cuban Revolution, various Latin American scholars called for the implementation of social thought in economic models.

Their notion of "dependency theory" continued at the center of Latin American thought into the mid-eighties, through Immanuel Wallerstein's world-systems theory.

Wallerstein proposed that capitalism simultaneously produced development in some areas and underdevelopment in others, providing the theoretical framework to link transnational exploitation with internal colonialism. Under these models, the centers of economic power are not opposed to peripheral regions, but rather all areas appear linked by unequal exchange, largely rooted in the imposition of capitalism on historically colonized nations. Dependency theory and world-systems theory showed the dynamics of global capital *from* the periphery. In the 1990s, a group of Latin American intellectuals inspired by the subaltern studies of South Asian scholars further insisted on placing Latin America from the perspective of its vulnerable populations, in order to show the continuation of colonial histories in "independent" nations. Under this light, national projects emerge as part and parcel of global systems of power.

For Michael Kearney, transnationalism "anchors" global processes (1995, 548): "Transnational processes are *anchored* in and transcend one or more nation-states. Thus transnational is the term of choice when referring, for example, to migration of nationals across the borders of one or of more nations" (author emphasis). Thus, while globalization has become a general term to describe—and often justify—current global dynamics, transnationalism "grounds" globalization by looking at *how* it unfolds in specific place and time. This is markedly present in what is known as the "transnational turn" in American studies.

The Transnational Turn in American Studies

In 2004, Shelley Fishkin (2005) celebrated the gradual move to an understanding of the Americas as a region including not only the United States but also Latin America, the Caribbean, and Canada. Reacting against US exceptionalism, scholars participating in this "turn" argue that placing Latin America requires placing the United States and vice versa.

Other scholars help us to further place transnationalism by denouncing globalization as an empty placeholder that describes our present historical period as a sequel to the colonial period and the industrial period. They warn that such a "designed" view of history makes current inequities based on class, race, and gender, for instance, seem like exceptions to globalization rather than intrinsic to it. Conversely, the transnational approach argues that definitions of "globalization" and of "nation" emerge from a long history of inequalities:

> Transnationalism has been a diverse, contested, cross-disciplinary intellectual movement that in some of its manifestations has been bound together by a particular insight: in place of a long and deeply embedded modernist tradition of taking the nation as the framework within which one can study things (literatures, histories, and so forth), the nation itself has to be a question—not untrue and therefore trivial, but an ideology that changes over time, and whose precise elaboration at any point has profound effects on wars, economies, cultures, the movements of people, and relations of domination. (Briggs, McCormick, and Way 2008, 628)

Thus, transnationalism requires turning the nation into a question—that is, not taking the nation for granted.

While much of the transnational turn in American studies found inspiration in Latin American scholarship, it is also heavily influenced by intellectuals writing from the "margins" of the United States, such as African Americans, Chicanos/as, Native Americans, women, and LGBTQ populations, who have emphasized the intersections between class, race, ethnicity, gender, and sexuality in systems of oppression locally and globally. Scholars writing *from* these traditions have arguably always conducted transnational work, simply because they have experienced the ruptures between their lives and grand narratives on a daily basis. In *Borderlands/La Frontera*, Gloria Anzaldúa describes the "mestiza consciousness" as the ability to think *from* outside the nation, *from* its "borders," or, as described by Fishkin, "questioning the naturalness." Historicizing the nation, just like historicizing globalization, allows us to challenge ideologies of power that work both globally and locally and that are supported by certain "naturalized" categories of race, gender and sexuality, ethnicity, class, and nationality.

Let's now work through the theoretical and conceptual implications of the transnational lens, but turning to one of its most vivid manifestations: the movement of people across national borders and their place in labor history and migration dynamics. How can the transnational lens help us analyze and understand human movements and displacements?

The Transnational Turn in Migration Studies

The transnational lens requires an epistemological position—a theory of knowledge that historicizes "the natural"—a way of turning assumptions into questions. It follows that a transnational approach to human movement requires that we turn "immigration" into questions addressing multiple and interrelated scales: What are the global processes (labor dynamics, environmental factors, trade agreements, popular media, etc.) influencing decisions to migrate and choices of destination? How do local practices play into these processes? What are the class, gender, and racial dynamics underlying migrations in both the country of origin and the country of destination? What do they tell us about the larger histories of human migration from and to those regions? Who is more likely to immigrate, and why? How do geographies of power in the society of origin play out in the place of destination and vice versa? How does the nation-state—the people joined together in a formal political unit—place the migrant through legal structures, stratified labor, media portrayals, and so on, in both the societies of origin and destination?

Michael Kearney (1995) addresses migration as a historical process, calling attention to how long trends and tendencies shape migrant communities. The transnational turn in migration studies shows how migration dynamics are not exclusively the outcome of global structures of inequality (push-pull factors), nor of individual "decision making" (equilibrium theory). Instead, migrants' place in their societies of origin *and* destination are tied to multiple and historically specific factors that frame—and limit—individual choice. Thus, class and citizenship status, for instance, influence the degree to which migrants participate in transnationalism.

Transnationalism became popular in migration studies in the 1990s through the work of a group of cultural anthropologists. They proposed a transnational approach that recognized the actual experiences of migrants, whom they defined as individuals with lives of constant and multiple interconnections across international borders and with public identities configured in relation to more than one nation-state. In dialogue with the transnational turn in American studies, the transnational framework emphasizes the critical stance toward oversimplified bipolar models (here/there, center/periphery, local/global), working instead through a multiplicity of scales to challenge homogenizing research on migration.

The transnational turn to migration as a lived and grounded process attracted scholars in the field of geography, who since the late 1980s had highlighted the importance of places as outcomes of social processes. As a result, several geographers have called for further attention on migrants' initiatives to make sense of new locations in the construction of their daily lives. These efforts have helped to delineate relations between economic globalization, transnational migration, and the construction of places, bridging the political, economic, social, and cultural. Thus emerges another key feature of transnationalism: it is necessarily transdisciplinary. Let's now think about how transnationalism, both as theory and method, helps us place Latin America.

Human Movements and Displacements: A Defining Feature of Latin America and the Caribbean

The history of Latin America began with population movements dating prior to thirty thousand years ago. Several scholars have argued that the indigenous populations of the Americas are the outcome of various migrations, some through the Bering Strait and others through the Pacific Ocean (Kam Ríos n.d.), though many of the patterns of migration remain unclear.

To get a feel for the dimensions of human movements, settlements, and displacements in Latin America, let's look at one of its largest urban centers, Mexico City. In its historical center, national and international students and tourists visit the archaeological remains of Tenochtitlán, one of the largest cities in the world in the fifteenth century and the center of an empire that dominated most of Mesoamerica (see chapter 4). Historical documents and legend merge to narrate its foundation following the migration of various indigenous Nahua groups from Aztlán, possibly located around what today is the US Southwest. As capital of the Aztec Empire, Tenochtitlán was a destination for people from tribes all over the region, through both volunteer migrations and forms of forced labor. Following its conquest by the Spanish in 1521, it became the capital of the viceroyalty of New Spain and the political, administrative, and financial center of the Spanish colonial empire (see chapter 2). It remained a destination for people from all over, including Spaniards (many of them Jews escaping persecution in Spain), people of other European nationalities, and forcefully displaced populations of indigenous and African labor. Today Mexico, D.F., is one of the largest metropolitan areas in the Western Hemisphere and one of the most important financial centers in North America (see chapter 4). Its population of nearly twenty-two million includes indigenous people and mestizos from all over Mexico as well as migrant communities from other Latin American countries (mainly from Argentina, Colombia, Guatemala, and Salvador), but also from the Caribbean region (Cuba and Haiti), as well as from Europe (largely from Spain and Germany, but also from Eastern Europe, France, and Italy), the Middle East (mainly from Egypt, Lebanon, and Syria), and recently growing Asian populations from China and South Korea. It also has the largest population of US citizens outside of the United States. In addition to communities of foreign-born retirees, the city attracts visitors from all over the world through the tourist industries and multiple study-abroad programs.

Latin America as a whole experienced large human movements throughout the colonial period, including the forced displacements of indigenous and African labor. Following Latin America's independence movements during the eighteenth and nineteenth centuries, many countries incentivized large migrations from Europe, oftentimes in response to racial ideologies emerging during the turn to the nineteenth century, which paralleled "development" with "whiteness" (see chapter 2). Despite the preference for European migrants, many people arrived in Latin America from Asia and the Middle East, mainly as contract laborers for the agriculture and fishing industries. Signs of their historical ongoing presence are the Chinatowns in Havana, Panama City, Buenos Aires, Lima, and Mexico City, but also popular customs, such as the consumption of rice as one of the staple foods of many Latin American countries. During Japan's Meiji era (1868–1912) many Japanese also migrated to Latin America, and today cities like Lima, Perú, and São Paulo, Brazil, have the largest populations of Japanese outside of Japan. In recent decades, in a process that many scholars term "reverse migration," many Japanese Latin Americans have migrated to Japan in response to the negative effects of the global economy on local communities, adding to the shared histories between these regions.

The transnational lens shows that migration patterns result from the combination of structural factors such as global and national economic policies, local conditions, and personal decision making in contexts of limited choice. For example, neoliberal politics and their associated cuts in social services have enhanced human movements and displacements throughout Latin America, particularly since the 1990s. But migrants are not just going from "here" to "there." They carry their own experiences and capacities, generating additional transnational flows between their locations of origin and destination, which Manuel Orozco classifies as "5 Ts"— money transfers (remittances), transport, telecommunications, tourism, and trade.

Migrants have become the agents of transnational development initiatives worldwide. In 2003, remittances to Latin America and the Caribbean comprised one-third of all global remittances, the highest share of all the world regions and more than quadruple the total official development assistance to the region (Orozco 2005, 318–19). Following the financial crisis in 2009, remittances dropped by 15 percent. Today, money transfers to the region have stabilized. According to the Interamerican Development Bank, by 2012, the Latin American and Caribbean regions received $61.3 billion in remittances. In Mexico, Central America, the Caribbean, and other countries with a large exodus, such as Perú, Bolivia, and Ecuador, remittances are crucial to the gross national product. The centrality of remittances to Latin American economies fuels governments' incentives to maintain the loyalty of their citizens abroad (health benefits, property rights, expatriate vote, etc.). At the same time, migrants' sense of belonging to more than one nation becomes more pronounced.

But economic remittances are not the only reason for the inclusion of citizens abroad in national politics. Migrants themselves organize in social movements and intervene politically in their countries of residency and of origin (see chapter 10). Remittances can be read as a positive outcome of migrants' transnational practices, but Peggy Levitt and Ninna Nyberg-Sørensen warn that "while some see migrants as a force for greater democratization and accountability, others hold them responsible for rising materialism and individualism" (2004, 8). The following two case studies further illustrate the complexity of migrants' transnational dynamics. The first addresses Mexican hometown associations in the United States, whereas the second offers a transnational analysis of Ecuadorians in Spain looking at the concepts of "home" and "gender."

Case Study I: Mexico in the US Midwest

Approximately twelve million residents in the United States were born in Mexico, with remittances that comfortably exceed $22 billion per year (see chapters 13 and 15). This sum refers mainly to amounts sent directly to individuals. In addition, there are other forms of transnational practices such as hometown associations (HTAs), which finance public projects in the societies of origin, such as wells, stadiums, roads and highways, churches, and plazas. Through HTAs, migrants have financed local music bands, sports teams, and scholarships, as well as donated and/or sent money to purchase instruments, food, clothing, and medical and industrial equipment for their hometowns.

A telling example of migrants' transnational practices in the United States, HTAs work on multiple scales (local, regional, national, and global) and share a commitment to cultural, political, economic, and social initiatives. Orozco provides data on Mexican towns where 50 percent of the total municipal budget comes from HTAs in the United States (2005, 323). In 1999, responding to the macroeconomic effects of these initiatives, the Mexican government implemented Plan 3x1, whereby for every peso raised by the HTAs, Mexico donates three, one for each of the government's administrative levels: the municipal, regional, and national. In addition, HTAs are also largely involved in domestic issues, including improvements of collective remittances infrastructures, immigration and education reforms, and other advocacy efforts, such as work on labor rights or efforts to obtain temporary protected status for all undocumented victims following Hurricane Katrina. On a larger scale, HTAs in the Midwestern United States, for instance, joined to form the Confederation of Mexican Federations in the Midwest, which in turn belongs to the larger National Allegiance of Latin American and Caribbean Countries (NALACC).

Casa Guanajuato Quad Cities was an illustrative example of the processes described above. Located in Moline (Illinois), on the Illinois-Iowa border,[2] it was founded in 1998 as a community and cultural organization, funded through local and state governments in the United States, as well as through the government of Guanajuato, Mexico. Although it kept its name, Casa Guanajuato no longer works as an HTA. Instead, it is mostly an office for legal and referral services. Yet, its emergence and trajectory are telling of the area's local Mexican histories. Not surprisingly, despite Moline's general invisibility within the United States, most people in various locations throughout Guanajuato know the city well, as the main US destination and residence of family members and friends.

Guanajuatenses have arrived to the Quad Cities since the 1900s, escaping the violence of the Mexican Revolution and filling the jobs of soldiers gone to war, mainly in the railroad and foundries. After World War I, many returned to Guanajuato, either voluntarily or as part of a US nationwide deportation of Mexicans following the economic crisis of 1929.[3] Moline remained a central referent in the region circulating through the stories of returned migrants and in the letters and visits to the hometowns of those that made it their permanent residency. In the context of World War II, new job opportunities emerged in "el Norte," while second-generation Mexicans of US citizenship living in Moline enlisted for war. Circular migrations, temporary visits, and movement of people, ideas, and objects between the Quad Cities and Guanajuato continued, leading to the configuration of organizations like Casa Guanajuato as official transnational arenas. Despite the constraints on migrants' rights, members in such organizations share a willingness to intervene both "here" and "there," showing new configurations of citizenship between Mexico and the United States, regardless of their legal status or length of stay in the United States. For over a decade, artists, scholars, politicians, and public workers circulated between Casa Guanajuato Quad Cities and Guanajuato, offering opportunities for its members to join social networks and obtain personal, economic, and legal support (figures 14.1 and 14.2). In addition, other smaller hometown associations turned to Casa Guanajuato Quad Cities for advice on how to become "official" and gain access to resources and services both in the United States and in Mexico (figure 14.3). Such hometown associations overflow definitions of citizenship based on national borders. They are ways for migrants to generate community and advocate for the safety of their *home* in both their place of origin and their place of residency. Keeping this in mind, let's undertake a brief approximation to Ecuadorian migration to Spain through the transnational lens, focusing on two concepts: gender and home.

Figure 14.1. Performance of the group from Guanajuato 'Los Tiempos Pasados' on September 15, 2007, at the Moline Public Library. Picture by Rafael González, courtesy of Rafael González and Casa Guanajuato Quad Cities.

Figure 14.2. Visit of the Mexican Consulate to Casa Guanajuato on August 2, 2007. Picture by Rafael González, courtesy of Rafael González and Casa Guanajuato Quad Cities.

Figure 14.3. Casa Guanajuato leading the Migrant March in May 2006. Picture by Rafael González, courtesy of Rafael González and Casa Guanajuato Quad Cities.

Case Study II: Ecuador in Madrid, Spain

Spain became the main destination for Ecuadorian migrants in the 1990s, with an estimated population of four hundred thousand. As in Mexico, remittances are central to Ecuador's GNP. Approved on September 2008, Ecuador's last constitution affirmed the centrality of Ecuadorian migrants by including them as the country's fifth region. While this shows Ecuador's interest in keeping the loyalty of its citizens abroad, economic remittances are not the only reason for this inclusion. Ecuadorian migrants organized to influence the Ecuadorian government through their activism abroad. Here, social remittances became as central as economic ones. Much of the success of Ecuadorian migrants' transnational practices in Spain relates to the fact that they had constituted an educated urban majority in Ecuador. Even if in Spain they worked primarily as domestic and construction workers, many of them had professional degrees. Further, the political activity of Ecuadorians in Spain inspired Ecuadorian migrants in other parts of the world, including New York and Chicago, two destinations for Ecuadorians since the 1950s. To conduct a transnational analysis of recent human movements between Ecuador and Spain, let's work from two central ideas: gender and home.

The scholarship on gender and migration has been a key player in the transnational turn in migration studies, shedding light on migration processes as a combination of structural factors and social dynamics (Pessar and Mahler 2003). These studies look at how gender relations facilitate or constrain people's decisions to migrate, and their material and/or imagined possibilities for settlement, and transnational practices. For example, gender dynamics are key to transnational systems of labor. As in many countries, Spain's cuts in social services and the expansion of professional opportunities for women have increased the demand for caregiving services and domestic work, positions traditionally occupied by women. Thus, while some women enter the professional arena, other women, normally racially marked, occupy their place in the home as domestic workers and caregivers. Shellee Colen (2006) describes these transnational dynamics as "stratified reproduction," unveiling the power relations that establish who is empowered to nurture and reproduce and who is not. Many migrant women worldwide face the irony of the transnational experience, by which in order to ensure the reproduction of their homes (the well-being of their parents and children), they must abandon them.

Women were the initial protagonists of migrations from Ecuador to Spain in the 1990s. They migrated as part of larger family projects and in response to the demand for domestic work and services most prevalent in Spain's urban centers. They took care of others' children and parents while arranging the necessary networks to sustain social reproduction back "home." Yet, the media in Ecuador and in Spain have offered an image of the migrant as predominately male. A transnational analysis would not only question the material and political implications of this erasure but would also seek to understand its reasons, analyzing gender dynamics both in Ecuador and in Spain (Masterson 2006). One of the conclusions from such analysis reveals that the historical image of the "provider" as male contributes to women's vulnerability in the workplace. In domestic work, for instance, the lack of regulations puts women in jeopardy, while favoring a continuous flow of cheap labor. There are multiple readings and implications that we can unravel if we keep following this thread.

While Ecuadorian women led migration dynamics to Spain, largely due to the high demand for domestic work and caregivers, men shortly followed. Their arrival at the end of the nineties coincided with the beginning of a period of unprecedented construction activity in Spain. This construction boom was accompanied by the "aggressiveness" of the financial sector in the country's realty market. In Madrid, construction grew by 80 percent in just nine years, becoming one of the main sources of employment and the main labor niche for most male migrants arriving to the city. After their first years in Madrid, many Ecuadorians began investing in homes. By 2004, Spain's realty market included advertisement campaigns geared to potential migrant homebuyers. Further, following the first signs of a deceleration in the real estate market in Spain, which would later develop into the housing crisis of 2008, Spain's joint ventures of construction firms and real estate agencies turned to Latin America for additional areas of growth. Many Ecuadorians who could not purchase a home in Madrid opted to invest in a home in Ecuador instead. With the growth of Spanish construction and real estate companies in Ecuador, migrants in Spain began choosing their homes in Ecuador through the catalogs available in real estate agencies in Madrid (Acosta, López and Villamar 2006; Ospina Lozano 2010; Masterson-Algar 2016).

Piecing the above observations with our prior analysis of Ecuadorian women's employment in Spain further reveals transnational threads. Ecuadorian women and men guarantee the reproduction of their homes in Ecuador and in Madrid while investing in houses in Madrid and in Ecuador. Mainly employed in domestic work and care, Ecuadorian women ensure the social reproduction of Madrid's homes, while Ecuadorian men, mostly employed in the construction sector, build them. Their earnings from these efforts pay the mortgages of houses in Ecuador that are often promoted and constructed through Spanish foreign investments in the region. The "global design" becomes even clearer when factoring in the large numbers of migrants arriving to Ecuador from Colombia and Perú to build the houses of Ecuadorian migrants abroad.

Spain's frenzied real estate activity explains why during the 2008 economic crises it became the second most affected country behind the United States. Those employed in the construction sector, largely migrants, suffered the consequences of the crises most directly. In this context, CONADEE (Coordinadora Nacional de Entidades Ecuatorianas) emerged as one of the most active organizations against Spain real state practices, and a key actor in Spain's 15-M movement. Representing the over four hundred thousand Ecuadorians facing the consequences of Spain's real estate crises, but also in the interest of Spain's population at large, CONADEE has denounced the practices of financial institutions in Spain. On March 21, 2009, hundreds of Ecuadorians took to Madrid's streets to denounce Madrid's transnational housing industry from its very streets. Finally, the situation in Spain influenced a serious decrease in the demand for homes in Ecuador, and those who migrated to Ecuador to meet the construction demand joined the numbers of Ecuadorians unemployed in Spain.

Conclusion

In sum, transnationalism addresses histories of crossings of ideas, people, and products. The concept of transnationalism also attempts to better capture the interface between national identities, domestic interests, and foreign relations. Several chapters in this book, whether they discuss market dynamics, tourism, or social movements, all address these processes. Placing Latin America necessarily involves a transnational approach to the movement, settlement, and displacement of people within and outside the region. These processes are part of global systems of inequality at play since the colonial period, albeit today they take different forms in response to global dynamics of capital.

Another point we have emphasized is that a transnational approach to human movements and displacements requires that we turn the "nation" into a question. Throughout the chapter, we have seen examples of migrants' social dynamics that do not overlap with the nation, such as hometown associations, and other transnational alliances that support "migrant rights" worldwide. Guanajuatenses in the Quad Cities and Ecuadorians in Madrid create their own transnational networks through practices that branch to multiple locations and transcend scales. These alliances, however, do not translate into the demise of the power of the nation-state. State governments continue to be the main voice in defining who can and/or cannot be a citizen, and the power of the state to control national borders results in the loss of thousands of human lives, as experiences of migrants along the US-Mexico border demonstrate (see chapter 13). In addition, Latin American populations within the region (Central Americans in Mexico, Nicaraguans in Costa Rica, Peruvians and Colombians in Ecuador, or Bolivians in Argentina) are sometimes stripped of rights in their countries of residency while their remittances feed the GNP of their countries of origin. Thus, while migrant networks open new opportunities to counter the limitations posed by national borders, these processes are embedded in systems of global capitalism that often rely on undocumented and cheap labor. In addition, the increasing legal restrictions and monitoring of borders raise serious questions about the well-being of thousands of people on the move and are a continuous reminder of the burden placed on migrants, who are maintaining economies and social networks "here and there."

The transnational lens recognizes migration as constituting and constitutive of the interface between the power of the nation and local and global processes. Under this light, migrants become people with specific histories, and globalization is no longer an empty placeholder for a new era but a historical process rooted in systems of inequality from the beginning. Keeping all scales in mind—the global, the national, and the local—is key to understanding migration dynamics as both worldwide and local reality in a complex interface influencing migration at all levels: decision to migrate, choice of destination, and the development and maintenance of transnational networks.

Finally, transnational work deepens the interdisciplinary possibilities of geographic research, demanding historical depth as well as unveiling the ties between human mobilizations and economic, social, political, and cultural processes. Through the transnational lens, we can place Latin America in multiple and intertwined scales (global, regional, national, and local), transforming it from "abstract" space to contact zone. Under this light, it becomes clear that migrants cannot arrive and then leave, because humans' lives always unfold through social networks and practices of citizenship—regardless of citizenship status. The transnational lens shows the unproductive nature of arguments that address migration based on prescribed degrees of assimilation and integration, simply because migrants are not additions to space but part of it.

Let's return, for the sake of closure, to Vargas Llosa's character in *The Dream of the Celt*, who had to work in Congo and Perú to place Ireland's position in relation to Great Britain. Similarly, for us to place Latin America, we must travel through its presence worldwide and unveil its shared histories and influences from and in other regions. The United States, the country with the second-largest number of Spanish speakers in the world after Mexico and the main destination of Latin American migrants, is an excellent point of departure. And while references to US Latinos are often paralleled with discussions of migration, the transnational lens reminds us that the United States and Latin America have emerged from shared histories that comfortably predate the arrival of the Mayflower to Plymouth Rock in 1620.

Key Terms

migration: Traditional approaches to migration studies differentiated between leaving (emigration and emigrants) and arriving (immigration and immigrants). Eliminating the suffixes counters this duality by defining migration as a process involving continuities, simultaneities, and overlaps between the society of origin and the society of destination.

scale: In critical geography, scale does not refer to size, but to a socially constructed process that has real and material implications in cultural and political landscapes. It is a term that helps geographers to articulate the relationships between global dynamics and lived experiences in specific place and time.

social geographies of power: Power is localized, specific, and relational. "Social geographies of power" refers to the relations and processes underlying constructions of meaning about different groups of people in particular places.

transnationalism: A theory and a practice that works to understand the interface between local, national, and global processes through analyzing the historical processes underlying the construction of the nation. Transnationalism "grounds" global processes to show how they are lived and imagined by people in specific time and place.

US exceptionalism: Rather than showing the ties between the United States and world history, US exceptionalism perpetuates ideas of the United States as a "contained" territory, largely exempt from a Western tradition configured through systems of inequality, imperialism, and war.

Notes

1. All translations mine.
2. According to the Pew Hispanic Center, Latinos in Illinois constitute 16 percent of the total population in the state, 80 percent of whom are of Mexican origin. State data for Iowa shows that Latinos have become the largest racial or ethnic "minority," with an increase in population to 168,806 people from 82,473 in 2000.
3. Mass deportations of Mexicans during the Depression are estimated at between five hundred thousand and two million nationwide, many of whom were residents. Although Mexicans were only 1 percent of the US population, they made up over 46 percent of the persons deported during the decade (Cruz and Carpenter 2011, 55).

Suggested Additional Resources

Acosta, Alberto, Susana López, and David Villamar. *La migración en el Ecuador. Oportunidades y amenazas*. Quito: Corporación Editora Nacional, 2006.
APJ. Asociación Peruano-Japonesa. www.apj.org.pe/quienes-somos/nosotros.
National Allegiance of Latin American and Caribbean Communities (NALACC). www.nalacc.org/.
Rivera, Alex. *La Sexta Sección*. 2003. 27 min. Subcine Independent Latino Film and Video, New York.
Smithsonian Institution. Migrations in History. Last accessed May 5, 2011. www.smithsonianeducation.org/migrations/start.html.
Yamasaki, Tizuka. *Gaijin. Ama-me como sou*. 2005. 131 min. Scena Filmes.

References

Acosta, Alberto, Susana López, and David Villamar. *La migración en el Ecuador. Oportunidades y amenazas*. Quito: Corporación Editora Nacional, 2006.
Anzaldúa, Gloria. *La Frontera/Borderlands*. San Francisco: Aunt Lute Books, 1987.
Briggs, Laura, Gladys McCormick, and J. T. Way. "Trasnationalism: A Category of Analysis." *American Quarterly* 60, no. 3 (2008): 625–48.
Colen, Shellee. "Like a Mother to Them: Stratified Reproduction and West Indian Childcare Workers and Employers in New York." In *Feminist Anthropology: A Reader*, edited by Ellen Lewin, 380–96. Malden, MA: Blackwell Publishers, 2006.
Cruz, Evelyn, and Shawn Carpenter. "We Want You When We Need You, Otherwise Get Out: The Historical Struggle of Mexican Migrants to Obtain Lawful Permanent Residency in the United States." *Law Journal for Social Justice at Arizona State University* 1, no. 1 (2011): 50–74.
Fishkin, Shelley Fisher. "Crossroads of Cultures: The Transnational Turn in American Studies—Presidential Address to the American Studies Association, November 12, 2004." *American Quarterly* 57, no. 1 (2005): 17–57.
Glick Schiller, Nina, Linda Basch, and Christina Szanton Blanc. *Nations Unbound. Transnational Projects, Postcolonial Predicaments, and Deterritorialized Nation-States*. London: Routledge, 1994.
Harvey, David. *The Urban Experience*. Baltimore: Johns Hopkins University Press, 1989.
Kam Ríos, Jorge. "Los primerospobladores o descubridores del continente americano." Biblioteca Monseñor Marcos Gregorio McGrath. Universidad Católica Santa María La Antigua, Panamá. Last accessed May 5, 2011. www.usma.ac.pa/biblioteca/ Profesores/JorgeKam/Temas%20de%20Historia/Los%20pobladores%20de%20América.pdf
Kearney, Michael. "The Local and the Global. The Anthropology of Globalization and Transnationalism." *Annual Review in Anthropology* 24 (1995): 547–65.

Lefebvre, Henri. *The Production of Space*. Oxford, MA: Basil Blackwell, 1991.

Levitt, Peggy, and Ninna Nyberg-Sørensen. "The Transnational Turn in Migration Studies." Global Migration Perspectives 6. Geneva: Global Commission on International Migration, 2004. Last accessed on May 5, 2011. www.gcim.org/gmp/Global%20Migration% 20Perspectives%20No%206.pdf

Martí, José. *Nuestra América*. Buenos Aires: Editorial 33 orientales, 1891/2005.

Massey, Doreen. *Space, Place and Gender*. Minneapolis: University of Minnesota Press, 1994.

Masterson, Araceli. "NosOtras: Construcciones de identidad de las mujeres ecuatorianas en Madrid." Coord. Mari Carmen Albert. In *Migraciones en las Américas. Viejos y Nuevos Destinos*. Alicante: Librería Compás, 2006.

Masterson-Algar, Araceli. *Ecuadorians in Madrid: Migrants Place in Urban History*. Hispanic Urban Studies Series. London: Palgrave (2016).

Mignolo, Walter. *Local Histories/Global Designs*. Princeton, NJ: Princeton University Press, 2000.

Orozco, Manuel. "Transnationalism and Development: Trends and Opportunities for Latin America." In *Remittance: Development Impact and Future Prospects*, edited by Samuel Munzele Maimbo and Dilip Ratha, 307–31. Washington, DC: World Bank, 2005.

Ortiz, Fernando. *Cuban Counterpoint of Tobacco and Sugar*. Durham, NC: Duke University Press, 1995.

Ospina Lozano, Óscar Raúl. *Dolarización y desarrollo urbano. Mercado de vivienda nueva en Quito*. Quito: Abya Yala, 2010.

Palma Mora, Mónica. "Asociaciones de inmigrantes extranjeros en la Ciudad de México. Una mirada a fines del siglo XX." *Migraciones Internacionales* 3, no. 2 (2005): 29–57.

Pessar, Patricia, and Sarah Mahler. "Bringing Gender In." *International Migration Review* 37, no. 3 (2003): 812–46.

"Remittances Flows to Latin America and the Caribbean Remain Stable at $61bn." Inter-American Development Bank (IDB). April 29, 2013. http://www.iadb.org/en/news/news-releases/2013-04-29/2012-latin-america-remittance-flows,10432.html

Rivera-Salgado, Gaspar, Xóchitl Bada, and Luis Escala Rabadán. "Mexican Migrant Civic and Political Participation in the US: The Case of Hometown Associations in Los Angeles and Chicago." Paper presented at Mexican Migrant Social and Civil Participation in the United States. Washington DC, November 4–5, 2005. http://wilsoncenter.org/news/ docs/riverabadaescala1.pdf

Sassen, Saskia. *Cities in a World Economy*. New York: Columbia University Press, 2006.

Smith, Michael Peter. *Transnational Urbanism: Locating Globalization*. Oxford: Blackwell Publishers, 2000.

Vargas Llosa, Mario. *El Sueño del Celta*. Madrid: Alfaguara, 2010.

Wallerstein, Immanuel. *The Modern World-System*. 3 vols. San Diego: Academic Press, 1974.

Chapter 15

Remapping Latin America

US Latino Immigration and Immigration Enforcement on Localized Scales

Joseph Wiltberger

THE GROWING PRESENCE OF Latinos in the United States challenges us to reconceptualize the space, place, and borders of Latin America (see Introduction). Many neighborhoods, workplaces, towns, and cities in the United States, are, in many ways, also Latin American places. Walking down the streets of some parts of Los Angeles, for example, you may hear Spanish and some indigenous languages spoken and see *panaderias, pupuserias,* and many other kinds of businesses run by and directed toward residents of Latin American heritage. Although Latinos have a long-standing presence in the United States (see chapter 13), the relatively sudden arrival over the last two decades of Latino immigrants, mainly from Mexico and Central America, has been received with hostile and xenophobic local reactions, particularly in rural and suburban areas of the United States where the Latino population, until then, may have been relatively small. We can see that even as these spaces, in the interior of the United States, have become more Latin American in character, they have also experienced new kinds of racial, economic, and social divisions. In other words, they have become *bordered* spaces, as new spatial constructions have emerged within local communities that delimit the influence of the Latino population and the possibilities for immigrant integration.

In this chapter, we will look at recent changes linked to US Latino immigration,[1] focusing on an emergent trend toward involving local officials in federal immigration enforcement efforts. These have included a range of locally and state-enacted immigration enforcement initiatives, as well as federal programs that empower local officials with immigration enforcement authority. These efforts have emerged in response to social and economic concerns surrounding unauthorized immigration, and they have had a significant impact on the lives of Latino immigrants and the Latino population as a whole. They have particularly caught the interest of small towns and cities in the South and other areas of the United States that have suddenly seen a spike in Latino immigration since the 1990s. We will examine how such exclusionary policies reproduce the literal and symbolic power of the US-Mexico border throughout US communities by guarding the boundaries of US citizenship and by constructing and reinforcing messages about belonging and non-belonging in the United States.

To explore how Latino immigration is remapping the spaces and boundaries of Latin America and the United States, we will first review theoretical perspectives that reconceptualize the political geography of Latin America and the US-Mexico border. After reviewing some background on the US Latino population and the US legacy of anti-immigration measures, we will examine the recent rise of localized immigration enforcement initiatives and the exclusionary and "bordering" effects they have had in local communities. Finally, we will explore a few of the responses to such changes by Latino immigrant advocates.

Reconceptualizing the Space, Place, and Borders of Latin America

What if there were no political border dividing Latin America and the United States? How might we understand the Americas and see our world differently? According to cultural theorist Walter Mignolo (2005), Latin America, as we have long understood it—its geography and meanings—was an invention of European colonists. In other words, the naming of the region, and the national borders that were eventually drawn, all stem from Conquest and colonial legacies. Guatemala's contemporary political boundaries, for example, would not exist as they are today at fixed latitudes/longitudes had it not been for initial cartographic renderings made at the time of independence, which were based on the descriptive charting of places for the Spanish Empire throughout the colonial period (Sellers-Garcia 2014).

Mignolo suggests that a new imagination of the region's geography may have decolonizing effects. Following this "de-colonial" line of thought, a more relational and fluid understanding of Latin America also helps to decolonize long-standing ideas about racial superiority and inferiority built on colonial logics that privileged white European ancestries over others. Recognizing the significance of migrations throughout the Americas further destabilizes conventional notions of a bounded space and place of Latin America. Just as political borders derived from colonial legacies have an immediate and powerful impact on people's lives, so do the cross-border flows of people, goods, ideas, and cultural practices. Rather than sticking to a singular definition rooted in colonialism, from this view, we can imagine Latin America as a space without clear boundaries and with changing and multiple meanings (see chapter 14).

In his artwork (figure 15.1), Mexican artist Pedro Lasch depicts the Americas as a much less bounded, more fluid space. Spacing the title of his work, "Latino/a-America," across the entire territorial space of the Americas gives the impression that North, Central, and South America are all "Latinized." By combining the words "Latino" and "America," Lasch implies that this space is at once made up indistinguishably by Latinos and Latin American people and characteristics. As a hyphenated version of the Spanish translation for "Latin America," the renaming also privileges Latin America's most widely spoken language. Such an alternative imagination of the geography of Latin America destabilizes the widely accepted narrative that presumes that the dominant character of the United States should rest upon a legacy of Anglo-European immigration and Conquest.[2] As some scholars suggest, such a singular and reductionist narrative of US immigration and identity is inherently Eurocentric, favoring white privilege while marginalizing other histories of immigration, as well as those of American Indian peoples (Grosfoguel et al. 2006). In other words, this simple re-rendering of American cartography also challenges us to reconceptualize popularly accepted notions of American history, meaning, and identity.

Recognizing plurality, diversity, and dynamism makes it possible to view US places differently. After doing research about the lives of working-class Mexican immigrants in Chicago—an immigrant population that has grown out of a long history of immigration to that metropolitan area and now has an expansive presence there—anthropologist Nicholas De Genova (2005) began referring to the area as "Mexican Chicago." Writing against the common

Figure 15.1. "Latino/a-America," by Pedro Lasch. Picture courtesy of Pedro Lasch.

tendency to speak of Chicago Mexicans as a minority pertaining solely to one iconic "ethnic" neighborhood called Pilsen, his renaming suggests that the entire Chicago metropolitan area is not simply a place geographically located within and belonging to the United States. Rather, he argues that Chicago is a place that actually very much *belongs to Mexico*, since the valuable work and presence of many Mexicans there has, importantly, made Chicago the place that it is today. Cities like Los Angeles are considerably Latin American in character, and in 2014, Latinos surpassed whites as the largest racial/ethnic group in California (Lopez 2014).[3] According to the US Census Bureau, Latinos are expected to comprise the majority of US inhabitants by 2044 (Krogstad 2014). US Latino immigration continues to contribute to the Latin American character of US spaces and places, an ongoing change that challenges us to move beyond singular narratives about the geographic meanings and boundaries of the United States and Latin America (see chapters 13 and 14).

Places that have taken on more Latin American characteristics are perhaps most detectable in parts of the United States where the population of Latino residents has grown significantly in a short period of time, particularly in rural and suburban areas that until recently were home to mainly white and/or black residents. As Latino residents with ties to Mexico, Central America, and other parts of Latin America have settled in these places, they have introduced families, started businesses, and established social and political networks, transforming the places where they reside. Geographer Doreen Massey (2005) reminds us that places are made through particular convergences of time and space; as such, they are constantly changing and experienced differently by different people. That is, the same physical space may be experienced very differently by an immigrant from El Salvador and a native-born white resident. Always works-in-progress, places are continuously being made and remade. Their boundaries, meanings, and identities are fluid and understood differently according to diverse subjective viewpoints. Furthermore, it is important to recognize that places and social groups cannot be viewed as bounded entities, especially as they continue to adopt more transnational characteristics and linkages through globalization and migration (Gupta and Ferguson 1992) (see chapter 14).

Based on research in Latino neighborhoods in Tennessee, geographer Jamie Winders suggests that the US South, a region that has experienced unexpectedly high levels of Latino immigration since the 1990s, has seen local areas get "re-placed" in recent years as southern neighborhoods continue to be transformed by Latino residents (Winders 2011). Now referred to as the "Nuevo South" by some, the recent wave of Latino immigration has changed the region significantly, in some ways redefining what it means to be "Southern," despite the long history of Mexican agricultural labor migration to the region, which dates back to at least 1910 (Fink 2003; Cravey 2005; Winders 2007; Weise 2012). The jump in Latino immigration to rural and semi-urban areas in the US South by the 1990s marked a remarkable shift away from "traditional" destinations for Latino immigrants, such as California, Arizona, and Texas and large cities such as Los Angeles or Houston (see figure 15.2).

Not everyone welcomes these types of changes, and in some places they have been fiercely contested. In rural and suburban communities in the US South and elsewhere that have seen a demographic shift away from a white majority as the Latino population has grown significantly in the span of only a decade or two, some residents feel as though the US-Mexico border is crossing over them. Reactions to these transformations of local places are sometimes hostile, as more attention turns to border enforcement and concerns around unauthorized immigration. Latino immigrants tend to be the focus of policy attention since the majority of unauthorized immigrants have arrived from Latin America, with the largest of those groups coming from Mexico and Central American countries. The attention to Latino immigration as a subject of

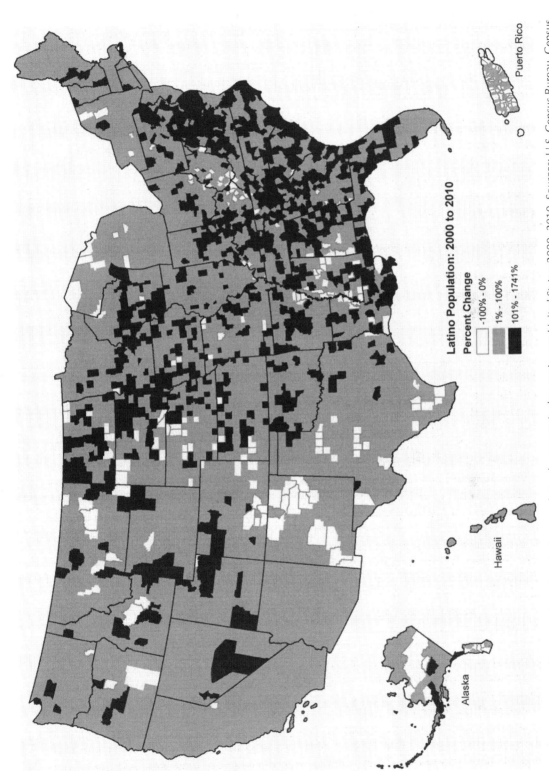

Figure 15.2. Percent change in Hispanic or Latino population by county in the contiguous United States: 2000–2010. Sources: U.S. Census Bureau, Census 2000 Summary File 1 and Census 2010 Summary File 1.

Latino Population: 2000 to 2010

Percent Change

-100% - 0%

1% - 100%

101% - 1741%

Puerto Rico

Hawaii

Alaska

political debate has led some news media and politicians to express concerns that immigrants from Latin America are "invading" the United States, "threatening" US national identity, and have a propensity for criminal activity (Chavez 2008).

Just as Latin American spaces are always being reproduced and remade in places throughout the United States in fluid and changing ways, so are the material and symbolic effects of the US-Mexico border, through xenophobic reactions and exclusionary practices and policies. The US-Mexico border has social, political, and economic effects that are both symbolic and literal. It has the literal effect of dividing and separating the US population from Mexico and other Latin American neighbors. However, it is also laden with meaning, having the effect of dividing people along the lines of race, class, and nationality. As a symbolic marker of the value, strength, and coercive force behind immigration enforcement, the border naturalizes ideas about race and class-based power relations and inequalities between Latinos and non-Latinos in US society.

In some places, mainly in urban areas, a wall or fence visibly marks the US-Mexico border to block cross-border movement. In other areas, including hundreds of miles of rural desert land, the border is invisible and not marked. Instead, the US Border Patrol uses aircraft, all-terrain vehicles, and surveillance technology, such as sensors and towers with cameras, to spot unauthorized border crossings. Anthropologist Josiah Heyman suggests that both the steel wall and this "virtual wall" are an expression of "symbolic border fear," and "an effort to keep outside separate from inside, to preserve an imagined purity that defies the many decades of interpenetration" between the United States and Mexico (Heyman 2008, 2009, 83). This symbolic delineation is further marked by the growing presence of US detention centers near the border, which are equipped to incarcerate thousands of unauthorized immigrants for. days, months, or years while they await deportation proceedings or court hearings.

As a material and symbolic marker of power relations, the border reinforces racial and economic divisions and inequalities in the United States. As more attention has turned toward the US-Mexico border and immigration enforcement to respond to the question of unauthorized immigration, US Latinos often find that they are treated with suspicion and judgment about their immigration status based on race. Racialized ideas that circulate in the United States about individuals' "illegality" and "deportability" stigmatize Latinos and affect the mistreatment of immigrants, reproducing race and class inequality (De Genova 2002). Restrictive immigration controls and the perpetuation of these stigmas each contributes to the normalization and maintenance of a flexible and precarious low-wage labor pool of unauthorized and marginalized immigrants in the US economy.

Background: Latinos in the United States and Immigration Enforcement

Since public policy and media debates tend to frame Latino immigration as a relatively recent phenomenon, its historical formations and transnational context are often overlooked. However, understanding the significant and growing US population with ties to Latin America requires a look into long-range history. The section that follows offers a window into the long history of US Latino immigration and belonging, though the history presented here is far from complete, and emphasis here is put on Mexican and Central American experiences. It also offers a look at the legacy of anti-immigrant legislation and enforcement initiatives, and new ways that unauthorized immigration has become criminalized.

It is important to recognize that much of the southwestern United States actually belonged to Mexico until cessations of land were made in the mid-nineteenth century as a result of the Mexican American War and the Treaty of Guadalupe Hidalgo. Those who resided in the region at the time did not migrate from Mexico; rather, as the border crossed over them, they were no longer legally Mexican and suddenly lived in the United States (see chapter 13).

The first significant waves of Latin American migration to the United States date back to the 1850s, when the United States began to depend on immigrant labor from Latin America. Immigrants from Mexico and other parts of Latin America worked in mining along with immigrants from China and elsewhere during the California gold rush and on the construction of US railroads throughout the late nineteenth and early twentieth century (Garcilazo 2012). Many of them settled in the United States and took on work in other sectors. A different stream of early migrants came from the Hispanic Caribbean. The first significant wave of Cubans arrived after the Cuban revolt in 1868, when thousands left the island in search of better conditions in the United States and Europe.

Throughout the twentieth century, the Latino population became much more significant. At times, immigrants from Latin America were welcomed, and at other times, Latinos faced harsh anti-immigrant policies and xenophobic reactions. With its close geographic proximity, the United States has long turned to Mexico to fill labor needs, and today Mexican Americans comprise the largest US Latino group. During World War I, when many US men were abroad, Mexicans were encouraged to come to the United States as temporary workers to fill the labor gap. At the same time, the United States established a literacy requirement for immigrants and started restricting immigration for the first time. The US Border Patrol was established in 1925, and the 1930s saw the first mass deportation of Mexicans, when an estimated 300,000 to 500,000 were deported. Beginning in 1942, the Bracero Program initially brought in Mexican workers temporarily contracted to meet a demand for low-paid agricultural labor during World War II. Formalized in 1951 as the Mexican Farm Labor Supply Program and the Mexican Labor Agreement, the program brought in millions of workers at an average of 350,000 Mexican workers yearly. Under "Operation Wetback" in 1954, nearly four million people of Mexican descent would be deported in a span of four years. The Bracero Program officially ended in 1964, but US farms continued to depend on seasonal Mexican farm workers to maintain production. By then, a farmworker movement had developed in California with the leadership of Cesar Chavez to protest working conditions and demand civil rights.

When Guatemala, El Salvador, and Nicaragua became engulfed in civil wars in the 1980s, migration from the region surged. More than a million displaced people came to the United States seeking refuge. Due to US foreign policy in the region, Guatemalans and Salvadorans were not legally recognized as refugees or granted asylum. Initially viewed as labor migrants, Guatemalan and Salvadoran immigrant activists spent years advocating for legal recognition throughout the 1980s and 1990s (Coutin 2007).

During the 1990s and 2000s, neoliberal reforms and free trade agreements spread and strengthened throughout Latin America, deepening economic inequalities. The North American Free Trade Association (NAFTA), which went into effect in 1994, solidified Mexican domestic policies that decimated Mexico's rural economic sector, driving people to seek jobs elsewhere. Similarly, Central America—much of which is still struggling to recover from the effects of recent wars—has been affected by a wave of austere economic policies and privatizations since the 1990s, as well as the approval of the Dominican Republic-Central American Free Trade Agreement in 2005. Economic challenges have led millions from Central America and Mexico to migrate to the United States, following migrant social networks and routes that had already been established through earlier migrations.

The growing US population of immigrants from Mexico and Central America began to encounter significant backlash. Latino immigration increasingly became a source of polarized political debates. Those concerned about soft immigration laws argued that unauthorized immigrants are costly to US taxpayers and responsible for social ills. These arguments and debates gained momentum after the 1986 passage of the Immigration Reform and Control Act, which granted amnesty to hundreds of thousands of immigrants (Newton 2008). By the late 1980s and early 1990s, a new narrative had developed that blamed Latino immigrants, in particular, as those primarily responsible for problems linked to unauthorized immigration. Perpetuated through the news media and politicians, the narrative constructed Latinos as a "threat" to US national identity, by emphasizing cultural difference and assuming that the basis of such a "national" identity rests on having a white majority and privileging the legacy of US immigration from Europe over other immigrant groups or native histories (Chavez 2008). Since the 1990s, new convergences have emerged between immigration law and criminal justice, which has affected unauthorized immigrants who have been arrested by law enforcement officers (Coutin 2013).

One of the first examples of this new wave of backlash was the "Save Our State" initiative in California, or Proposition 187, a ballot initiative passed by California voters in 1994. Proposition 187, later declared unconstitutional, would have prohibited unauthorized immigrants from accessing health care, public education, and other state services. Based on the assumption that unauthorized immigrants were not lawfully entitled to such services, it set a precedent for future US legislative initiatives on immigration.

Later, in 1996, US President Clinton passed the Illegal Immigration Reform and Immigrant Responsibility Act (IIRIRA), a piece of legislation that made sweeping restrictions on immigration. Among other reforms to the US immigration system, IIRIRA enhanced the US Border Patrol, allowed for potential deportees to be held in jail for as long as two years, restricted benefits for unauthorized immigrants, and imposed stiff penalties for illegal activities such as the use of fraudulent documents, alien smuggling, and racketeering.

The terrorist attacks on September 11, 2001, provoked xenophobic reactions to immigrants and further measures to control immigration, particularly through border enforcement. More funding, equipment, and personnel were given to the US Border Patrol. Along the border in parts of Texas and Arizona, a federal initiative called "Operation Streamline" was implemented in 2005. Under Operation Streamline, unauthorized immigrants caught by the Border Patrol, rather than facing trial in civil deportation proceedings, are instead tried in Federal District Courts with a criminal charge of "illegal entry" or "illegal re-entry." The initiative "streamlined" deportation because, rather than having individual hearings, individuals can be tried all at once in large groups shortly after getting caught so that they can be deported immediately. Hundreds of thousands of immigrants have been prosecuted at the border under Operation Streamline, with "illegal re-entry," a criminal charge that carries a prison sentence, now ranking as the most common immigration charge (Santos 2014; Lydgate 2010).

In the spring of 2006, millions of immigrants and sympathizers took to the streets in cities across the United States to protest H.R. 4437, a bill proposed by Congress that, along with a number of other restrictive immigration measures, would make it a felony to live in the United States without legal immigration status. Protesters marched in the streets in more than a hundred US cities, with the largest gatherings reaching the hundreds of thousands. The mega-marches marked a historic moment of visibility for the millions of immigrants that would have been affected by the legislation.

Although the protests inspired further mobilization and coalition building among immigrant rights advocates, they were also received with strong backlash. A voluntary civilian border watchdog group, known as the Minutemen, emerged. They charged themselves with looking out for potentially unauthorized immigrants near the US-Mexico border, and they opened chapters within several local communities in the interior of the United States. Other reactions were explicitly motivated by racism and xenophobia; the number of white supremacy groups surged, and many of them started taking on anti-immigrant and anti-Latino agendas, which informed their protest actions (Shively et al. 2013).

Immigration has continued to be a polarizing subject of political debate. Between 2003 and 2013, the number of yearly deportations more than doubled, climbing from around 211,000 to more than 438,000 and reaching new record levels as each year passed (Gonzalez-Barrera and Krogstad 2014). The surge in deportations was largely linked to the nationwide shift toward immigration enforcement by local and state officials. The section that follows discusses this trend.

The Rise of Immigration Enforcement on Localized Scales

On July 13, 2006, city officials in Hazleton, Pennsylvania, signed into law the Illegal Alien Relief Act, commonly called the "Hazleton Ordinance." Hazleton is a small city of a little over twenty-five thousand residents in the mountains of rural northeastern Pennsylvania. According to the US Census Bureau, city residents who identified as Hispanic or Latino rose from just under 5 percent of the population in 2000 to 37 percent of the population by 2010 (US Census Bureau 2011). As the city experienced demographic change, residents perceived that the growth of Latino immigration was contributing to an increase in crime and was placing a burden on local schools, health care, and other services. The Hazleton Ordinance was intended to create an environment that was much more hostile to the local settlement of unauthorized immigrants. It prohibited employers from contracting unauthorized immigrants and landlords from renting to them, and it established English as the city's only official language.

By creating and enacting immigration law on a local scale, the Hazleton Ordinance challenged federal jurisdiction over immigration law in an unprecedented way. Within two months, six other US towns established local ordinances modeled after Hazleton, and within a year, 125 local communities had considered local immigration enforcement ordinances.

As debates on immigration enforcement continued among policymakers, in the media, and in the courts, local governments and, before long, states continued to experiment with policies that assumed what had been solely federal immigration enforcement responsibilities. Arizona became the first state to adopt Hazleton-like immigration enforcement measures aimed at creating an environment difficult for unauthorized immigrants to live and work in. In 2007, Arizona began requiring employers to use the recently established national E-Verify system to check the immigration status of employees. The state's 2010 enactment of SB 107 became what was perhaps the strongest anti-immigration bill ever adopted by a US state.

Many of the immigration enforcement initiatives written into proposed or passed state and city legislation were controversial and were later challenged in court on the pretext that they overstepped federal immigration authority. In 2007, the Hazleton Ordinance was ruled unconstitutional in district court, as was a similar ordinance in Farmer's Ranch, Texas, the following year. Despite the years of legal limbo, by 2010, more than a hundred local anti-immigration initiatives had been signed into law by US towns, cities, and counties. Finally, in 2014 the US Supreme Court refused to review the federal appellate decisions for Hazleton and Farmer's Ranch, which brought final clarity that these local immigration enforcement measures were unconstitutional (Chishti and Bergeron 2014).

Such policy initiatives have also engendered the idea that unauthorized immigrants warrant law enforcement treatment similar to that of serious criminals. They have also enabled exclusionary practices designed to drive immigrants out of certain places. According to Cecilia Menjivar (2013), they can constitute a form of "legal violence," or an excessive use of the law in a way that perpetuates social and economic inequalities and the meanings and ideas linked to them. By acting as a barrier to newcomers' ability to settle and integrate into local communities, and by codifying into law exclusionary policies that target Latino immigrants, the emergence of anti-immigrant legal initiatives reproduces the symbolic and literal effects of the US-Mexico border on localized scales within the United States.

While discriminatory local ordinances and state initiatives to regulate immigration were challenged in the courts on the grounds that they interfered with the authority of federal immigration officials, Immigration and Customs Enforcement (ICE) began implementing federal programs that would allow local law enforcement officials to carry out federal immigration enforcement tasks.

The first of these federal programs drew on the existing but little-known Section 287(g) of the Illegal Immigration Reform and Responsibility Act (IIRRA), the federal immigration bill signed into law by US president Clinton in 1996. ICE began rapidly expanding 287(g)'s reach by offering financial support for local law enforcement agencies to undergo training in immigration enforcement tasks and responsibilities that had until that point only been assigned to federal immigration authorities. Local agencies that opted into the program could carry out immigration status checks and detain potentially unauthorized immigrants during routine law enforcement activities.

Stemming from post-9/11 national security and immigration concerns and in the wake of the 2006 immigrant protests, the 287(g) program quickly caught on, particularly among municipalities in southeastern states and other new immigrant destination areas, as a legal alternative to the creation of controversial local immigration ordinances. Between 2006 and 2012, sixty-eight local or state law enforcement agencies across twenty-four states had begun participating in the program (Nguyen and Gill 2015, 2010).

In 2008, ICE piloted a new program similar to 287(g) called Secure Communities. Secure Communities incorporated a biometric identification system to enable local law enforcement to log and match fingerprints to check immigration status of arrested and detained individuals. ICE began obligating local participation and eventually expanded the program throughout the United States. Between its inception in 2008 and its full implementation in 2013, deportations from the United States reached a record yearly high with each passing year. The stated objective of the program, like 287(g), was to identify "criminal aliens" who could be a threat to public safety. However, as an ICE-led initiative similar to 287(g), Secure Communities had minimal oversight, leaving discretion with local officials in determining whether an immigrant should be deported (Kubrin 2014). Hundreds of thousands of immigrants have been deported through the program.

As a national approach to immigration enforcement, both Secure Communities and 287(g) have played a significant role in handing over federal immigration authority to local officials.

Textbox 15.1. The Impact of the 287(g) Program in North Carolina

North Carolina has had one of the fastest growing Latino populations of any state in the country. Like other states in the southeastern United States, since the 1990s, a wave of Latino immigrants arrived there to meet new demand for labor in agriculture, construction, and other sectors. Businesses in meatpacking, textile production, and other industries that depended on low-wage immigrant labor began relocating from other parts of the United States to the South, and some employers actively recruited immigrant workers at the border and in Mexico (Fink 2003; Gill 2010). Between 2000 and 2010, North Carolina's population grew by 111 percent, on par with several other states in the South (Ennis et al. 2011). From 1990 to 2000, it grew by 393 percent, with some small cities and rural counties in the state seeing the local Latino population grow by more than 1000 percent (Nguyen and Gill 2010).

In response to the dramatic rise of Latino immigration, cities and counties in the South took a strong interest in the 287(g) program. North Carolina quickly became the state with the most jurisdictions collaborating with ICE to implement the program.

Recognizing the need for a better public understanding of immigration dynamics and the Latino population in North Carolina, as well as the need to understand the actual impact of the sudden widespread implementation of the 287(g) program across the state, an interdisciplinary working group of researchers was formed at the University of North Carolina at Chapel Hill. The author of this chapter participated in this group, which, as a whole, sought to conduct various lines of research about the impact and experience Latino immigration and the 287(g) program in North Carolina, and to disseminate research findings in ways that would reach local communities and policymakers working on these issues.

The proliferation of 287(g) program enrollment in North Carolina appeared to be in large part based on a general perception that the rise in Latino immigration was increasing crime rates. This concern was used to justify deportations. By examining crime, immigration, and Latino population growth rates in all of the state's counties, some of the researchers tested the credibility of this perception. According to their report published in 2010, the researchers found no evidence that the Latino population growth or immigration were linked to higher crime rates. Rather, crime had been decreasing throughout North Carolina since 1993, when the state began to see the most notable increase in Latino immigration.

The researchers evaluated other impacts and effects of the 287(g) program. According to ICE, 287(g) was intended to help identify individuals who were not legally authorized to be in the United States and who had committed serious crimes, including "violent crimes, human smuggling, gang/organized crime activity, sexual-related offenses, narcotics smuggling and money laundering" (Nguyen and Gill 2010). The researchers examined the kinds of arrests made under the 287(g) program to determine whether it was being used to arrest and deport immigrants with violent and serious criminal offenses. Contrary to the program's stated intention, they found that 86.7 percent of those arrested were charged with misdemeanors, and that only 13.3 percent were charged with felonies. Traffic violations represented the most common charge at 32.7 percent, and the second most common charge, at 22.5 percent of total charges, was another driving-related charge, driving while intoxicated. Since immigrants were detained and deported mainly for misdemeanors and driving-related infractions, the researchers suggest that the 287(g) program in North Carolina was not prioritizing high-risk criminal charges.

(continued)

Textbox 15.1. *Continued*

Their report also highlighted how, in some cases, the 287(g) program had been used in "excessive" ways. For example, Latino immigrants were detained for fishing without a license, health clinics were raided by law enforcement in search of unauthorized immigrant patients, and even US citizens were mistakenly deported. Following the researchers' push for policy change, a multiyear Department of Justice federal investigation found that the Sheriff's Office of Alamance County, North Carolina, was consistently using the 287(g) program to carry out discriminatory policing practices. The findings included racial profiling tactics, such as targeting Latinos at traffic stops, and through checkpoints in Latino neighborhoods. In response, ICE terminated its 287(g) partnership with Alamance County's sheriff's office, and the Department of Justice filed a civil rights lawsuit against Sheriff Terry Johnson (Ball 2014, 2012).[1] The large percentage of immigrant deportations from North Carolina based on traffic-related infractions raises questions as to whether discriminatory policing under the 287(g) program was actually much more widespread.

The researchers also found that in municipalities implementing the 287(g) Program, immigrant residents were more reluctant to report crimes to the police. Focus groups and in-depth interviews with more than fifty Latino and non-Latino informants in 287(g) jurisdictions, including law enforcement, revealed that many violent crimes were going unreported because immigrant residents were more reluctant to cooperate with police to report crimes. This trend signaled a growing climate of distrust of local authorities and a deteriorating relationship between police and communities, and therefore more vulnerability of local residents, particularly immigrants, to violent crime.

---

1. At the time of the author's writing, there has not yet been a verdict for this trial.

As a result, deportations surged as more immigrants have been arrested in local communities where they were living. Deportation can have a significant economic and emotional toll for families, particularly for children who see a parent or parents getting deported. Nguyen and Gill's (2015) research suggests that such ICE-led federal initiatives tend to lack adequate oversight and transparency and may enable racial profiling and discriminatory policing. They also found that they often produce distrust between law enforcement and local residents, having a "chill effect." In other words, immigrants, regardless of their immigration status, were less likely to leave their homes or drive anywhere to avoid encountering police.

We can see how such experimental local policy initiatives have reproduced the symbolic and literal effects of the US-Mexico border by enacting policies and enforcement practices that define the boundaries of citizenship and belonging in exclusionary ways. Operating as a border of different sorts, they work to drive immigrants out through fast-tracked deportations and new regulations that make immigrant settlement more difficult. As the US Latino population continues to grow and transform the spaces and places in the United States, these initiatives continue to engender racially discriminatory practices and ideas about inequality of Latinos and non-Latinos. In the section that follows, we will look into the way advocates are challenging these policies and the divisions they reproduce.

Advocacy for Change

Latino and non-Latino immigrant rights advocates have actively responded to the recent emergence of new exclusionary local, state, and federal immigration policy initiatives and the social and racial divisions they engender. Organizations such as the American Civil Liberties Union and other civil rights groups have raised awareness about, and led lawsuits to take down, local policies that may violate civil rights and overstep the boundaries of federal immigration authority, such as the Hazleton Ordinance. Other prominent national organizations, such as the National Council of La Raza, have worked to influence immigration policy and to defend the political interests of the US Latino population. Countless grassroots organizations throughout the United States that work closely with immigrants and the Latino community also engage in advocacy to reform the immigration system and to reduce discrimination and xenophobia. Although these organizations and advocacy groups share many political issues of concern, forming a consistent political agenda is challenging, given the remarkable diversity of experiences of the many communities, nationalities, and social groups they collectively represent. Nonetheless, they have worked out alliances and shared political messages through various types of gatherings, coalition building, the use of social and other kinds of media, and large-scale demonstrations and campaigns.

One national network that works to help grassroots organizations find common ground and work together to influence political changes is the National Alliance of Latin American and Caribbean Communities (NALACC), which represents dozens of community-based organizations led by Latin American and Caribbean immigrants from around the United States. As a national network representing diverse communities, NALACC brings visibility to the presence and influence of Latin American peoples and cultures throughout the geography of the United States. The network extends its reach beyond the US-Mexico border to advocate for sustainable and just conditions in Latin America and the Caribbean, since much of the Latino population in the United States keeps close transnational ties to places and people in Latin America itself.

One of NALACC's campaigns, called "Somos/We Are," uses media and local initiatives to "challenge mistaken negative perceptions of Latino immigrants," promote "a common sense of humanity" through "meaningful personal interactions between native and foreign born nationals," and "empower Latino immigrant communities by emphasizing their strengths and contributions."[4] One of the local strategies employed in this campaign has been to encourage casual neighborhood gatherings among immigrants and nonimmigrants so that personal stories and experiences are exchanged among neighbors. In this way, "Somos/We Are" is intended to break down the social divisions and invisible internal borders along racial, ethnic, class, and other lines that have been constructed and perpetuated in local communities through exclusionary immigration policies and dehumanizing anti-immigrant rhetoric.

Along with other advocacy networks and organizations, NALACC has pushed for reform of the US immigration system, called for an end to unjust deportations under ICE initiatives such as Secure Communities, and has supported youth-led activism to pass the DREAM Act, a proposed bill that would offer a legalization path for some unauthorized immigrant youth. The pressures of advocates are having an effect. A bill that would have comprehensively reformed US immigration policy nearly passed in Congress in 2013. The proposal was supported by some immigrant rights advocates who recognized that it could legalize millions of immigrants, while other advocates opposed it, recognizing flaws. Advocates continue to pressure for immigration reform measures that will offer fair legalization paths for millions of unauthorized immigrants who live and work in the United States.

In 2014, in response to the failure of Congress to pass comprehensive immigration reform, President Obama announced he would take executive action to make several changes to the US immigration system, including the creation of a program to offer deportation relief to some parents of US-citizen children. He also called for the discontinuation of the Secure Communities program. A record high of more than two million immigrants had been deported during Obama's administration, leading some advocates, including a leader of the National Council of La Raza, to label him "Deporter-in-Chief." For advocates, the program's termination served as an implicit recognition that local officials were using Secure Communities to detain and deport immigrants for minor legal infractions and traffic violations rather than serious crimes. ICE then replaced it with a similar program under a different name, the Priority Enforcement Program, which is intended to only allow for deportations of those who had been convicted of specifically enumerated serious crimes (Cantu 2015).[5]

Youth advocates have perhaps played the most prominent role in pressuring the US government to grant immigration relief to unauthorized immigrant youth. These young people share the common experience of having come to the United States at a young age, and they have built their lives and plans for the future in the United States. However, without legal immigration status, they face the threat of deportation, and many are not able to attend college because they would be denied admission or financial aid because of their immigration status.

United We Dream, which calls itself "the largest immigrant youth-led network," has played a leading role in advocacy on behalf of unauthorized immigrant youth. Making themselves visible through public demonstrations, by approaching members of Congress directly on Capitol Hill, and the use of social media, the "Dreamers" of United We Dream have been pressuring the US government to pass the DREAM Act. After proposed DREAM Act legislation, initially introduced in 2001, did not pass in Congress despite multiple efforts to do so for more than a decade, in 2012 Obama created the Deferred Action for Childhood Arrivals program, which allowed unauthorized immigrant youth who met certain requirements to apply for a temporary, renewable legal status. "Dreamers" continue to influence policy by sharing their stories, courageously making their unauthorized status publicly known, and even risking arrest and deportation during some protest actions.

As a younger generation, a significant portion of whom have cultural ties to Latin America, Dreamers are remaking—and remapping—the present and future of "Latino/a-America." They have formed a powerful movement to confront exclusionary policies that are based on the notion that they should be understood as perpetual "outsiders" who are not entitled to basic rights or citizenship, despite their sense of belonging and contributions in the United States. By making their struggles visible, they are working to change an immigration system that does not recognize their presence or the value of their future aspirations, and challenging the boundaries of belonging and not belonging in the United States.

Conclusion

As federal immigration enforcement has become more localized through initiatives such as Secure Communities, the 287(g) program, and ordinances and legislation enacted by states and cities, the effects of the US-Mexico border are felt within local places in the interior of the United States.

Reproducing the literal and material impact of the border, many of these new locally executed policies and enforcement initiatives prohibit, or make difficult, unauthorized immigrants from accessing housing, employment, and basic resources. They make immigrant settlement more difficult, and can drive people out of local areas to look for more hospitable places to live, similar to the way the actual border aims to prevent or reduce unauthorized entries. Also, they are focused on facilitating the arrest, detention, and deportation processing of unauthorized immigrants in places where they already reside, as though they had just been caught crossing the border. In other ways, a "virtual border" is being constructed in invisible and infinite ways throughout US communities through the use of advanced technology, such as Secure Communities' biometric identification system, to register and arrest unauthorized immigrants, much like the increased use of surveillance technology and biometrics along the US-Mexico border. The employment of local officials to carry out federal immigration enforcement tasks greatly extends the reach of ICE officials and the US Border Patrol.

The symbolic role of the US-Mexico border is also reproduced within local places through the proliferation of these local enforcement initiatives. Those that contain exclusionary policies and practices can marginalize Latino immigrants, engendering economic inequality and reinforcing misguided ideas that Latinos should be treated as permanent "outsiders" in US society. As we have seen, sometimes the vague language of such policies can lead to problems such as racial profiling and contribute to distrust and tension between Latinos and non-Latinos, or immigrants and nonimmigrants. Furthermore, the convergence of criminal justice and immigration law enforcement may give the false impression that immigration is linked to crime and that immigrants are somehow more likely to be criminals. The social, racial, economic, and political divisions that stem from these stereotypes and ideas have a "bordering" effect internally in places throughout the United States and reproduce the meanings and messages that the US-Mexico border has come to represent. Regardless of the divisive effects that such initiatives may have, the Latino population in the United States is remaking spaces and places of Latin America.

Recent efforts to more locally facilitate federal immigration enforcement define and codify into law who is allowed and who belongs in the United States and who does not. However, even as boundaries and borders that symbolically and literally divide Latin America in the United States are getting redrawn in localized spaces, Latin American spaces themselves are continuously getting remapped onto what has long been understood to be US territory in fluid and diverse ways through Latino immigration. Latino immigrant advocates are working for social and political change that will recognize and value the presence and contribution of immigrants who have cultural ties to Latin America. These changes, and the changing experience and continuous growth of the US Latino population, challenge us to rethink the space, place, and borders of Latin America.

Key Terms

racialized ideas: Race-based stereotypical ideas and presuppositions about individuals or groups.

transnational: A characteristic by which flows of people, culture, ideas, resources, and other things can circulate across national boundaries despite the presence of borders, forming new and hybridized forms of identity.

unauthorized immigration: The movement across a national border of a person or people that has not received a legal approval to enter the destination country.

Notes

1. For the purposes of simplicity, the author uses the imperfect term "Latino" to refer to people of Latin American heritage, although some of the cited literature may use the term "Hispanic" or other terms to refer to those with ties to Spanish-speaking countries of Latin America or Latin America as a whole. "Latino immigration," in this chapter, refers to the immigration of people of Latin America to the United States.
2. This is the author's interpretation of the artwork, which may differ from Lasch's perspective.
3. U.S. Census Bureau statistical estimations come from the aggregate responses of individuals who must elect one of a small selection of racial categories on surveys. Such surveys are based on a binary notion of racial identification that problematically attempts to differentiate categories such as "white," "Hispanic," "black," "American Indian," or "Asian American." when in reality the boundaries of these categories can be blurred and overlapping. Racial phenotypical categories are always imperfect, and for many individuals who respond to such surveys, none of the electable options may appropriately represent their sense of racial identification.
4. Quotations from http://67.205.16.44/our-work/somos-we-are-telling-our-stories/, accessed July 16, 2015. The remaining additional perspective about the campaign and NALACC in general is also informed by author's interview with NALACC's director in October 2013.
5. Some advocates, however, are concerned that, as an ICE-led initiative like 287(g) and Secure Communities, the new program lacks adequate oversight and may be misused by local officials.

References

Ball, Billy. "The Department of Justice Lays out Its Case against the Alamance County Sheriff." *Indy Week (online edition).* August 20, 2014.

———. "DOJ Ends Federal Immigration Program in Alamance County." *Indy Week (online edition).* September 26, 2012.

Cantú, Tony. "New Name, Same Game." *Austin Chronicle (online edition),* July 10, 2015.

Chavez, Leo R. *The Latino Threat: Constructing Immigrants, Citizens, and the Nation.* Stanford, CA: Stanford University Press, 2008.

Chishti, Muzaffar, and Claire Bergeron. "Hazleton Immigration Ordinance That Began with a Bang Goes Out with a Whimper." Migration Policy Institute. Policy Beat, March 28, 2014.

Coutin, Susan. *Nations of Emigrants: Shifting Boundaries of Citizenship in El Salvador and the United States.* Ithaca, NY: Cornell University Press, 2007.

Coutin, Susan Bibler. "Exiled by Law: Deportation and the Inviability of Life." In *Governing Immigration Through Crime: A Reader,* edited by Julie A. Dowling and Jonathan Xavier Inda, 234–51. Stanford, CA: Stanford Social Sciences, an imprint of Stanford University Press, 2013.

Cravey, Altha J. "Desire, Work and Transnational Identity." *Ethnography* 6, no. 3 (2005): 357–83.

De Genova, Nicholas. "Migrant 'Illegality' and Deportability in Everyday Life." *Annual Review of Anthropology* 31 (2002): 419–47.

———. *Working the Boundaries: Race, Space, and "Illegality" in Mexican Chicago.* Durham, NC: Duke University Press, 2005.

Ennis, Sharon, Merarys Rios-Vargas, and Nora Albert. "The Hispanic Population: 2010." Census Briefs. U.S. Census Bureau, May 2011.

Fink, Leon. *The Maya of Morganton: Work and Community in the Nuevo New South.* 1st edition. Chapel Hill: The University of North Carolina Press, 2003.

Garcilazo, Jeffrey Marcos. *Traqueros: Mexican Railroad Workers in the United States, 1870 to 1930.* Number 6 in the Al Filo: Mexican American Studies Series. Denton, TX: UNT Press, 2012.

Gill, Hannah. *The Latino Migration Experience in North Carolina: New Roots in the Old North State.* 1st edition. Chapel Hill: The University of North Carolina Press, 2010.

Gonzalez-Barrera, Ana, and Jens Manuel Krogstad. "U.S. Deportations of Immigrants Reach Record High in 2013." Pew Research Center Fact Tank, October 2, 2014.

Grosfoguel, Ramon, Nelson Maldonado-Torres, and Jose David Saldivar, eds. *Latino/as in the World-System: Decolonization Struggles in the 21st Century U.S. Empire.* Boulder, CO: Paradigm Publishers, 2006.

Gupta, Akhil, and James Ferguson. "Beyond 'Culture': Space, Identity, and the Politics of Difference." *Cultural Anthropology* 7, no. 1 (1992): 6–23.

Heyman, Josiah McC. "Constructing a Virtual Wall: Race and Citizenship in U.S.-Mexico Border Policing." *Journal of the Southwest* 50, no. 3 (2008): 305–33.

———. "A Border That Divides. A Border That Joins." *Anthropology Now* 1, no. 3 (2009): 79–85.

Krogstad, Jens Manuel. "With Fewer New Arrivals, Census Lowers Hispanic Population Projections." Pew Research Center Fact Tank, December 16, 2014.

Kubrin, Charis E. "Secure or Insecure Communities?" *Criminology & Public Policy* 13, no. 2 (2014): 323–38.

Lopez, Mark Hugo. "In 2014, Latinos Will Surpass Whites as Largest Racial/Ethnic Group in California." Pew Research Center Fact Tank, January 24, 2014.

Lydgate, Joanna. "Assembly-Line Justice: A Review of Operation Streamline." Policy Brief. The Chief Justice Earl Warren Institute on Race, Ethnicity & Diversity, University of California, Berkeley, Law School, January 2010.

Massey, Doreen B. *For Space.* Thousand Oaks, CA: Sage, 2005.

Menjívar, Cecilia. "Central American Immigrant Workers and Legal Violence in Phoenix, Arizona." *Latino Studies* 11, no. 2 (2013): 228–52.

Mignolo, Walter D. *The Idea of Latin America.* 1st edition. Malden, MA; Oxford: Blackwell Publishing, 2005.

Newton, Lina. *Illegal, Alien, or Immigrant: The Politics of Immigration Reform.* New York: NYU Press, 2008.

Nguyen, Mai Thi, and Hannah Gill. "The 287(g) Program: The Costs and Consequences of Local Immigration Enforcement in North Carolina Communities." Chapel Hill: Institute for the Study of the Americas & the Center for Global Initiatives, University of North Carolina at Chapel Hill, 2010.

———. "Interior Immigration Enforcement: The Impacts of Expanding Local Law Enforcement Authority." *Urban Studies*, January 8, 2015, 1–22.

Santos, Fernanda. "Detainees Sentenced in Seconds in 'Streamline' Justice on Border." *New York Times (online edition)*, February 11, 2014.

Sellers-García, Sylvia. *Distance and Documents at the Spanish Empire's Periphery.* Stanford, CA: Stanford University Press, 2014.

Shively, Michael, Rajen Subramanian, Omri Drucker, Jack McDevitt, Amy Farrell, and Janice Iwama. "Understanding Trends in Hate Crimes Against Immigrants and Hispanic-Americans," Report prepared for the U.S. Department of Justice. December 27, 2013.

U.S. Census Bureau. "2010 and 2000 Census Summary File 1—Hazleton, PA [Machine Readable Data Files]/prepared by the U.S. Census Bureau." U.S. Census Bureau, 2011.

Weise, Julie M. "Dispatches from the 'Viejo' New South: Historicizing Recent Latino Migrations." *Latino Studies* 10, no. 1 (2012): 41–59.

Winders, Jamie. "Bringing Back the (B)order: Post-9/11 Politics of Immigration, Borders, and Belonging in the Contemporary US South." *Antipode* 39, no. 5 (2007): 920–42.

———. "Re-Placing Southern Geographies: The Role of Latino Migration in Transforming the South, Its Identities, and Its Study." *Southeastern Geographer* 51, no. 2 (2011): 342–58.

Index

ACP (African-Caribbean-Pacific) countries, 82
Africans, 3, 33
Alianza Bolivariana para los Pueblos de Nuestra América (ALBA), 78
Allende, Salvador, 44, 46, 124
Amazon: basin, 9, 11, 17, 126; Brazilian, 119, 152–56, *153*; rainforest, 122, 125–26; Peruvian, 15, 124, 219–20
Amazonian, 136, 141, 220
anti-American, 35, 46
anti-immigrant, 215, 238–39, 241–42, 245
Andes Mountains, 10–11, 17, 20–21, 33, 116, 124, 193
Anzaldúa, Gloria, 206, 222
Argentina, 3, 6, 21, 26–28, 33–34, 37, 40, 46–48, 73, 117, 178, 184, 223, 229; agriculture, 118, 125; Buenos Aires, 53, *59*, 62; children, 189, 193; "dirty war", 169; economic crisis in, 39, 45, 54; exports from, 60; HIJOS, *160*, 169, 171; Import-Substitution Industrialization in, 64, 113; inflation in, 46; Madres de la Plaza de Mayo, 163–67, *168*; mate, 135; migration from, 223; oil in, 123; social movements, 159–61, *160*, 163–164; tourism in, *100–101*, 108–9; urbanization in, 54, *63*, 65, 70
Atacama Desert, 9, 20–21, 34, 124
Audiencias, 27–28, *29*
Aztec, 10, 26, 28, 57, 223

Bahamas, 11; tourism in, 98, *100–101*
bananas, 32, 40, *41*, 42, 82–84, *117*

Barbados, 87, 100, *100–101*, 139
Belize, *110*, 143; retirement tourism in, 6, 104–105; tourism in, 100, *100–101*
biomes, 9, 15, *16*, 17–21, 23
Black Legend, 27
Bolívar, Simón, 28, 33
Bolivarian Revolution, 33, 39, 48
Bolivia, 6–7, 11, 28, 34, *41*, 47, 54, 113, 115, 118, 121, 123–24, 159, 181, 224, 229; children in, 192–93; coca in, 137, 141; inflation in, 45–46; social movements in, 160–61, 163; tourism, *100–101*; urbanization in, 59, 62, *63*, 65; water in, 182–84
Bourbon Reforms, 28
Bracero Program, 208, 215, 239
Brazil, 17, 20, 27–28, 34, 40, *41*, 44, 58, 78, 113, 118–20, 123, 152–54, 181, 195; agriculture in, 118, 125–26, 155–56; Bahia, *119*, 120; Bolsa Família, 46, *47*; children in, 196–97, *198*, 199–200; colonialism in, 31–32, 139; Curitiba, 7, 54, 72–74, *72–73*, 184–85; deforestation in, 15, 23, 149; exports from, 40, *47*, 48, 120; favelas in, 107; independence, 34, 36; inflation in, 46; informal workers in, 180; Japanese in, 224; Mato Grosso, 153, *153*; migration from, 223; military dictatorship in, 152; Movement of Rural Landless Workers (MST), *160*, 162–63; petroleum, 121–22, *122*; Rio de Janeiro, 57, 109–110, *110*; Rondonia, 153, *153*; São Paulo, 53, 62–63, *63*, 67–68, *69*, 70, 121, 126, 180, 183, 224; social movements in, 159, *160*, 161,

163; soy in, 125–26, *125*; sugar, 117; tourism in, *100–101*, 107–8; trade, 84; urbanization, 54, 62, *63*, 67, 70
Bush, George W., 46, 87, 127

Cancún, 65, 97–98, 107
the Caribbean, 3–4, 17, *18*, 25, 27, 36–37, 41–42, 57, 62, 78–79, 82–87, 89–90, 116–17, 137, 141, 221, 223, 239; cities in, 53–54, *55*, 58, *62*; colonialism, 31–32, 139–41; cruises, *106*; exports from, 40; reforestation in, *19*; sugar in, 32, 41, 82, 105, 117–18, 139; remittances to, 224; tourism, 95, 97–98, *99–101*, 102–3, 105, 109–10
Caribbean Plate, 11, *13*, 14, *16*, 17
Casa Guanajuato, Quad Cities, 225, *226–27*
Central America, 11, *13*, 17, 21, 23, 60, 78–79, 97, 99, 137, 193, 238–39; Banana War in, 82–84; children in, 195, 199; coffee in, 116; exports from, 40–41, 85, 89; independence in, 31; maquiladoras in, 85–86; Mayans of, 26; migrants from, 143, 213–14, 229, 233, 236, 240; neoliberalism in, 84; physical geography of, *18*; remittances to, 224; tourism in, 95, 98, 100, *100–101*; U.S. intervention in, 36
Chávez, Hugo, 33, 46, 78, 121
Chicago Boys, 44
Chicano, 221
Chile, 9, 11, 20–21, 26, 33–34, *35*, 46–47, 60, 118–20, 123–25, 167, 184, 193; copper in, 124; exports from, 40, *41*; neoliberalism in, 44; social movements in, 159, 162–63; tourism in, *100–101*; U.S. intervention in, 36; urbanization in, 62, *63*
China, 21, 25, 37, 78–79, 85–86, 90, 142, 239; "Effect" or "Cycle", 113; exports to, 113, 125; investment by, 48, 123; migration to Mexico City, 223
chinampas, 10
Christian Base Communities (CBEs), 152
CIA, 42, 44, 46
cocaine, 133–34, 137, 141–42, 144
coffee, 21, *22–23*, 32, 40–41, 41–42, 82, 113–134, 116, 118, 126, 133–4, 139–40, 144–45, 154
Colombia, 28, 35, 47, 62, 82–83, 123, 141, 159, 180, 195, 199; coffee in, 22, 116; drug cartels, 141, 143–44; drug war in, 133, 142; exports from, 40, *41*; Gran Colombia, 31, 33; migration from, 223, 228–29; National Federation of Coffee Growers in, 116; social movements in, 160, 163–64; tourism in, 97, *100–101*

colonialism, 25, 27, 40–41, 138, 182, 191, 219, 221, 234
commodity chains, 114
Conquistadores, 27, 32–33, 57
conucos, 10
Costa Rica, 28, 31, 86, 116, 229; exports from, *41*; tourism in, 96, *100–101*, 110; urbanization in, *63*
criollo, 31, 33–34, 66
Cuba, 11, 28, 78, 80, 114, 121, 220; exports from, 40–41, *41*; Havana, 53; migration from, 223, 239; socialist, 77; sugar in, 117; tobacco in, 138; tourism in, 87, 97, *100–101*, 102; U.S. intervention in, 36; urbanization, *63*
Cuzco/Cusco, 57, *59*, 138, 196–97

de las Casas, Bartolomé, 26, 32
debt crisis, 43–44, 64–65, 80, 82, 152; in Argentina, 48; in Mexico, 44
dependency, 5, 37, 42–43, 47, 79, 82–83, 110, 141
dependency theory, 2, 80, 115, 220–21
diaspora, 84, 96; African, 140
direct foreign investment (DFI), 40
Dominica, *81*, 82–84; tourism in, *100–101*; urbanization in, *63*
Dominican Republic, 36, 85, 144, 239; exports from, *41*; sugar in, 117; tourism in, 87, 100, *100–101*; urbanization in, 62, *63*
drug smuggling, 207, 213
drug war, 36, 143, 201

ecology, 176, 184
Economic Commission for Latin America and the Caribbean (ECLAC, originally ECLA), 42, 46
ecotourism, 5, 90, 104
Ecuador, 6, 20, 26, 28, 47, 53, 83, 115, 121; cacao in, 138; exports, 41; Guayaquil, 182; indigenous in, 159, 191, 193; migration from, 7, 219, 224–25, 227–29; oil in, 122–23; Quito, 65; social movements, *160*, 160–61; street children in, *194*, 196, *197–98*, 200; tourism in, *100–101*; urbanization in, *63*; water in, 181–82, 184
El Nino, 18
El Salvador, 6, 31, 120, *121*, 199; coffee in, 116; drug war in, 143; exports from, *41*; human rights in, 159; migration from, 89, 199, 213, 236, 239; social movements in, *160*, 165; tourism in, 100, *100–101*; U.S. intervention in, 36; urbanization in, *63*
ELN (Ejército de Liberación Nacional), 141

encomienda, 32
England, 27–28, 31, 60, 139, 190,
environmental determinism, 9
environmental justice, 176, 178
environmental possibilism, 9
European Union (EU), 48, 82–83, 125
export processing zones (EPZs), 85–86

fair trade (general concept or movement), 84,
    103, 116
favelas, 6, 53–48, 70, 107
France, 25, 28, 31, 33, 40, 82, 223
FARC (Fuerzas Armadas Revolucionarias de
    Colombia), 141

gated communities, 68, 70, 191
GONGOS, government-organized NGOS, 149
Great Britain, 28, 35, 40, 60, 219, 230
Great Depression (U.S.), 42, 64, 113, 215
Greater Antilles, 10, 17
Guatemala, 47, 88, *88*, 115–16, 162, 180, 234; drug
    production, 141, 143; exports, *41*; Guatemala
    City, 31, *63*; human rights activities in, 159;
    Kingdom of, 31; migrants from, 199, 213,
    223, 239; Pan-Mayan movement in, 161; rain
    forests in, 89; social movements in, 160, 171;
    tourism in, 98, *100–101*; U.S. intervention in,
    36, 42; urbanization, 54, *63*
Guyana, 11, 28, 89; gold mining in, 125; tourist
    arrivals, *100*

Haiti, 139, 223; earthquake in, 10–11, *18*;
    education, 193; exports, *41*; independence, 33;
    maquiladoras in, 85–86; Port au Prince, 62, *63*;
    remittances, 85; tourism, 97; U.S. intervention
    in, 36, 41; urbanization, 54, *62–63*
haciendas, 32, 33
hallucinogens, 133–38
HIJOS (Hijos por la Identidad y la Justicia y
    contra el Olvido y el Silencio), *160*, 169–71
    170, 192
Hispanic, 4, 205, *237*, 239, 241
H-2A, 215
historical persistence, 3
hometown associations (HTAs), 224, 225, 229
Honduras: drug trade, 143; education, 193;
    exports, *41*; geo-hazards, *18*; independence, 31;
    maquiladoras in, 86; refugees of, 199; tourism
    in, *100–101*; urbanization, 54, *63*
hunter-gatherer, 9

Hurricane Mitch, *18*
hybrid cultures, 4, 10

import substitution industrialization (ISI), 42–44,
    49, 64, 152, 210, *210*
Inca, 10, 26, 57
empire, 28, *59*, 138
Incaic, 138
indigenous movements, 6, 123, 159–53, *160*
indigenous people, 2, 26, 32, 33, 37,113, 149–54,
    183, 191, 220, 223
inflation, 44–46, 5, 78
informal economy, 7, 65, 209, 213–15
informal housing, 53, *62*, 70, 71, 74
informal sector, 65, 69, 200
Inter-American Development Bank (IDB), 65, 97
Intermediate Area (archaeology), 137
international financial institutions (IFIs), 79
International Labor Organization (ILO), 86, 192
International Monetary Fund (IMF), 34, 43, 45,
    46, 48, 65, 80, 90, 124, 152–53
Intertropical Convergence Zone, 17

Japan, 224

karst, 10, 11, 20

Latin American City Model, 65–67, *66*, 70, 71
Latino, Latina, 2, 4, 8, 230, 233–42, *243–44*,
    245–47
Lesser Antilles, 10, 17, *19*, 139, 144
Liberation Theology, 151
Llosa, Mario Vargas, 219–20, 230
Lomé/Cotonou, 83
The Lost Decade, 46
"Lula" (Luiz Inácio da Silva), 46–47

Machu Picchu, 26, 57, *57*, 138
Madres de Plaza de Mayo, *164*, 164–69, *165–66*,
    168
maquiladora, 5, 7, 65, 79, 84, 85–86, 91, 165,
    207–9, 211
mecca (as in tourist), 96, 98
megacities, 53, 61–64, 73, 74
megaslums, 70, *71*
Mesoamerica, 57, 137, 223
Mexico, 3, 4, 6, *12*, 34, 35, 44, 47, *55*, 91, 128,
    138, 159, 180, 213, 230; 3x1 Plan, 225; Aztec,
    10, 26; Acapulco, 65, 97; border, 7, 8, 65, 85,
    199, 205–13, *206*, 216, 229, 238; Campeche,

107; Cancún, 65; Ciudad Juarez, 65, 165, 214; climate, 20; drug cartel, 142, 144, 214; economic growth in, 42, 86, 113; exports, 40, *41*, 77; Guanajuato, 225, *226*, *227*; heroin production in, 141; immigration from, 89, 215, 233, 236–47, *237*, *243*; independence, 31, 34; indigenous in, 223; landforms in, 10–11; marijuana in, 140–41; natural resources, 113, 115, 121–24, *122*, 126–27; Oaxaca,7; PEMEX, 127; Puebla, *98*; Quintana Roo, 97, *99*; remittances, 89, 224; social movements in, 159–61, *160*, 165, 171; tourism, 87, 97–102, *101*, 105–7, *106*, 208; urbanization, 54, *63*, 64; Youth Alternative Resistance or Jóvenes en Resistencia Alternativa (JRA) in, 201; youth violence in, 199; Zapatistas, 161, 169
Mexico City, 28, *30*, 53, 57, *61*, *63*, 67, 70–72, 195, 223–24
Metropoles, 139
milongas, 3
Montego Bay (Jamaica), 96
Morales, Evo, 123, 183
multinational corporations (MNCs), 36

narcoterrorism, 142
nation-state, 4, 5, 37, 46, 113, 159, 221–22
natural hazards/disasters, *18*, 97
NAFTA (North American Free Trade Agreement), 7, 86, 127, 209–13, 239
neocolonialism, 5, 25, 37, 39, 41, 60
neoliberal, 2, 5, 7, *19*, 39, 44–49, 65, 79, 80–85, 90, 114, 115, 121, 124, 127–28, 141, 152, 156, 160–63, 178, 181, 194, 209–11, *210*, 213–14, 216, 224, 239
Neolithic Revolution, 136
New Spain, 28, *30*, 31, 223
Nicaragua, 28, 31, 45, 47, 78, 86, 93, 200, 229; exports from, *41*, 113, 117; immigration from, 239; tourism in, 98, *100–101*; U.S. intervention in, 36; urbanization in, 53–54, *63*, 99
North American Plate, 14
Nongovernmental organizations (NGOs), 2, 6–7, 147–58, 167
NPO (nonprofit organization), 148–49, 156

OAS (Organization of American States), 77
OECD (Organization for Economic Cooperation and Development), 87, 148
oil, 6, *15*, 34, 36, *41*, 47, 82, 88–89, 121–23, *122*, 161, 182; in Mexico, 126–29; in Venezuela, 40, 48, 78, 121

offshore gambling, 86
Overseas Department of France (Martinique and Guadeloupe), 31
overurbanization, 45, 64, 74

pampas, 21, 60, 119
Panama, 28, 31, 35–36, 40, 78, 98, 193; exports from, 41; tourism in, 100, *100*; urbanization in, *63*
Panama Canal, 78
Pan-Mayan, 161
Paraguay, 20, 28, 34, 47, 118; exports from, *41*; tourism, *100–101*; urbanization in, 54, 62, *63*; War of the Triple Alliance, 34
Perú, 20, 26–27, 47, 118, 137, 192, 219, 228, 230; Atacama Desert, 9, 20–21, 34, 124; cocaine in, 137, 141; Cuzco, 57, *59*, 96–97, 138; exports from, *41*, 118, 120, 124; foreign investment in, 182, 220; gold production, *15*, 123–24; independence, 33–34; inflation in, 45–46; Lima, 27, 28, 61–62, *63*, 68, 70–71, *71*, 73, 181, 224; remittances, 224, 229; Sendero Luminoso, 141; soybeans in, 15; tourism in, *100*; urbanization, *63*; Viceroyalty of, 28
Peruvian Amazon Company, 220
Petén rainforest, *88*
PetroCaribe, 78
petroleum. *See* oil
phantom landscapes, 88–89
Pinochet, Augusto, 44, 124
Plan 3x1, 225
politics of scale, 6, 149–50, 157, 167
Potosí, 11, 28, 124, 128
Prebisch, Raúl, 42
privatization, 36, 44–45, 49, 53, 70, 114–15, 127–29, 162, 178, 181–84, 210–11
Precambrian cratons, 11
Puerto Rico, 10, 28, 31, 41, *41*, *101*, 102, 105, 117; Viejo San Juan, 105

Reagan, Ronald, 80
reais (plural of Brazilian real), *47*
Rebellion of Tupac Amarú II, 31
remittances, *19*, 85, 89, 91, 224–25, *227*, 229, 255
retirement tourism, 6, 104
Río de la Plata, 28
Rondônia (Brazil), 153–56
Rousseff, Dilma Vana, 47
rural-to-urban migration, 43, *62*, 64, 70, 74, 179, 195

San Martín, José de, 33

Sauer, Carl, 136

segregation, 68–70, 117

shantytowns, 70, 107

Southern Cone, 3, 33, 53

soybeans, *15*, 21, *41*, 78, 114, 118–19, 125–26, *125*, 155–56

Spain, 3, 7, 25, 27, 31, 33–34, 37, 58, 82, 117, 139, 171, 220, 223; Ecuadorian migration to, 219, 224–25, 227–29

Spaniards, 26–27, 31, 57, 124, 138, 223

squatter settlements, 67, 97, 107

St. Lucia, 82–83

St. Vincent, 82

street children, 196–97, *198*, 199, 201

structural adjustment programs (SAPs), 44, 65, 153, 194

stupefacients, 134

subducted, 10, 11

sugarcane/sugar, 27, 31, 32, 40–41, *41*, *81*, 82, 105, 113, 117–18, 128, 133, 134, *135*, 139–40, 144

sustainable development, 5, 6, 79, 83, 90, 95, 103–5, 108, 109

Taino, 10

Tenochtitlán, 26, 57, 138, 223

Teotihuacán, 57, 98

tobacco, 41, 133–40, *135*, 144–45

transnational corporations (TNCs), 46, 114–16, 118–19, 121–28

Treaty of Tordesillas, 27, 58

Triangular Trade, 139, *140*, 144

Transnationalism, 7, 219–23, 229–30

United Fruit Company (Chiquita Brands), 41–42, 82–83

United States, 21, 28, 31, 33–36, 40–43, 46–48, 60, 67, 85, 87, 89, 96, 98, 101, 104–5, 109, 115–18, 122, 127, 182, 191–92, 205–9, 213, 221, 223, 229–30, 233–34, 236, *237*, 239, 240–42, 245–47; 287 (g) program in, *243–44*, 244; activists in, 169; drug production/use in, 142; geopolitics, 77–78; hometown associations in, 224–25; imports from/exports to, 79–80, 85–86, 90; migration to, 89, 143, 161, 208–9, 213–16, 219–20, 238; NGOs in, 147, 154; war with Mexico, 34; and the WTO, 82–83

urban primacy, 53, 61–62, *62*, 65, 71, 74

Uruguay, 21, 28, 33–34, 47, 118, 119, 184, 193; exports from, 40, *41*; tourism in, 53, *100–101*; urbanization in, 54, 62, *63*

USAN (Union of South American Nations), 48

Venezuela, 5, 28, 33–34, 46–47, 90, 128–29; exports from, 11, *41*, 138; oil in, 40, 48, 78, 114, 121, *122*; tourism in, *100–101*; U.S. involvement in, 36, 77; urbanization in, *63*

Viceroyalty, 27–28, *30*, 223

War of the Pacific, 34, 124

War of the Triple Alliance, 34

Washington Consensus, 48

Windward Islands, 83

World Bank (WB), 34, 43, 45, 48, 65, 69, 78, 80, 86, 89, 90, 148, 150, 152–55, 178, 181

World Tourism Organization (WTO), 97–98

World Trade Organization (WTO), *19*, 45, 83, 95–96

World War I, 42, 225, 239

World War II, 42, 43, 54, 64, 80, 82, 142, 208, 215, 225, 239

Yucatán Peninsula, 26, 97, *99*

About the Contributors

Fernando J. Bosco is professor of geography at San Diego State University. His research interests include geographic dimensions of social movements and informal politics; geographies of children; families and communities; and food, ethnicity, and place. His articles have been published in *The Annals of the Association of American Geographers, Social and Cultural Geography, Gender, Place and Culture* and *Children's Geographies*, among others.

Christian Brannstrom is professor of geography and director of environmental programs in geosciences at Texas A&M University. His publications include two edited books: *Land Change Science, Political Ecology, and Sustainability* and *Territories, Commodities and Knowledges*. His research focuses on governance of environmental resources and energy development. He co-edits the *Journal of Historical Geography* and has served as chair of the Conference of Latin Americanist Geographers.

J. Christopher Brown is professor of geography and environmental studies, University of Kansas. His work spans the areas of biogeography, political ecology, and moral geography. His current work focuses on environmental governance in Amazonia; social movements, civil society, and the environment; and farmers' land-use decisions vis-à-vis changes in the bio-fuel economy in Brazil and the US Great Plains.

Altha J. Cravey is a feminist and political economic geographer concerned with how globalization shapes daily life and how ordinary people effect social change. Her book *Women and Work in Mexico's Maquiladoras* used a gender analytic to explore transformations in daily household activities, government social programs, national development strategies, and waged work in Mexico. In recent years she has published many papers about Mexican lives in the United States' South, including a special issue of the *Southeastern Geographer* (2011) about Latinization in the region. She has produced three video documentaries—*People's Guelaguetza: Oaxacans Take it to the Streets* (2007); *The Virgin Appears in* La Maldita Vecindad (2009); *Seed Spirits: The Otomi of* Carolina del Norte (2011)—and is working on a fourth that concerns life after genocide in rural, highland Guatemala. Cravey's research has been supported by the

North Carolina Arts Council, the National Institute of Health, the Iowa Fellowship, and the National Institute of Environmental Health Sciences.

James J. Hayes is assistant professor of geography at University of Nebraska, Omaha. His research and teaching focus on the relationship between people and the environment, especially the effects of land use and development on vegetation and ecosystems. His publications address spatial environmental analysis of human-environment interaction and implications for conservation and sustainability.

Edward L. Jackiewicz is professor and chair of geography at California State University, Northridge. His research interests are in development/postdevelopment, lifestyle migration, and tourism. He has recently published in *The Professional Geographer, Annals of Tourism Research*, and *Latin American Perspectives*.

Thomas Klak is professor of environmental studies at the University of New England, Biddeford, Maine. His research analyzes the theories, discourses, practices, and ecological consequences of development. He annually convenes a course in the eastern Caribbean on sustainable development. He is the coauthor of *Alternative Capitalisms: Geographies of "Emerging Regions"* (2003) and *The Contemporary Caribbean* (2004). He is an Editorial Board member for *the Journal of Latin American Geography*.

Araceli Masterson-Algar is associate professor at Augustana College in Rock Island, Illinois, and associate editor of the *Journal of Urban Cultural Studies*. She is the author of *Ecuadorians in Madrid: Migrants' Place in Urban History* (Palgrave-Macmillan 2015). In the Quad Cities (Illinois-Iowa) she teaches courses on Latin/o America, often with a focus on the cultural expressions of human mobility in transnational urban contexts. In addition to her research in Spain and Ecuador, she has conducted research on the US-Mexico border. In the Quad Cities, she is co-founder of the Palomares Social Justice Center, a grassroots organization that works with Mexican residents in the area, most of them with ties to the Mexican state of Guanajuato.

Kent Mathewson is professor of geography and anthropology at Louisiana State University in Baton Rouge. His research focuses on cultural/historical geography and the history of geography. His travel and fieldwork has taken him to Mexico, Central America, Andean America, Brazil, and the Caribbean. He is author, editor, and co-editor of various books, including: *Irrigation Horticulture in Highland Guatemala* (1984); *Prehispanic Agricultural Fields in the Andean Region* (1987); *Dangerous Harvest: Drug Plants and the Transformation of Indigenous Landscapes* (2004); *Ethno- and Historical Geographic Studies in Latin America* (2008); and *Carl Sauer on Culture and Landscape* (2009). Current projects include an edited book on Elisée Reclus's Colombian travels and Latin American writings.

Sarah A. Moore is assistant professor of geography at the University of Wisconsin, Madison. Her research focuses on the politics of the environment, including issues of urban development, struggles over environmental justice, and contradictions between the uses and hazards of garbage. Her work, involving long-term fieldwork and archival research in Oaxaca, Mexico, is funded by a grant from the National Science Foundation. She has also explored the historical geography of urban gardening, race, and development in the United States, and contributed to collaborative projects on the development of nongovernmental organization networks in southern Mexico.

Linda Quiquivix is a United States–based writer and researcher.

Zia Salim is assistant professor in the Department of Geography at California State University, Fullerton. His research focuses on urban and social geography, with particular interest in urban inequality, uneven development, and cultural landscapes. More specifically, his work has examined central city redevelopment, affordable housing, homelessness, gated communities, nonprofit service provision, and public art. Some of his publications have appeared in *Urban Geography, Urban Studies, City, The Yearbook of the Association of Pacific Coast Geographers,* and *The California Geographer.*

Kate Swanson is associate professor of geography at San Diego State University. Her research currently focuses on youth, poverty, migration, and marginality in Latin America and the US-Mexico border region. Some of her publications have appeared in *Antipode, Urban Geography, NACLA, Gender, Place & Culture, Children's Geographies,* and *Area.* She is author of *Begging as a Path to Progress: Indigenous Women and Children and the Struggle for Ecuador's Urban Spaces* (2010) and co-editor of *Young People, Border Spaces and Revolutionary Imaginations* (2011).

Benjamin Timms is associate professor of geography at California Polytechnic State University. His research focuses on environmental conservation, land-use and land-cover change, political ecology, and sustainable tourism development in Latin America and the Caribbean with publications appearing in the journals *Antipode, International Development Planning Review, Global Development Studies,* and *Tourism Geographies,* among others. Ben also serves as the resident director for the Cal Poly Peru Study Abroad program and in his spare time enjoys traveling, hiking, and exploring wine country with his lovely wife Erika and dog Stella.

Joseph Wiltberger is assistant professor of Central American Studies at California State University, Northridge. Focusing ethnographically on the experience of El Salvador and Salvadoran migrants, his research explores the economic, social, and cultural effects of international migration between Central America and the United States. His publications have addressed migration-related issues including remittances, development, immigration policy, and migrant rights activism.